Thomas P. Malone and Patrick T. Malone
previously coauthored
THE ART OF INTIMACY

Thomas P. Malone coauthored
THE ROOTS OF PSYCHOTHERAPY
with Dr. Carl Whitaker

The
WINDOWS
of
EXPERIENCE

Moving Beyond Recovery
to Wholeness

PATRICK THOMAS MALONE, M.D.

THOMAS PATRICK MALONE, M.D., PH.D.

SIMON & SCHUSTER

NEW YORK • LONDON • TORONTO

SYDNEY • TOKYO • SINGAPORE

SIMON & SCHUSTER
Simon & Schuster Building
Rockefeller Center
1230 Avenue of the Americas
New York, New York 10020

Designed by Edith Fowler
Manufactured in the United States of America

10   9   8   7   6   5   4   3   2   1

Library of Congress Cataloging-in-Publication Data

Malone, Patrick Thomas, date
    The windows of experience : moving beyond
recovery to wholeness / Patrick Thomas Malone,
Thomas Patrick Malone.
        p.   cm.
    Includes bibliographical references and index.
    1. Self-actualization (Psychology) 2. Conduct
of life. I. Malone, Thomas Patrick, date.   II. Title.
BF637.S4M336   1992
158'.1—dc20   92-15609
                                               CIP

ISBN: 0-671-76707-0

The authors gratefully acknowledge permission from
the following sources to reprint material in their control:

From "St. Francis and the Sow" in Mortal Acts, Mor-
tal Words by Galway Kinnell. Copyright © 1980 by
Galway Kinnell. Reprinted by permission of Hough-
ton Mifflin Co. All rights reserved.
From "Esthétique du Mal" in Collected Poems by
Wallace Stevens. Copyright © 1947 by Wallace
Stevens. Reprinted by permission of Alfred A. Knopf,
Inc.
From "Ceremony" in Ceremony and Other Poems by
Richard Wilbur. Copyright © 1950 by Richard
Wilbur. Renewed 1978 by Richard Wilbur. Reprinted
by permission of Harcourt, Brace, Jovanovich, Inc.
From The Precious Present by Spencer Johnson, M.D.
Copyright © 1981 by Spencer Johnson. Copyright ©
1984 by Candle Communications Corp. Used by per-
mission of Doubleday, a division of Bantam Double-
day Dell Publishing Group, Inc.

To my mother and father
T.P.M.

To Elaine, Tom, and Shannon
P.T.M.

Acknowledgments

We would like to thank our colleagues at the Atlanta Psychiatric Clinic for their support and assistance. The many hours we have spent sharing ideas and experiences together are manifest in this manuscript.

Michael Malone for the original editing of the book. His willingness to share his gift has been invaluable to us.

Elaine Malone for her assistance in editing and her patience with the long process of bringing a manuscript to final form.

Joan Hussey for her preliminary editing and preparation of the manuscript, and the many hours she gave to working on the book.

Thomas P. Malone II for the computer programming and word processing time and skill he gave.

Phil Pochoda for his support and assistance.

Toni Sciarra for her encouragement and guidance during the process of bringing this work to fruition and the final editing of the manuscript.

Gail Winston for bringing the book and the authors through the publication process.

Isolde Sauer for putting the book in its final form.

Lastly, we would like to thank the many wonderful persons we have had the pleasure of seeing professionally over the years who have taught us most of what we know.

Contents

INTRODUCTION:
Becoming
the Person We Are

There is an invisible garment woven around us from our earliest years; it is made of the way we eat, the way we walk, the way we greet people, woven of tastes and colors and perfumes which our senses spin in childhood.

—JEAN GIRAUDOUX

Being unhealthy as persons—being less than whole—is like living alone in a small room with the windows shuttered, with only slits of light coming through. The door is shut and sometimes has more than one latch. The furnishings are never changed because we feel secure only if we are familiar with everything in our room. There is a vague feeling of being imprisoned, even though we may protest that we are in control. It is not surprising that when the latches come off and the door is opened—when we walk out into a world filled with light and life—we will be disoriented. We may even shuffle back into the room and close the door, leaving it cracked open only a little, in order to summon up courage to go back out.

Few people who grow as persons have not had that unsettling experience to some degree. It makes no difference whether we began our growth in counseling, in therapy, at church, at school, or on our own: sooner or later we come to "how do I live as the real person I am, in the world as it is?" That is the crux of the question of life for all of us: "How can I be the person I have always wanted to be? How can I be who I really am?"

One of the paradoxes of psychotherapy lies in the psychological difficulties people encounter even *after* they have become more emotionally real, more relationally sensitive, more expressively themselves. Enabling us to reach those maturational states is the goal of many self-help books, but even people who succeed at such growth—whether through self-help or professional help—do not feel whole. They often speak, instead, of feeling confused. That is because it takes people considerable time to readjust to the world in which they live. Nor is this adjusting something that someone else can tell anyone how to do. The readjustment happens only *in relationship* to that world—a cultural world that does not support wholeness—and is the sole responsibility of the individual *self*.

It simply takes time for a healthy adult who has found his or her emotional health in adulthood to adjust in an unhealthy world. This book sets forth the critical and fundamental *experiential bridges* that facilitate these two transitions: (1) Our becoming our real *selves* (2) our learning to live as those *selves* in the real world. In many ways, what we will be describing are the basic psychological capacities of the healthy child. Sadly, however, most of us do not escape childhood unscathed, and thus lose some of those capacities for human wholeness.

The need for the first transition is clear to most of us, the need for the second less so. For example, a person may come to adulthood depressed, dependent, anxious, or angry, with a very poor sense of personal worth. She courageously struggles and works toward change. Finally she succeeds. She becomes more emotionally whole, more involved in her own life. She has come to live out of her own feelings rather than simply react to the feelings of others. She is less dependent and thus less ambivalent; she has transcended the chronic anger that unchosen dependence breeds, and clearly has a better self-image. Having come to care for herself, she expects at that point—as well she might—that life will be easier, more comfortable, and more natural.

Usually it is not. Why? The woman assumes, as therapists also often do, that being more mature, more relationally capable, automatically makes being in the world easier and simpler. Such, however, is not the case. Changes occur that can be confusing, difficult, and painful. For example, one of the earliest indications that a client is growing in psychotherapy is that he or she begins to experience a diminished interest in some old friends—not necessarily a dislike, but a discovery that they have less in common than they had previously felt. Concurrently, there is a beginning of new friendships. These shifts are harbingers of further changes, and, almost always, of a second painful and anxious period of transition. Becoming *whole* requires both transitions.

Such change requires relearning experiences. Therefore, it takes time and effort. We easily forget that security is wed to familiarity. This addiction to familiarity underlies many of our unhealthy ways of being in the world. These ways are familiar because they are the ways we grew up. Familiar, after all, means family. They also have become what we know and are accustomed to today. For both these reasons, we tend to retreat to self-defeating ways of being in the world even when they do not feel good, simply because they *are* familiar. For example, the person who felt he must appease his parents when he was five years old will probably be appeasing his boss, his friends, and his spouse or lover at age fifty.

To leave these patterns behind is not easy, even if we are becoming a more loving and sensitive person. Personal maturation is not automatic. There is an active process of *becoming*—becoming whole as a person. Such becoming leads to the kind of wholeness described by American Indian Black Elk:

> The first peace, which is the most important, is that which comes within the souls of people when they realize their relationship, their oneness, with the universe and all its powers, and when they realize that at the center of the universe dwells the Great Spirit, and that this center is really everywhere, it is within each of us.

The transitional relearning required involves sorrow, anxiety, and uncertainty. We feel sad because we have left our childhood and given up our lifelong familiar dreams and hopes. A patient of mine (Pat) remarked just after a session, "What I guess I've learned so far is that this is all up to me. These are my decisions, my choices, and I am going to have to be in charge of my own life." She paused a moment, then asked softly, "Why does it make me feel so sad?"

The only answer we can offer is that most of us have spent our life dreaming of the family or the parent or the savior who will show us the way, make it easy, and bring us out into the light. Giving up that fantasy *is* sad. But doing so opens the door to full selfbeing.

Anxiety is present because we are not prepared to *be* in this new, albeit healthier, way of living. Confusion is present because we do for a time feel adrift in a new and different world. We have lost many of the familiar personal benchmarks by which we have lived all of our previous life. We have to take the time to *relearn* the wholeness and naturalness we once possessed as a child, but, in most instances, have neglected to exercise since childhood.

The behavioral sciences have developed many sophisticated ways, ranging from cognitive reeducation to drug therapy, of altering unhealthy behaviors. We naively assume that when a person becomes less unhealthy, he will automatically become more natural. In a *natural* world that, indeed, might be so. But in our culturally driven world, becoming more natural requires further learning experiences. Such wholeness comes with *new and present experiences*—which are always available—not through an *alteration of the past*—which is never available. We can *grow;* we cannot *change past history.*

Unless we have the growing experiences, culture—both *social* and *personal*—will recapture us. We will too easily move back to the security of being unwhole. But then, if we are like most people, we cannot simply return to the unhealthy confinements of that small room. The old is gone, the new not fully found. We stand on the threshold, only vaguely remembering the time when we moved in that larger world freely. We yearn for the wholeness we were born with.

A six-year-old girl sits in a session with her mother and father. Her parents are having difficulty in their marriage. The woman says of her husband, "He just won't talk to me."

The six-year-old speaks up. "Talk to him."

The mother responds, "I do talk to him and you know it."

The child replies, "Not like you talk to me. When you talk to me you touch me."

The mother begins to defend. "That's not quite true. Sometimes I'm in the kitchen and you're in the family room and I'm talking to you but I'm not touching you."

The child stays in the reality of natural relationship, saying, "You can be in the kitchen talking to me and I can be in the other room, and you can still touch me."

If you are taught to be "adult" when you are a child, your

naturalness is undermined. When we start to unlearn this pseudo-adultness, we become anxious and confused. Each of us needs to spend some time reexperiencing what we once so naturally knew. These are the experiences, or, if you will, the reexperiences, that constitute the framework of growth. The six-year-old felt fully capable of being present in the here-and-now and knew the power of *intimate* relationship. She spoke directly to her immediate, present experience. She will learn, however, to sacrifice this presence and natural intimacy in order to be secure. In later life if she wishes to be whole, she will be faced with the task of relearning the natural capacity.

Relearning these natural capacities involves relearning to love and, equally, to enjoy being loved. Since love is natural, it is then perplexing that we are so afraid of it. I (Tom) spent more than a decade doing psychotherapy with schizophrenics. A central problem for these people often seemed to be the fear of loving and the fear of being loved. They seemed convinced that love killed. I once asked a young man why he considered love to be lethal. He smiled and suggested that I collect at random a hundred examples of what is done, said, felt, or shared under the label of love. If, then, I still wondered why he was suspicious of love, perhaps I needed to talk with a psychiatrist myself. To some extent, we all participate in that struggle.

The same fear is present in our dealing with our greater ecology. We cannot keep our planet healthy because we do not know how to let ourselves be part of our earth without controlling it or being controlled by it. We do not know how to *love* nature—including our own. We seem no longer to have faith in love, and the *relational* issue among humans is always love. And, since we cannot *not* relate to our environment, *all our issues* are relational. We are inevitably part of what we love and what we are loved by. Love is the energy-blood of life.

The word *love* has a history that it carries with it, whether we are consciously aware of it or not. The word comes from the Old English *leif* or *leave*, which originally meant to give permission, to allow. "I give you leave" meant "I give you permission." I give you leave. I allow you to be yourself. From that, leave came to mean depart. "I give you permission to do as you would do, to go if you would, to be yourself." To give the other permission—leave—to be himself or herself is the underpinning of what love means.

Love enhances the ability of the loved person to be himself or herself, to grow and change, to be in the world in good faith. It is easy, then, to understand why loving and being loved makes people anxious and uncertain. Love challenges our need for security and familiarity. If love means to give leave, then the windows to true experience are the windows to love.

The Windows of Experience is about the ways in which each of us is removed from loving our own self and loving others. It describes the ways each of us harms the natural ecology—what we call the *psychoecology*—of our lives. We hope to describe pathways by which we may return to being *whole* human beings.

We began our journey as therapists trained with the understanding of the central importance of pathology—that is, a sensitivity to what is *wrong* with people. As we grew in our own experience as therapists, it became clear to both of us—as we think it does to all good therapists—that our awareness and sensitivity to what was *healthy* and *growthful* in our clients had to become the central focus of our therapy. What the true therapist really understands is the natural human thrust to wholeness. The *ways of being* described in this book therefore comprise those pathways to health that we gradually came to recognize as the ways in which human beings move toward harmony and wholeness.

We are psychiatrists at the Atlanta Psychiatric Clinic, a father and son who feel strongly that the return to such a natural state is the goal of all therapy. I (Tom) and I (Pat)—which is how we will identify ourselves—together have over seventy years of experience as experiential therapists in which we have found these ways of being to be the major pathways to restoring our internal balance as persons. We wrote this book because we believe that we as a culture will only save our world when individually we each learn to save ourselves.

1
Beginning

To be nobody—but—yourself—in a world which is doing
its best, night and day, to make you everybody else—
means to fight the hardest battle which any human being
can fight; and never stop fighting.

—e. e. cummings

In our first book, *The Art of Intimacy*, we introduced the concept of *selficide*, and used it to describe the "leaking away" of personhood, the ways in which we make ourselves less than whole. Such a lack of wholeness is certainly far more prevalent and, in a certain sense, much more malignant than the abrupt end of life found in suicide. Since we remain conscious of our loss of relational being, our lack of wholeness is a living death. *Loss of our relational being* means we are not able to be who we are, *while* and *when* we support others in being who or what they are. We are, in that way, like barely conscious robots, aware of our wishes and hopes, but not able to live as we would. This loss of being is the personal process wherein we injure, stunt, immobilize, damage, and deaden our psychoecology, our *selfbeing*. It is actually psychological cancer, and we bring it on ourselves. As Emerson said, "We are always getting ready to live, but never living."

Our lack of wholeness has profound implications. With few exceptions, both the minor and major failures of human beings are self-engendered. Climate, bacteria and viruses, and natural

19

disasters are the major exceptions. Even with these problems, we humans often seem to have a hidden complicity. It is almost as if we wish to assure that their destructiveness will be maximal. Whether it be the poor use of land, the overuse of antibiotics, or the depletion of the ozone, we participate in ways that increase problems even in processes we do not cause.

Other social and ecological disasters are sadly but inexorably engineered by ourselves. In these, there is no hidden complicity— the fault is gross. Who else can be held responsible for war, acid rain and other pollutions, the starvation of children, the social destitution of our elders, racial and ethnic genocides (whether biological, social, or psychological), and, more mundanely, what appears to be our unending abrasive interpersonal dehumanization of one another? Our sins hardly need belaboring. Evolutionists, ecologists, and scientists of all facets of the human pilgrimage have graphically documented our culpability. Somehow we do not learn. We are not *educated*, that is, led out of ourselves. Instead, we are *trained*, that is, drawn along or handled. The result is our inability to learn from history.

The microcosm of that macrocosm is the unique, solitary individual human being. And self-destructiveness seems as characteristic of the individual as it is of society; the problem is that it seems less documentable in the individual. Less documentable unless, of course, we are willing to look at our folklore, myths, and literature, and in the memories and files of the teachers, priests, and therapists of our culture.

There—as Freud and Jung well knew—in songs and poems, books and tales, stories and memories, we may learn something of why humans live in such unhealthy ways, why we are less than the whole persons we might be. We may learn something of why and how we come to be so *unnaturally* self-destructive. Our folklore, mythology, and literature tell a tale that is unswerving and consistent, a tale crystallized by Shakespeare in Hamlet's soliloquy: *To be or not to be.* That indeed is the question for each of us. What better description of self-destructiveness than "not to be" or by a sleep to end "the thousand natural shocks that flesh is heir to," to end the "heartache." On the other hand, "to be," to dream of being, indeed, that is the rub. For therein lie the beginnings of "those enterprises of great pith and action"—the enterprise of moving from dispassion and abject compliance to our familiar pasts into passion and being in the world in good faith.

So much of the time you and I are accommodating, compromising, being other than *who* we really are in order to stay *where* we are—sacrificing self in order to be secure in a relationship—at the enormous personal expense of never becoming who we really are. We do not *exist* in our relationships; and worse, we seldom have any real sense of why we do not. And those of us who know we are significantly less than we could be, or could have been, rest in the pain of that awareness. We usually live with little sense of any possible way to change.

Out of the internal discomfort, many of us move to geographic or occupational escapes, affairs, senseless divorces, alcohol and drugs, retreating illnesses, or distorting ideologies. More often than we care to know, like those stylized robots, we sit staring night after night, hour after hour, at a television screen—or its emotional equivalent—which neither knows nor cares who we are. That nonreflective mirror becomes the most addictive drug of all. Like the giant vacuum tube it is, television becomes the modern symbol for the leaking away of our *selves* into the vacuum. We creep down the hall to bed, wondering but empty, and usually dream with the same meaningless and disconnected metaphors with which we spent our evening.

Unhealthy Living

Rarely do we live in our world with a healthy awareness of our responsibility for self. Sometimes, of course, we have short-lived, episodic experiences of creative self-responsibility. These usually result in personal change. But far more commonly we blame our troubles on parents, spouse, lover, work, authority, government, drugs, foods, culture, history, and even our "stars." Seldom do we blame ourselves—except for the pathological self-blamers, and their position is self-deceptive rather than self-motivating, for it is not accepting responsibility; it is simply blaming the "self." Thus, even as blaming it is dishonest, for it is more like blaming God than their real selves.

When we blame, we suffer the loss of true self; we forget our dreams—both our night and day dreams—and become frozen without a sense of freedom, shriveling in the cocoon of a pained and damaged self. Even so, we stubbornly continue to hold the other responsible. We learn nothing from the price we pay, the pain we feel. Unable to acknowledge that we do the damage to ourselves, we are impotent to change it. We passively wait for the world around us to do the changing. The Great Pill is always something outside of ourselves—the capricious, all-powerful *other*.

This loss of self-responsibility begins the pervasive, insidious erosion of selfbeing that inevitably ensues. Much as our world's ecology is ruined by our irresponsible living, our internal ecology is destroyed by our lack of self-responsibility. Fragmentation of personality, repressive role playing, codependency, deadening compulsive repetition of uncreative behavior, addictiveness—in general all the ways of living once removed from the energies of life—are the predictable results. Healthily alive in neither self nor relationship, removed from the balanced being in the world in good faith—from *being self in relationship*—we use up our time of living. Neither the unending dull personal pain of such "living" nor the absence of gratification and excitement seems sufficient to move us to be different. We bemoan the symptoms. We seek all kinds of outside things to ameliorate these same symptoms. Yet we do little or nothing to confront the underlying problem: the loss of *our* responsibility for *our* living.

Motivation to change apparently does not come out of pain and lack of gratification, even when they endure for years. Something else appears to be needed. Otherwise the escalating statistics of human personal suffering and tragedies make little sense. Obviously living as ourselves in our world is puzzlingly difficult for us humans. Being one's self is the exception, not the rule. We described such *self* in *The Art of Intimacy* as the ecological dimension of the human psyche—that particular and invaluable part of the human being that enables him or her to live fully and gratifyingly in relationship to his surrounding personal, social, and cultural coinhabitants, whether they be persons, corporations, trees, or stars.

Our loss of wholeness is the spoilage, the diseasing of that critical psychoecology. As in all ecological crises, the major problem is a loss of a critical natural balance, a loss of a nourishing balance between self and other. On the small scale, for example, a pond is thermally polluted by the hot waste water runoff from a mill. There is a change in the system—temperature goes up, oxygenation increases, the plant and animal life change. In the crises in the psychoecology, the truth is the same; it is simply more difficult to identify and document. It is no less disastrous for both the disrupter and the disrupted. The metaphor of the disrupted pond and the difficulties encountered in reestablishing its natural ecology are just as true of the psychoecological disruption of a human being. Only it is more than a metaphor. It is the same phenomena with one possible significant difference. The pond does not participate in its own "pondicide." On the contrary, it usually resists courageously. It fights to be whole.

Our movement away from wholeness differs from nonhuman ecological disruptions in that the human being is usually, at the adult stage of life, his own disrupter. Nevertheless, the cost is as great, and the difficulty in returning to the healthy state as real. We are not what we would be as persons, and we are responsible for that. Not always, but usually. "Yet is everyman his greatest enemy," wrote Sir Thomas Browne, "and, as it were, his own executioner."

Systems and Selves: Closeness and Intimacy

In exploring the various significant ways in which such disruptive imbalances develop in persons, it is clear that the *self* is the main force in controlling the delicate homeostasis of the psychoecological system. Each of us exists both as an individual and as a part of various systems. These systems maybe marriages and families within which there may be many other subsystems. Or, they may be business organizations, churches, schools, ethnic groups, neighborhoods, governments, cultures and subcultures, the whole of humanity, even planetary systems. Or, most commonly, they may be systems of our past, personal systems of living that we cannot shed. We are all closely involved in these systems. More often than not, we are involved in ways we are not even aware of. We are captured by our systems and are usually unaware of being captured.

Our behavior reflects those systems. Our choices are often mitigated by the ethos of those systems, with little conscious participation on our part. We belong to our systems without knowing that we are belonging. In such ways, we exist not as selves but as components of systems. This part of our living is not always negative. To be functional in systems is half of being a mature, creative, healthy human being. *Keeping healthily functional* will depend, of course, on our continuing ability to be our own persons while in those systems. When we can do so, systems not only provide us with stability and safety, but also reinforce and mature our persons.

More and more, however, we are less healthily functional in our systems. We abrogate our responsibility to attend to our individual personhood. Increasingly cut off from the rest of nature, we have fewer correcting experiences. We live in a world in which life is more often seen as entertainment than as experience. Our systems "feed" us, and in return we agree to forgo being individuals and live docilely as mere parts of those systems. We surrender our individual experience for external security. "Experience," as Henry James wrote, "is never limited, and it is never complete; it is an immense sensibility, a kind of huge spider web of the finest silken threads suspended in the chamber of consciousness, and catching every air-borne particle in its tissue." But such real experience requires wholeness. It is not possible for us when we are living as part-persons.

This experiential reality—what e. e. cummings termed "isness"—has become, in our Western culture, more and more compromised and attenuated, until it is near extinguishment. The *system* has become overriding. We are out of balance. *And it would be equally frightening were the system to be in jeopardy,* for the balance between the two is essential to the survival of each. One cannot exist without the other, and we cannot exist as whole persons without both.

The truth of our current unhealthy living, however, is that we have become disconnected, unlinked, from our "isness," and thus from our universality, or our "selving" as the poet Gerard Manley Hopkins called it. Captured by our systems, we have compromised our ability to live fully as selves; we have diminished our selfbeing and become less than whole. *Natural closeness*—healthily being part of natural systems—is an essential part of healthy life. The other part is *natural intimacy*—the natural and energizing dyadic (one-to-one) interactive connection of self and other. Only in this balance do we feel what Hopkins called the "instress" (the individual unity of things) and live in the "inscape" (the energy of life).

Me, Myself, and I

What does living in balance mean? We feel and experience closeness in the space we share with an other. By *other* we mean whatever we are in relation to: lover, landscape, or culture. We can be close to the idiosyncrasies or even idiocies of our boss, to a neighbor to whom we seldom speak, or to the traffic on the way to work. In traffic, we can peripherally be aware that those other people are probably more like us than different from us. At work, we can realize occasionally that, like our boss, we, too, have idiosyncrasies and idiocies. As we drive by our neighbors, we can vaguely sense that their mailbox is not too different from our mailbox, and, perhaps, they are not too different from us. We recognize both their humanness and our own. To do so allows healthy closeness.

The closeness we feel with those persons in our lives who are most significant—our spouses, lovers, parents, and children—provides us with the safety and stability that enables us to grow, to risk being ourselves, to live as selves in good faith. That closeness is a very intense awareness of the feelings and being of the others as we live in relationship with them. We are as aware of these others as we are of ourselves. In fact, more often than not, we are more aware of their feelings, thoughts, dreams, and behaviors, than we are of our own. We are more sensitive and responsive to their needs, defenses, and wants, than we are to our own needs, defenses, and wants.

We give up significant parts of ourselves to deepen our awareness of significant others. We most often do this not to please or placate, or even manipulate, but to enhance our experience in the relationship. We accommodate to the other, as well we should when we are close. Living in this way—*healthily* close—is the main function of what we have called the *I* in each of us: our personality, the gift giver, the facilitator of closeness. The *I* learns to live lovingly and sensitively with the reality and experience of the other. The *I* is happy to do so because it enables us to know the other better, and concurrently know ourselves better as well.

The equally important component in the healthy self is the component we have designated as the *me*. *Me* is what we experience when we are in our personal space, simply being in the world without the distraction of attending to anyone or anything. *Me* directs our separate personal experience. *Me* meditates. *Me* is our character, our psychological etching, the difficult-to-erase early engravings of our person. *Me* is internal, more germinal, and comes from the deeper recesses of our person, our very early experiences, even our genes. It is what makes us recognizable to others at the thirtieth college reunion even though we are older, somewhat gray, and twenty pounds heavier. Character, *me*, articulates our origins and comprises the deepest imprints of our person. These imprints provide those few, extremely powerful, persistent motivational systems that identify us as persons regardless of the vagaries of our personality over time. Character sits in the bottom well of our persons and wills us toward those broad behaviors that we hope will meet the basic emotional needs prescribed in our early life experience.

What then is *self?* It is neither *me* nor *I*, but the natural and beautiful synchronous *balance* of the two. It is a pairing in which the sum is more than the total of the parts. So much so, that in the experience of *self*, we wonderfully lose any sense that *me* and *I* compete, or are even different from each other. Perhaps that is what people mean by centering. In the intimate experience of being fully *me* while in full relationship with the other, *self* is found. When I am *close*, I know *you* fully in your presence. When I am *intimate*, I know *myself* fully in your presence. Intimately, I can be joyfully and freely who I am, connected with everything else in the universe, without blunting or compromising anyone or anything outside of me from being itself. Only in intimacy can *self* be experienced.

We intuitively recognize *self* experience because it feels so natural. For example, when we suddenly see some truth about ourselves while sharing our experience with our child in a discussion about his problems, we *know* we are being our real selves. When we are living so, we are most in creative contact with our unconscious. *Self* experience brings us connection, animation, and personal aliveness. It allows us to experience ourselves in our personal space while we live sensitively in our shared spaces with others. It allows us to express our *intima,* our innermost core, while at the same time facilitating the expressive being of others. It puts us in touch with who we are, what our wholeness is. Then, through the reexperience of healthy closeness, these new ways of knowing ourselves become part of our ordinary lives.

Spiritual Selfbeing

We feel this reality of self when it occurs. We feel the connecting, linking reality of our person being there without judging, blaming, prejudging, or distorting. We live in the here and now with the other. We forgo the futility of continually preconstructing worlds, of preconceiving things that will be, of reliving long dead past relationships. As Sartre hoped, we come to "being in the world in good faith." In such selfbeing, we are the active creator as well as the creation of "isness." Being our real selves brings us to our soul, our spirit, the breathing in and out of which exuberant life is made. When being our *selves,* we learn to be whole.

Such experiences then provide the ongoing nourishment necessary for the healthy existence of both the *I* and the *me.* They allow us to be truly spiritual, to live in a way that involves our breath of life, our soul. And make no mistake: whatever intellectual embarrassment we may feel as pragmatic scientists when dealing with the spirit and soul, if we ignore them we will never fully comprehend humans and their relationship to each other or to their world. Whatever spirit and soul may be, they are a most *pragmatic* part of life.

William James, in his classic *The Varieties of Religious Experience,* spoke to the pragmatics of religion:

> Primarily, religion is a biological reaction. Its simplest terms are an uneasiness and a deliverance from that uneasiness. We are saved from that uneasiness by making proper connection with the universe . . . at bottom the whole concern of religion is with the manner of our acceptance of the universe.

This religion, a spiritual concern so very different from what passes for religion in our current world, centers on two central concepts. These concepts—*relationship* and *the enthusiasm of passion*—are the quintessential experiences of the intimate being, of connectivity, of the fully animated self.

Psychoanalyst Carl Jung saw this religious experience as an effort creatively to connect ourselves to our cultural and biological history. He used religious in its original meaning, coming from the Latin, *ligamentum*, meaning anything that ties one part to another. Religion then means to retie: a connecting, energizing, spiritual activity. To retie to the past, to the present, and to the future, to each other, and to ourselves, to the very experience of religion—that of constantly reconnecting. Only in this way can spirit be constantly re-created. And if humans stop being spiritual in this way, they will become personal evolutionary anomalies. In all probability, they will not survive as evolving human beings—as *selves*.

Unfortunately, as psychiatrist Leston Havens writes in *Making Contact*, "interest in the self waxes and wanes through the history of psychiatry." The same, sadly, is true of psychology and the other social sciences, as well as of philosophy and religious studies. But in recent decades, psychologists such as Rogers, Laing, and May have written of this connectivity and its vital importance in the growth of the *I* and the *me*, that is, in our ongoing animation and maturation as persons. We see the same emphasis in the "weness" of Martin Buber and, in a broader sense, in the concept of God as ground substance in the writings of Paul Tillich. Currently such therapists as Alfred Margulies, Alex Comfort, Alice Miller, and others, including the late Gregory Bateson, have sensitively labored to illuminate the realities of self in the world. In somewhat different ways, writers such as information scientist Douglas Hofstader, animal scientist Vicki Hearne, mathematical scientist Rudy Rucker, physical scientist David Bohm, and chemical scientist Ilya Prigogine are also attempting to describe this *being and becoming*.

Just as important, poets, artists, and novelists are primarily engaged in the same task. *Meaningful* art, as opposed to propaganda, may bring us to understanding self more readily than science. Such art may simply be a more direct experience of self. Music conductor Robert Shaw wrote:

> Art on the heroic scale is the most pervasive, persistent, powerful affirmation of the life-force in the man thing . . . it is a true transubstantiation: pitch into sonata—form into spir-

it—paint onto canvas into tears; words on paper across a pro-
scenium into the heart of man . . . it is finally the flesh become
word.

To visit the Louvre, the Prado, the Metropolitan, or the Smith-
sonian museums affords us a chance to see the myriad of ways
man and woman have spoken of the realities of self. A visit to any
library or symphony hall can do the same.

Understanding *self* as this spiritual connectedness, as the *ecological dimension* of the human psyche, underlies any effort to
move to full selfbeing, to end our alienation from our intima, our
"isness." In the imbalance between *me* and *I*, in the loss of connection to either ourselves or to the rest of what is in our world,
there is diminishment of *self*, and *I* and *me* become malnourished.
The psychoecology that is selfbeing is disrupted, and our ability to
be ourselves in relationship to another is seriously compromised.
Selfbeing is undermined, and we are less than whole.

Selfbeing's Absence—Selficide

> But warm, eager, living life—to be rooted in life—to
> learn, to desire, to know, to feel, to think, to act. That is
> what I want. And nothing less. That is what I must
> try for.
>
> —Katherine Mansfield

What is this imbalance? Unlike suicide, the abrupt ending of
life, selficide is far more common, slower, more insidious, and in
some ways more formidable. We seldom consciously know that
we are killing our *selves* when we commit selficide. Workaholics,
alcoholics, the man who cannot say how he feels, and the woman
who cannot accept the lover who is different from her are all
destroying their wholeness. More frightening, we seldom are
aware that we are dying, psychologically, relationally, or even
physically. A lack of playfulness, an inability to share, a lack of
internal integrity, or a fear of choosing are all ways of slowly
ceasing to be.

Suicide, of course, also has its long, preparatory, insidious beginnings. It never simply comes out of the blue, but always has its prior hidden agenda. But when it happens it is final—for too many people a permanent solution to a temporary problem. Those who commit suicide for unique reasons, such as a painful terminal illness, really present what is more an ethical problem than a psychological one. We should, in truth, have a separate name for such acts.

Suicide, indescribably painful to those who are left behind, is the most senseless ending to an individual's life struggle to attain wholeness—because it *is* the end of that struggle. The saddest thing about suicide is precisely its finality. Most people who succeed in killing themselves have no such intention. Their deaths are usually accidental, in the sense that they had no true intent to die. They are really trying to communicate a feeling, to change something.

Usually these people die because they are uninformed, not because they actually want or intend to die. Most who survive the attempt furiously fight to recover what life they have left. Those few who succeed in suicide because they really mean to die show that clear intent in the incisive, unequivocal manner in which they kill themselves. A shotgun in the mouth leaves little room for error. But the majority of people who attempt suicide have no such intention. The opposite, in fact, is true; they want to be listened to, heard, and sensitively attended. But ignorance can be deadly, as Mary McCarthy described in *On the Contrary:*

> In moments of despair, we look on ourselves leadenly as objects; we see ourselves, our lives, as someone else might see them and even may be driven to kill ourselves if the separation, "the knowledge," seems sufficiently final.

Overcoming Personal Inertia

With suicide, one cannot change one's mind. Most humans probably would, had they the chance. The singular, redeemable quality of the myriad ways of selficide, in contrast to suicide, is simply that—we *can* change our mind. What does it take to change our mind? Obviously, some new experience. But for most of us such experiences come only serendipitously. And although we often seem to, we cannot depend on serendipity in such important matters as life and death. As therapists, can we improvise these experiences? Many counselors certainly believe we can. For example, workshops are such improvisations. We, however, are not sure about such a structured, intentional approach. We are not sure that spirituality ever really, integrally develops out of the revival experience.

We suspect that such staged revival experiences can give us a taste of life, but seldom a genuine appetite for it. Most people who participate in workshops become spirited briefly in the communal experience, but then rather quickly slip back into the mundanity of their need for security and unhealthy closeness. Community is not maintained after the meeting—the communality is quickly lost. It is a start, but more often than not, a start that stops. It leaves us with a taste, but without the enduring appetite for life. Something else is needed beyond revival.

What then does it take to change our person? How do we gain a real appetite? How do we regain our communality with our world? A single experience can change a mind. To change our person, however, takes much more than one experience, much more than a workshop. It takes extended, repeated, and continually changing *self*-energizing experience—experience that creates new experience that creates more and further new experience. Personal change of any significance requires *momental* experience, experience that creates personal momentum.

This process is not unlike that of physical inertia. Persons tend to remain at rest, as they do in all forms of selficide, unless impacted by significant other experience. Significant in this particular psychological sense simply means different. The experience has to be new in order for it to have sufficient momental thrust to overcome the inertia of our self-diminishing behavior. "There was that law of life, so cruel and so just," Norman Mailer wrote in *The Deer Park*, "that one must grow or else pay more for remaining the same." The cost of remaining the same, staying inert, is being less than whole.

Equally true, once a person has developed psychological momentum, he or she tends to remain in a growing experiential *self* development. Unless one is significantly impacted by other experiences (such as divorce, chronic illness, some overwhelming loss, or senility), the thrust of growth continues. The greater the psychological momentum, the more powerful the negative impact experience needed to stop that growthful inertial thrust.

Seen in this conceptual context, humans exist in a continuum of nonexperience and experience. Anyone who exists has experience. If, however, the experiences are unendingly repetitious, at some point they cease to be *experience* and become habit or personal rote. This "rigor mortis" is selficide. The person literally "lives out" his life, with little difference in his experience when he is five, sixteen, forty, or seventy years old. *Self* never emerges. On the other end of the continuum is the person whose emergent psychological inertia constantly engenders new and different experiences. The fact that the experiences are continually different leads to growth, openness, change, and the capacity to be who one is: whenever one is, wherever one is, and truly with whomever one is with. Such a person has moved to wholeness.

Between these two extremes is where most of us live. But to stay in *any* one place on the continuum is self-diminishing, *wherever we are on the continuum.* Personal growth is the only alternative to such self-diminishment. Regardless of what we individually see as the ground substance, to be natural simply means that we constantly grow toward that ground substance, our communal reality. Perhaps few in history have come close to realizing it, but that is far less important than our continuing our momental thrust to more experience. Standing still is unnatural.

Other Words for Selficide

Why describe this lack of momentum, this lack of wholeness, as ecological selficide? By making clearer that human relationships are not different from planetary relationships, or the way that flowers, bees, birds, and trees successfully live together, perhaps we can add a useful perspective.

There are thousands of other terms that describe in detail the varied forms of selficide. Our textbooks of psychology recount many types of self-diminishment—obsessive-compulsive behaviors, phobias, paranoia, for example. Interestingly, however, many of the ways we make ourselves less than *whole* are not analyzed. For example, there is no diagnostic description of the person who is not curious. Nor is there one for the person who is seldom, if ever, passionate; persons who lose their sexuality in their sixties; persons who progressively lose the capacity for new experience. There is no diagnosis for the normal, well-adjusted person who has not been excited about anything for decades.

To be sure, all of the above personal deficits could easily be included under terms like depression, or situational reactions, or marital maladjustments. We are not suggesting that these carefully documented diagnostic categories are not valid, or enormously useful for research or statistical purposes. They are indeed. Nonetheless, the diagnostic designation is of no personal help to the person so labeled. It tells him or her nothing. It does not help him or her to any real sense of what they have to deal with in their lives. We need a more personal language, just as science needs its more impersonal language. Both can coexist, and, perhaps, even fertilize each other.

The language of selficide and selfbeing may provide such a discourse. Descriptions of self varying from extremes of spaced-out, bananas, goofy, or crazy, to dud, square, and stick-in-the-mud do not really help us grow. The most commonly used term—for it has now become personal—for most forms of self-diminishment is "neurotic." He is neurotic. She is neurotic. Even the dog or cat can be neurotic. But what does neurotic mean to the person using it to describe someone else, or to the person so described? Does it lead them in any way to greater selfbeing?

No. Subjectively it means little or nothing. As the word itself suggests, neurotic is essentially a neurological term, having no personal referent. The person who uses it generally does so as a frustrated epithet. The person so described generally experiences it as a social judgment, and, more often than not, as an insult. We seldom use the term neurotic either in reference to ourselves or to anyone else in order to be sincerely helpful. It really does not matter that its technical meaning is not so different from our concept of selficide. People do not live in the world of technical meanings.

The essential dynamic of neuroticism is that of *repetition compulsion*. A person repeats behavior compulsively because his original experience was unfinished, unsatisfactory, and ungrowthful. He does it again and again in order to have it come out right. Unfortunately he always does it in the same way he did it originally, so it always has the same outcome. That is neurotic. Or, as we would say, it is selficidal. When people live in those ways, it is painful, and it affects more than just the individual alone. "Those who cannot live fully often become destroyers of life," wrote Anaïs Nin in her *Diaries*. With our own self-diminishment, we often damage others.

Language, in its nontechnical sense, is critically important in human experience. If a therapist suggests to a person that she is neurotic, it not only means little that is helpful to her, it creates an experiential vacuum. By its judgmentalness, it may even create an unbridgeable distance. On the other hand, if we suggest to the same person that she seems to have problems being herself even with us, or that she seems to care less for herself than she does for others, or that she seems unable to be wholly herself, then she hears us differently. Of course, merely using different words is not enough. The therapist has to feel, know, and experience the person's lack of selfbeing *with* her. The therapist has to *miss* the patient's person, not just know about it clinically. Only then is the language personal. And only when it is personal does it make a difference to the other person.

Selficide and selfbeing, too, as words or concepts, make little difference unless we can identify those experiences that assure self-emergence, and those nonexperiences that occur, particularly in early life, which predispose one to self-diminishment. How can *nonexperiences* occur? A simple example will help explain. If I tell my mother that I hate my brother, and she tells me that I really do not hate my brother; if I then give greater credence to my mother's description of reality than I do to my own feelings, then a nonexperience has occurred. I decide that I did not really hate my brother, and that is a nonexperience. Actually, we should call it a *disexperience*.

I (Tom) remember one such "disexperience." My mother told me when I was six years old that I could have a birthday party, and I could invite all of my friends. I happily announced whom I wanted at my birthday party, including my friend Mike. She said, "You don't want to have Mike at your party."

I said, "I like Mike."

"No, you don't," she said. "You and Mike are always fighting."

I thought to myself, "I really like Mike," and told her that.

She replied, "You don't like Mike. You two are always fighting."

I thought to myself some more. "Fighting with Mike is fun, that is why I like him so much. But she said I did not like him. She is the one who knows. Do I really like Mike or not?"

At that moment I did not know. I was experiencing nonexperience. By denying my experience of myself in deference to my overpowering dependence on my mother, I was losing my wholeness. I was allowing needs related to what was outside me to displace what was inside me. In just that specific sense can we experience nonexperience. I was six years old—most of us are still deferring to nonexperience when we are sixty years old.

2

The Windows
to Experience

The most beautiful thing we can experience is the mysterious.

—Albert Einstein

What then are the growthful experiences, the ones that facilitate and energize our consciousness of selfbeing? In *The Art of Intimacy*, we said that this issue is not a matter of *doing* but of *being*, and that there is no prescription for being. Contrary to the unending destructive belief of so many people, *being cannot be prescribed.* Nothing outside us—not drugs, not exercise, not lovers, not religions, not governments, not status, not power, not position—can give us the answer to being ourselves. Humans look for such answers in the mistaken belief that others can somehow tell them how to be themselves. Our loss of wholeness frequently comes out of that very illusion. Prescriptive answers of any kind do not work. No one else can tell *us* who *we* are. Only *self* can prescribe being in the world in good faith. When we try to be what the other defines, whether that other is a drug or a prescribing guru, selfbeing does not evolve. We must *be* out of our own person. The essential ingredients of personhood are resident within each of us, and we must learn to pay passionate attention to them. When we do not, we lose our wholeness.

Such inattention is common. As psychoanalyst Erich Fromm wrote in *Man for Himself*:

> We listen to every voice and to everybody but not ourselves. We are constantly exposed to the noise of opinions and ideas hammering at us from everywhere: motion pictures, newspapers, radio, idle chatter. If we had planned intentionally to prevent ourselves from ever listening to ourselves, we could have done no better.

In listening to every other voice, we never hear our own. There is no *other* who can tell us the essential ingredients of our own personhood. There is no *recipe for us* written by someone else.

How, then, do we learn for ourselves these essential ingredients for personhood? In what areas must we search, in our listening to ourselves, in order to become whole? There are two very critical areas to which a person must attend in order to increase his or her availability to selfbeing. (1) One must develop the capacity to be aware of *self* and *other* concurrently, be "a part of" without losing self. (2) One must have an awareness of one's communality with one's world, one's connection to that world, and one's identity in that world. In order for someone to fully *be* the person he or she is, both capacities are needed.

Defining Windows to Experience

This awareness is not simply cognitive. Thought alone cannot engender being. Nor can feeling and desire, or simple rote behavior. Thought, feeling, and behavior in their full *congruency* are all required. Real awareness only comes out of that sense of a congruent self. Both ourselves and others recognize such real knowing. It impacts our being. In contrast, we are all unsure when we only think, or simply feel, or just behave. *Knowing* in the wholeness of our persons is the essence of experience.

We all know when we move into that space of being our most real selves, because we feel a clearing in our vision of both ourselves and others, a poignant sense of being fully open, aware, and present. We know honestly in that moment who we *really are* and what we *really think and feel.* We also know then what our *real experience* of the other is. From such real selfbeing—and the real experience it brings—we can learn and grow.

An ordinary example will help to make the point. I (Pat) went one Saturday morning with my wife, Elaine, to have a picture framed for our daughter's birthday. We drove some considerable distance to the shop, but, upon our arrival, I discovered I had forgotten to bring the picture. With an anger that I myself recognized only in retrospect, I led Elaine into the shop and began to show her frames and mats, asking her which ones she wanted. She, of course, looked at me as if I were crazy, and, after several further efforts on my part to get her to make a choice, she pointed out to me that she could not make a choice without having the picture. By this time I was overtly if sullenly angry, and we left the store. On the way across the parking lot she asked gently, "Why are you angry with me?"

I was not angry with her; I was angry with myself for forgetting the picture. But I was living with her as a person who was angry with her. My "eyes" were closed and I was unknowing about both myself and her. I could not see that she was not the person who was causing my pain—she was, instead, a real person herself. And I could not see how the child in me—unable to feel okay doing something "wrong"—was controlling my current living. In short, I was not conscious of myself; I was not aware. In that moment in the parking lot, in her being accepting of me instead of reacting to me, I experienced the fact that I was not being accepting of her, was not being responsible for myself, was not being very playful, and was not living in a way that recognized our connection to each other. Some windows opened for me and I *knew* myself for the moment—and grew a bit.

A simple example—even mundane—but one that points out how we must open ourselves to *awareness of self* if we would change and grow. We will attempt to define these critical areas of *consciousness of self*, these thoughts, feelings, and behaviors that engender and enhance experience. We call them the *windows to experience.* Intimacy creates experience, experience assures our growth into selfbeing, growth into selfbeing is consolidated by the reexperience of healthy closeness, and selfbeing ensures against self-diminishment. If these windows to experience can be identified and described, then we very likely can also identify and describe the nonexperiences that make us less than whole.

There are fourteen windows to human wholeness that we will briefly define. In later chapters, we will look more closely at each window individually and see how it helps us rediscover our wholeness as human beings.

Acceptance

She likes herself, yet others hates
For that which in herself she prizes;
And while she laughs at them, forgets
She is the thing that she despises.

—WILLIAM CONGREVE, *Amoret*

The first window is *acceptance*. It is a wide and beautiful window to experience, with impressive precedents. Jesus said to accept and love the sinner while you condemn the sin. That is acceptance. Buddha said we must accept and love the sinner and know that sinning is simply part of life. That is acceptance. If we realize that neither Jesus nor Buddha were passive beings, that they were in fact passionately confrontive beings, then we begin to sense the vitality of acceptance. It is not simply a matter of being resigned or forgiving. It is instead an active part of love and nature. Unable to accept, we are unable to know ourselves.

We accept so that we may go on to experience with the other without the selficidal estrangement of judgment. Blaming others for being who they are ends meaningful relationships. Criminals should be judged, not lovers or friends. Judgment separates us from further experience. Judgmentalism is clearly the polarity of acceptance and engenders self-diminishment.

Responsibility for Self

The second window is *responsibility for self*. No one else can *be* for us. We are in the world as we want to be. We may despise it, decry it, or complain mightily about it, but we are responsible for our living, for our selfbeing. We have to accept the fact that we live as we choose, however we lament that living. We are responsible for what we have become or have not become. This window clears when we accept the terrible but beautifully freeing realization that we must take the initiative for what we want and who we are. That acknowledgment frees us to experience and enables being. The opposite of self-responsibility is dependence and blame, in which our lives are turned over to others. Unhealthy dependency and blaming of others for who we are guarantees a lack of wholeness. If we are not responsible for our own selves, how can we ever envision being fully who we are?

Innocence: Naturalness

The third window is *innocence* or *naturalness*. Innocence does not mean naïveté. It means the delight of the person with his or her experience of belonging to the connected mosaic of the world he or she lives in. It is childlike but not childish. An openness to experiencing the other permeates innocence. It renders us free and creative, risking and curious, sensual and sexual without contrivance or need to manipulate or exploit. We are joyful and continually learning from the other. Without constructing a world of our own, one that we so often mistakenly believe will better allow us to be who we are, we share ourselves. When we do not rejoice in the energy of the surrounding real world, we become a world unto ourselves, and, sterile and stagnant, we become mired in it.

Self-Discipline: Participation

The fourth window is *self-discipline* or *participation*. "The notion of looking on at life," wrote Antoine de Saint-Exupéry in *Flight to Arras*, "has always been hateful to me. What am I if I am not a participant? In order to be, I must participate." Young children accept the authority of their parents. They listen for a variety of reasons, perhaps out of fear, but just as likely out of

THE WINDOWS TO EXPERIENCE 41

respect. Either way, children listen with deference, and thus the voice of conscience is established. Such a voice, though necessary, leaves growing persons with the subsequent labor of establishing their own voices. Yet only through that process can they determine how *they* will participate in the world. They may well adopt many of their parents' values. But by first *questioning* them and then finally *choosing* them, they make the values their own.

They will then be listening to themselves with self-discipline and becoming their own persons. That is literally what self-discipline means: to follow ourselves out of love and respect for ourselves, to be disciples of ourselves. It is not enough simply to listen to ourselves; we must follow ourselves because we love ourselves. This ensures that love will be included in all our behavior, so that we are more apt to do what we will like and respect ourselves for doing. Being *self-full* is the best guardian against being selfish.

The opposite of self-discipline is abject subservience to some other—a voice from outside of ourselves—as the basis of our conscience. Someone other than ourselves decides how we are to be in the world. Our commitment in life becomes rote, a robotical compliance to external dictates from, for example, a rigid church, a totalitarian state, a nationalistic fervor, a corporate culture, or, more directly, a needy spouse or lover. Such living is self-diminishing. The opposite of self-discipline is fearful, or dutiful, obedience to another. Only when the choice is freely ours—even when our choice is no different from what the other said it should be—are we being in the world in good faith. Only then do we *participate* in life as ourselves.

Congruence

The fifth window is *congruence*. It is an essential quality of self. Congruence means personal harmony. More concretely, it refers to the harmonious integration of a person's thoughts, feelings, and behaviors. The absence of such harmony characterizes all forms of self-diminishment. If our thinking is different from our feeling, then our personalities are literally split. If we are angry at our lover about doing something for him, but we do it because we think we are being helpful to him, we are diminished as persons. If our behavior does not honestly reflect how we think and feel, then we are not really ourselves. These incongruences or disharmonies in people are a substrate of all personal psychological "illnesses." The experience of living in the harmony of thought, feeling, and behavior is essential to the healthy self. It is the true *being* of being in the world in good faith. Congruence is most commonly referred to as integrity.

Presence

The sixth window is *presence*, which means being there, in the world. We see presence dramatically in young children before they are socialized by the world in general and the educational system in particular. I (Pat) recently sat with a depressed mother and her seven-year-old son. The mother was complaining in a rambling way, and I was simply looking at her. The boy was looking at a comic book he had brought with him. The mother was silent for a moment, and then asked, "Why are you looking at me?" Without looking up, the son answered for me, "Because you are more important than the telephone." That is a clear experiential description of presence.

The child is likely to lose much of that direct insight into presence. Most of us do as we are socialized. But one hopes he will regain enough of it in his adult life to make selfbeing possible. *Absence* characterizes selficide—either the absence of our being or the absence of our relationship to the world we live in. Thomas Wolfe was speaking about such absence in *Of Time and the River:* "We get together and talk, and say we think and feel and believe in such a way, and yet what we really think and feel and believe we never say at all." Unlike children, most adults are seldom present.

Freedom: Free Choice

The seventh window is *freedom* or *free choice*. We tend to think of freedom as being free *from* someone or something. Free from debt. Free from disease. Free from obligation. In its original meaning, however, the word had much more to do with being free to *be* someone. Freedom is an inner capacity to be who we are, free from inner, personal restraints, even though there can be external restraints on our being. In that sense, as Nelson Mandela demonstrated, one can be free even if one is in jail, or living under a dictatorship, or, more immediately, living with a controlling spouse or lover. "Everything can be taken from a man but one thing," wrote psychoanalyst Viktor Frankl. "The last of human freedoms—to choose one's attitude in any given set of circumstances—to choose one's own way."

Freedom describes one's ability to choose, not simply where to be, or what to do, or when to do it (for sometimes those choices *are* restrained), but rather to choose to be, to think our own thoughts, to feel our own feelings, and to choose how we live within the confines of the realities of the world we live in—even if that world is confining and arbitrary. To be peaceful, loving, and passionately present in the presence of another who is trying to control us is our true freedom. Not to be free in this sense—to cease making personal choices—leads to the loss of our full selfbeing.

Making Do: Personal Surrender

The eighth window is *making do* or *personal surrender*. Making do has to do with our capacity to fit together with others. It has to do with the learned ability to be in the world, to commingle with that world while at the same time maintaining our own being. Making do is a major relational component of one's self. Simply being ourselves would amount merely to being narcissistic. We must live as ourselves in our world as it is. We must live in our relationships with other people as they are. We must live where we are, with whom we are, doing what we are doing together, when we are doing it. We must make do. We surrender our own special needs in order to maximize the experience available to us. Those developmental experiences that teach the value of making do, without suggesting either passivity or rebellion, increase our capacity for selfbeing.

Attentiveness:
Environmental Nourishment
of the Self

The ninth window is *attentiveness*, the ability easily and constantly to use our environment to nourish ourselves. It is clear when we think of our breathing and air, our energy and food, our survival and mutual protection, that we do not live alone in the world—albeit how we deal with our ecology and nutrition suggest that our awareness of this fact is not *very* clear. We tend to forget that we rely on others in general to help nourish our selfbeing. Other persons, other beauty, other truth, other life—the rest of nature nurtures us. "Everything that lives," wrote William Blake in *The Book of Thel*, "lives not alone, nor for itself." Our being has to attend as well as be attended to, just as do other's beings; otherwise, all beings shrivel and die. Our early years must concretize that attentiveness, an important precursor of subsequent selfbeing. Without it we are at risk.

Play

We shall not cease from exploration
And the end of all our exploring
Will be to arrive where we started from
And know the place for the first time.

—T. S. Eliot, *Little Gidding*

The tenth window is *play*. Children, of course, are natural players. They frolic if given half a chance. Play is a natural capacity of enormous intensity and vital energy that often is diminished through unrelenting socialization. Nonetheless, it remains the most powerful window to growth experience for the developing child, and continues as such for the adult. It is as the Chinese philosopher Mencius said: "The great man is he who does not lose his child's heart." Through play, we explore our external and internal worlds.

Language (like most of our fundamental nonverbal communicative sensitivities) is learned through play. The books used to teach the three- or four-year-old child to read are almost always literature of play. Dr. Seuss's books are a wonderful example. Our basic moral and personal ethical values are by and large learned in play, usually in the play of children with each other. Thus, play is the experience in which we most readily learn to be both intimate and close.

This is why it is a striking paradox that most adults come to believe that being intimate means being serious. Nothing could be further from the truth. Being serious in our sexual experiences provides sex therapists with more of their clients than all other reasons combined! If we were able to observe and tabulate all of the genuine and meaningful intimate experiences between couples, the majority would be playful, and the very best would be more like frolic. Lose the capacity for play, and we make self-diminishment not only likely, but almost a certainty.

Aesthetic Morality

The eleventh window is *aesthetic morality*. Aesthetic refers to our experience of beauty. Morality speaks to our experience of goodness. This window contains the polarities of ugliness and evil as well. There are critical experiences in humans, particularly in the developing experience of the child, in which the person learns to see beauty as good and goodness as beautiful. That connection seems to be vital to the subsequent emergence and personal growth of self in adults. It is further reinforced by its antithesis, experiencing ugliness as evil, and evilness as ugly. Such a connection seems to better assure that the person will stay responsible for self, will remain congruent, will live out of his or her own self-discipline, and will maintain a constancy of personal choices.

Psychologist Carol Gilligan, in *In a Different Voice*, wrote that the "essence of moral decision is the experience of choice and the willingness to accept responsibility for that choice." Such choice comes most reliably out of an aesthetic sense. Experiencing evil as ugly seems to be an incomparably more powerful motivation to choice or change than any social feeling that something is wrong. And an inner sense of the beauty of goodness appears to be a far stronger reinforcement of personal morality than the usual religious or social reinforcement. Perhaps we see this power more vividly because both are such deeply personal and inner experiences. Goodness and beauty resonate with self while evil and ugliness both seem almost synonymous with nonexperience.

Connectedness: Reciprocity

The twelfth window is *connectedness* or *reciprocity*. All experience is reciprocal and involves a connection to some other. Much of psychotherapy is the task of helping a person understand that they always participate in what happens in their relational experiences. This does not mean that they are at fault. It simply means that they participate, they are indeed connected, and they have to acknowledge the ongoing reciprocity in the experience. They can persist in trying to change the other person to make the relationship better, but doing so is a losing endeavor. We can only change ourselves. As Thomas à Kempis said in *The Imitation of Christ*, "Be not angry that you cannot make others as you wish them to be, since you cannot make yourself as you wish to be."

That fact is true of all relationships, even in psychotherapy. A therapist cannot change another person. Growth is always emergent, and ways of growing—or not growing—are learned early in life. If a child has a playmate whom she has continued to play with over a period of time, and she comes complaining to her father about how badly that other child has treated her, and if he deals with his child by suggesting that there are some people who are so messed up that you simply cannot get along with them, then he is being irresponsible. He is undermining in the child an important awareness—that regardless of the other child's problems, his own child has something to do with what has happened in that relationship. She is the *creator* in her ordinary living, not just the *created*. The father forgets the truth of which John Ruskin spoke in *Time and Tide:* "To make your children *capable of honesty* is the beginning of education." There is no honesty in living in a nonreciprocal world.

Even in our solitary experiences, our dreams, our meditative reflections, our planning, our worrying, or our fantasies, we are dealing with reciprocities—reciprocities with memories, expectations, and lingering consciousness. We must always remember that we are participating in the unending reciprocity of life. Otherwise, we are seduced by the notion that others are doing it to us; we are seduced into becoming less than whole.

Physicalness: Risking

The thirteenth window is *physicalness* or *risking*. Humans too readily forget that their bodies speak loudly to their close and ongoing relationship to their evolutionary past. We are still animals, and, in certain ways, still closely connected to the plants. We must not forget that we are a part of *all living things*. Animals and plants do not destroy their bodies. They take risks to live, but they do not undo themselves for unnatural reasons. Humans do, particularly in their self-diminishment. Animals and plants do not pity themselves in their ecological survival struggles. Humans do. Animals and plants seldom appear to be plagued with problems of self-destructiveness. Humans are.

Animals and plants seldom forgo the important part that taking risks plays in their continuing being. They dare to try, to evolve. We can come to know this through unending attentiveness to the physical—to the animal and plant world and to our own bodies and souls. To stay alive we have to experience the beautiful exhilaration of *being*, experiencing ourselves in our physicalness—when we just walk, much less dance. To repress or forgo that exhilaration is to jeopardize our selfbeing.

Growth and Death: Creativity

The fourteenth window to experience is *growth and death* or *creativity*. Children seldom seem to be concerned with or even aware of maturation and death. Their natural thrust in life is unending creativity. We usually attribute this lack of concern to a lack of experience with the concept of growth and death.

Strangely, it may be that the opposite is true. Children may, paradoxically, be less concerned and less aware because they are constantly experiencing both growth *and* death. This is easy to see with regard to growth, but what of death?

The precursive experiences of death are endings, and children experience endings in superabundance. As psychoanalyst Otto Rank suggested, they first have to come to terms with the end of their uterine bliss. Then they have to come to terms with the end of their early childhood omnipotence. In their first five years, they have to deal with many other momentous endings. Is this not a primitive preparation for later deaths, including our own ultimate death? We should learn by these experiences that all creative self-emergence involves a constant succession of growth and dying. If we cannot accept the death or ending of present experience, then we have problems moving on to create new experiences. We learn this truth as children—we must continue to learn it as adults.

Clouded Windows

These windows to experience are present in all stages of our lives. Some, however, are more critically open in childhood, others in adolescence, others in adulthood, and still others in the final aging experience. Every age in humans has its primary developmental tasks. It helps to be aware of this evolution even though all of the tasks continue throughout all of life. There is nothing that the child struggles with that the old person does not continue to struggle with. There is nothing that the adult struggles with that is not part of the experience of the child. Humans of any age must be able to see through all of their windows in order to be whole. When the windows cloud, we begin to lose our personhood.

Such cloudings are the precursors of our losing our wholeness. We will attempt to describe them in a meaningful and useful way—the windows that enhance selfbeing, as well as those shutters that preclude experience and lead to a lack of wholeness. Perhaps even more important is seeing the ordinary, often insidious, ways in which nonexperiences mitigate and even abort the thrust of our human beingness. We can see how we participate in our lives if we will but look. But first we need to know where to look and, even more important, how to look.

> People "died" all the time in their lives. Parts of them died when they made the wrong kinds of decisions—decisions against life. Sometimes they died bit by bit until finally they were just living corpses walking around. If you were perceptive you could see it in their eyes; the fire had gone out . . . but you always knew when you were making a decision against life. When you denied life you were warned. The cock crowed, always, somewhere inside of you. The door clicked and you were safe inside—safe and dead.
> —ANNE MORROW LINDBERGH, *The Steep Ascent*

We hope to document the crowing of the cock and the clicking of the door, so that each of us is *less* likely to become one of the living dead. We hope to look at those ways of experiencing ourselves that make it *more* likely we will move to our wholeness as persons.

3
Using
Our Windows

Nothing ever becomes real till it is experienced.

—John Keats

How do we use these windows to see who we really are? How do we go about experiencing in ways that help us move to greater wholeness as persons? Before looking at each individual window, we must understand what *experiencing* in these terms means. Beth is a case in point.

Beth, now in her early forties, is having difficulty sleeping, has lost her appetite, has little energy, and is functioning poorly both at home and work. In therapy, she shares her depression verbally and nonverbally. Being in the room with her, one can feel it. She has also shared in some detail the reasons for her depression. These "reasons" consist of Marshall, her husband. She has described his behavior, his thoughts, his feelings, and his motivations. Her judgments about these are all very real to her. She would acknowledge, if confronted, that her statements are only the way she sees him, but on a deeper level, Beth feels that she really knows her husband. Sadly, she also really believes that he is making her depressed.

Marshall reluctantly comes with her to a session. He is initially quiet and obviously unsure about being there. He has already heard many times what she has shared with the therapist. The depth of her pain and the misery of her depression are all clear to him. She often has shared with him the barren lack of satisfaction she feels in their marriage, how everything has changed since the children were born. She has often screamed with her hurt at his lack of sexual interest, a lack she sees as a direct result of his drinking too much. He has heard it all many times before, and he knows he will hear it again today. He has his own pain and his own anger, but they are more manifest in his pounding arteries than in his voice.

Beth begins by talking about her husband's plans for separating from her. Marshall begins to look impatient and angry. She continues by saying that she has done everything she could to make the marriage better, including arranging for these sessions. Beth's pain, depression, and frustration are very real and certainly present to the therapist, but so also are her anger, righteousness, self-pity, confused dependence, and collusion in what is happening to her. Beth, however, does not see these parts of herself. She is so sure that Marshall is making her experience of life unbearable that she has stopped experiencing her own living.

Beth looks older than her forty-three years. She looks bone-tired, gray. Her face, wrinkled with hurt and bitterness, reflects the long struggle their marriage has become. She seems embattled, like a soldier who has lost the battle but is going to fight on to the end anyway. Such is her experience of life. She is losing everything that is important to her, and losing it in a relationship that seems terribly unfair to her. She is unaware that she is also losing *herself*, that she has closed the windows to her own *real* experience.

Marshall is dressed in a suit and tie. He came to the interview from work. According to Beth, he lives at work twelve hours a day. He, too, looks tired and old, as gray as she. In contrast to Beth's angry frustration, he seems sad and resigned. It is more as if he has hopes that if he can begin again, with someone else, he can still make it—a not uncommon illusion in those who have taken little or no responsibility for the failure of a relationship and have, consequently, learned nothing as persons. He begins slowly, but soon responds loudly with his own judgments and accusations against Beth.

Marshall sees getting away from Beth as the only way he can

be free, be himself, really live. He believes Beth is making him the way he is just as tenaciously as she believes he makes her life unbearable. Like her, he has long since lost his self-responsibility. His windows, too, are closed. They sit and look at each other, sure in their knowledge and accusations. Both are far out of touch with the other, out of touch with what Sir Thomas Browne long ago noted in *Religio Medici:* "No man can justly censure or condemn another, because indeed no man truly knows another." We can only know ourselves, know our own experience. Yet we seldom do even that. Refusing to know ourselves, we are unable to learn and grow. We are unable to be whole.

Beth and Marshall's painful lack of touching is especially evident. Perhaps, in time, love and personhood will be manifest as well. The therapist will, of course, come to know more about their families, their marriage, and their individual life experiences. After all, one can collect *conscious* information. But unconsciously, Beth and Marshall know much more of these histories than a therapist could ever know in a millennium. A therapist will need their *unconscious* participation and help for any success in the task at hand. The windows will have to open for change to occur. For what Beth truly needs to know is what is *her experience of herself* with Marshall? and what Marshall truly needs to know is what is *his experience of himself* with Beth? What is the experience each has of him- or herself when they are together?

The Intensity, Importance, and Impact of Experience

The answers to those questions depend on what we mean by *experience.* But is experience singular? Are experiences simply occurrences, each one being psychologically equivalent to the others? In that sense, all consciousness is experience. Anger, fear, frustration, and depression are all experiences. Breathing and talking are experiences. Touching and making love are experiences. Taking a walk with our daughter is an experience. Paying the bills and washing the dishes are experiences. Dreaming and dying are experiences. Are these experiences in any way equivalents? Is the difference only that some experiences are more important or more intense than others? Perhaps the difference lies in the extent to which experiences affect our own lives or the lives of others.

By all of these criteria, Beth's anger is a full and total experience. It is important, it is intense, and it certainly affects her as well as others. But suppose that Beth's experience is not really of herself, and her experience of Marshall is not really of him. Such false experiencing is common in all of our lives. For example, Beth's father, like her husband, was a workaholic. Beth's mother was long-suffering and angry, much as Beth is now. Are Beth's feelings about her husband, or about her father? Are her feelings her own, or feelings that her mother had with which Beth identified and now believes are her own? And if both are true, which they probably are, is Beth's experience of herself and her husband any less of an experience? It is certainly no less important, intense, or impactive.

If Beth and Marshall were self-responsible in their behavior in the relationship, would they have more real experience? If each would allow him- or herself to be honestly present, and if they then lived naturally out of that presence, would they not have a different experience? If they could be playful with each other, bringing something new and creative to the relationship rather than always reliving the old, or if each could actually accept the other as he or she is, would they not have a more growthful experience? Intensity, importance, and impact alone do not seem to define experience.

There is another and very different meaning to the concept of experience. If we could isolate and identify the experience that both Ben and Marshall have with each other as presently living persons, would not such *real experience* provide a healthy and sufficient nucleus for an expanding and current relationship with each other? Various therapeutic disciplines have certainly seen things that way. However, as psychiatrist James Gustafson described in *The Complex Secret of Brief Psychotherapy*, the emphasis on how to get there has almost invariably focused on different aspects of the *past* experience. The therapist's effort has been to clean up the past. Only the point of attack would be different among the various approaches.

As Gustafson points out, there may be other ways to grow. Suppose we concern ourselves with *present* experience. More important, suppose present experience has an emergent and powerful thrust to create even more present experience. Suppose synthesis is more powerful than analysis. Then, perhaps, people could grow in their ordinary lives without the aid of therapy. We could relearn to learn. The quest for wholeness could then be an ongoing activity.

What if these two angry people could relearn acceptance, or naturalness, or responsibility for self, or play, or any of the other windows to experience? Would opening these windows not quickly propel them into fuller personhood? Being fully who we are with other humans we fully accept as who they are, even in a single moment, has infinitely more power to change our persons than a multitude of notions about who we are not being, even if those interpretations are quite correct. It may even be that an extended relational experience that is constantly annotated and interpreted decreases our capacity for experience, despite the increase in our understanding. Many of us use understanding to blame our past for our present, and in so doing guarantee a future devoid of change and growth.

Defenses Against Experience

Personal experience as we are presently describing it does not have to be a significant event. All ordinary living *can* be experience. All events *can* be experience, but often are not for the simple reason that we will not let them be. We foolishly shutter, as it were, our windows to selfhood. We remove ourselves from the world of what is valued above all price.

Experience literally means "to try out." It has the same root as the words "experiment" and "peril." Have Beth and Marshall tried out, or experimented, or periled in their living with each other? No. Trying out requires an honest personal participation while remaining aware of the ever-present connection in the relationship. Instead, Beth and Marshall have chosen the *security* of already knowing and blaming a separate other. In so doing, they are missing the chance to see that all of life is available to us to learn about our own nature, human nature, and, thus, nature itself—*the world we really live in.* They have set aside and ignored that awareness at great risk. It might sound self-evident to say that we have to be *ourselves* to have our own experience. It obviously is not self-evident, however, to Beth and Marshall.

Experience, then, *can* be any thought, feeling, behavior, sensation, relation, fantasy, dream, movement, or perception. When, however, these events in our lives are mitigated by our *defenses*, they turn into qualitatively different experiences. These defenses are the shutters to our windows to true experience. None of us is without defenses, ways of removing ourselves from what is real, self-diminishing ways of making that space between us and the other somewhat opaque. Psychotherapist Carl Rogers wrote in *On Becoming a Person*, "In a person who is open to experience each stimulus is freely relayed through the nervous system, without being distorted by any process of defensiveness." Defensiveness assures nonexperience, and we are all defended to some extent.

Against what are these defenses formed? Clearly, the answer is experience itself. Humans form defenses to block the very thing we are describing, the direct experiencing of themselves in their world as it is. The child, fully experiencing, is overwhelmed by fear, shame, rage, sadness, and other feelings. These feelings are often imposed by anxious and defended adults—usually their parents—but are at other times simply an inevitable part of life. Unable to remain unknowing in the midst of such feeling—that is, without enough support and safety to be able to live unsure—the child forms a defense. The child moves away from her wholeness—the naturally experiencing self—to a part self, a defended self. She collects a thousand defenses, rehearses them endlessly, and then, as an adult, lives in the world with those defenses as a partial person.

The manifestations of our defensiveness may be casual and incidental. For example, someone asks us how we feel, and we answer, "How are you?" That response basically halts the interaction, although it is not consciously meant to block intimacy. Or, the manifestation can be more direct: someone asks us how we feel, and we answer, "I feel fine," when, in fact, we feel desperately depressed. That response, too, stops intimacy. Both are forms of self-diminishment. Both cut us off from the real experience of our world and make us less whole.

Some defenses are very transient and personally inconsequential, others are permanent and very consequential. Some matter for just moments, others matter for a lifetime, but all of them diminish life. All of them diminish *self*. All shuttering of our windows guarantees some form of nonexperience. To really experience is to live and grow; to avoid experience is to become one of the living dead. The degree to which any one of us limits our experience, opaques or shutters our windows, will determine how healthy or unhealthy, joyful or unjoyful, growing or ungrowing, we will be in our lives.

Time Living and Time Being

If experience were simply everything that happens, we would all be equally experiential, and so equally alive and growing. How then would we account for the depressed, the anxious, the bored, the resigned? Is it correct to say that the depressed person is equally as experiencing, equally as growing, as the passionate and relating person? No. Just because something occurs does not mean that it is experienced. Time lived is not necessarily experienced. Experience is time *being*. Beth and Marshall are spending time living, but know little of how to spend time being. Their experiences are mostly occurrences and reoccurrences. There is little or no *being* in them, especially with each other. Therefore, they do not grow, do not find joy, and are not healthy. They choose to remain secure in their unhappening, however miserable.

If every occurrence were experienced in the sense that we are describing, all humans would be equally nourished by experience. Beth and Marshall would be alive, passionate, in harmony with nature, and growing in relationship as they celebrated their living, simply because they lived together. We know that does not happen. Too much of the occurrence of our lives is not real experience in the sense of trying out, risking, or fully being. It is not even useful reexperiencing. It is mostly reoccurrence, the uncreative repetition of nonexperience.

All humans accumulate, to some extent, defensive shells that preclude experience. Doing so is simply a part of life. More damaging, however, is the fact that we integrate those defenses into our persons early in life and then believe that those defenses are a natural part of our being human. We accept as natural and human the personal postures that in actuality *prevent* us from being fully human and natural, from being whole.

These defenses then block the very experiences we need in order to grow, change, and become whole. Occurrence, or reoccurrence, as we have called it, merely perpetuates *time living*. It usually precludes *time being*. The person who is most defended is the least experiential, and in contrast, the undefended and vulnerable person is most experiential. It is not reserved to therapists to know that. We all sense the same thing in our ordinary relationships. The person who is real and open seems present and whole. The defensive person seems somewhere else, cut off from large portions of life.

Contrary to common assumptions, giving up our defenses and being vulnerable does not mean being naive, unreal, or passive. Far from it. People who give up their defensiveness are usually passionate, real, and self-caring. The notion that if we are undefended we are apt to be used or abused is a major human delusion. In truth, defensiveness weakens us and makes us much more available to use and abuse by others. It makes us much more likely to be captured by systems. But defenselessness is frightening to us. We equate *defended* with *secure*. Consequently, we seldom allow ourselves to live openly in the world in which we live. We seldom fully open our windows. In our fear, we lose our strength, our energy, and our resilience, and live shut off from those experiences that would assure our continued aliveness. We board up the windows in our small rooms of self to keep out the light of life and experience.

Art and Experience

An internal resonance of thinking, feeling, and behaving characterizes those undefended moments, our epiphanies, moments of grace, what are now called personal highs. There is a difference between recognizing something (thinking), doing something (behaving), or sensing something (feeling), and really knowing something (experiencing). It is the difference between saying "that makes me sad" and being tearful. The first is a feeling. The second is an experience for both you and the other person. It is the difference between taking up a pencil to write a poem and writing the poem. Japanese playwright Monzaemon Chikamatsu said it succinctly in his *Preface to Hozumi Ikan:* "It is essential that one not say of a thing that 'It is sad,' but that it be sad of itself."

It is not surprising that an artist sees through such windows so clearly. Art is one of the quintessential expressions of full experience. Politics, economics, and other social movements are more like occurrences. They are more *craft* than *art*. That distinction is the essential difference between occurrence and experience. The *art* of wholeness cannot be accomplished solely by craft regardless of how good a craftsperson one is. Counseling—craft—will not work because we cannot tell others what they see through their windows. Occurrence and craft are important, but they do not change the *nature* of things. Changing the nature of things requires artistic experience. As Martin Luther King, Jr., wrote in *Strength to Love*, "Human salvation lies in the hands of the creatively maladjusted."

We see that truth operatively. The nature of our systems appears to change significantly only when infused with the energy of art. The Beatles influenced American sexual mores more than Lyndon Johnson. Individuals who truly experience war, poverty, or social causes, and convert their experiences into shared art, certainly have more substantial effect on us than simple reports of the news. The democratic idea is maintained more by its artistic merit than its economic or political merit.

However, not all music, literature, philosophy, or design is impactive. Much of such work is not art at all but part of the systems themselves. Most art simply reflects its culture; it does not change it. Such art is not creative; it does not infuse our society, insistently move it toward more human experience, the way art that is creative does. Craft, which is the direct manifestation of the reexperience of such real, creative art, also moves us to experience. The well-made ceramic bowl, or quilt, or cabinet also leads us to understanding the order and disorder of our world. *Real* art and craft trace *real* experience.

Art in this sense is the transmission of real experience from one human being to another. In his Nobel lecture, Aleksandr Solzhenitsyn said, "The sole substitute for an experience which we have not ourselves lived through is art and literature." In this way, song and chanting are languages of experience. So is poetry. But only the song or poem that is not a sexualization of power or money conveys such experience. We know the difference in our real selves—by and large we recognize bad poetry much as we recognize bad singing—and cannot learn from such nonexperience.

At some level we know better. We watch television indiscriminately. We seem to watch simply to be watching. What we watch has the same meaningless quality as does so much of our personal living. Thus it seems as if television shows are really about us. We read computerized books and periodicals for the same reason. Turned out in mass, word-processed into predigested form, they are paper televisions. They comfort us, and sedate our pain at our deadness. More distressing, we act as if we believe they are meaningful. Years ago English historian George Trevelyan wrote, "our education has produced a vast population able to read, but unable to distinguish what is worth reading." He could have just as easily been speaking of any of our mass media today.

Being Poets in Our Lives

Our lack of discrimination has nothing to do with our aesthetic sensibilities or literary expertise. It has to do with experiential constriction, a phobic avoidance of the aliveness of being. The aged, uneducated mountaineer from Appalachia, if he could read, would not only understand Shakespeare, he would exult in it—*if*, that is, he had led a full life, a life unendingly emergent in experience. Responsiveness is not a matter of one's age or education, but one's connection to the life process. This connection is the basis of all real art. Poets intuitively know the creative power of immediate experience. William Blake, the poet of tigers, wrote, "To see a world in a grain of sand/And heaven in a wild flower,/ Hold infinity in the palm of your hand,/And eternity in an hour." Being good poets in our own lives requires such wide open windows to experience.

Our general disquietude, restlessness, and haunting search for something else reflect our generally nonexperiential lives. We healthily long for the real, but persist in the rut. We wait for our life to happen. But as long as we are frozen in fear of any new and different experience, it is unlikely ever to happen. The distortion and impasse are always with us, because they *are* us. We remain responsible for what happens and for what does not happen. We cannot change ourselves or alter our lives by blaming others, or getting them to feel for us or make us feel. We engender, that is create, our own experience. No one else can. Other people can only engender responses.

We have no choice but to be the poet of our own life, constantly to write its unique poem. In defaulting the choice, we simply become poor poets. "But it is not so easy for most people to become poets," says Japanese psychiatrist Takeo Doi in *The Anatomy of Self*, "no matter how trying it becomes for them to live in modern society." Indeed, it is not easy at all. The only punishment for unbeing is our loss of wholeness. Its only reward is the security that keeps us less than whole. Only alive as the poets we really are do we live in full selfbeing. If we write our own real poetry, we will be listened to. If we do not, we will be confined to the unending soap opera of our dependent expectations.

Jack is thirty-eight. He has two children he seldom sees, from a marriage of fourteen years to Marie that ended in divorce. They married in college and he now firmly believes that she went to college just to get a husband. She got Jack. He says, "All I wanted was someone to love me." He got Marie. Once they had each other, they became more and more unhappy. Jack, she felt, was distant, unaffectionate, and really uninvolved with either her or the children. Marie, Jack says, was not sexual, was just one of the kids, and lived mostly for them. In therapy, he spends most of his time talking about her. He seldom talks about himself. It is almost as if he does not exist. He lives as if he is a response, not a person. His "experience" is Marie and his past. He still longs to be loved.

Whatever Marie's problems were, and we are sure she had her share, she appropriately abhorred and avoided the awesome responsibility of making Jack happy or living for him. That she could not do anyhow. She could only be happy *with* him. Under the circumstances, how likely or even possible was that? One day Jack asks the therapist, "Where are all the women who like to play and make love? They must all be at home doing what their husbands want them to do." Jack is a poor poet of his own life. He may be well informed about the occurrences in his life—Marie undoubtedly did behave in many of the ways he describes, his children undoubtedly did cause their share of problems—but he has no awareness of his own absence of experience. He has no appreciation of the real relational world in which he lives. He does not know himself, even if he were totally correct about Marie. And that is the real sadness.

Brain and Experience

The resistance of the mind in going beyond the boundaries of particular divisions of subjects, and more generally, its resistance to change in fundamental notions of all kinds, is particularly dangerous where the idea of fundamental truth is involved.

—DAVID BOHM and F. DAVID PEAT,
Science, Order, and Creativity

We are poor poets of our lives when we live disconnected and lonely in our already known and prejudged worlds. Such worlds will always preprogram what our experience will be. What occurs, therefore, is never experience at all but only occurrence. With such expectations we live once removed from what really is. This description of life is not simply philosophical; it reflects the very way our brains operate. Brain function has more to do with personhood than we have assumed for years, and we are just beginning to understand that a person's experiencing has more to do with the basic dynamics of brain function than we have ever imagined. Healthy brain function may directly depend on healthy experiential exercise.

Current research clearly suggests that the brain reacts to the difference between what is expected and what actually occurs. The more the brain expects a given input, the less it will react to an input that does not differ from that expectation. One might say that the brain, then, not surprisingly, is quite like people. It is constricted and confined by the very familiar that it constantly seeks out, as it prefers in most ways to live with the already known. It resists the intimate and different despite the fact that its evolution and growth depend on input that bypasses that familiarity barrier, despite the fact that there is a powerful desire for the new.

Our brain must meet *both* needs: ongoing stability and the

capacity to change. The whole person possesses a balance of the two. But living in a world of preset expectations, disconnected from the "isness" of the other, we miss the differences. We are not balanced. *We do not experience.* When our windows are closed and we do not try out each new input for what it is, we forgo the enriching, invigorating newness, the challenging strangeness, and the beautiful uniqueness that can impel and assure our growth. We become less than whole.

Risking, Knowing, and Responding

We must risk to experience, for experience never occurs without some element of risk. That is the nature of trying out. It is our brain's being willing to alter its known state. Real experience always has some element of the exhilarating for that reason. An alive person *experiences* it when his or her brain changes—the two are the same thing. Otherwise, what happens is more likely only occurrence or reoccurrence, flat and opaque, dispassionate and already experienced. The risk is not only real—clearly to allow the new does indeed alter our lives—but important, because what does not change mortifies and deadens. Ultimately, risking is necessary regardless of the outcome of the risking.

Taoism, a religious philosophy that emphasizes the interchangeability of experience and reality, holds the belief that the same thing never happens exactly the same way ever again. Everything is always new. And everything is always renewing. Such understandings, whether coming from the mysticism of the East, or the more pragmatic, empirical world of Western science, have provided us with a substantive definition of experience. We experience only when we try out the new reality of every new stimulus. It also explains why we can have a *new experience* every moment with someone we have lived with for fifty years.

Can we make such new experiences an integral part of our ongoing living? Not have them be something special or separate? *Ordinary experience* is the basic building block of reality and, consequently, for growth to occur should be momental and creative. Difference provides us opportunity. That opportunity does not depend on the difference being extraordinary or special. It depends far more on its simply being momental and creative of other and new experiences. We can all appreciate from our own individual lives that the special and extraordinary experience most often isolates us. It becomes an end in itself. For example, when someone we love is dying, it is difficult for us to experience losing them as momental to our own growth, difficult for us to experience any momentum to growth even though the experience itself may be growthful for us. Often, special experience simply overwhelms us. The ordinary and simple experience, in contrast, recreates itself as it goes and grows.

Risking, trying out, being what we really are with the other in the ordinary context of our lives, moves us to the kind of momental and emergent experiences that are the assurance of selfbeing, that are the best insurance against selficide. Living in those ways connect us—brain, body, and soul—with our ecology. We are a part of what is. Our beings connect with the uniqueness and continuity of each moment's sensation. "Man's main task in life," wrote Erich Fromm in *Man for Himself*, "is to give birth to himself." In our birthing, we learn to be in the world in good faith.

Clearly we do not continuously live this way. It frightens most of us to think that we might. We fear that were we to stay in that more passionate, excited, and creative way of being in the world, we would not attend to business, even the business of dealing with the everyday and ordinary world. We fear we would have neither the time nor the interest to attend to matters of everyday life. How very odd. Had we the energy and enthusiasm of such being, would we not do the things that need to be done? The alive person *would* live responsibly. There is no chasm between the real and the passionate. Contrary to usual belief, the passionate depends on the practical, and how real and effective the practical is depends on its passionate context. Neither is *functional* without the other. Such an understanding is basic to any concept of wholeness.

If we are passionate without regard to practicality, we are disconnected. If we are practical to the exclusion of passion, we are despairingly captured. If we achieve a balance between the two, we are beautifully participating humans, being in the world in the best of faith. A balance of both the experiencing and processing parts of ourselves is essential to our healthy living. They are two different ways of being in the world, and either *alone* is self-diminishing. They are inextricably dependent on one another.

We are unhealthy if we are either being ourselves regardless of the other, or only being ourselves if others allow us to be. We cannot be ourselves if we are not related. We cannot be related if we are not being ourselves.

Only when we come to see these two ways of being in the world as a natural pairing rather than exclusive opposites can we learn to be in the world in good faith. They are mutually *interdependent*. We cannot know hot if we do not know cold. We cannot know order if we do not know chaos. We cannot know life if we do not know death. All *being* depends on our simultaneous experience of such polarities. Only then are our windows open; only then do we truly *experience*.

This balancing can be described in many ways:

1. Being who we are honestly and openly is essential to our selfbeing but is fruitless unless at the same time we can be sensitive and responsive to others.

2. How intimate we can be depends on how able we are to be close, and how close we can be depends on how able we are to be intimate.

3. How healthy an *I* we have depends on how healthy a *me* we have, and how healthy a *me* we have depends on how healthy an *I* we have.

The point is that only having a balance leads to an open, emergent, and creative *self*. Our windows open only when we live in the union of the two. We must remain aware that each time we are captured by *any* fixed way of believing or being, we become less conscious of self, we become less whole.

Awareness

" 'Consciousness' is consciousness of," as Sartre said. It is awareness. But we do not live just consciously; *true awareness is multilevel*. Consciousness means that we know that we know. On the other hand, preconsciousness means that we have some sense that we know, but we do not know why. Nonetheless, we pay more attention to this sensing than we do to our consciousness. There also is the unconscious with its own kind of awareness. With it, we do not have even a sense of, we simply know for no reason. And, in truth, we pay more attention to that knowing than we do to either the conscious or the preconscious. It is a much more powerful determinant in our actual living than either of them. *Knowing*, as an experience that determines what we do and feel, is clearly not a simple awareness.

For example, recognition is much less powerful than knowing. People will frequently say, "Why didn't you tell me that before?" They have heard the same thing—that they, for example, are sharp-voiced when they speak—many times before, but at those times, while it was recognized as probably true, it changed nothing. This time they *know* it as truth and use it to change and grow. They *experience* the truth of themselves. Preconscious and unconscious experience are crucial because they allow us to be aware on that level.

Similarly, the preconscious and unconscious experiences of both therapist and client are equally important and determinant of growth and change in therapy. They must both be available to the process, because consciousness alone is not sufficient. The most important and productive interventions therapists make in their pilgrimages with people are probably preconscious and unconscious. Conscious interventions are usually a waiting experience, waiting for some more natural experience to happen. When used well, as in the cognitive therapies, they allow good counseling, but counseling is different from therapy. No less important, but very different.

Counseling involves teaching. In counseling, the therapist assumes responsibility for the interaction and tries to help the client adapt, cope, and find better ways to deal with the issues of closeness. The client learns within his or her capacity to learn, and the therapist pays attention to the problematic needs presented. Therapy, on the other hand, involves learning. In therapy, the client remains responsible for the interaction, and the issue is growth. Therapy, for the most part, involves issues of intimacy. The therapist pays attention to his or her own internal state, and the client learns how to learn.

This distinction is inevitable, since no person, not even the very best counselor or therapist, can teach another person how to be him- or herself. Growth is up to each individual self. A guide is very useful, but we must each choose our own destination. The experience may provide the garden, but we are each our own seed. Because of this distinction, the conscious world is the arena of much of counseling and the unconscious world the arena of much of therapy. Done well, both move into the interfaces with the preconscious. Good *psychotherapy* involves both, as both are necessary to becoming whole.

The same appears to be true in ordinary relational experience. We consciously dance with each other, hoping that we may happen into more of the natural preconscious and unconscious dance of life. We sincerely desire to be whole, to be all of ourselves. We *naturally* live with each other primarily preconsciously and unconsciously—an evolutionary truth, not an academic one. Nonetheless, thoughtfulness and consciousness are not opposites of naturalness. They also are part of what we naturally are. It is becoming imbalanced that distorts us. Most healthily (most wholly), we live in a congruence of our conscious, preconscious, and unconscious.

We associate the unconscious experience with being creative and the conscious experience with being responsible. The creative and responsible drives are thus woven into the very fabric of our lives. The truly creative experience is new, spontaneous, and almost always generative and growthful. The truly responsible experience is almost always a reexperience that allows stability. It is the necessary companion of the creative experience. It is not sufficient just to be intimate and creatively experiencing. We have to integrate that experience and make it part of our enduring living. We integrate by being responsible. We grow into being able to respond to others with what we have learned about ourselves in our creative experiences.

We learn this ability to respond through conscious reexperiencing. In our familiar closeness, we reexperience the creative newness we have discovered in our unconscious. We literally practice being ourselves. This exercise is not to be confused with repeating the old, familiar, and rote. They need no practice. Indeed, they are known all too well. The securely known is far different from the creative newness of present personal experience and the subsequent weaving of that newness into the cloth of our beings. The former represents our shuttered windows. The latter represents our throwing the shutters open.

If we practice the old and familiar, usually we are avoiding real experience. In healthy reexperience, we continue to relearn our newfound being. In nonexperience, we learn nothing, except to reinforce being out of touch with our*selves*. In healthy relearning, we increase our capacity to be intimate and so engender further experience. The balance between creative, intimate experience and the responsible reexperiencing of those new experiences enable us to be in this world in good faith, to be growing up continually, to become more whole.

In reexperience, we practice the truth that in closeness we enhance the other person's ability to relate to us in a way that enables us to be ourselves with them. We enhance responsibility, the ability to respond. Spontaneous, creative experience without subsequent reexperiencing would amount to a life of unrelated and meaningless anarchy. There is a difference between the natural and the anarchic, the same difference which exists between art and nonsense. Nature is always relational, just as real art is. Both have to be shared and experienced with some other in order to exist and have meaning. We are all in this together.

4

THE FIRST WINDOW:

Acceptance

These fellow mortals, every one, must be accepted as they are.

—George Eliot

Any increase in our capacity to be who we are reflects itself in our increased ability to respond to others. It is in our relationship to others, in our relationship to our world, that our wholeness manifests itself. If we were to have but one window unshuttered, it would be healthiest to be able to accept others. Out of that acceptance of our world, we might learn how naturally to open our other windows. In opening ourselves to the experience of what is outside us—which only happens when we accept it for what it is—we learn more of who *we* are.

In the movie *A Thousand Clowns*, Martin Balsam says to Jason Robards: "You come to my office today like George God. Everybody's supposed to come up and audition for human being in front of you." Most people seem to think you *do* have to audition for human being. But *being* is not judgeable. Our acceptability to our universe is not deniable, negotiable, or judgeable. No one has to audition to be a person.

Rob is tall, athletically built, and well tanned. He wears gold necklaces under his tailored shirts. Hiding inside his expensive suit, he is a success to the outside world. Rob is impressive as an investment counselor, civic leader, and father of two children graduated from prestigious schools. The world sees him married to an intelligent, attractive woman who is apparently very much in love with him. To the external world, Rob seems to have everything in life. However, his internal world is very different, and he shares those inside feelings painfully. Rob speaks to us while looking down at the floor or looking out the window at the trees. He is on the verge of tears, his voice heavy and tremulous.

"I don't know what to do anymore. I've got all this shit . . . the expensive house, the cars, the beach house. But it doesn't mean a damn. I'm a phony. No one else knows it, but I do. I'm either scared or I'm full of it. You know, like I'm a coward or a pompous ass. I'm fifty-two years old. I've been working all these years and I still don't know a damn thing about my wife, my kids, or even me. I'm a lousy excuse for a person."

What is Rob asking? Is he asking us to help him change? We do not believe so. Were we to try immediately to help him change, we most likely would never see him again. And his not returning would be understandable. Rob has a more important and immediate agenda than his being phony or pompous, even though his real agenda may be unconscious. In therapy, he presents the desire for *acceptance* as the issue he struggles with. He *insists* that acceptance be the issue. He seeks neither approval nor confrontation. He wants to know if we can accept him as a human being—as a coward, a phony, a pompous ass, and, most importantly, as a frightened man. Before he can do any constructive changing, he must first know that he is accepted as he is.

Being Accepted

All people who come to therapy need to know first that they are accepted. Accepting them is the first experiential task of any therapist, and it may remain the primary task for some considerable period of time. We say *experiential task* because it is not enough simply to have an accepting attitude. Acceptance has to be constantly processed in relationship; it is an active way of being, not an attribute of the person. It is far different from passive acquiescence in and indifference to what is wrong with the person. It is not tolerance of his problems.

The other person is well aware that the therapist may know what needs to change for him to be healthier. That knowledge alone, however, has little to do with helping someone change. Change occurs *relationally*, not *intellectually*. Change depends on our feeling accepted as we are, not understood as what we are not. Acceptance has to do with the experiencing of unconditional love in a relationship. A person wants to feel that however messed up she may be, she is yet a worthwhile, valuable human being, deserving of love and respect. She wants to experience this feeling in the other person despite the fact that she does not feel it to be true within herself. More to the point, she needs to experience it in the other precisely *because* she does not feel it to be true within herself.

If we say to a person that we will both love and respect her *if* she changes and is different, then she *has* to stay the same. She has no choice. She must continue struggling against our judgment in order to continue being herself. This is why feeling accepted as we are is the foundation of becoming a fully realized person. It gives us the freedom to choose to change not because someone else wants us to, but for our own growth and fulfillment, for our own becoming whole. In this sense, acceptance is crucial to our unfolding humanness. It is a basic prerequisite for living in the world in good faith.

If we can accept Rob with all of his struggles, and if he stays in the therapeutic relationship with us, he will eventually get around to being cowardly with us, as well as phony and pompous. When he is *being* those ways with us, and not just talking *about* them, we will confront him, as well we should. We will confront the ways he diminishes his person while he is with us. We must accept his experience of himself but confront his nonexperiential—his reoccurrent—ways of being with us.

"I wish Sara would stop spending money like it floated down the Chattahoochee from Lake Lanier and all I had to do was go out with a net and scoop some more up. She buys more clothes and jewelry than she has room to store."

"So why are you smiling?"

"What do you mean?"

"If you are really upset about her spending, why are you

smiling? I suspect you like it. You like her spending all that money."

"Why would I like it? I work my ass off."

"Maybe that's why you work your ass off, Rob."

"That's crazy."

"It sure is."

Rob's self-deception, what he calls his phoniness, does indeed need honest confrontation. However, it is exquisitely important that we, at this point of confronting, are aware of our basic acceptance of Rob. Only in that context can we effectively and usefully feed back to him his nonexperience, the pseudoself he has been presenting to us as if it were his true self. Within the germinal experience of acceptance, perhaps he may hear and use the confrontation, not simply internalize it as just one more failure to understand him and then defend himself against it. To be useful, the confrontation must be experienced as a genuine relational sharing. When we are defending, we are closed to experience.

In *The Drama of the Gifted Child*, psychoanalyst Alice Miller describes the development of a "healthy self feeling" that comes out of such acceptance. She describes the acceptance between mother and child, but this process must occur in all growing relationships:

> I understand a healthy self-feeling to mean the unquestioned certainty that the feelings and wishes one experiences are a part of one's self . . . this automatic, natural contact with his own emotions and wishes gives an individual strength and self esteem.

One would think that, never having had enough of such acceptance as a child, the adult finding it would be happy and gratified. Not so. More often, we are confused and frightened, sometimes, as psychoanalyst Karen Horney said, even terrified: "A neurotic person may have a feeling of terror when he approaches the realization that some genuine fondness is being offered him." When such "genuine fondness" does, indeed, terrify, it suggests that the recipient is aware on a deep level of both the acceptance being offered and its newness to his experience. Acceptance has effects that go far beyond the simple passive reception of some good feeling.

Acceptance forces the other person to look at him- or herself. When we are accepted, therefore, we are unavoidably faced with seeing ourselves. That self-reflective experience is the root of our anxiety and confusion. It is always ourselves of whom we are most afraid; our innermost fears, angers, hurts, and loves are what most powerfully frighten us. Since this fright is inevitable, acceptance must be an ongoing relational process. People do not usually remain accepted after a single experience. In ordinary life, just as in therapy, acceptance must be an ever present and available part of relationship.

Most of us feel a deficit of such acceptance. Both in our childhoods and in our adult years, we do not experience enough unconditional positive regard and love. We are left then with the task of filling that void, of gaining that experience. The only way we can move to such wholeness *by our own choosing*, however, is by finding the experience of acceptance in the ongoing personal process of accepting others.

Accepting Others

Julie is twenty-seven, divorced once, and trying to deal with the opposing pulls she feels between career and desire to again be in a primary relationship. Much of her hurt lies in an internal sense of unacceptability to men, a feeling going directly back to her sense of never having been accepted by her father.

She asks weeping softly, "How can I get what he's never going to give me?"

The therapist responds with a smile, "Well, it wouldn't really make any difference if he did anyway. The feeling is inside you now, and you're the only one who has access to that part of you anymore."

She looks up. "So how will I ever change?"

There is only one answer the therapist can give. "You need the *experience* of unconditional love. There's only one way you can give yourself that experience. Unconditionally love *him* yourself."

She resists. "You mean I have to give in to him?"

"No. I mean you have to give in to you. It's an experience of *self*, not of *him*. Just for example, you're walking through the mall and see something that your inner self would like to give him . . .

and, yes, I know he won't understand or want it because you're giving it to the part of him he's out of touch with . . . and I also know that that inner part of you is saying, 'But I did that so many times so long ago and the rejection hurt so much.' But if you go ahead and be you, then you recapture a part of yourself, you become more whole. If you stay in that process long enough, you'll start to feel that love you long for.''

Knowing that acceptance must be such an ongoing personal process helps us understand that it is not simply an attitude. It involves hard psychological work and personal moral commitment. This work and commitment in turn require spiritual energy and mean that accepting others must be a priority in our lives. Acceptance of others ultimately becomes a resonant experience in ourselves, and acceptance of ourselves is a primary window to experiencing the world. We feel acceptance for others and gradually surround ourselves with the same feeling. As Max Ehrmann wrote in his prose poem *Desiderata*, we then become "gentle with ourselves."

Through acceptance we come to know most deeply the basic equivalence of the other person and ourselves. Finding that equivalence will be a rediscovery of something we knew innately at one time as children, but lost in being socialized without sufficient unconditional love. Finding it again as an adult is a first and clear step toward wholeness. To accept the other—be it person or thing, idea or sensation—without slight, anger, or judgment, allows us to experience unconditional love. It allows *us* to be as *we* are.

The word *acceptance* has roots which are illuminating; it comes from Latin origins meaning "to receive" and "to take." To receive another, and in that touching take something that we can grow with, is the essence of full experiencing. Acceptance is to take the other as he or she is and receive much from that taking. The basic equivalence of humans in their relationships is seen in this union of taking and receiving. Thus acceptance is the first window to our spiritual participation in the universe.

Undefended, living as a whole member of our universe, we can be ourselves naturally. We can freely choose to be as we really are. Acceptance not only allows that choosing, it makes it likely. Accepting the other is, then, clearly important to that other in the relationship, but not nearly as important as that same acceptance is for the person who accepts. It immediately enables us to be ourselves more fully, expressively, and honestly.

That paradox of acceptance is what most of us have such difficulty understanding: if we genuinely accept the other person, we can more easily and readily be ourselves. We tend to believe that acceptance is capitulation and amounts to our giving up ourselves. It is as if we believe that "it's either him or me." We seem to have little sense of the truth that "only when I let him be him can I be me." In our unhealthy living, we believe that if we quietly accept the other, then somehow we passively acquiesce to them, are willing to be controlled by them, do what they want, condone what they do, and generally abandon our own being. This conclusion is a sad misunderstanding of what acceptance actually is. It is instead a socialized mislearning. Acceptance, in truth, has the opposite effect. Acceptance makes the other more moral, not more complacent in their immorality.

Mutuality

The most common problem in relationships is our notion that whenever two people disagree, one is wrong and the other is right. It is apparently very difficult for us to believe that when two people disagree, both can be right. We live in an *either/or* world instead of a *both/and* world. But knowing that both persons can be right is fundamental to acceptance. Every person's honest experience of the world is equally valid. To believe otherwise is to adhere to the relationally disastrous belief that there is but one right way to be. If we come to know that two people can honestly disagree and both can be right even while they disagree, then we have some basis for growthful relating. We can accept the validity of each person as him- or herself, accept the validity of their experience of the world.

John and Maureen have been married for thirty-five years. They come to therapy because she has become suicidal after years of being chronically depressed. As best I (Tom) can tell, they have not actually communicated with each other for several decades. When asked to describe his or her own experience, each tells me exhaustively about the other. Almost all of what each says comes from an absolute, total belief that the other is wrong about everything. They talk at each other about how much the other weighs, how much money he or she spends, how neat he or she is, even how he or she loves. Each claims to be *an accepting and loving person,* but each not only has no concept of the other being valid as the person he or she is but also has no idea what *his or her own real experience is.* And the two issues are really the same thing.

Mutuality involves validating the other and respecting them as the person they are. It does not mean respecting what they do or agreeing with how they are; *it means unconditionally loving them as the person they are.* Such respect and love are profound parts of how we exist in our world. They acknowledge that the other is valid unto him- or herself and is as right in that validity as we are in our own.

The Accepting Person

Perry and Christy are in their early thirties and have been living together for four years. The relationship is pleasant and close, at least on the surface. Christy, however, is vaguely disquieted and feels that something is not right, although she is not at all clear why she feels that way. In fact, she is upset because she does not know what she is really concerned about. She would describe Perry as an accepting person, but, nonetheless, her disquietude stems from her feeling that she is not accepted. She often feels judged and unaccepted, and these feelings puzzle her. Perry seems to be such an accepting person that Christy wonders if she might be overly sensitive to criticism.

"I feel badly about bringing this up, since our relationship is very good. I think it must really be me and not him. I'm confused. We seldom fight. We really care about each other. It's mostly good. Sometimes I think I'm crazy. I'm not sure anybody could make me happy."

What is Christy actually struggling with? She *consciously* perceives Perry as being accepting. He says the right things and appears to be accepting her as she is as a person. But she is uncertain and disquieted. With her fragile sense of her own worth, she predictably decides that her uncertainty is her own problem. Her insecurity is undoubtedly partly a cause of what she feels, but it is rather unlikely that the problem belongs only to her. It is true that there are some people who are almost incapable of accepting love. They are so damaged that almost any genuine feeling is rejected. Such people live in the world painfully, both to themselves and to others. But Christy is not that wounded.

It is convenient and comfortable for most of us to assume that, when a person feels rejected despite our loving ministrations, he or she has real problems that account for the sense of being unloved and unaccepted. It is much more useful, however, to wonder if, indeed, the person may be right to feel in some way rejected. Like Perry, we may be more an accepting person than actually accepting of another's personhood. The difference is subtle but very real. And, just as it has been to Christy, that difference can be confusing to other people.

This truth does not really indict Perry, just as it does not indict most of us. We are being consciously honest when we are being accepting persons. But being accepting persons is not enough. Real acceptance is always received because it dissolves defenses. We can be mistaken about our loving another person, but we are seldom mistaken about being loved by another, not if that other genuinely loves and accepts us. When Christy is uncertain, we are wiser and closer to the truth if we assume she is valid in her experience. A person might be psychotic, or severely neurotic, or distorted in her own personality, and those issues certainly might mitigate that truth, but even under those conditions we should listen carefully to her experience.

Christy is probably healthy in wondering if she is, indeed, being accepted. Acceptance is not simply an *intrapersonal* experience. It is also an *interpersonal* experience. It has occurred only when the other person feels it. The connection must be there for the real experience to happen, and that connection manifests itself unconsciously all the time. Sadly, unlike Christy, most of us give in to our own self-doubts and never really question what we "don't feel."

In many relationships, this difference between being an accepting person and being truly accepting causes pain. To see another person as somehow *less than us*—less intelligent, too much into feelings, too involved in sports, too caring about poor people, not caring enough about being on time, etc.—and then in some way be accepting about it, is unhealthy. It is destructive of the other person, the person we are, and the relationship.

I (Pat) struggled with this existential distinction in my relationship with my stepmother for many years. I was confused as to why we were so conflicted in our relationship when I was young. I knew, with the clarity that only children have, that she was an accepting person. I also knew that I, too, was an accepting person. But we seemed for a long time unable to connect. As in most step relationships, we struggled to find a way really and honestly to be with each other. I think we eventually gave up trying, gave up trying to be accepting persons, and then came to share expressively a real acceptance of each other. Over the many years since, we have had a very intimate as well as close relationship. Why the difference? Only accepting another, a *particular* person in a *particular* relational experience at a *particular* moment of time, actively felt and actively expressed without condition, is acceptance. It is very concrete and relationally intense. In contrast, being an accepting person, however genuine and real, is a quality of personality. It is an attitude, a personal potential, that may or may not be actualized in any given relational experience. It is only intrapersonal, not interpersonal.

> From the beginning, you ought to be diligent to make no distinction between yourself and others. Happiness or distress for me is the same as for others. Thus, I must take care of others as I do myself.
>
> —PRAJNAKARMITI, *Santideva's Bodhicharyavatara*

Love and Acceptance

We can be a loving person and not be at all loving in many particular, concrete experiences with those we love. We can often falsify our experiences by assuming that we are being loving in particular moments simply because we know ourselves to be loving persons. But we may not be living that way in any particular experience.

This claim to being a loving person, in the face of this professed love not being experienced, confuses the other person, just as it confused our client Christy. More important, it stultifies the person who feels that he is being loving simply because he is a loving person. It is self-diminishing; it blocks us from knowing our own experience. Perry felt misunderstood and unappreciated when, in fact, he was clearly understood and appropriately unappreciated in the concrete personal "isness" of Christy's experience. Like so many of us, Perry does not *live* his love and accepting.

The French philosopher Pierre Carlet de Marivaux once said, "In this world you must be a bit too kind in order to be kind enough." Similarly, we must be a bit too accepting to be accepting enough. Acceptance must be total and fully expressive. When it is, the other person knows it without question.

If the other person experiences being accepted without alternative motive, reservation, condescension, or patronizing attached to it, then, and only then, is the acceptance truly real. Something new is born then in the being of the *accepting* person. Growth happens in that moment. Self is enhanced, not in a superficial social or narcissistic sense, but in the sense of becoming capable of being in the world more fully, becoming more whole.

Acceptance is, in this way, natural. It is evolutionarily derived as a way of thrusting our growth forward. Its presence is evident everywhere in nature. The natural order, no matter how violent it appears, is operative acceptance. We never think of pine trees as being unaccepting of oak trees or honeysuckle of azaleas. When animals feed on plants, it never occurs to us that they are unaccepting of those plants. We watch birds eat worms or lions eat gazelles without any sense of nonacceptance. On the contrary, it seems ordinary. It never occurs to us to attribute *judging* to natural relationships.

But in human relationships, we know we are often extremely judgmental. All humans judge and must struggle with their inability to wholly accept others.

> I have, and I think everyone has, incontrovertible evidence that some persons do sometimes persecute, deprive, and oppress. Where is such evidence found? While I may have suspicions of other persons, of course, simple reasoning requires me to admit that I cannot *know* the wills and intentions of others, but only speculate about them. They are not *in* my experience, as my own will and intention would be, if only I would consider them carefully. The incontrovertible evidence

that I do have, therefore, comes from my knowledge that *I* sometimes persecute, deprive, and oppress. . . .

—RICHARD MITCHELL, *The Gift of Fire*

Righteousness

Our lack of acceptance is born of our righteousness. The bird eating the worm is not righteous. The lion eating the zebra is violent but not righteous. Wild animals in their pecking order are not righteous. The pine tree which will be displaced by the hardwood does not even then feel righteous. There is no righteousness in nature except for that of humans, and possibly of animals humans have taught to act similarly. Family dogs *often* express family prejudices.

Righteousness is the antithesis of acceptance. It represents the belief that we, and only we and those who agree with us, know the way things should be. It is devoid of spirituality. The power of Christianity is its message of acceptance, a message to love other humans, to transcend judging. The power of Buddhism is likewise its message of acceptance of the least of all in nature. The power of all great religions and humanist creeds is their insight into the power of acceptance. When, in contrast, Christians, Buddhists, or humanists live righteously, and condescendingly abhor those differences, they demean the human spirit and falter in their convictions.

We diminish ourselves in our unwillingness to accept others in this way. The most common examples (sadly all too common) are prejudice, bigotry, chauvinism, racism, sexism, and religious fanaticism. Nazi Germans dehumanized themselves by treating Jews inhumanely; religious inquisitions, ancient (witch hunts and heresy trials) or recent (censorship of the arts), destroy the spirituality of those religions. Whites who demean blacks, men who demean women, Christians who demean Muslims and vice versa demean all of humanity, most of all themselves.

In personal relationships, it is our unending compulsion to define and control other persons, righteously to know what they should do, feel, and be, that makes us less than whole. When we are partial persons, experience stops. It simply freezes. The relationship becomes cold and dead. Warmth is the quality of life, but warmth is absent in relationships marked by righteousness.

Even to talk about righteous people makes us painfully aware of the personal struggle necessitated by acceptance. We become angry at their wrongfulness. But at the point that we condemn or belittle them, we become exactly like them. And it is frightening how easily and frequently we all do just that.

If, on the other hand, we can stay involved in the patterns of nature, we can accept people as they are without in any way acquiescing to their view of the world, without letting ourselves become captured by the same system of living. The problem of accepting the sinner while shunning the sin is always a struggle. But that struggle, while a dilemma, is also the road to growth. It is opening a window to wholeness. While struggling, we deal with our being and that is the foundation of growth. Out of our growth we may better be able to accept others. And acceptance, or grace if you will, is the only organic way to transform the righteous or any other "sinner."

"Cultural" Nonacceptance

Sadly, nonacceptance is our cultural norm. Nonacceptance in our culture has too often been equated with independence, social assertiveness, standing up for what we believe, and, in a sense, being adult. For example, we often feel that participating in another person's religious beliefs in some way diminishes or weakens our own. This distortion is well illustrated by another common example of the form such social nonacceptance takes: being a "man." To "be a man" involves the loss of the ability to accept women as equals. Not only are women themselves "less than" in some ill-defined way, but similarly any "feminine" characteristics (such as sensitivity, relatedness, and reciprocity) are to be avoided. In that tortuous process there is no way one can truly become a man, since being a man in any meaningful sense is naturally and totally dependent on the full, feeling capacity to accept women. Nor is this paradox confined to men; it is equally true for women. Being a woman is naturally and totally dependent on the full and feeling capacity to accept men and the masculine. Nonacceptance always diminishes personhood, regardless

ACCEPTANCE 81

of gender. The same is true of issues of race, creed, faith, education, or socioeconomic status. To whatever extent "they" are seen
as less than "us," we are less than ourselves. We cannot be empowered when we seek power over others.

Most particularly, we cannot be naturally related when we
believe that we are right and the other person is wrong. That way
of living is not nature's way. Nature clearly teaches that our
acceptance of the different, even the righteous, is the only way *to
be most fully what we are* in the natural world. The righteous cut
themselves off because they insist on being separate and unconnected from the rest of nature. Alone, they become static. They
lose the ability to evolve and grow. If we remain connected to the
universe, we survive and grow into something more, something
different. We move toward greater wholeness.

This stasis is too often seen in our organized religions. The
problem with such religion, whatever its particular form, is its
lack of spirituality. *Spiritus* means hope, and hope underlies all
acceptance. Acceptance—*grace*—is the essence of all spirituality.
To see God as righteous and without grace is to suggest that God
is not spiritual, has no hope, and is effectively dead. A God without grace and acceptance would be a horror and an evil. There
would be no connection, no creation, no animation, no resurrection. The same is true for us as humans.

Learning Acceptance

Active and relationally expressed acceptance of people is the
most meaningful basis of successful psychotherapy. Without it,
we can educate, counsel, or behaviorally modify, but we cannot
facilitate personal growth which becomes indigenous to the person and is not dependent on the therapist. No learning-how-to-
learn takes place. Such *deutero-learning*, as anthropologist
Gregory Bateson defined it, comes only with felt acceptance. The
same is true in all personal relationships. If we wish other people
to change, we must accept them as they are. The experience of
that acceptance opens the way to trust in the relationship.

We can see the results of the lack of this *unconditional positive regard*, as Rogers called it, in our self-talk. When we make
a mistake or err in some way, we most often self-negate. We call

ourselves names, aloud or silently, judging ourselves as persons. So infrequently do we gently support ourselves, hold and love ourselves. In truth, it seems that we do not know how to live with ourselves.

It is but the old issue of the child and the spilled milk. Do the parents accept the child unconditionally—confirm and support worth, lovability, and acceptability as separate from the behavior? Or do they look judgingly, speak harshly, and identify the behavior in that way as a *definition* of the child? The adult's self-talk is but those same voices. The truth of the power of unconditional positive regard is that *one moment* of a parent's completely looking into a child's eyes and totally accepting her is more important than hours, days, or even years of time simply spent with the child. Only being accepted allows the child to grow into *her own wholeness*.

Everything we know about parenting clearly underlines the basic importance of trust and acceptance—the basic components of unconditional love. To love in that way does not, as many assume, mean that we cannot discipline. On the contrary, only when such unconditional love is present can we truly and effectively discipline. Such *positive discipline*—discipline that empowers the child rather than diminishing her—exists only through the power of such love. The child can, for example, learn that while always spilling milk does not define her worth, in the real world it may make others less inclined to invite her to dinner. The only alternative to such positive discipline is a hurt obedience. An obedience that, even when maintained throughout life, produces a depressed, unlearning, unrelated, less-than-whole person.

When, as therapists, we cannot accept a client, and sometimes we cannot, we must accept that truth about ourselves and help the person find another therapist who perhaps can accept him. None of us can be ideal. I (Tom) have found during my forty years of seeing clients in therapy that there is no way of knowing immediately when such acceptance is not possible for me. The realization takes time. The best I can do is to be sensitive to the issue and recognize when I know that I cannot accept the person. I find that I am sometimes able to tolerate, forgive, understand, and endure, but still I cannot accept. Such a relationship will not allow real change in the other person to occur.

At that point, I will refer the person to another therapist. I have never discovered any pattern to my inability to accept another person—there does not seem to be a particular kind of person, or race, or sex, or religion, or particular personality type. Perhaps someone I think of as an evil person, a person who seems to me to be totally unrelated to the world in which he lives, will feel unacceptable to me. Even so, he deserves acceptance, not of his behavior or actions, but of his humanness. If I cannot give it, perhaps someone else can.

We must understand that our difficulty in accepting does not mean that the other person is unacceptable. All of us have our own personal struggles with our capacity to accept. We each have our wounds, the places we are stuck, the closed windows that make us less than whole. Another person, no more or less loving than ourselves, may be capable of accepting someone we cannot. It suggests nothing as to our relative maturities or values. It simply reflects our different personal pasts and growths. These differences in our persons make each of us unique, and give each of us our own particular work to do in our quest for wholeness.

The Struggle to Accept

Gerald sees himself as a good father. He talks to his children on their terms and in their language and says he can appreciate their problems. He goes out of his way to let them have their space. He prides himself on letting them do their own thing. He lives this way in all good faith and earnestness, even though he sometimes feels vaguely troubled. He is unclear about whether his children need him to set limits for them. They do. In order to be truly free to explore and risk, children need clear limits. They need responsible parents, who are knowledgeable about the real world, quietly protective, and able to educate their children about life. At the same time, such parents must be willing to let their children explore. A delicate balance is required. Acceptance is neither permissiveness nor caretaking.

The balancing act between allowing risk and setting limits is a moment-to-moment reality. Such relational decisions are always precarious, subjective judgments, which have to be made immediately in real relationships. A long-distance love affair may always leave time for careful reflection, but real lovers tend to look into each other's eyes in the immediate moment. Certainly, most of parenting happens in the here-and-now moment. The immediacy of this kind of relating means that risk will be real, both the risk of being ourselves and the risk of accepting the other person.

Angela struggles with her feelings about her roommate at school. They have lived together for three semesters. Charlotte is at times very demanding and can be insensitive and petulant. On the other hand, she is for the most part honest and forthright, loyal, and seems genuinely to care for Angela. Angela wants to get along and on principle is usually willing to let people just be people. She always tries to be grown-up about things, and will usually try to go along with Charlotte and give her the benefit of the doubt. She tries to work with her feelings whenever issues arise and make a choice about what to do. Is this acceptance? Or is it, instead, a passive accommodation that will eventually destroy the relationship? If the relationship grows into more intimacy and closeness, then, indeed, Angela's feeling was acceptance. If not, then it was simply tolerance. Tolerance does not feed growth. It does not make us more whole.

Ultimately, the proof of true acceptance is only in the outcome. Acceptance is, in that way, *operative* in the world. It makes things change. It does not guarantee *how* they will change, only that growth will occur. Acceptance changes the accepting person as much as the accepted one. It feels clean, clear, and joyful. We actually know when we accept others because we then know more deeply what *we* feel and who *we* are.

Nathan has always been bothered by his friends' drug use. He is bored with their behavior when they are using drugs, and has strong feelings that using drugs is not healthy. But he tells himself, "They are my friends, and they do not have a *serious* drug problem. They do not hurt me with their drugs. Anyway, who am I to talk?" Nathan is different from Angela. He would like to have his say but feels unwilling to commit his whole self to the relationship. Where she is uncertain but participating, he seems to know underneath that his feeling is only a tolerance that has none of the energy of a loving acceptance. Nathan is stranded because only the latter would allow him honestly to confront them.

It is not that Nathan simply knows what he feels better than Angela does because using drugs is more troublesome than just being demanding and insensitive. The difference is that while

Nathan knows on some level that something inside *himself* is not as he wishes, he is not unconditionally accepting of his friends. Angela, equally unsure about what to do in her relationship, seems, however, actively engaged in the process of accepting Charlotte as well as herself.

Neither is simply right or wrong. When we know that something is not right within ourselves, we are troubled and feel the need for change. If we love and accept, we can honestly confront both ourselves and the other. When we are uncertain about our love and acceptance, however, we must resist confronting because we will only be judging the other person. We must learn to know the difference, for in such knowledge resides our growing edge. For Nathan to confront his friends without acceptance would be a disaster. For Nathan *not* to confront them, when he finally finds that acceptance, would also be a disaster.

Gene's sister Marne has had a lifetime of "bad luck" with men. She consistently seems to choose men who hurt and damage her. Some have even physically hurt her, yet she has continued to stay with them. Gene loves Marne and has always felt close to her. He hurts with her repeated pain. He feels both protective of her and sorry for her, and he is usually there for her when she is in trouble and needs him. But is Gene accepting of Marne? Is such caring acceptance?

He is there, he is loyal, and he cares, but none of those feelings are acceptance. Supporting self-destructiveness is not acceptance. Facilitating another's unhappiness is not acceptance. Codependency is not acceptance. Acceptance not only makes the other person aware of our love but also of our concern with their self-destructive behavior. Acceptance conveys our love while at the same time powerfully confronting the other person's unhealthiness.

Were Gene genuinely accepting, we are not so sure that he would always be there, certainly not in the same way. He would be there, but in a way that would make the relationship to Marne different. Acceptance energizes growth because it loves at the same time that it confronts. Acceptance energizes growth because it moves the other person to their choice, and *the ability to choose is the essence of being a growing, free, and mature human being.* Acceptance makes possible that movement toward wholeness. It does not assure or guarantee the growth but does make it possible. Accepting the other person guarantees change, even if the only change is that person's inability to relate to us further. Our unconditional love will be experienced by the other, but they retain the choice of how they will respond to it.

It is for exactly the same reasons that we must equally accept ourselves. Accepting ourselves—stopping the self-negating and judging ways we live with ourselves—energizes our own growth, moves us to our own choice, and loves as well as confronts ourselves. It makes possible our own movement toward wholeness. Unconditional love for *self* and *other* are woven into a fabric of one piece—one cannot exist without the other. When our self-talk moves from the false self's judging, unaccepting voice to the real self's unconditionally loving, accepting voice, we begin to rediscover our true selfbeing.

The Work of Acceptance

Acceptance is a profound and personally demanding experience that requires constant attention to our inner feelings. It is often, however, confused with other social feelings that we consider good and desirable. For example, feelings of acquiescence and forgiveness are often mistakenly felt to be acceptance. But tolerance, patience, caring, forgiveness, understanding, acquiescence, and other related positive feelings are not acceptance. They may be forerunners of acceptance, but they are not the same thing. In acceptance we know that the other person is more like us than different from us. True acceptance recognizes a connection to the other person in which self/other is not seen as a polarity, but as a union. None of those other positive feelings contain that sense. They are for the most part *I-You* states as opposed to true *I-Thou* states. There is a subject-object sense that is not present in true acceptance, and that is why acceptance is so critically different and important.

Simon and Nan are both in college and have lived together for the past two years. They plan eventually to get married. Nan has to work long hours and to study extensively. She withdraws during this time and is distant from him. Simon understands this, even though academics come much more easily to him. He feels that once they are finished with school and are married, everything will be different, their roles will be more clearly defined. So he waits and is admirably tolerant and understanding. He does not want to put any more stress on Nan than she is already under. Is that accepting? Of course not. His thoughts suggest that he is simply waiting for some other "Nan" in a nonrelationship. He is condescending and is judging her.

Simon says that he accepts the fact that Nan cannot be related to him while she is involved in something else that is significant and meaningful to her. But no union is possible on that basis. He, in essence, sees who she is as being incompatible with her loving him, although he would never acknowledge it. He not only judges her in that way, but clearly would choose for her to live as the person who "loves" him. His tolerance is destructive of the relationship and of her personhood.

Acceptance is much more overt and intrusive. It never diminishes the other person. It says, "I love you. I know that there is currently something that makes it difficult for you to be both with me and going about your own business, but I want you to know that when that happens I miss you and want you and still feel connected to you. *But I insist on your continuing to be you.* I want you to be able to go about your own business and continue to enjoy loving me. When you do not, I miss the real you. I hope you and I can discover that we can do what we want to do and still be truly with each other." That relationship represents true acceptance. It is very different from tolerance or understanding. Those qualities may help. They are certainly more helpful in closeness than sarcastic complaints would be. But they do not make a significant difference in intimate relationship. Acceptance does make such a difference, but it is hard work.

Daniel has had a rough year. He earns too little at his current job to pay for training for a different job, so he has to continue to work in a situation he genuinely dislikes. He lives in a chronically bad mood. He is bitter toward his work, toward the school he feels he cannot attend, toward society in general. His girlfriend Patricia understands and accepts his anger and his bad moods. She believes that she is accepting him as he is, but in reality, she only endures and takes care of him.

Patricia's enduring and care taking are of no help, however, for they do not move either the relationship or Daniel to growth. Instead, they help keep both people mired where they are. Patricia would be more accepting to tell Daniel how much she loves him and wants him to live out his personal choices, to get on with his growth. In genuine acceptance, she would *insist* that he do so. Acceptance is not patience, codependency, timidity, or going along with the other in their unhealthiness. It is an active, passionate statement of belief in the other, even if they might fail, *even if they do fail.* Success or failure is not the issue. Selfbeing is the issue, selfbeing based on personal choosing.

Nick and Dave have lived together for six years. More often than not, Nick comes back from work to find their apartment a mess. Nick finds the mess upsetting, but says to himself, "I remember when I burned a hole in the couch. None of us is perfect. I guess I just need to accept Dave the way he is." In truth, Nick puts up with Dave. He outwardly tolerates and forgives the behavior which inside he finds intolerable. He says, "I have been the same way, so I can't complain too much."

Nick's putting up with Dave's personal irresponsibility is not loving. It is actually a disrespectful and hostile willingness by Nick to sacrifice his own person to Dave's lack of responsibility in the relationship. It is disrespectful, for it sees neither of them as whole persons. It is hostile, for over time it will destroy their love for each other. Such permissiveness is not acceptance. Acceptance is much more demanding, much more honest, and much more work.

Permissiveness is not acceptance. It contains no healthy love. Permissiveness on the part of parents is experienced by children as unloving, detached, and uncaring. The same is true when any of us are being permissive with another person. Tolerance is not acceptance. Toleration conveys a patronizing willingness to put up with the other person. It demeans the other, seeing them as less than us. Acquiescence is not acceptance. It is simply an avoidance of relationship. It cannot be acceptance because it is not even relational.

Not-confronting is not acceptance. It is simply another way of judging the other. Sympathy is not acceptance. Sympathy means literally to "feel with." Acceptance means to "be with," when, indeed, we do not "feel with." Sympathy is a poor substitute for empathy. Being with someone is radically different from standing apart from them and being sympathetic. Acceptance involves and is felt by both persons. In acceptance, both of us know deeply that we are more alike than we are different. Opening us to experience and growth, acceptance allows the light to stream in.

5

THE SECOND WINDOW:
Responsibility
for Self

It is no use to blame the looking glass if your face is awry.

—Nikolai Gogol

One of our colleagues tells a story about his two youngest children. His daughter, just sixteen, was asking permission to go to a concert, but he was reluctant to say yes because he was worried about what else might be going on at the event. They fussed back and forth for some time, with his thirteen-year-old son sitting there quietly watching. Finally, his son spoke up: "Dad, what's the problem?"

"Well, I'm worried and not sure I should let her go."

"But, Dad, it's your job to worry . . . and you can't get her to live just so you won't have to do your job."

"Well, I'm doing my job. I'm worrying!"

"Yeah, but she wants you to worry *quieter*."

The notion that we are all *self-responsible* often seems clearer to children than to adults. They seem more intuitively in touch with what educator Harriet Wiseman Elliott meant when she said "people, not systems, are important." Family rules, like all cultural systems, cannot be allowed to displace selfbeing if a person is to remain whole. And self-being is only possible when based on self-responsibility.

Self-Esteem and Self-Responsibility

It is far more important that one's life should be perceived than that it should be transformed; for no sooner has it been perceived, than it transforms itself of its own accord.

—MAURICE MAETERLINCK, *The Treasure of the Humble*

Self-perception on that deep level—seeing ourselves for who we really are, knowing what we feel and think—is the basis of self-responsibility. Out of it, we can grow and change; without it, we are forever self-diminished. Such self-perception is how we experience our self-esteem. Our everyday use of the concept self-esteem is confused. We often use it to refer to how much we value ourselves inside. Apart from others, and in my private introspective experience, I may feel wonderful about me. But how much does such a completely internal concept tell us about the wholeness of the person?

The paranoid personality sitting comfortably in the garden behind his home, with no one else in his space or in his sight, can feel an enormous *me*-esteem in the sense of feeling powerful, capable, and in charge. However, all of those feelings are dependent on his being separate from others, including, we suspect, not just other people but even the plants in his garden. This pseudo-self-esteem disappears when such a person comes in contact with others and the paranoid feelings become predominant. Obviously, despite his enormous *me*-esteem when alone, he has very poor *self*-esteem when related, one person to another.

If *self* is our energizing and creative connection with the world around us, then what we feel in solitude does not reflect our *self*-esteem. Our self-esteem can only be accurately assessed when we are connected to other people and the rest of our world. That real self-esteem will then determine how viable our self-responsibility is in the presence of others, how comfortably and firmly we assume our responsibility for the way we are in the world. Such real self-esteem is then intimately connected to whether we live as self-responsible persons.

Self-responsibility is much easier to understand if taken literally—that is, as the ability to *respond to self*. Such a definition, while etymologically obvious, is not the way most of us usually see self-responsibility. Most of us deal with self-responsibility as if it meant "living as if someone else is watching" instead of "perceiving ourselves." That destructive interpretation does not describe self-responsibility at all, but can, at least, lead us back to the origins of our problems about our ability to respond to self.

We learn or mislearn self-responsibility in childhood. As with acceptance, our capacity for self-responsibility forms in our early years. In childhood, we learn either to predominantly respond to self or respond to other. Also in childhood, we learn whether or not to be conscious of the difference. We learn whether or not we have a choice. To be whole, we must ultimately *choose* to respond to our*selves*. If I simply respond to *me*, I have no awareness of my relationship to the other. If I simply respond to *others*, I have no awareness of me. When I have an awareness, a sensitive awareness, of my relationship to the other, *and an equally sensitive awareness* of the feelings within me, then my responses are coming from my *self*. Self-responsibility is not isolative, egocentric, or narcissistic. It is rather a sensitive and communicative response which represents an awareness of both me and the other.

Healthy responses are not simply reflexive. They reflect, instead, an awareness of our inner feelings at a particular moment in the presence of a particular person, and are modified by our experience of that relationship to the other. As children, we might learn to respond only to our *me*—our own feelings and needs— with total insensitivity to other people. Much more commonly, however, we are taught to avoid our own feelings and respond primarily from an overawareness of the other person's feelings. That preoccupation, of course, is a fundamental characteristic of most unhealthy behavior—what is commonly called neurosis. The rarer phenomena of simply being aware of one's own feelings and totally ignoring the feelings of others is the common denominator of more severely disturbed behavior—psychosis and severe character disorder.

The Issue of Dependence

A star looks down at me,
And says, "Here I and you
Stand, each in our own degree:
What do you mean to do?"

—Thomas Hardy,
"Waiting Both"

We must be primarily responsible to our inner world as the basis for making choices and decisions in our lives. Those internal experiences are the foundation of our being. That inner world, experienced in context, that is, in connected relationship—for that is the difference between being self-responsible and being severely disturbed—allows us to live as whole persons. Self-responsible living, not independence, is the opposite of dependence. "The questions which one asks oneself," wrote James Baldwin in *Nobody Knows My Name*, "begin at last to illuminate the world, and become one's key to the experience of others."

We are dependent on others when we allow them to tell us what we feel, who we are, or how we should be. We are dependent when we do not ask and answer those questions ourselves. When parents do not allow children their own feelings, they foster such dependency. When they do not allow children to ask their own questions and to find their own answers, they teach them to be un-self-responsible. However innocent or helpful their intentions may be, when they tell their children how to feel about someone or something, they are depriving them of their self-responsibility.

Watley comes in for therapy at his employer's insistence. A salesman in a growing local business, Watley is a serious person. He is always stressed and anxious, and his employer, who cares about him, worries about Watley's suddenly dropping dead. Unlike pure workaholics, whose problems are closer to those of the addicted person, serious people are usually overtly invested in security. Watley's family could tell us how disproportionate the time he spends on business, how much he worries, how little fun they have together, how oppressively high his expectations are. They know him to be a good person, but they do not understand why he chooses to be as driven and unhappy as he is.

If we ask Watley why he puts so much pressure on himself, he will tell us that he does what he does for his family, and that life *is* serious, and that bad things *can* happen, so preparations must be made. He sees himself as being very responsible. He sees himself as choosing to be how he is. In fact, however, Watley has lost his wholeness in his pursuit of security. He responds very little to his real inner self. Instead, living his life out of his fear of dependency—out of responding to what is outside him—he ends up totally dependent on what is outside him. He is neither choosing nor *being responsible for himself.*

The Depressive Dependent

The majority of us struggle with the problems of dependency, problems born in the unchosen dependence of the child. Like most of the problems we struggle with, dependency issues arise from this unfinished business of our childhood. These child issues contain within them the notion that someone or something outside us holds the answer to our needs. The particular ways in which these problems will appear in adulthood may vary, but their genesis is in the unresolved issues of our childhood.

Childhood struggles left unresolved will be expressed later in life in nonexperiential living. The dependent person, in particular, abdicates the sense of being responsible for him- or herself and lives in response to others. Since dependence is always ambivalent—we are needy of others but resent them for having such power over us—the problem will be manifest in one of two ways. If the dependency is primary, we will be depressive, helpless, and self-deprecating, victims of our environment and particularly of the people in it. We will find thousands of reasons for our lot in life, but *we* assume no responsibility for it. We lament our fate in various ways: "It has nothing to do with me, I didn't do anything. Some people have all the luck. What did I do to deserve this? Why me?"

In such living, we see ourselves as helpless victims, innocent and self-effacing. The world gives us a hard time and if things were only different—be it lover, child, job, neighbor, or just the times—then things might be wonderful. We are misunderstood. This is a "germ theory" of life; we are forever catching the illnesses of the *other*. Moreover, it is a mistake to see this attitude as passive, whining, or helpless. Indeed, in their own way, such people are often aggressive, demanding, and controlling. It is, in truth, fascinating to see how often in life it is the passive, helpless person who controls the dynamics of any given situation.

The Hostile Dependent

At the age of forty-seven, Laura has finally succeeded in becoming alone. She rails constantly against the husband who left her, the children who rarely visit her, and the friends who deserted her. She will tell anyone who will listen all the reasons for her misery, and all the reasons boil down to "him" and "them." She is chronically angry, and speaks with a voice and expression that barely contain her rage. She is a difficult person to be with. For that reason, few people choose to be with her. The resultant isolation from others then only fuels her conviction that others do not love her.

Laura displays the second common manifestation of dependency: anger. If a dependent person lives primarily with the hostile feelings accompanying dependent ambivalence, he or she will not be passive and helpless but, instead, will be active and militant. It is the same psychological germ theory of life—all the reasons for their distress lie outside them and impinge on them not by chance but by intention. They are as innocent as the depressive dependent, but feel angry and righteous toward the world in which they live.

For humans caught on either side of the dependency struggle, life is full of nonexperience. Either form of dependency will control a relationship with another if that other person allows it. With *everything* predefined, *nothing* can be what it is in itself, and thus, nothing can be experienced. Living dependent on what is outside us leaves a large window to experience shuttered. We lose any sense that we are the prime mover in our own existence.

When responding only to what is outside, *we are dependent on it*. We are living as if what is outside us can define our *selves*. We all struggle with dependency in this way to some extent. And we all struggle in both passive and angry ways with the abdication of responsibility that dependency brings. We all sometimes feel

helpless and depressed and at other times feel hostile and paranoid.

In most of us, unhealthy dependency hides within our ordinary beha   vior. We may be thirty or forty years old, parents of
our own children, yet we will still wait for our parents to pick up
the check whenever we go out to eat together. Or we may expect
our parents or some other older adult to help us out of the tight
spots we get ourselves into—not to assist us, as a peer might, but
to make everything okay for us. Or we may expect that big
present or gift of money at a holiday or birthday and then feel
somehow betrayed when we do not receive it. There are endless
everyday examples: the fifty-year-old husband who expects his
wife to maintain *his* personal necessities, the forty-year-old wife
who expects her husband to make all her decisions in life, the
thirty-year-old woman who quits her job because she does not get
her way, the sixty-year-old man who will never go out or get
involved in any activities on his own because his children do not
invite him to theirs, the forty-five-year-old man who is awaiting
the death of a parent to get his inheritance. These are not strange
or abnormal people. They are us, diminishing ourselves as persons.

Healthy Dependency

With unhealthy dependency comes self-diminishing nonexperience, comes living in the world of what-is-not, comes being
what we are not, comes relating with others without even sensing
what they really are. In *healthy dependency*, we choose to be
dependent when our healthy self wants to be. For example, when
we are ill, we may ask another person to help us. We choose to
accept help and thus we relate to the other person in a way that
helps them to help us. Instead of being demanding, critical, and
full of expectation, we are cooperative, positive, and try to retain
our sense of humor. We then resume responsibility for ourselves
as soon as we are able.

Such *chosen* dependence breeds no anger or passivity. It is a
self-responsible act in itself. We must all learn to stand alone, but
not separate from others. We all need help. "Independence is
never absolute," wrote psychoanalyst and pediatrician D. W.

Winnicott in *The Maturational Process and the Facilitating Environment.* "The healthy individual does not become isolated, but becomes related to the environment in such a way that the individual and the environment can be said to be interdependent." A balance of healthy dependence and healthy independence is one of the clearest outgrowths of heightened responsibility for self.

Experiencing
Responsibility for Self

George was a businessman in his early fifties when I (Tom) first saw him. He was highly successful in his particular business, regarded as astute, aggressive, and competent. He came to me for a rather common problem. He explained in our first meeting that for the past year he had had difficulty with his potency. In that area he was not being successful. As he said, using his business-like speech, he had difficulty "getting up for it." He told me he had made the appointment to see me because just recently in desperation he had decided to go to his bank and get a thousand new one-dollar bills. He took them home, spread them over the bed, then went out to the living room to tell his wife to come back to the bedroom. He told her that he wanted to make love. She came to the bedroom, and they stood by the bed, which he had covered with the money. She slowly sank down by the edge of the bed and cried.

George decided in that moment that there was something deep within him which he needed to look at much more honestly and openly than he had up to that point. He sensed that his sexual problem was a symptom of a much larger problem, one he had been avoiding for years. He was unclear as to just what this problem was, but it became very clear to him that there was something deeply wrong with how he was living in his world.

George stayed in therapy for several years, dealing mostly with his chronic depression. The depression was not, for the most part, manifest in a passive, plaintive, or self-derisive dependency. It was expressed more often in an angry blaming of others for whatever befell him that was not to his liking. George was not paranoid, but he obviously was *not being responsible for himself* either. That absence of self-responsibility was the issue we had to deal with. We had to deal with his feeling that because he was successful and moneyed, he was owed. And we had to deal with the much older needs those feelings represented. George felt he had done his part, and the question in his mind was why others, including his wife, had not done their part.

The first significant experience George and I had in our working together was his calling me one afternoon and saying that he thought he was having a heart attack. He said that he had seen his internist, who had examined him and reassured him that the problem was not cardiac and he was not in any immediate danger. George, however, said that he was still concerned and wanted to know if I would see him. I told him I had no time that afternoon. He said he really needed to see me. I told him I would see him after I had seen my last patient for the day. At that time, I sat with him for an hour while he described his fear, his insistent and frightening chest pains, and his puzzlement about whether this episode was the end or simply another way he had of being either dependent or angry. When he left, he was free of pain.

I left my office shortly afterward, and on the way home found myself developing chest pains. Later in the evening I called George and told him that I had something that belonged to him and that I would like to come over to his house, which was not too distant from mine, and give it back to him. He said fine. I drove to his home and explained to him that I had gotten these chest pains which I did not feel belonged to me. I thought they were his, and his responsibility, and that he ought to have them back. I thought his having them back might help him resolve some other important issues.

My keeping the pains might have, indeed, helped *me* resolve some immediate issues—such as taking better care of myself by not staying late to see people, and not taking upon myself their burdens in life—but the real gain would come for *him* if he accepted the responsibility for his own pain, his own dying, and did not one more time relieve his issues by placing them on another. In this particular instance, the other had been myself. George said he could accept his own pain back, although he was now clearer than ever that he did not want it. We both grew some in the experience.

The next important experience I had with George came many years later when he suffered a regression in his depressive feelings after his wife died. I had not seen him for quite some time. He came to me and said that he had done well for years but now was feeling as bad as he had ever felt. He complained that he had gotten nowhere, that he was right back where he had started, and that he had the same painful feelings he had felt when he had first come to see me. I looked directly at him and said, "Well, if that's true, George, then we need to go back to the drawing board and start all over."

He sat up sharply in the chair and shouted, "Goddamn you, you son of a bitch! What do you mean we have to start all over? I've done a great deal of growing in all these years, and I know it. And I really resent your lack of faith. I resent even more the fact that you feel that simply because I have a bad time for a little while, that all the growing I've achieved and worked hard for has been meaningless. I mostly resent your feeling that I have become no more responsible for myself than I was when I first knew you."

George had had an experience. He had had an experience that he would be able to reexperience from then on in his life. It represented a *knowing* rather than just a *recognizing* and thus was very different from what would have occurred had I just pointed out to him his participation in his own depression and what that participation was doing for him (just like the many times in the past when I had pointed out to him that he was not innocent, that he participated in everything that happened to him). Such interactions are educational, mostly aimed at preparing someone for the *experience* of feeling responsible for himself. The crux of our current interaction, however, was returning him to the *experience* itself.

Self-responsibility itself is always experiential. A therapist cannot simply retrain attitudes in a cognitive manner or generate enthusiastic feelings for self-responsibility like a cheerleader. A therapist must have the faith that experience will allow the imprinting of the cognitive/emotional/behavioral changes in the person, and that these experiences will arise between the therapist and the client *in their relationship.*

Therapists must also deal with the cognitive, emotional, and behavioral *work*, but that work is only meaningful as reexperience. The *experience* of self-responsibility must come first. We are all aware, for example, that if a person's attitude is just the cognitive iteration, "Of course I am responsible for myself," that the "self-responsibility" will collapse in the face of any real experience in which the person's underlying conviction that he or she is the innocent victim of a cruel world will resurface. The experience itself is *crucial* because we must come to know ourselves. To insist that a person reexperience what has not yet happened is a waste of time. For a therapist to insist that clients know a way of being that they have yet to experience is exactly the same waste of time. It cannot be done. The therapist must continue being available for experience in the relationship in order for clients to have the opportunity to give up their nonexperience, their not being whole.

The same truths hold for each of us individually striving to become more whole. We must experience our self-responsibility first so we can then practice—that is, reexperience—it. Experiencing our self-responsibility will only come with our being in the world in that way. The shuttered window of believing that others make us feel the way we do, make us make our mistakes, or make us less than we could be, cuts us off from any chance to have that self-responsible experience.

At twenty-eight, Larry appears to be intent on never making a mistake in life. He loses himself in thinking about things. Like the person who is always collecting information but never acting, Larry never wants to do anything until he has already done it. He wants to make sure he can live up to any "self-responsibility" before he assumes it. Of course, such a life position makes decision-making very difficult, so most of Larry's choices are made by default. While he is still thinking, the time to choose comes and passes, or someone else makes the choice. Larry thinks he is protecting himself, making himself secure, but in reality he diminishes himself. He thinks he is being self-responsible, but, in fact, he entirely separates himself from that experience. There is no experiencing without risk. The person who avoids self-responsibility avoids risk and experience, and thus will never be whole. If we remember that self-responsibility is *the ability to respond to self*, and that *self* is by definition connection to others, then living in that way is easier to understand and seems less lonely. We may be alone, but we do not have to be lonely.

Responsibility and Causation

Most of us confuse responsibility with causation. The fact that each of us is responsible to and for what happens to us does not mean we *cause* it. We do not *cause* everything that happens to us. However, we are *responsible* for everything that happens to us. Since self-responsibility is the ability to respond to *self*, the whole person has no choice but to be responsible for everything in her life if she would be a *self*, if she would *experience* life.

I (Pat), spend much of my time with clients attempting to return them to some sense of their responsibility for their own lives. The most difficult thing for us to learn seems to be that we are being what we want to be, doing what we want to do, and doing it with those with whom we want to be doing it. I do not mean that people want to be poor, or raped, or airplane-crash victims. I mean that in our ordinary relations in life, our pairings, families, parentings, workings, playings, and strugglings, we are what we choose to be, so that *has* to be what we want. Therefore, I do not look at what clients say they want, I look at what they have and what they are doing. I then assume that the latter is what they really want, at least for the time being. I do, however, encounter unending protests and disbelief, as from Joe:

"You mean I really want to be this anxious?"

"Of course, some part of you must. Why else would you be so anxious, Joe?"

"That's crazy; I hate being anxious, I can't see why I would want to be anxious."

"That's because you don't see what your anxiety is doing for you. If you could see that it is satisfying some need, then it wouldn't seem so crazy to you."

"What on earth could being this anxious be doing for me?"

"It could be your way of telling people how helpless you are. Or, it could be your way of controlling everyone around you. You must know that your anxiety does that with most people . . . controls them. It's also contagious. It makes people either want to fix the problem or to get away from you. It ends up giving them a feeling of inadequacy, a frustration at their inability to make you feel better. After dealing with you they may well wonder what is wrong with them."

"Why would I want to make anybody feel that way?"

"Maybe you're afraid, and maybe your fear is more important to you than anything else, even feeling good. I don't know you well enough to know any of the whys yet. But there has to be something pretty important to make it worthwhile to you to feel that bad. You need to realize that what you want is important to you, but the way you're going about getting it is self-destructive. You may be afraid, but you're afraid in a way that is more destructive of yourself than whatever you're afraid of could ever be. What you're doing in your life with what appears to be your fear, and its attendant behaviors, is very important and meaningful to you. It needs to be done. It needs, however, to be done in a way that is less self-destructive of you."

Explaining things to Joe is reflective and cognitive. It may help, but it will not change him. Joe has to experience his self-responsibility in a more immediate interpersonal context. The experience he has in the relationship to the therapist can be how he grows—it may provide him the experiential opportunity—but the teaching itself will not. No one can teach experience.

The fact that we cannot teach someone either the nature of their own experience or how they individually might experience, is why all our arguments with others, in which we try to tell *them* how *they* are, are destructive wastes of time. If we stick to our own experience—know and say what we can know and say about *our* inner world—we will carry the relationship further. Likewise, it does no good for our spouses, lovers, families, or friends simply to point out the error of our ways. Regardless of whether they are correct or not—and they may well be factually correct—we will only learn when we experience being those ways with them ourselves.

Experience involves *learning*, and learning is very different from being *taught*. We cannot experience that for which we are unwilling to be responsible. The truth of that fact has nothing to do with cause. That we cause so many of our own problems is simply one more thing, a very important thing, that we must be responsible for. "We are spinning our own fates," wrote William James in *The Principles of Psychology*, "good or evil, and never to be undone . . . so our self-feeling in this world depends entirely on what we *back* ourselves to be and do."

Growing Responsibly

Frequently, people come into therapy depressed, and we go through a similar initial interaction with those clients. It may be that they are saying that they are angry about something that they do not feel comfortable being angry about. It may be that they are saying that they feel uncared for, unsupported in their life. We tell them that regardless of the source, what is most important is that they realize that their depression is trying to do something for them, something important and real, meaningful, and genuine. The problem, again, lies in the fact that they are going about their struggles in ways that are self-destructive and almost certainly guaranteed to make sure that they do not get what they want. They are actively diminishing their selfbeing.

The problem is to find another, more constructive, way of doing what the depression was attempting to do. Most of our unhealthiness comes when we attempt to achieve something that is valuable, significant, and growthful, but do it in unhealthy ways and with behaviors that we mislearned as children. We fall back into our old security loops again and again, into behaviors that are inherently self-defeating and self-destructive. Because such behaviors are ways of looking *outside* for solutions, they are part of a lack of self-responsibility. They block experience.

Certainly, we must learn to deal with how parents, lovers, and children *do* affect us, how viruses, how genes, how biochemistry, how social structures affect us. But if we are to live with any of these as *ourselves*, we must be self-responsible for them. Regardless of what the *other* does, *I* am responsible for me. I must take full and complete responsibility for my thinking, feeling, and behaving. My ways of relating and my hopes are my responsibility, regardless of the situation outside me.

The Jamesons have two children—Terry, seventeen, and Jon, nineteen. As is common in families, the children often act out the parents' issues and struggles. Jon lives out his mother's conforming, uptight behaviors, and Terry her father's rebellious, nonconforming feelings. Jon is always punctual, meets external expectations, has difficulty talking about his feelings, and is somewhat rigid in his interactions and speech. He can seem withdrawn and hostile to others, although he will deny he means to be that way. He has trouble being "different." Terry, on the other hand, appears driven to be different. She will not meet schedules or outside demands even if to do so would be in her own best interest. She is very aware, but often seems uncaring. Both of these adolescents are already full of mislearnings with windows of self-responsibility already partially shuttered.

The conformists of the world renounce their responsibility for self by living with their choices determined, molded, and dictated for the most part by someone or something outside them. The same is also true of the rebels of this world. Their choices are equally dictated by what or whom they are rebelling against. In that sense, they are as conforming as the robots whom they so despise and denigrate. The only difference is the former are dependent in one way—passive and compliant—while the latter are dependent in another way—angry, unwilling to participate, and convinced that the world is responsible for everything that is wrong in their lives.

Neither the conformist nor the rebel, or the conformist or rebel that is in each of us, is self-responsible, for neither really *responds to self*. The two merely have different external programs or roles for their responses. But in both instances, the program is nonexperiential. Each way of living cuts us off from being whole. The eventual result is the sad diminishment of self. No one else causes us to be us. No one can respond to our *selves* but us. Neither conforming nor rebelling are growthful because, being roles, neither are self-responsible.

Irresponsibility as Nonexperience

Oliver Wendell Holmes wrote that "Life is an end in itself, and the only question as to whether it is worth living is whether you have enough of it." Having enough of life requires experiencing it. Just putting in time is not living in this real sense, but putting in time is exactly what people who live in roles are doing. Roles can range from overt caricatures—such as the macho, the flirt, or the seducer—to the more subtle living out of a fixed life philosophy such as friendliness, optimism, pessimism, loneliness, or stoicism. The same is true of living out fixed ideologies—

religious, social, or political. In none of these roles do we truly experience. We live in a play written by someone else.

More often the role is not a type, but is specific to the person who lives it. To live this way is to become the main character in our own idiosyncratic play. The role is easily mistaken for our real life. Many of us not only blindly live inside our play but even assign roles to other people to whom we relate. Unfortunately, they do not know they are in our play and thus do not know the roles we would have them fill. We are then further frustrated by their not fulfilling our needs and become even more nonexperiential as we struggle with them to correct their "wrong" approach to their parts.

A few simple examples from therapy will show the momentary *experiences* that can critically reinforce the hours of cognitive education, behavioral queries, and affective confrontations that are all attempts to bring clients out of their roles and into their self-responsibility. Such experiences are by and large ordinary experiences, just as the experiences that created the roles and distorted the *self*-images of people have been ordinary experiences. Many of us may have spent years being undermined by anxious parents, controlled by frightened ones, or even neglected by depressed ones. Ordinary experience is the ordinary way most of us have mislearned. In therapy, or on our own, we can only relearn in similar ordinary experience.

Cognitive, behavioral, and affective interactions are ways of touching one another through ordinary experience. For example, the therapist may say:

Cognitive education: "I hear what you are saying about your husband, but what was your part in the fight? That is the only part you and I can do anything about. We both already know that you think he always starts these things."

Behavioral query (asked of a client who repeatedly comes into the office and begins emptying the cups, gathering up Coke bottles, etc.): "Are you always cleaning up other people's trash?"

Affective confrontation: To the client who, just as always, says, "If you don't mind . . ." we reply, "What if I do mind?"

The rules for therapy are no different from those for ordinary life. All three approaches, in *any* relationship, must be congruent for the interaction to be experiential. Without congruence, the interactions will not be experienced. Instead, the other person will defend against what he or she experiences as judgment and attack. Only in the experiential moment can change occur. It is only then that the hard work of reexperiencing can become meaningful.

The common conflicts in our relationships reflect this difficulty. Without being self-responsible, we tell the other about him- or herself. We do not share *our experience;* we *define* the other and tell them about *their experience.* Since we are not self-responsible, our cognitive, affective, or behavioral confrontation is blaming and judging and is correctly experienced as such by the other person. Our message—even if it is about something we perceive accurately—is *not* experienced, and the other person learns nothing. The other is simply reconfirmed in the belief that we judge and attack. Our desire to be right and righteous overwhelms our desire to love and be loved. We have trouble living *our* life, and, instead, try to live the life of the *other.*

Don is in his mid-twenties. He is depressed about a consistent pattern of almost succeeding in school and work, but then at the crucial moment folding his tent and leaving. He relates a dream in which he has just had a book published that gets the lead review in *The New York Times.* The review is very positive and he wants to share the good news, so he calls the therapist at home. He is told that the therapist is in the hospital and wakes up deeply concerned.

After relating this dream at his next session, Don asks his therapist, "*Are* you having any serious medical problems?" The therapist replies, "Don't you know that was *your* dream?"

There is a slow smile, then a chuckle, and Don says, "Yes it was, wasn't it?" He pauses. "You know, that's important. It *was* my dream."

The moment is an experience. Don could not, at that moment, have individually separated out his thinking, feeling, behaving, or his connection to his world or his hope in life. He knew, at least for that moment, the experience of his *responsibility for self.* And surrounding that experience were multitudes of other secondary insights. For example, he knew that his thoughts were not magical, that he could be successful without *really* harming someone he loved, and that the therapist, like other people, was responsible for himself. He knew his *role* was not who he was, for *it was not real.* He owned his own dream and experienced being responsible for himself. As he and the therapist reexperience these knowings in the future, Don can generalize this moment into a way of being and learn how to be a more whole Don.

Often we come to see our roles by having an ordinary but profound experience of ourselves *not being responsible for self*. An example: Michelle is an intelligent, warm businesswoman in her late forties. She arrives at her appointment for a therapy session more than thirty minutes late. Coming into the office she says, "I'm terribly sorry I'm late. I was on the phone at work, and I couldn't get off."

Later, as the end of the hour nears, the therapist gets up to go. Michelle says, "Is our time up? It's only been about thirty minutes." She is still sitting. The therapist, who is standing, replies, "Yes, you were late today and I'd like to stay on schedule." Michelle stands up rather hesitantly and asks, "I've been late before and you've stayed over a little with me. What's different today?"

The therapist responds, "We are. I've gotten to know you better, and I don't think of you as such a helpless person that I have to continue to sacrifice myself for you. You can make better choices about how you live if you are clear about the fact you are not so helpless or needy."

As they reach the door Michelle says, "You know, I got more out of these last few minutes than all the time before. Why haven't you done this earlier?" The therapist responds, "Because either you wouldn't have heard me, or I wasn't sure enough of our relationship to say it. Before, I wasn't ready. Today I feel okay with both me and you about it. Now I'm ready."

The Reparative Experience

One of our therapist colleagues has often noted that "there is no more frustrating and dismal experience than trying to educate people who are just not interested in being educated." We would expand the thought: there is nothing more disastrous in therapy or ordinary life than trying to bring about an experience, even though it may be good for the person, before the relationship can permit it—not before the person is ready for it, for humans are innately ready for growth, but before the relationship can *permit* it. Readiness and permission are not the same. For human relational experience, the proper timing of an experience has less to do with whether the individual can have it, than it has to do with whether the relationship between the two people will allow it, contain it, and enhance it.

In addition to this close tie between the stage of the relationship and what experiences are possible, the interaction with Michelle illustrates another significant factor in a person's experience of responsibility for self. In therapy, the two most activating events in bringing about this *experience* in a client are: (1) the client's experience of the therapist's being self-responsible, or (2) the therapist's *knowing*, and then sharing the knowledge, that he or she is *not* being self-responsible with the client. The same seems true in any relationship in life, whether parent-child, lover-lover, friend-friend, or boss-employee. The other person learns and changes only through our being self-responsible, or through our sharing with them the ways in which we are not being responsible for ourselves. *Experience* brings change, not judgments or explanations.

In Michelle's case, she experiences the therapist's *being responsible for himself*. The therapist is *responding to his self*. More significant to Michelle is the fact that the therapist is in relationship with her at the very moment of that self-responsibility. The therapist is *experiencing* responsibility, not simply promising it, or retrospectively reflecting on it. In a different situation, a therapist could as well have shared his or her experience of *not* being self-responsible. If it were shared in the moment, that too would foster change. If it were *subsequently* shared, however—for example, if the therapist brought this up at their next appointment—it might have some educative value, but it could have little power to actualize Michelle's experience of her responsibility for self. Acknowledgment—"Oh, I have a bad temper" or "I have a problem being late"—is not the same as becoming responsible for self. Similarly, sharing the fact later is not the same as experiencing our lack of responsibility *with* the other person.

It sounds banal when looked at directly in this way, but, in truth, few of us live self-responsibly. Most of us seem *not* to know that we are responsible for how we feel, and, of course, we feel all the time. We can blame our pasts, our parents, our lovers, our fates, our diets, our heredity, our therapists, or even our God, but *we* are still responsible for how *we* feel. We pay a high price both individually and as a society for our inability to acknowledge this truth. Our current ecological, political, and social messes clearly reflect such a lack of self-responsibility.

Culture and Our Lack of Self-Responsibility

While individual lack of self-responsibility brings individual selficide, societal lack of self-responsibility makes the culture a more and more potent reinforcement of increasing lack of self-responsibility among its members. Our current culture does so powerfully. Simply to scan the newspaper, to spend an evening watching television, or to listen to our leaders speak can educate us to our lack of self-responsibility. For example: politicians cannot deal with budgets or international affairs as responsible adults; corporate executives show no sense of responsibility for our environment or the people who work for them. Irresponsibility has become in many ways institutionalized.

In the entitled society, nothing is my own responsibility. Regardless of what has happened, *the fault is always someone else's*. If something happens to me, I am entitled to be paid back in some way. If I encourage my child to play football and then he is hurt in the course of the game, it still must be someone else's fault. If I do not get my promotion at work, it must be because someone is treating me unfairly, not because the other person is, indeed, more qualified. We have moved to a childish society: *dependency forever.*

Without self-responsibility, we do not seem able to learn from our mistakes, to learn how to be different. An unhealthy dependency seems to have captured us. And parents are not the only culprits. Perhaps no group in society has been more culpable in diminishing self-responsibility than psychiatrists, psychologists, sociologists, anthropologists, and all the other professionals who believe there is a reason for everything. These reasons are all too often *explanations*. Rather than using our intellectual understandings to increase our commitment to self-responsibility, we use it as if "reasons" determined human behavior.

There may well be reasons (psychological and sociological) why a man beats his wife, a woman abuses her children, a juvenile steals, a student cheats on exams, a politician lies, a robber robs, or a killer kills, but none of these *reasons*, except in cases of actual mental incompetence, make the people involved any less responsible for themselves. Insight is useful, but reasons do not define us or take away our self-responsibility.

These are not inconsequential problems: over five million women abused every year, about five thousand a year beaten to death, half a million husbands abused, three or more out of every hundred children abused, eight thousand killed a year. Sexual abuse is far, far more common than has been thought in the past. Alcohol and drug abuse are so widespread in the United States that they have become a national *tragedy*. We are not responsible in these problem areas because the culture does not support our being responsible in ordinary areas.

It is a culture that lives out irresponsibility: politics based on image, not integrity; position bought, not earned; media use of images for consumption based on manipulation of people and taking no moral responsibility. Seldom do those in leadership positions stand for what is mature, growthful, and responsible. Instead, as a culture, we live out of expediency. Whether collecting souls, money, power, or viewers, we see the same lack of any *internal* sense of accountability. We live in a social system in which nobody is responsible for anything. Too often, we all just want to get by.

Well, getting by does not get it. The personal diminishment of self that comes from such ways of living eventually brings about a cultural diminishment. In most areas of our society today we see the effects all too clearly: an educational system unable to educate, a government system unable to govern, an economic system unable to provide many people meaningful work or human dignity, religious systems unable to provide people spiritual comfort and growth. Without a different concept of self-responsibility, we will not survive. Is this the best we can do?

Might we learn something from examining special areas of personal achievement, like entertainment or athletics? Not in the sense of their financial rewards or celebrity status—which is so much of what those fields mean to people and is so representative of our very problem—but in the core sense of personal achievement, would these areas teach us anything? What makes for a Larry Bird or Jackie Robinson, a Roberta Peters or a Helen Hayes, a Mikhail Baryshnikov or a Laurence Olivier, a Wilma Rudolph or

Martina Navratilova? What do those who rise to the highest level in some area have that the rest of us do not?

Certainly they have talent, but they also need will and discipline. How else can they put out total effort over and over? We would suggest it is because—at least in this particular area of their existence—they are incredibly self-responsible. Such people do what they do because of themselves, not for fame or money. At the important moments, their responsibility to self is total. Their colleagues will say about a Michael Jordan or a Chris Evert, that they "leave it all on the court," "they don't bring anything back with them." Such people give everything they have in the moment because that *is* them. Such self-responsible living provides us the added satisfaction of knowing that, after "the game," regardless of outcome, we "left it all on the court." And, yet, we still have it all with us as we walk in the front door of our homes. Living that way moment-to-moment *in our ordinary lives* is a window to wholeness.

How many of us leave it all at the office, at the plant, or on the job anywhere? Even more meaningfully, how many of us are fully self-responsible with our lovers, spouses, children, parents, friends, or neighbors? Most important, how many of us do this within ourselves, challenging ourselves to total effort if only by having the courage to know how we feel about another person? How many of us live self-responsibly? Not enough. Not enough to move the culture in another direction. Not enough to change our social selficide. Too many of us, just like so many athletes and entertainers, cannot generalize the moments of self-responsibility we do have into our ordinary living.

Regaining Self-Responsibility

How do we change? We must return to the child who holds her head up, sits up, walks, and finally talks, with little regard for whether her parents particularly want her to or not. She is naturally able to respond to self. Given a minimum of necessary feeding, touching, communication, and unconditional love, she is self-responsible. This child is the *phenomenologic* child, the child who lives in the here-and-now experiential moment of doing what she is doing, being what she is being. The *epiphenomenologic* child, on the other hand, speaks to the needs of the environment, he responds as he believes his family (his culture) expects him to respond. Such an ability is necessary, but it *must be chosen*. We must be able to respond to self *and* other, and must know when we are doing each, in order to be whole. Many of us, sadly, come out of our childhoods without that ability.

Sally is forty-eight years old. A physical therapist, mother of three, she has been married for twenty-six years. After being depressed for years, she went into therapy and grew out of her depression. Today, she comes in to her session angry: "Dick and I went down to Savannah for his convention. We stayed with my brother and sister-in-law, and, just like every other year, he and Dick played golf and drank for three days. It's a bore for me and it makes me angry. I tried to talk to him. I wasn't angry when we talked. I just said I didn't want to go anymore. . . . I was fine with his going, but I would rather stay home. He got real angry and stomped off. The next day he sat down and calmly said that if I would go, he wouldn't drink so much and would spend more time with me. So I told him I'd go."

The therapist looks directly at her and says, "And so now you are *really* angry. Why did you stop being responsible for yourself?"

Sally sits back. The anger recedes, her muscles relax, and she speaks out into the room, talking mostly to herself, "And I guess I know he'll be angry, too."

Sally experienced in that moment her lack of self-responsibility. She knew that she had not chosen, that she was not living as the person she really was. She understood in the experience that she had given away her wholeness for her dependency, and, as he always did, Dick responded to the control he felt in her dependent need (and the surfacing of his own dependent needs) with anger. She experienced the truth of her responsibility for herself and that experience provided her the chance to grow.

What happens when someone experiences herself as being responsible for herself? What in our childhood is revisited and reexperienced in a positive, useful way? It has something to do with that sitting up, that walking and talking, that self-responsible movement into the child's environment—the child who is responsible for herself before she becomes enveloped with her dependent concern with how others will feel about how she sits, how she walks, or what she says. Or, for that matter, what she does not say. Experience brings phenomenological reexperience, the only kind that has any real meaning. Having more self-experience is the only way we can refind responsibility. Without self-responsibility, we are less than whole. We die a little each time we refuse to be self-responsible, and our culture dies with us.

Responsibility for self is the experience that occurs as a person's responsiveness to what is going on within her own person is the primary source of her participation in life. When our primary source of participation in life comes from our connection to the other, whether another person or a system of the culture, our experience is lessened. This fact is equally true for our dreams, for our anger, for our bad habits, or for our most mundane activities. Experience increases as dependence decreases. Responsibility *to* self in relationship becomes responsibility *for* self in retrospect, in reexperience. We all need to have good memories of our *selves* if we are to go on *experiencing*, and so, unendingly collecting good memories of *ourselves*.

6

THE THIRD WINDOW:

Self-Discipline/
Participation

Do not consider painful what is good for you.

—Euripides

Selfishness and obedience frequently interfere with the growing person's capacity to live fully and joyously in the world. Paradoxically, many parents and teachers consider them the cornerstones of how to raise a child properly. They reason that if we can help the child learn *not* to be selfish, then he will develop affection and care, or, perhaps, even love, for others. If we teach him to be obedient, he will learn to respect other people, to take care of himself, behave well, and be responsible. But are such assumptions true?

Bobby is four years old. He is sitting in my (Tom's) office with his family. He is looking curiously about the room, which has a great deal of personal memorabilia in it, and he begins to hum. After a while, he adds words and begins singing, still quietly, but with a little more volume. His mother turns to him. "Bobby, stop that. Can't you see we're trying to talk? I thought you knew better than to be so selfish." I can only wonder how many such experiences of being judged selfish it will take before Bobby hesitates ever to sing out loud, or even inside to himself, how many it would take before he hesitated to speak up in a class when he had something to say, how many it would take to bring him to the point where he felt no freedom to be expressive, excited, or joyous at all.

Another session with another family. This time the child is five years old. She is walking about my office, not bothering anything, mostly looking and occasionally touching. The mother says, "Meg, sit down and be still. You're bothering the doctor." At that point, of course, Meg looked at me, and I could immediately feel the distance as she withdrew from me and the moment. She then walked back to the chair in which she had originally been sitting and emphatically sat down. She sat there for the rest of the interview looking at me quizzically. Squirming and fidgeting, but not saying anything, she sat looking both disquieted and uncomfortable. She had obeyed. How many experiences of such obedience will it take for Meg to sit squirming uneasily and disquieted, in thousands of chairs, for the rest of her life?

Parents too frequently confuse self-love, or "self-fullness," with selfishness. I (Pat) once saw a middle-aged man who had begun dating a woman I had seen in therapy for some time. I had first met her at the time of her divorce. She had grown from being an overly accommodating, dissatisfied person into someone capable of being much more herself. Her new friend said that he had come to see me because of a conversation the two of them had shared the previous week. He had said to her that he loved her more than anyone else in the world, including himself. She had responded, much to his amazement, with the comment, "I'm sorry to hear that."

The man said that he had come to discuss with me whether that kind of selfishness was part of being a healthy human being. I told him that I did not consider her response to be about being selfish; I considered it to be a mature understanding of the importance of his need to love himself before he could honestly and fully love her. He asked me if I felt that way about my own love relationships. I said yes. He asked, "Well, suppose your wife is walking across the street and a car is coming and you're standing there. You know that if you don't run out and push her out of the way that she's going to be hit by the car. Now if you love yourself more than your wife, and there's a good chance that you may be killed rescuing her, what would you do?"

I said, "I would rush out and push her out of the way so she wouldn't be hurt."

He replied quickly, "Why would you do that if you didn't love her more than you did yourself?"

My response was, "I would do that *because* I loved myself more. If I did not do that, I could not live with *myself* the rest of *my* life."

We are all constantly struggling with this issue of selfishness. For most people, the problem with "selfishness" is their shortsighted view of their lives. They do not understand life in terms of what is most important to them in the long term, that is, their wholeness. In most instances, then, we are not really talking about selfishness. We are talking about self-love and self-fullness. We are talking about *self-discipline*.

The same confusion arises in our concept of obedience. The failure on the part of parents and teachers to distinguish obedience from discipline is tragic, as is the failure to trust discipline in those who *do* distinguish between the two. Discipline comes from the word *disciple* and basically means someone who is "following out of love." Obedience is acting upon the instructions of another. Even granting that the other person loves us, obedience does not facilitate the experience of learning to care for ourselves out of love for ourselves. It does not facilitate our naturally attending to both our own needs and the needs of others. Instead, obedience makes for reflexive, and often resentful, behavior.

There are, of course, life-threatening situations in which parents must intervene abruptly and demand immediate obedience. If our three-year-old child is running out into the street in front of an oncoming car, we are not in the business at that moment of helping him develop his self-discipline. Even so, we can integrate that experience by spending some time with the child afterward and helping him develop a sense of love of self and love of life to go along with a heightened awareness of his environment. The areas in which obedience is necessary are those concerning ways of *doing*. Obedience is not applicable to ways of *being*.

What Self-Discipline Is Not: False Responsibility as Selficide

David is a competent surgeon in his mid-forties. He had been waking up late at night obsessing about his work and his family, and found himself feeling intermittently depressed, troubled by lethargy and a growing disinterest in life. He decided to get some help with his problems, more at the behest of his wife than because of his own inclinations. As she said, "He's quite willing to tough it out. He always has been."

David spent long hours at work. He described frequent self-sacrificial behavior in regard to his patients—behavior that was not really necessary. Even on vacations, for example, David would accept calls from patients. He was very responsible and very unhappy. But he seldom experienced his unhappiness as unhappiness. He would complain only of inconvenience, or discontent, or, at worst, the absence of something he could not describe.

Had he been able to describe those missing things, I (Tom) think he would have mentioned words like freedom, play, and joy. He searched for an easiness, a sense of escape from his feelings of responsibility for others. David felt responsible for everything and everyone, and he was unaccepting of failures or laziness in himself or others. He even made extensive and meticulously detailed plans for his family to have fun. As a consequence of all his planning and his insistence that the family relax with each other, his family dreaded going anywhere with him. This pattern of excessive responsibility was repeated in most areas of his life. After hearing him on a number of occasions describe events on the golf course, I asked him why he referred to what he did as playing golf. I told him it sounded to me like serious business.

David knows exactly how he needs to live, exactly how his wife needs to live, and exactly how his three children need to live. He is puzzled when his wife describes him as being constantly angry and irritated. He does not see himself as being angry, but rather as being helpful. When he says he is helpful, he means he is "helping my wife use her time more fruitfully for her own benefit." He is always helping other people be better.

There was only one area in which David was not responsible. Most of us do have some area of our living which remains uncaptured by our particular ways of making ourselves less whole. For David, that area was his sexuality. But even his freedom with sexuality was such that it was not constructive. He had very little awareness of his wife's sexual feelings, needs, and responses. In addition, he overgenitalized his own sexuality, and was cut off from its other meanings. Even in this area, David was less than whole.

Like the rest of us, David was a result of what he had been taught. He had been raised by a father whose two major beliefs in life were, first, that he needed to teach his children to be responsible and that they should obey his dictates since he knew what was best for them, and, second, that he needed to teach them that selfishness was the deadliest of all sins. David's mother was practically nonexistent as a person, a shadow on the wall who subsequently disappeared into a bottle of gin. Not only was she unable to provide a balance to his father's dictates, she also became the living example of what irresponsibility leads to. As a result, David learned obedience but not self-discipline. He did not learn how to *participate* in his own life.

To be self-responsible, it is necessary to respond to one's *self* as opposed simply to one's *environment*. However, experience *is* modified by reality. External reality can either facilitate experience or significantly diminish it. The modification of experience by reality is our *participation* in life. *How* we participate will be largely determined by our *self-discipline*. Knowing our communality as well as our uniqueness as a self, we are able to participate in life in a self-fulfilling rather than self-diminishing way. Self-discipline is fundamental to fully experiencing. It involves self-love, self-following, and self-esteem.

In *The Myth of Freedom*, Buddhist teacher Chogyam Trungpa speaks to the value of such self-discipline:

> You are not a nuisance to yourself anymore; you are good company, an inspiration to yourself. You do not have to control yourself so as to avoid temptations or follow rules or laws. You find temptations less relevant and guidelines less necessary, because you naturally follow the appropriate patterns.

With discipline, we live in the world naturally. Without it, we move further and further from our wholeness.

A person does not, of course, determine alone the fullness of his or her experience. In the dyadic pairing of self-other, the other is half of the relationship. There is clearly a connection between experience and the environment. Experience increases as our participation in the world increases. As experience increases, the awareness and responsiveness that come with seeing similarity and difference between self and other increase. We increase our responsibility to self and our ability to respond to the other and thus increase our own experience. To do so requires self-discipline: the ability to follow ourselves out of love. This attunement to self heightens our appreciation of and responsiveness to the experiences of others around us. Therefore, *self-discipline* is naturally the other face of *self-responsibility*.

Obedience as Selficide

Adriane is twenty-nine years old, single, and desperately trying to finish a training program at work. She is bright and capable of working hard, but finds it more and more difficult to do so. In the past, she has always applied herself diligently. In school she met her teachers' expectations; now she is trying hard to meet her employer's expectations. She keeps her apartment neat to meet her mother's expectations. She very much needs to do the right thing.

Adriane does not behave in these ways in the role of a little girl, a sycophant, or a teacher-pleaser. She is intelligent and certainly capable of thinking for herself. She simply does *not* think for herself. She has much the same difficulty in her relationships with men or friends and in her other activities. Adriane lives in the world in terms of obedience, not self-discipline.

The loss of herself in her ritualized orderliness or in her need to do right is manifested in many forms. She plays tennis as if being graded; she has a dinner party as if inspectors were coming. Slowly, however, Adriane is losing the capacity to continue making herself live in this way. She feels an increasing resentment. Her obedience training is breaking down.

We need only watch the evening news to see how poorly our rules of obedience are working. Our social failures are all too evident. Those social failures demonstrate the inadequacy of obedience training as the basis for community. In addition, the loss of self involved in such training leaves all of us angry. Historian David Rothman addresses this point directly in *The Discovery of the Asylum*. He looks at the *institutionalization* of our culture, in the field of mental health especially, but also in other areas:

> At the root of this popular insistence on the primacy of
> obedience was a conception of individual respect for authority

as the cornerstone of an orderly society. Like almost all others in this period [the nineteenth century] who thought about deviancy and dependency, the authors of these tracts [writings on child rearing] remained convinced that only a rigorous training in obedience could stabilize individual behavior and the social order.

Such convictions have a long history and grow from a distrust of the basic nature of human beings, a belief that without outside coercion human beings cannot live together healthily. Philosophers like Confucius and Mencius were dealing with this question thousands of years ago. While Confucius tended to see humans as needing outside control, Mencius felt that, "Man's nature is naturally good, just as water naturally flows downward." Mencius's position has seldom been the operative opinion in Western cultures. There is always an investment, by those who want control, in making obedience the foundation for *other people's* living.

The alternative of self-discipline to obedience only gradually appears as people grow in awareness. Much as acceptance gradually develops as an alternative to dependent placation or righteous judging, and as responsibility for self gradually develops as an alternative to the hostile or depressive postures of total dependence on what is outside the self, so self-discipline—responsible participation in life—gradually develops as an alternative to blind obedience. Self-discipline enhances experience. It creates new experiences. With self-discipline, we know both our communality and our differences—we live in the world as a peer part of nature. With obedience, we know only our differences from others, we live in the world as being "less than" something else, usually in a frightened, angry, and undeveloped way.

Obedience comes from Latin origins meaning "to hear before" or "to hear against," and that is exactly what obedience is. Obedient people live out what the other person has told them—in the past or in the present—before they live life on their own. The obedient person listens to the outside voices and never hears the inner one. Obedience contains in it the terribly negating assumption that those who listen to their own *selves* would not behave in a proper or loving way.

The question too rarely dealt with is whether listening to others is itself proper. The Nazis were obedient; the secret police in South Africa were obedient. They lived out of "what they heard before." Why do people think that children are learning to be good when they are taught to be obedient? Once learned, obedience can be used to any end by any authority. It is life as other-controlled. One does not learn ethics or morality out of obedience. One does not learn choice.

The Meaning of Discipline

Self-discipline, in contrast, means being a disciple of one's self and listening to one's self. It is grounded in the conviction that a *self* is naturally healthy and naturally responsible, both to itself and to others. That conviction is the *natural* faith and hope of all humans. With self-discipline, one participates in life with the faith that one is a good, functional, and caring part of all that exists, and with the hope that growth together is possible.

David was clearly obeying external voices. One of those voices was almost certainly that of his father. He was hearing that voice when he told himself that it was weak not to do what he "should do," even if doing so made him feel bad. He heard it again when it told him that it was weak to be helped or comforted, even if doing so made him feel better. When he took calls while on vacation, he was hearing that voice saying, "Work hard, don't be selfish." It was that same voice that told him to help others have a better life by telling them precisely how to have one. He was captured by voices outside himself.

Participation in life based on self-discipline opens for each human being his capacity to experience other persons or things without being *captured* by them. Self-discipline allows the development of wholeness as opposed to the diminishment of self that comes with obedience. We can all fulfill our hunger for living if we participate in the world with self-discipline.

Boredom and Hyperactivity as Selficide

At eighteen, Luke is bored with life. He has little interest in school, in his home life, in others, or even in himself. He goes through the motions, but does not really participate. He seldom does his course work and never involves himself in school activities. At home, he shows an equal lack of interest in family activities. Luke is not merely depressed. He has lost himself in boredom as a direct result of his not participating in life, as a direct result of his lack of self-discipline. He resists the efforts of others to engage him. He does not live in the world with hope or faith. He does not really live in the world at all.

A loss of self in boredom, like spending the majority of one's time sleeping, is often the refuge of those who know only obedience and obligation but who do not want to live in the world that way. The only way they know *not* to live compulsively is to not really live. Paradoxically, the person who is *continually* busy likewise has no time for being. Often such people have trouble believing that fact. But in truth, just like bored persons, they are avoiding being themselves.

Compulsive living, regardless of what the compulsion is, denotes a lack of self-discipline. The compulsive person *does not choose* his actions; therefore he is not participating in the world as a whole person. There are many different ways we can live without participating in life as our whole selves.

The Problem of Duty

Much as Adriane lived in a world of "doing what she has been told to do," Ben lives in a world of *duty*. At thirty-eight, Ben has already been treated twice for ulcers. He is literally eating his *self* up. When the ulcers returned for the third time, his internist suggested he talk to a therapist. But Ben is very anxious about seeing anyone. He feels confused about why it is he could be making himself sick by doing what he is supposed to do. He intuitively knows what is acidifying him, but does not understand why it should. Like most of us, he is afraid really to look at what he is doing to himself.

Ben lives in the world in terms of duty. "Duty" comes from the word for "debt." Duty is conduct that is owed. It means participating in the world under obligation. Living in this way creates nonexperience, for we cannot obligatorily be whole. Ben does his duty in his family, both the nuclear and the extended one. He also does his duty to his company, often creating much anger in his family. He then feels guilty about not doing his duty to his family. This vicious cycle is eating holes in Ben's stomach. He says that he had to work out of town through the Thanksgiving holidays. Since he had done the same thing last year, it was not really his turn to do it this time, but when the company requested it of him, he felt *obligated*. Ben always responds to his duty. Unlike David, who saw obedient behavior as being right, Ben does not wish to live in this way, but he feels that it is his duty to do so. He spends his life on duty, just as if he were in the Army.

I (Pat) noticed during my years as a Navy psychiatrist how people would use "duty" in two distinctly different ways. I think the distinction is both important and instructive about how we participate in the world. On one hand I would hear people say, "Hey, I pulled the duty tonight" or "I got a bad duty assignment." They were referring to some owed conduct. On the other hand, when talking to sailors or marines on a deeper level—for example, when talking to Vietnam combat personnel about their war experiences—I heard "duty" used in a very different way. If I asked a corpsman why he had crawled out under fire to help a wounded marine, he might reply, "Because it was my duty." There is some healthy quality represented in certain kinds of duty when they have to do with how we live in response to our environment. It is dignified to pay a *real* debt that is owed. It is absurd to continue to pay an imagined debt, as we do when we act out of involuntary obligation. Duty to oneself is a voluntary, chosen behavior. Our love of self depends on our attending to such *healthy duty*.

Perhaps commitment would be a better word for healthy duty, for the self-disciplined way of participating in life. Committed people feel no owed conduct to others in terms of externally obligatory feelings. Instead, they feel strongly that *doing what they do is a manifestation of who they are*, a material and expressive part of their being.

True duty, true responsibility to the other, is direct evidence of self-discipline. It is the only kind of duty that withstands the horrors of war, the terrors of death, the powers of temptation. Obedience will not—not over the long run. No compulsive behavior will give us the strength to be ourselves when we most need to be. The old cliché, "When the going gets tough, the tough get going" means (or should mean—since it is frequently misused) exactly that. The living toughness of self-discipline is infinitely stronger than the stasis of obedience. When academies—military or otherwise—teach self-discipline, they increase that higher sense of duty. When they teach obedience, they create less than full human beings. The world has all too often felt the consequences of traveling down the latter road.

Ben's ulcers speak to him painfully about unhealthy duty. He is confused by them, just as he is puzzled by his family's anger and their feeling that he does not do his duty toward them. Ben feels that if he were any more dutiful it would kill him, and in that feeling he is correct, for false duty exhausts and diminishes. He neglects his true duty—his duty to himself; his concept of duty is always *external*. True duty, even duty that costs life, is accompanied by a sense of health and power, a congruence of soul and behavior that transcends the immediate price. Whether seen in Martin Luther King, Jr., Mother Teresa, or in the many members of the armed forces who have lovingly given of their lives for others, such self-discipline elevates all of us. True duty is part of wholeness.

Following Self Out of Love

Denise has struggled with mild depression and moderate anxiety for some time. She is underweight and wants to talk about why she is obsessed about controlling her eating. At thirty-four, she reports that her weight has been up and down over the years, but that it has always been an issue to her.

There are many causes of eating disorders. The first cause may be simply our definition of what a disorder is. Certainly our models for human body shape have become quite distorted. Anorexia is not healthiness. The anorexic is not unlike the bored person who when asked says, "I'm fine. I really don't want to do anything." The anorexic says, "I'm fine. I really don't want anything to eat." Neither is participating healthily in life.

The overeater, always hopeful that he will find the "sacred treasure"—usually peace and love—is at least still grasping, still trying to fill himself up. The anorexic, on the other hand, has given up. It is, however, an angry and dishonest giving up. How much better if we could say, "Hell, there is no use in looking for the answer outside me (food), but I might try looking inside me."

Many other causes for eating disorders have been proposed: genetics, hormones, addictive behavior, or incorrect early eating patterns. But labeling overeating or refusal to eat as an addiction, attributing it to genetics or hormones, or any of the other ways we remove responsibility for self from the person, does not really help Denise with her problems. It is Denise's body, and she must deal with it.

Denise tells me (Tom) that she has been able to gain weight, but that as soon as her weight is up to a healthy level, she stops eating and loses weight again, usually getting more depressed in the process. I myself watch this process occurring over a period of time. It becomes clear to me that there is no way I can help alter the cycle as long as we focus on the problem of her weight or her eating. The imperative to gain weight was for Denise a matter of obedience to what we call an *introject*, a part of her parent whose voice she had internalized. In eating, she was simply dependently doing what she felt she had to do in order to be loved and accepted. Inevitably, she was equally in need of doing just the opposite in order to establish her right to be herself. It seemed to me that, in those terms, the seemingly inescapable cycle of gaining and relosing weight was perfectly understandable.

How to resolve this Catch-22 dilemma? Suppose I could find something for Denise to use as a way of being herself other than being underweight—something that was not self-destructive, something she enjoyed doing, something she would *want* to do rather than feeling she *needed* to do? What if I asked her to do it with the same perseverance, continuity, and regularity that she has applied over the years to eating and dieting? That is, suppose I ask her to engage in behavior that she enjoyed with all her previous compulsiveness, but without the feeling that she was giving up her right to her own identity and without the resultant underlying anger? What if I insisted that she retain her right to be herself? In order for her to follow this mandate, she would have to be living out a choice.

At this point, Denise weighed less than eighty pounds. After all of her cycles of gaining and losing weight, she had come to feel that she was no longer in charge of herself. This conviction led her to behaviors that were contrary to what she *said* she wanted to do. She felt a victim of her unconscious. This all too common feeling of not being in charge of ourselves is immobilizing and debilitating. It is a feeling we see in many of the people who come to therapy. It probably atrophies growth as much as any other feeling.

I suggested to Denise that she give up her focus on eating and dieting, and as far as possible *any* concern with her weight. I then asked her if there was something she really wanted to do, as opposed to her compulsive obsession with weight. She said, somewhat apologetically, that she always wanted some time for herself after her husband came home, before supper: "If I could just have a half hour to myself it would make a world of difference to me." I suggested that she take the half hour for herself, beginning precisely at five-thirty. She was to do this every day, regardless of any demands her husband or children might make. She was to do it with the same dedication that she always followed in her struggle with her weight. The difference would be that she would now be dedicated to doing something she wanted to do. It would be something she enjoyed, something she was doing to *follow self out of love* rather than something she felt she *should* do.

Of course, she had trouble staying with this goal at first. But we worked on it, and eventually she did stay with it. After about ten months her body size became healthy, and it has stayed that way for many years now. Denise says that she does not know why her weight increased to a healthy level. She was not trying to gain.

I have tried this approach many times since. Failures seem almost always to come from the inability of a person to sustain healthy behavior in the face of the guilt induced by the other people in their environment. They give up following themselves out of love in order to obey what others tell them. In my experience, the practice of "I'll make myself obey" never works—not for eating disorders, alcohol disorders, drug disorders, sexual disorders, neurotic disorders, or any of our myriad other problems. We cannot *make* ourselves anything. Our *selves* already are something. Our real need is to allow them to be what they are. That is the true root of self-discipline. Personal success is not a question of effort, or reason, or urgency; *it is an outcome of self-discipline.* The same is true communally. As a community, we do out of love of ourselves and others what, indeed, needs to be done. We do if we wish to survive.

The Power
of Being in Charge

One of the wonderful things that happens when we live with self-discipline is the enormous power and energy that come with the feeling of being in charge of ourselves. Self-discipline accounts for the highs experienced by many people who *healthily* exercise, play musical instruments, cook, do crafts, paint, or engage in other creative and growthful activities in a disciplined way. They will often say that the good feeling comes from being in shape or from expressing themselves, and those reasons are undoubtedly valid. However, these people are also experiencing the exhilarating feeling that comes with self-discipline, the feeling of being in charge of themselves. This capacity resides within all of us. It is the discipline that comes from within, not the discipline that one imposes on oneself from outside.

It is important to realize that, in living this way, we are not doing something because it is *good for us.* As Mark Twain frequently remarked, he avoided more than anything else in life anything someone suggested was good for him. That type of behavior is simply another way of responding to the internalized parent. The most insidiously destructive parents may appear well intentioned. It makes a positive and critical difference that we do not *what is good for us,* but *what is loving of us.* It is the difference between need and want.

Most people, when they first come into therapy, speak unendingly of their needs. Like all the rest of us, the unwholeness they suffer is manifest most clearly in their needing something outside themselves to fix it. Given that motivation, the progress any of us makes in our growth as persons—as well as our realization of what we want of ourselves in life—is quite slow. It is enlightening to see what happens, however, when these people begin to speak not of need but of want. The acceleration of the growth process is impressive, with far fewer reverses, setbacks, or regressions.

There is a fundamental difference between behavior that is based on need and behavior that evolves out of the process of desire. Need is based on the feeling that control lies outside of us. We feel that what we are doing or being is not really for ourselves, not really as ourselves, but for the other person. This external focus minimizes the total personal motivation needed to accomplish those things we so desperately say we need to accomplish. It also inevitably brings into the picture that undercurrent of resentment at doing for others rather than for ourselves which eventually undoes us. We ultimately sabotage the commitment made, and our goals, however worthwhile, are never accomplished. We are confused about how we participate in our lives. We forget that Christ did not say do unto others *instead* of yourself, but *as* yourself.

Good intentions based on need create more failed commitments than any other human characteristic. When the focus shifts to desire, however, the underlying resentment and sabotage disappear and a process of workable, successful, and enjoyable commitment begins. It is our inability to understand that commitment must be based on want rather than need which makes it very difficult for us to achieve change. Whether personal or cultural, goals that are relationally important to us—such as being more intimate with our children or caring more about the homeless—go unmet because we continue to struggle with them as needs. Our schools, our environment, and our impoverished fellow citizens, among many others, suffer as a result.

An excellent example of this issue on the social level is our fruitless (though intensive) effort to deal with the drug problem. The continuing emphasis on need rather than want makes it most unlikely that anything will change. Essentially we say to the addict, "We need you to stop, and you need to stop being a drug addict. You need to rely on something other than drugs in your life." But we are reticent to address the issue of motivation. We do not attempt to understand what might bring these people to *want* to be drug-free for *themselves* rather than to *need* to be drug-free for *us*. This same dilemma is seen in most of our other social and ecological catastrophes, as well as in most of our personal problems.

I (Tom) recently was seeing in therapy a middle-aged man I have known for some time. He was in a particularly good mood. He sat on the sofa rather than in the straight-backed chair he usually used, and he was unusually relaxed and playful. He said jokingly, "You know, Tom, it's such a gorgeous day out, why don't you and I go out and play some golf instead of sitting here working on my head?"

I laughed and said, "Mitch, I'm going to share with you something about me and golf. Many years ago when I played golf fairly regularly, I took a lesson with an elder Scotsman who was supposed to be a wonderful golf teacher. He was about seventy years old at the time. I was an average golfer, and I wanted extra instruction so that I could play better. Decked out in his knickers and a tam, he walked with me to the practice tee, dropped five balls, and told me to hit them with a five iron. But I thought that first I should let him know what my problems were, so I explained to him in great detail what was wrong with my swing. He looked at me patiently during my long recitation of my foibles. After I finished, he continued to stare at me without comment. Two minutes feels like quite some time in that situation. Finally, I blurted out, 'Well, what should I do?' Without any change in expression, and maintaining direct eye contact, he answered, 'Hit the ball.' "

It was the best golf lesson I ever had. It may even be one of the best therapeutic interactions I've ever had. I told Mitch that if we could go out and hit the ball, I thought it might be fun, indeed, but that if we went out and found ourselves "needing" to hit the ball, we might as well stay here. He laughed. I had shared with him my learning that we all have to participate in life out of our own desire to be whole persons; we have to be committed to being ourselves fully.

The inability to understand that commitment is an expression of a *want* and *not a need* is one of the most destructive elements in our current culture, where dependency is the major organizing principle. It is most directly manifest in our divorce, drug and alcohol, and physical and sexual abuse rates, and in a degeneration of our value system to a level at which the need for money is the be-all and end-all.

The Meaning of Will

Self-discipline represents the true nature of will. Psychologists William James and Wilhelm Reich both defined will as "choosing to choose." From a similar perspective, Otto Rank elaborated a type of therapy he called *will therapy*. His concept was that therapy was a duel of wills between client and therapist. Not that the therapist's will would overcome the will of the client, but that the client would be forced to choose his or her own will. The client would be brought to the reality of needing to choose to choose, to make decisions in his or her own life, to move away from the depressing selficidal nonexperience of not having will.

Making decisions and being depressed are almost mutually exclusive experiences. If we are making the decisions in our lives, we cannot be depressed in that sense. We can be sad, grieving, or a host of other real feelings, but we cannot be depressed. Conversely, if we are depressed, we are not making the decisions in our own living.

Making decisions is an integral part of self-discipline. The procrastinator diminishes wholeness with each decision he or she avoids. If life is what happens to us while we wait, we are not living. Thus, to deal with decisions, even about inconsequential matters, is a vitally important experience in therapy, or life. Whenever a client comes to a decision in therapy, the therapist is wise to bring her face to face with that experience of will. In it she can find her self-discipline and will, and through it, the energy and power of living as herself.

Many people never develop self-discipline. They live out of compulsive obedient behaviors all their lives. As a result, it is difficult for them to live in the world with pleasure rather than anger. Such people have no sense that they are doing what *they* choose to do in their living. This dilemma and its resultant fallout are seen consistently in our workplaces. Employee theft, sabotage, sickness (both real and feigned), and absenteeism are all manifestations of obedient living, and the reactive failure thereof. The current talk about the need for new management styles, methods, and approaches is a reflection of the dilemma. In fact, the basic issue is self-discipline. In the long run, only management styles rooted in such *participation* in life, in the work, in the company, can be profitable—in all senses of the word.

Wendy works as a nurse on the three-to-eleven shift at a local hospital. She went into nursing because that is the only education her parents would pay for. Her authoritarian father effectively ran her life for her first twenty-two years. She is now twenty-seven, unmarried, and in an inner turmoil. She knows how she is *supposed* to be, but is confused about how she *wants* to be. Thus she often finds herself resistant. We see this struggle in the problems she has relating to co-workers—either in being supervised by others or in supervising others herself. We also see it in the passive way she exists in the rest of her living.

We could say that Wendy does not have the will power to live the right way. But doing so would simply add to her problem; we would become just one more outside figure, like her father before, demanding her obedience. Or, we could realize the damage being done to her *will,* and help her restore herself to healthy living. The latter is the only workable approach. No one can be whole unless she wills to be so. She walks this path only when *she* chooses, even if it might be true that for right now we could provide her with a seemingly better choice.

Psychotherapist Jean Miller speaks to this issue, particularly in women, in her book *Toward a New Psychology of Women,* where she talks about *productive conflict,* in which the will is engaged, and *blocked conflict,* in which the will is broken and defeated. In such destructive conflict, the person loses hope that she can ever restore herself to a state of wholeness. Restoring ourselves involves coming to grips with the blocked conflict with which our obedience training leaves us. The loss of will, the feeling, as Miller says, that one must move away from one's deeply felt motives, is, of course, just as common in men as it is in women.

Wendy must find and accept her *participation* in her lack of wholeness. By then choosing to live out her own personhood, she can begin learning self-discipline and making her conflict productive.

Self-Discipline in Our Schools

Perhaps in no area is the problem of will clearer than in our schools. School, like therapy, is an activity that must involve both learning and teaching, experiencing and reexperiencing, if it is to function well. As all teachers (and therapists) know, it is impossible to *make* people learn. But why would anyone not naturally *want* to learn, *want* to know more of the world of which he or she is a part? And why is the problem so common if it is not natural?

The difficulty is that we cannot teach what is not experienced. Students cannot learn without experiencing. On the student's part, this obviously requires self-discipline, the ability to participate in the process in a way that allows him or her to experience. Students also must be in school in a way that enhances their self-discipline. Otherwise, they are taught as the compulsive David and the passive Wendy were taught, and with the same sad outcome.

In order to teach or help others learn, we must develop two broad capacities. First, we must learn to be who we are congruently with the person to whom we are relating. Second, we must be a person who invites, enhances, and supports others in *their* selfhood. The first is largely the capacity for intimacy; the second, largely the capacity for healthy closeness. The first is "sponsibility" (self-sponsorship), the second is "re-sponsibility." Both require self-discipline. Like the student, the teacher must be able to participate in the learning process in a way that does not oblige but, rather, enlarges the listener. We grow together, or no one grows.

In *The Teacher*, American philosopher Bronson Alcott wrote that, "the true teacher defends his pupils against his own personal influence, he inspires self trust, he guides their eyes from himself to the spirit that quickens him. He will have no disciple." He will have no disciple because he teaches out of self-discipline. In doing so he enhances self-discipline in the student. The same truth holds for therapy: the therapist who would have followers is not allowing others to learn how to lead in their own lives.

Self-discipline is learned, or not learned, in childhood. It does not come automatically. It becomes an issue as soon as a sense of external reality begins to emerge from, and intrude into, the early, totally dependent state of the newborn child. How much we will have to distort that reality will be largely determined by whether or not as we grow we develop self-discipline or compulsivity as our way of being in the world. In other words, whether we are able to deal with external reality with pleasure rather than anger will be determined by our ability to develop self-discipline. It is a powerful difference, just as educator Maria Montessori wrote in *The Montessori Method*:

> Discipline must come through liberty . . . if discipline is founded upon liberty, the discipline itself must necessarily be

active. We do not consider an individual disciplined only when he has been rendered as artificially silent as a mute and as immovable as a paralytic. He is an individual annihilated, not disciplined.

Obedience, owed conduct, and other compulsive behaviors annihilate personhood. They are self-diminishing and block experience. Those who owe their conduct to something outside of themselves cannot be congruent, are unlikely to feel connected, and have usually lost faith. They are unavailable to enlivening intimacy and incapable of healthy closeness.

Self-Discipline and Therapy

I (Tom) for several years supervised a therapist named Hilary. Hilary was an intelligent and hardworking person. She exercised hard, read hard, played hard, and in general lived hard. She followed a stringent diet, and approached the rest of her personal living in the same rigorous manner. Over time it became clear to me that there was a certain pride in her being so tough with herself, a sense in which she felt that these behaviors were what made her strong, independent, and autonomous. She saw them as her self-discipline. I wasn't sure.

It came to pass that Hilary began seeing a client who demonstrated very similar behaviors. It was very clear to me that the behavior in Hilary's client was compulsive. It did not come out of healthy self-discipline but, instead, arose from the behaviors of an obedient child, healthier than many, but still an obedient child. Hilary did not see this. Her difficulty in seeing her client's compulsiveness helped me to see Hilary's own compulsiveness much more clearly. It crystallized for me the idea that therapists cannot be useful to people in areas of self-discipline that they themselves lack.

I know my own difficulty in allowing myself to play, to goof off, which is a healthy form of self-discipline even though many mistakenly see it as just the opposite. My difficulty with goofing off makes it more difficult for me to help others in that way. It is not that I discourage them from letting go of their ambition, or encourage them to be serious. On the contrary, I am forever trying to get people to goof off! However, my capacity to succeed is diminished by my own lack of self-discipline in that area. A lack of self-discipline is just as self-diminishing in a therapist as it is in a client. It blocks experience for both, and without experience, neither therapist nor client can learn. The truth is that a lack of self-discipline in any of us is experienced directly by others, regardless of what we say. Self-discipline is a way of *being*, not something one does.

I (Pat) find this aversion to experience especially present in people I call "head-livers." Such people live in their thoughts instead of living in the world around them. They often come to therapy complaining that they do not feel as if they are a part of things, or that they do not seem able to let go, enjoy, and simply be like other people. Many therapists tend to be head-livers themselves. In fact, the habit of endlessly analyzing life can easily capture one. This makes it much more difficult for such therapists simply to be with people, especially with people who are similarly captured. Living in less-than-whole ways is ubiquitous. None of us is perfect, we cannot be experiential all the time. However, we can be aware of how we are and deal with ourselves as we really are. When I am clear that I am living too much in my head, that awareness helps me let go and try to return to living in the world. It helps me to *choose life*.

Self-discipline is *being* in the world in good faith. The good faith is our love of ourselves. Self-discipline is what enables us to bring ourselves out of dependent needs and into living as *full* selves, into living fully as ourselves in the world.

7

THE FOURTH WINDOW:
Innocence/
Naturalness

If there were no confusion, there would be no wisdom.

—CHOGYAM TRUNGPA

I (Pat) remember, from many years ago, a short conversation between my then nine-year-old brother David and my mother that illustrates what we mean by innocence. We had just finished eating supper on a hot, muggy southern night—in the times before air conditioning—and were sitting together around the table. Whatever we had eaten had been fairly light, and David turned to Mama and asked what was for dessert. Now, we seldom had dessert at our house, so Mama, turning around in the small kitchen alcove, grabbed a bowl with some oranges in it and said to him, "We've got oranges for dessert." He looked at her in disbelief. "Mama, oranges can't be dessert. Oranges are *good for you.*"

Adult innocence is difficult for most of us to understand because we persist in seeing innocence as this kind of naïveté. Although David simply *naturally* reflected a truth of his culture, adults insist on seeing such behavior in children only as cute and naive. Actually, the two concepts—innocence and naïveté—have little to do with each other. We use the word *naive* to describe someone who is inexperienced, sweet, gullible, even somewhat simpleminded. Such behavior is very different from what we mean by being natural or having innocence. *Innocence* literally means "incapable of doing harm" or "without intent to harm." Having no intent to harm is not naïveté.

True innocence is a characteristic of nature, though not of culture. Anyone who has ever experienced being in the middle of a hurricane, watching a lion stalk its prey, or dealing with the suffering of an ill child can testify that nature could never be described as either sweet or simple. Nature is not naive. However, nature does not have malevolent or manipulative intent, and, therein, it *is* characterized by innocence.

It is impossible for any of us to live without ever hurting others or without being hurt ourselves. Those experiences are a natural part of the life process. Hurting others in the process of living as ourselves does not preclude our innocence, however. Paradoxically, in many ways such experiences define innocence. Being in the life process with *all* its experiences is one of the chief characteristics of innocence.

In these terms, innocence is our *naturalness*. It is our ability to be as *selves* in our world, to live uncaptured by any system, be that system needs from the past, needs for the future, or needs of a particular person we may be in relationship with at the moment. If we are aware of ourselves as a natural part of our world, we are more able to risk being truly in the world, to *naturally* be a person, with all that being a person entails. We so often tend to categorize, to differentiate between good and bad, helpful and unhelpful, to dissect life rather than live it. However, nature does not acknowledge opposites like right or wrong. An animal may use deception to catch its prey, but it does this naturally in the service of real appetite needs. When people fake, con, manipulate, coerce, or force, they are most often motivated by something other than their human growth. They are certainly not being real in the experiential sense— the behavior is *not* moving them to a more whole selfbeing. One cannot be real unnaturally. Becoming only happens unintentionally and naturally. It is a process, not an accomplishment.

Reality and Appearance

The true appearance of innocence in humans we call realness. How very different this is from the "gives the appearance of" that we so often live out. When we try to get what we "need" by calculation, we often disclaim that we are "doing" anything. However, we *are* doing something. We are not being naturally who we are. We are not living in the world as a process. We are not planning or goal setting in the service of growth and wholeness. Instead, in the service of our unhealthy needs, we stop the process and, thus, stop growing. We are trying to be *secure,* but we end up being less than whole. We end up, as the writer Margery Williams described, with hard edges, with being hurt easily, and with the desire to be carefully kept.

When we are innocent and natural, we recognize that there is no such thing as absolute security. We come to grips with the reality of both sides of life's various dualities, and we live with the insecurities such reality brings. There are no easily defined boundaries between good and evil, pleasure and pain, love and hate, joy and sorrow, black and white, or even hot and cold. Knowing this truth *does* leave us unsure. The chaotic nature of the living process means that uncertainty is *always* a part of living. There are no fixed answers in life. Unfortunately, we take our unsureness and turn it into insecurity. We want to be sure—to have only one answer for each question and for that answer to be the "truth." What we fail to realize is that the only real truth is unpredictable nature itself. "One-channeled minds," wrote the psychologist Gordon Allport in *Becoming,* "can never comprehend that truth may have many channels."

When we try to deny or avoid the unsureness of life, we lose the ability to experience full living. We become limited by believing in any one side or aspect of natural processes, or even by believing that processes have "sides." In allowing all sides of experience, we are naturally of what Rainer Maria Rilke called our "whole blood" rather than grasping at one "truth"—reaching for security. Our whole blood is our innocent participation in our nature. Such innocent participation is the only reality available to us.

We do need dualities to understand and analyze the components of existence. However, we must remember that life is not actually made up of those discrete components. As Gregory Bateson so often said, the map is not the territory. There is no technical manual for life, whether religious, scientific, or philosophic. To believe that life can be defined in mechanical terms is to lose our innocence. Dualities must be seen as dyads, not as polarities. In *The Art of Intimacy*, we looked at several of these dualities, different "sides" of the sphere of life: intimacy and closeness, learning and teaching, dyad and system, art and craft, psychotherapy and counseling, sexual being and personal being. Natural life includes these pairings, among many others, in their *wholeness*. Living in life with innocence means interacting with others in ways that recognize this fact. Only then are we living life to its fullest.

Innocent Relating

Perhaps by looking at a struggle typical of our ordinary living we can best demonstrate these issues. Dale and Courtney are in their late forties. They have been married for twenty-eight years, and both of their two children are grown and living elsewhere. Courtney is a high school teacher who has always been somewhat "schoolmarmish." Dale, owner of a small business, tends to be a bit looser, a little more likely to kid around and be playful. The two have come to therapy after many years of unhappy tension in their relationship. This tension is most easily seen in their interactions over Dale's sexual jokes and behavior. Courtney has usually responded prudishly to his vocalizations and public demonstrations of affection. Dale has always felt torn between "acting like myself" and "doing what she wants me to do."

If Dale continues simply to share himself with Courtney, he continues living in life innocently. That is, if he shares his thoughts and behaviors without the intention of "teaching" her something, changing her, embarrassing her, or defying her— without in any way being defiant—then he is being in life in a way which recognizes both "sides" of the living process. He accepts as valid her right to be as she is, even if it is not, in *his* opinion, healthy for her. It is very difficult for most of us to do.

We so often are teaching, defying, or trying to change the other person whether we are aware of it, and will admit it, or not.

Dale shares himself at some risk, knowing Courtney's past responses. Each risk has a momentary history. It is an extending of his sexuality to her in a hope of a joining response from her. If innocent, this risk is new each time—it is a real risking and not just a repetition of fixed behavior. But we must remember that this dilemma is not simply Courtney's problem. It is but one facet of a reciprocal relationship between two people. In the presence of the therapist, Dale did not feel angry, or defiant, or controlling when he was sexually clowning with Courtney. He did convey a vague sense of guilt—his own struggle—but his risking felt genuine.

Continual innocent risking is the opposite of the unhealthy repetition of behaviors, thoughts, and feelings that characterizes so much of our living. Risking contains a faith that eventually a successful connection will be made. That innocent faith empowers us to take such small risks. If connection is made, reexperience (the closeness aspect of relationship) allows the growth then to be healthily integrated into our ordinary living. Reexperience, as opposed to nonexperience, diminishes the ongoing risk inherent in extending ourselves to others in these ways. Dale's being himself with Courtney becomes easier each time he makes a connection with her.

In contrast, the lack of innocence produces nonexperience. If Dale tells his jokes with *intent*, that is, to upset Courtney, to show her up as a prude, to teach her, to make fun of her, or to try to force her to be different, he diminishes himself and their relationship. Behaving in these ways, he cannot experience, and consequently reexperience, her as a person. Nothing will change. Courtney's energy in life will be expended on her defending her right to be as she is, on her insisting on the correctness of her life position. She will never deal with her sexuality at all. Both will live unnaturally and without innocence, having no real experience of self *or* other.

Having an agenda—having intent in the sense that our behavior has a certain purpose—locks us into unnatural relational patterns. Living locked into only one aspect of life, regardless of what it is or whether it is "right," is neither natural nor innocent. It always diminishes self. That is a difficult concept for most of us to accept: *being right does not equate with being healthy, or being loving, or even being useful.* Rightness can block experience completely when it itself becomes the issue. Living without an agenda, living out of the fullness of our hope, opens us to experience. It is the opposite of the compulsive repetition of *self-*destructive behaviors.

Dale and Courtney present this truth in process. People pair because they are different. They grow, and the relationship grows, if both learn from those differences. If not, they either become relational robots or they separate. We learn only in experience, and experience of the other is heightened through naturalness. Dale and Courtney are just beginning the long journey of reclaiming their innocence with each other.

Nancy is another example of this truth in process. She has been living with her lover, Ruth, for three years. At thirty-two, Nancy still feels unable to be who she is with her parents, who live several states away. Her mother and father, she believes, could not deal with her sexuality, so she has never told them that she is gay. Although everyone who is close to her is convinced there is no way that her parents cannot know that she is gay, and no way that Nancy cannot know that they know, both parents and child live in a perpetual state of nonreality with each other. The cost of not being real within themselves is not being able to be real with each other as persons. The nonexperiencing of love in such instances is tragic, and totally without innocence.

Living with each other as *who we are not* may be the simplest example of the lack of innocence. It certainly is the most direct example of how we diminish ourselves. Nancy's parents miss the wonderful person she is and the true love she has for them. Nancy misses the real love they have for the person she is and the support they could offer her if all three of them could ever regain their innocence.

Childlike Living

George Orwell wrote that "One of the effects of safe and civilized life is an immense oversensitiveness which makes all the primary emotions seem somewhat disgusting. Generosity is as painful as meanness, gratitude as hateful as ingratitude." The person so shut off from primary feeling is living without innocence and cannot truly experience or reexperience in his life. Thus, he is cut off from his wholeness. Our culture too often sees such *distancing from our feelings* as being adult. We view naturally having feelings as somehow childish.

Laverne is thirty-seven years old, works in merchandising for a local department store, and is the mother of two teenaged children. She has been living as a single parent for eight years. She comes into therapy with a question: "Why do I turn off all the men I date?" Laverne is intelligent and correctly perceives herself (at least she sees this intellectually) as an attractive and able person. What Laverne does not perceive is that when she is in a romantic relationship, she changes personality by taking on false roles. She becomes alternatively demanding and clinging or loud and angry, then quickly switches to being quiet and solicitous. This Laverne is not the same person she is in her relationships with her friends. Her peers would not recognize as the competent adult they know at work the "child" they would see in her dating personality.

People who see innocence as being naive also tend to see it as being childish. They fail to understand the difference between *childish* and *childlike*. *Childish* is a pejorative term and implies a demanding and inappropriate way of interacting with life. It is a ploy based on need, a way people behave to get what they insecurely feel they *must* have. It is a stereotypic way of eliciting the parenting that they feel they missed and must now have. It is the false vision of perfect dependency—the child gaining instant gratification from an all-loving parent.

Childishness does not work because it is not genuine. It is manipulative, hostile, and accusatory. It dramatically states, "I am owed something" while mocking the parent figure. It is demanding and petulant rather than healthily, truthfully dependent. It consists of neither choice nor self-responsibility. The hostility and mocking characteristic of childishness are part of the anger that always accompanies *unchosen* dependency.

Being childlike, on the other hand, entails not knowing. It is the recognition that none of us "knows" in that false sense of adult security. It is a statement of genuine faith in the world, a trust that the world contains for us whatever we need. It is without manipulation, hostility, or drama. Its request for help is natural, real, and congruent. When one is childlike, one experiences chosen dependency as a natural feeling state. When one is child-like, one accepts all feelings as being equally valid, a quality most adults have lost. If she were childlike, Laverne could simply be the *wanting* person she actually is, not the *needing* person she lives as.

The childlike person is much more willing to risk what others find uncomfortable. Trusting that the universe contains what they are looking for, they are willing to look. When I (Pat) was young and growing up in North Carolina, my mother would send me to the neighborhood store for milk or catsup—items we needed before the next trip to the supermarket. This little country store was about a dozen blocks away from our house. In simpler, slower times the walk was a reasonable undertaking for an eight-year-old alone. About two-thirds of the way there, the main road crossed a dirt street named Dollar Avenue.

Dollar Avenue was a city dirt road. That is, oiled and rocked, it was a residential street in the old southern style. I would in-evitably detour down Dollar Avenue for several blocks before returning to the main road to go on to the store. I was looking for dollars. I innocently assumed that it was called Dollar Avenue for a reason. In the *adult* sense this was naive, but that is not the point here. The point is that, childlike, I never gave up. I kept doing this, even though I never found any dollars. I did not become angry or blame the world for my lack of success, I simply assumed that someone else had already found the dollars that day. Of course, I never discussed this activity with the adults in my life, as I had long since realized that they would just give me "reasons" why what I was doing made no sense. Naive or not, I was willing innocently to risk my time, effort, and selfhood to be in the world.

Think of such living in terms of curiosity. After all, to be curious requires being willing to be our not-knowing selves, risk-ing what we may or may not find. Curiosity is seen in those who have a willingness to change their minds. *Literally* changing our minds is the only way we can grow. That willingness to be open to change is part of innocence. Innocence is knowing that we do not always know. Psychiatrist David Keith, in "The Self in Family Therapy," calls this way of living the freedom to advance or retreat from any position: "The self is not paralyzed by reason or consistency. It changes hypotheses so that any problem can be seen from a different perspective." Someone who knows every-thing has no curiosity; someone who insists he is right is unwill-ing to change his mind. It is an unnatural and nonexperiential way to be in life.

The Parkers have been in family therapy for several months. The parents, Randall and Miriam, come each time with their three adolescent children. Although the current difficulty pushing the family to treatment is the oldest son's depression and school prob-lems, the family quickly jumps on Dad as the focus of their meet-ings. Randall is a responsible, calm, and caring person. He is, however, no fun. He seems to have no curiosity in life—not about himself, his wife, or his children. Like a pack mule, he keeps his head down, puts one foot in front of the other, and gets done what must be done. He is reliable but dull.

And, indeed, these qualities in Randall are both valuable and meaningful. His care *is* real and valuable. His reliability *is* real and meaningful. But his lack of curiosity in life effectively cuts him off from large parts of himself as a person. It is self-diminishing. He does not live in the world with innocence and naturalness. Instead, with lowered eyes, he tries not to see all the "dangers" out there. The dangers are his wife's sexuality, his children's playfulness, and his own creativity, but even that realization is not allowed into his awareness. To Randall, things are either *out there* or *in here*. He has, up until now, not been willing to question his position that only what is in here is secure. Security seems right to him. Randall lives as if there is an unbridgeable difference between his inner world and his outer world. Moreover, he lives as if he believes that difference can be controlled. There is no innocence in such liv-ing.

There is no *out there* or *in here* to life. Knowing this truth is part of the foundation basis of innocence. Innocence is alive to faith and hope. It has a patent trust that we are a part of our world. Out of this faith comes a willingness to try the new and to go on. Such willingness is one of the prerequisites of any real experience. Limiting it leads to unhealthiness and self-diminishment in one form or another. Chronic depression, addic-tions, compulsive behaviors, and obsessive thoughts can all be thought of as ways in which humans are unwilling to try some-thing new or to progress toward wholeness.

Being a Part of Nature

Heartfelt naturalness means we recognize that we are *completely* a part of nature. Not just a little bit, but totally a part of nature. As adults, we have difficulty staying in touch with this fact. As if we had an option, we always respond with a "yes, but." We forget what the poet Wallace Stevens meant when he wrote, "I am a native in this world and think in it as a native thinks." There *is* no other option, not if we are to experience and be whole. In the only reality there is, all things are a part of one another. Nothing lives by itself.

I (Tom) had a remarkable learning experience about naturalness not long ago. Our psychiatric clinic has always been a family, in all the various senses of that word. In the early years, the staff members' children were constantly around the office. They provided a visible and noisy growing edge. But as the clinic has grown, so have they. Now the children of the newer and younger members are showing up. One is Will, the four-year-old son of a colleague. One day Will was out in the hall; as I came by, he asked me his usual question, "Who is that man?" "Tom," I replied. He looked at me in a concerned way and said, "You look thirsty." Then he grabbed my hand and led me to the water cooler. He took a cup, pushed the button to fill it, and quickly drank the water down himself. He repeated the action. Then, turning to me, he said, "You feel better?"

A cute story, if you will, but one which tells us something profound about our being a part of nature. We can understand from it that perhaps the child knows something we have lost sight of, that there is a real connection between all of us. We all exist as part of the same body. A version of this same "childlike notion" is currently held strongly by many adult scientists. They call it "The Gaia Hypothesis," a theory that the world itself is one large organism and that *all things* are literally connected. Whether one agrees with their hypothesis or not is less important than the fact that *humans* certainly are connected, and while one person's drinking water may not make another less thirsty, our being ourselves with each other, innocently, does allow the other to learn what we know, and that is all any of us can really do for one another. Naturalness also allows us to be more ourselves because it allows us to experience others as they really are and to learn from them. Innocence is a requirement for any learning experience. The trick for all of us is to learn—to grow up—and still keep our natural innocence.

Interestingly, we more easily get in touch with the naturalness in ourselves when we go on trips to ecosystems which are radically different from those we are used to. That is, they are not yet part of our preknowledge. The beach, the mountains, a swamp or bayou, the badlands, the mesas, or a deep forest can all elicit from us an internal pull. It is a pull to refind something inside of us. That something is our naturalness, our natural innocence as a part of nature. As the American Indian cultures so clearly felt, it is a profound and basic organizing principle of life. Without it we are less whole.

> *Gods, who dwell everywhere,*
> *Let us see, is this real,*
> *This life I am living?*
>
> —the Pawnee Indians,
> *Let Us See*

The healing power of nature is not a special knowledge of nomadic or hunter-gatherer cultures. David Bohm and F. David Peat speak to the same issue in *Science, Order, and Creativity:*

> In the very distant past, human beings obtained their sense of harmony within the cosmic dimension through direct contact with nature. When people were constantly immersed in the natural environment, their attention naturally turned in this direction and consciousness frequently moved into a dimension beyond time and the limited concerns of particular social groups. Even now, when people spend some time close to nature they may experience something of this "healing" quality in body and mind. In earlier times humans were in almost constant contact with nature so that "misinformation" arising, for example, from social contacts would have little or no ultimate significance, as it was completely "washed away."

Whereas traveling and being out in nature may help us reestablish innocence, few of us can, Kerouac-like, be "on the road" all the time. We must learn to keep in touch with naturalness in our ordinary lives. We must be aware of the constant turning over of life. System homeostasis, in the healthy ecological sense, is based on a continuing individual ability to change. That changing is part of the motion of life. An awareness of this ever-changing of our own minds, of our bodies, of our *selves*, is an integral part of innocence. It is a sense of aliveness to our connection to our world. Whether we will retain the innocence of our childhood depends on how much we are caught by *fixations*. Fixations on the unfinished business of the past—our pasts not being "washed away" in that healthy sense—prevent naturalness. The unnaturalness of the false self blocks experience. It is one of the most basic forms of selficide.

Natural Learning

Naomi sought help because her alcohol use was troubling her husband, Bob. He believes she has a serious problem. He sees that she drinks every day, is often intoxicated, and has embarrassed him at social occasions. Naomi, however, tends to minimize her drinking. She always has reasons for her behavior. The one area in which they both agree, however, is in their description of Naomi's aimlessness in life. Both say that she has few real interests, much less passions. There is little she wants to see, do, or try.

On a trip out West—something Bob had eagerly planned and anticipated for three years, Naomi was uninterested in the history, the scenery, or the people. She simply says, "I'm all right. I just wish he was a little more exciting. Then maybe I could get interested in him." Naomi may well be correct about Bob. He fully participates in the relational dance they do together and his actions comprise half of what is happening, or not happening, in their relationship. However, Naomi is wrong about herself. She is not all right. Her drinking, her chronic depression, and her lack of involvement in her own living are all destroying her. There is little naturalness in her ways of living. Without curiosity or openness to the new, we simply exist; we do not live.

The foremost advantage of being an integral part of nature is the direct experiencing, the natural learning, that such a way of being allows. It gives us the opportunity to avoid being trapped by our systems. In our adapting to systems, we frequently lose our selfbeing. Knowing how to be ourselves comes only through natural learning and can only be *learned*. It cannot be *taught*. No one else can tell us how to be ourselves.

The crucial aspects of such learning were discussed by philosopher Jacob Needleman and physicist Geoffrey Chew in *Parabola*. Needleman expresses the opinion that "we seem to be getting more removed from those sources of perception which are not just in the intellect," and should remember that "there is a difference between awareness and thought." Chew talks about the learning process as "gentle events" which Needleman defines "as a kind of reconciling principle between two opposing or contradictory forces." Natural reconciling principles come only to those who are open with innocence, that is, those who can learn as opposed to only being taught. We do not mean "only" in the pejorative sense, but in the limiting sense. True education comes only through the reexperience of teaching, but for something to be reexperienced, it must first be experienced. Awareness is indeed different from thought.

In natural learning there is a substructure of passionate questing. This questing is equally real whether it is applied to doing physics, going out West, enjoying music, or opening Christmas presents. I (Pat) learned something about healthy questing from my son Tom when he was selected for a summer honors program. He went off to work on a particular science project he had selected, and I spent the summer sending him the journal articles and hardware supplies he requested relevant to this project. In all his excited communications to me, however, there was no mention of the project. By the end of the summer, I finally realized that he was not simply *doing a project*. Rather, he was *having a learning experience*. There is an important and distinct difference between the two.

Instead of working on the project as a fixed, obligatory goal, Tom was enjoying himself with what he was doing. There was no progress report to make because there was no "work" being done. He was open to whatever might happen and thus joyfully learning. Those who are open to learning are never jaded or surfeited. They relish the last spoonful as much as the first. Their passion is tangible, always available, and experienced as such by those around them. An openness to learning is a natural life position, an innocence in being a part of the world we are in.

Unnatural learning is dangerous, for diminished people are the consequence of such "education." But natural learning has its own risk: there is no preset outcome. Natural learning does not constrain or restrain the one who is learning. Nor does it constrain or restrain what is learned. Natural learning, instead, allows the unfolding of the natural personhood of the learner.

What we value above all is the reality of ordinary experience, of being who we really are in a world which we allow to be as it is. The risks of natural learning are simply the risks of living. The constraints and restraints of trying to "educate" people—of trying to teach them without any risk—result in the blindness, deafness, and dumbness of the three proverbial monkeys. A perfect symbol for nonexperience, they clearly represent the selficidal truth that it is we who diminish ourselves.

If, as Shakespeare wrote, "The silence often of pure innocence/Persuades when speaking fails," perhaps it is because naturalness (the silence of pure innocence) is the only route to experiential truth. It allows us to know such truth when we come into contact with it. This capacity is as valuable to an adult's learning wisdom as it is to a young child's learning language. Living in the world with naturalness makes us available to its reality. It is the clearest manifestation of faith.

Personhood

Leslie is thirty-one. She has done well at her job in real estate, rising within the same company over the past several years. She makes friends easily, but has no boyfriends. She comes to therapy because of her increasing anxiety and depression about not having a permanent relationship. Although she is not conscious of her self-negation, Leslie is firmly convinced that she is not worthy of having such a relationship. She offers many reasons for her troubles, some of which are real and pertinent—men are intimidated by intelligent women, successful women scare men off—but underneath she still feels inadequate. Leslie invests in and works hard in her relationships with men, only to have the men depart, leaving her with the vague feeling that the problem lies with her. She feels she cannot *earn* their love. She finally decided to seek therapy, and to try to change how she sees herself.

Macy finds herself in a similar situation, but feels more desperate because she is already in her middle thirties and has not yet "found a man." She is attractive, successful, and, above all, intense. After some years of avidly but unsuccessfully seeking a permanent relationship, she sought therapy with me (Pat). During the first year of therapy, she continued her driven pursuit for a man—in bars, acting classes, bicycle clubs, and anywhere else she thought she might meet someone. Then one day she came in and announced to me that she had had it. She was going to settle for being single and would get out of her life whatever she could. She was going to start by getting in shape, so she began running at the track at a nearby university athletic field. A few weeks later, she came in and laughingly described a man she met there while running. They were married a year later.

People who live with innocence never experience love as *earned*. Instead, they live with the clear knowledge that there is an innate worth in being a part of all things. They may put forth effort, work hard, and invest in a relationship to make it healthier and more growthful, but they do not do so in order to earn love. To live in a world where love is earned is to live in a world where *being* has no intrinsic meaning. Preoccupied with constantly searching for meaning in the thing or person outside, there is no way for us to experience people or things for what they are. Consumed by finding ourselves in the other, there is no way to experience ourselves for what we are. This diminishes us painfully.

Naturalness means seeing ourselves and others as innately valuable, intrinsically lovable, and, therefore, far more alike than different. None of us are more special to life, either positively or negatively. Leslie is no more or no less meaningful in her own existence than anyone else. Her ignorance of this truth diminishes her personhood. Macy is lovable by virtue of her being. Until she recognized that truth, she felt less than whole and sought to complete herself through another.

Recognizing our self-diminishing tendencies means seeing the ways in which we block our full personhood. In our fear of life's basic uncertainty, we give up innocence and naturalness for the sake of security. In therapy, people will begin the return to some naturalness with anxiety. They become frightened, wondering whether they are getting worse. Such people need constant reassurance that this uneasy feeling is natural.

We create our miseries by making decisions to get us out of limbo. We must go back into limbo to make new decisions. Limbo is not a scary place in the middle of nowhere, nor is it a distant time in the past. Limbo is the space-time of reality. It is always here, always now, and we are always naturally a part of it as persons in the world. If the world were not in limbo—if it were, indeed, fixed—it would be dead. In just that way, our fixations make us "dead." They are the instruments which contribute to our selficide.

A modern-day folk myth about this truth can be seen in the popular *Star Wars* movies. During his training to be a Jedi, the hero, Luke Skywalker, must go through the place of evil. When he asks his guru/teacher, Yoda, what he will find there, he receives this reply: "Only what you take in." Each of us carries within us our own undoing. We silently move away from our innocence, our naturalness, and immediately become a little less ourselves. We move far away and we feel the terror of nonexperience. This death fear is inevitable, since nature—our individual natures as well as that of all other living things—can only be a *living* nature. Stasis is not living; it produces nonexperience, and diminishes us as persons. Neither does such stasis ever work to make us secure. It is an empty bargain. We, like Luke Skywalker, always carry our own self-destructiveness with us, no matter where we go.

Our own walk through the dark place is a journey. During this journey, we search to rediscover our innocence, our naturalness, our direct connection to the rest of what exists. We are all on such quests even if we do not recognize our travels. Sadly, too many humans see this journey as the province only of the special. In *Shamanism*, religious historian Mircea Eliade wrote:

> . . . candidate shamans or the heroes of certain myths sometimes find themselves in apparently desperate situations. They must go "where night and day meet," or find a gate in a wall, or go up to the sky through a passage that opens but for an instant, pass between two constantly moving milestones, two rocks that clash together, through the jaws of a monster, and the like . . . all these mythical images express the need to transcend opposites, to abolish the polarity typical of the human condition, in order to attain to ultimate reality.

But, in truth, we are *all* candidates for wholeness, and must *all* go where "night and day meet." We must *all* find our "ultimate reality." In truth, ultimate reality is the ordinary stuff of real experiencing. As such, it is in the nature of each and every one of us. The journey to innocence is the quest of every human, not just the shaman. Personhood is not confined to special people.

Innocence and Innocent

Pearson and Sue have stayed together for six years in a relationship that few of their friends understand. They are in constant conflict, appear unhappy with each other, and frequently complain about each other's behavior. Each spends most of the time explaining their own innocence, protesting that they only want a caring relationship. It is always the other one who causes the problems. In truth, both are causing the problems.

Pearson demands freedom—a freedom sometimes expressed in seeing other women or staying out late at night. He believes he will not be able to feel as he needs to feel if Sue does not live with him as he defines their life. Of course, he denies having any such feelings. Instead, he portrays Sue as withdrawn, cold, and uncaring. Sue, on the other hand, wants to escape from Pearson rather than risk genuinely relating. Unable to live as she is herself— always needing the approval of the other person—she can only "save herself" by pulling away. His neediness makes her feel controlled, and his anger makes her feel inadequate. Each time he asks her why she withdraws into reading or watching television, her own neediness makes her get angrier and pull farther away. Pearson then demands even more attention. His neediness grows with his escalating blaming and anger; hers, with her withdrawal and hostility. Their relationship is doomed to increasing pain and anger unless they find a way to begin to be truly innocent with each other.

When most people hear the word innocence, they think of being innocent, and by that they usually mean "Don't blame me, I'm not at fault." As Albert Camus wrote in *The Fall*, "we all want to appeal against something. Each of us insists on being innocent at all cost, even if he has to accuse the whole human race and heaven itself." And we do. Such insistence is, in many ways, the clearest indication of our loss of innocence.

When we are truly innocent, we know that no one can actually be "innocent." As living things, we are a part of all other living things—even the behaviors, thoughts, and feelings that we find most despicable. To claim no-fault lives is to be without responsibility and, therefore, unnatural. In nature, there is no blame and there is no one but ourselves to be responsible for us. Cursing the wind, the rain, or our God for the storm only makes us less ourselves. If bemoaning fate becomes our way of living in the world, we lose ourselves completely. The lack of suspicion and cynicism that naturalness fosters is not naïveté but a willingness to be part of the process. Hopefully, *both* Pearson and Sue can refind that process and begin their journey to finding a real relationship based on being natural persons.

At the age of forty-two, Ramon divorced his wife. After twenty-one years of marriage, he left her and the two children he helped bring into this world. Ramon is convinced that "they"—his wife, his children, his house, his obligations—were the problem. They were why his life was so painful, why everything was always going wrong. He felt cursed by living among people who could not or would not live as they "should." Over the years, his suspicious and cynical nature slowly wore his family down. Their willingness to confront him as who they really were finally burned out. They withdrew. Their disengagement only strengthened his conviction that they were the problem. Even now, living by himself, he continues to be angry and blames them for what has happened in his life.

Ramon, like most cynical and suspicious people, needs to keep the unhealthy cycle going. He needs to stay "innocent." Such people cannot afford to experience themselves because their life's investment lies in not feeling responsible for their own living. They are always protesting their "innocence," but their protesting only keeps them from being natural. Thus, they are shut off from the experience of *true* innocence.

In a society of laws, criminals should be blamed for their crimes. But in our ordinary living—in our struggle to be ourselves, to love others and to be loved—there is no blaming the guilty and no being "innocent." There is simply participation and experiencing. As D. W. Winnicott said, "The false self cannot experience." The false self—in its blaming of the other and its protestations of its own innocence—loses the ability to function in meaningful ways. We cannot learn. Our brains cannot get past searching for only those things that already agree with it. Unable to allow in the new, we are left with the suspicion, cynicism, and stasis that characterize so much of unhealthy living.

It is "through our own recovered innocence," as Thoreau wrote, that "we discern the innocence of our neighbors." Free of blaming, we may finally stop feeling blamed and guilty ourselves. I (Tom) remember an experience I had as a twelve-year-old child which, for me, points out the fear we have of such real experience. I was studying my catechism and had read that heaven was the beatific vision. I did not know what that meant, so I asked my priest, Father Fleming, who told me "The beatific vision is sitting and looking at God, Tom." Since I had always had trouble sitting for long periods of time, I asked him with some anxiety, "That's what heaven is? How long do you have to sit?"

He answered with a smile, "Oh, forever, you sit there forever."

"That doesn't sound like much fun to me," I said. "You mean you're good down here just so you can sit up there forever? Why would I want to do that?"

Father Fleming put his hand on my shoulder and said, "Tom, you would if you could just imagine how beautiful God is."

Although Father Fleming's answer is one I now, as a grown man, could be satisfied with, as a child I was not. I returned home and asked my mother to explain to me what heaven *really* was. She led me into the kitchen, and said, after closing the door, "I will tell you, Tom, but only if you promise never to tell Father Fleming." There was no smile on her face.

Now, my mother was a devout Catholic, and I took all this mysterious behavior quite seriously, as well I should have. And so I promised. "Heaven is this wonderful place that God has made because He is so wise and kind, and everybody goes there," she said.

"Everybody?" I asked. "Even Mr. Harrigan who gets drunk on beer and beats up on his wife?"

She glanced nervously at the closed door. "Yes, everyone. The only person in hell is the Devil. Everybody else is in heaven, because God loves everybody, even Mr. Harrigan."

I was still unsure.

"And Mr. Harrigan gets to drink lots of beer?"

"Yes," she replied. "I told you God is kind."

I persisted. "And he gets to get drunk just like at home?"

She looked me straight in the eyes. "No, God is wise as well as kind. You can't get drunk on God's beer."

I studied her face then asked, "How did God get to be so wise and kind?"

She replied without pause, "Because He had a good mother."

My mother's profound innocence had nothing at all to do with being innocent.

8

THE FIFTH WINDOW:
Congruence/
Systemic Detachment

*Each human being is a more complex structure than any
social system to which he belongs.*

—ALFRED NORTH WHITEHEAD

The world often appears to be overcrowded with human doings,
human thoughts, and human feelings, probably in that order.
However, in the midst of all this, there seems to be a frightening
scarcity of human *beings*. By "human being," we mean a person
whose behavior, thinking, and feeling are integrated, and who, on
the basis of that integration, is fully being in this world. This
concept of a human *being* is the simplest and clearest way to
describe what we mean by *congruence*. Much of the work of
therapy involves precisely the effort to increase such congruence
in the person involved.

Incongruence

In our society, the level of incongruence in individuals, couples, and families is quite high. We often behave out of partial
feelings or thoughts that are not our own but rather are parts of

systems to which we belong. These systems may be personal—for example, learning never to show anger or learning not to speak unless spoken to—as well as cultural (our race or nationality), economic (our class or status), social (our clubs or groups), or religious (our churches or faiths). We may believe that we are better than others, that another's faith is wrong, or that sexual feelings are evil. We are seldom aware of our systematized living. That loss of self-awareness is, indeed, one of the major effects of living incongruently. When entire families are captured by a system—as, for instance, when they believe that saying how one feels is harmful to others, or they believe that *not* saying how one feels is harmful to others—they become *dysfunctional*.

Incongruence, the disconnection between feeling, thinking, and behaving, closes a window to experience. Incongruence is not conscious or deliberate. It is more a deep wound than a surface falseness, but the word *incongruent* is often misused by therapists and others to describe other psychological states that are not really issues of congruence, but rather issues of honesty.

Dieter is a forty-four-year-old attorney who comes willingly to therapy with his wife. He appears solicitous and says he is more than happy to come in with Sandy, because he has a great deal of compassion for her pain and struggle. Her pain and struggle are essentially that she believes Dieter has been having an extramarital affair for many years. He denies it. She obsesses about this affair at length. It leaves her sleepless and, as one may imagine, not readily open to a relationship with her husband. In therapy, Dieter anxiously collaborated in his feelings with me (Tom), hoping that together we could help his wife get over these troubling, "paranoid" thoughts. His helpfulness made Sandy feel more confused: "These feelings seem so real, but when he talks like that, I wonder if I'm crazy."

I, too, felt that Dieter was being deceptive and manipulative. Subsequently and inadvertently I found this intuition to be true. A therapist whom I was supervising began talking to me about a case of hers. The therapist was treating a divorced woman who had been having a rather hectic affair for some years with a prominent attorney who was obviously my client Dieter. I sat and listened to the story of Dieter's "gaslighting" for some time. I could only deal with this information by myself, being in the bind of confidentiality, but it did make clear to me the truth of Sandy's marriage.

The point I want to make is that Dieter's behavior was not what we mean by incongruence. It was lying and deceptiveness, perhaps sociopathy. We are not being incongruent if we *know* our feelings, our behavior, or our thinking, and, for reasons of our own, falsify them or just do not share them. It is incongruence only when we have *no awareness* of the fact that our behavior, thinking, and feelings are not connected. The only deception in a lack of congruence is to ourselves. There is no overt dishonesty.

Real incongruence occurs when either our behavior, our feeling, or our thinking is being driven in an unconscious way to separate from the other components. Such incongruence is seen, for example, when our feeling or thinking is totally different from what we consciously express by our behavior in a relationship. Such incongruence frequently manifests itself in our sexuality.

I (Pat) see in therapy a very attractive woman named Carrie. She invests a great deal of her time and money on makeup, clothes, and her appearance in general. She is clearly flirtatious in her contacts with men, including me. She speaks in double en-tendres, and I wonder to myself if she can possibly not be aware of what she is saying. But she is not. She lives in a world full of the sexualization of relationships with men, but her behavior is unconscious. When she is approached by a man, even in some socially acceptable way, in response to her overtures, she ada-mantly protests her innocence and disclaims all interest: "I won-der why you got that idea?" She never follows through on the messages she behaviorally gives to men. In truth, she does not really recognize the messages she gives at all. Carrie is discon-nected within herself, incongruent in her living.

Carrie's behavior is not congruent with either her real feel-ings (she basically wants to be approved of and loved), or her real thinking (she does not think that going to bed with every man she interacts with is either what she needs or wants to do). The behavior does not reflect what she actually wants or who she actually is. Incongruence manifests itself in Carrie in other ways as well. She is a "shopping addict," who says she is unable to go to the mall without buying clothes and accessories she did not plan to buy and does not need. She is always going to do better about her extravagance and is sincere in that feeling, but her behavior does not change. Carrie is a competent, responsible busi-nesswoman, but when she goes off to meetings or conventions, she reverts to behaving in seductive ways without the intent of being sexual. In all these ways, Carrie shows the separation of feeling, thinking, and behaving that leaves a person less than whole.

Unlike Dieter, Carrie has no intent or motivation to deceive on a conscious level. Indeed, it pains her that she has not been able to grow into a congruent identity. Many of us are always "going to do better." We intend to exercise, eat a more nutritious diet, or be more gentle with ourselves, but rarely follow through. It is incongruence in this latter sense, rather than the sociopathic deceptive sense, that we must confront in ourselves in order to be whole. If we actively choose to be dishonest and deceitful, the issue of our congruence is not even available to us. Seeing ourselves as we really are is part of finding our wholeness.

The word *congruent* comes from Latin roots meaning "to come together, to be harmonious." Congruence is one of the cornerstones of all experiencing. Living harmoniously on various levels is a theme that runs through almost all psychological writing. As Carl Jung wrote in *The Undiscovered Self*, "The discrepancy between intellect and feeling, which get in each other's way at the best of times, is a particularly painful chapter in the history of the human psyche." Whether it is represented in the harmony of the conscious, the preconscious, and the unconscious, or in the harmony of thinking, feeling, and behaving, congruence is a prerequisite to life in the world in good faith. As the "being" component of our living, it is closest to the conscious part of our experiencing.

Systemic Detachment

I must create a system, or be enslav'd by another man's.

—WILLIAM BLAKE, *Jerusalem*

The various internal aspects of each of us must be free from external control if we are to be capable of integrating our thinking, feeling, and behaving. "Being free from external control" does not, however, mean being out of control or only doing what we want or being uncivilized. Culture and its systems have tremendous effects on who and how we are, and these effects are part of healthy closeness. But we must also have the ability to step back temporarily from our systems and culture in order to establish our congruent selves before we reenter those systems. That ability allows us to be part of our systems in good faith, that is, as whole persons. In the moment of stepping away, however, we cannot be *agents* of any outside force. We must be free to be the selves we are. *Congruence* is impossible without *systemic detachment*.

Most of us have difficulty with the notion of systemic detachment. We are too likely to see people who are "just being themselves" as potential anarchists. The dependency needs that are the hallmark of our culture make us afraid of rocking any boats. We have a powerful belief in systems—our governments, our religions, our politics, our creeds—and are trapped by our conviction that systems are right. In truth, systems are never "right." They are either functional or nonfunctional, and *humans* must be sure of what those functions are. Systems do not have feelings; people do. Systems do not define functionality; humans do. Systems can never include all truths, either about themselves or about what is outside the system. As mathematician Kurt Gödel demonstrated, systems are confined or constrained by their own construction. Systems are not living, they are merely *ways* of living. Learning not to be captured by our systems allows us to make better use of them, to make them more functional. It also allows us to remain congruent.

Systems are not always negative. That is, most systems are not founded on evil intent. They are simply driven by predetermined rules designed to meet some need other than the direct experience of who, where, and how a single human being is. They do not operate out of primary choosing by an individual as a basis for existing in the world. They are collective in nature and designed to maintain the status quo, as opposed to fostering change. This truth is glaringly evident in institutional systems, but much harder to grasp in ourselves. Our *personal* captures, by our own personal systems, are much more difficult for us to see. But they, too, support the status quo—security.

People usually will say they believe in the system. Even though they recognize their "believing," they are not aware of being captured by it. The radical free-market capitalist, the rigid Marxist, the diehard conservative, the doctrinaire liberal, and the intolerant religious fundamentalist are all clearly captured. They are more determined by the system than the person.

Contrast these ways of living with the individual who is paranoid or the one who is hysterical. Both of the latter are just as captured by systems, especially their original family systems, as the ideologue. The paranoid is captured by the dictum that it is not right to have murderous feelings, so he has externalized them. The hysterical is captured by early familial prohibitions associated with guilt about sexuality. Both persons are incongruent, but neither has any immediate awareness that they are captured by a powerful system of belief. We are not usually consciously aware of captures by our personal and familial systems.

I (Pat) recall a date I had when I was fifteen years old. I had invited over a young woman of whom I was enamored to baby-sit for my younger siblings with me. I cooked a spaghetti dinner, which I planned for us to eat romantically in the kitchen. For some reason my parents were late leaving, so Dad was trying to be unobtrusive while I was serving dinner (I must admit that I have no memory at all of just where my younger siblings were at the time). I was trying to give my date this huge plate of spaghetti, which she kept refusing—she only wanted a small portion. I kept placing it in front of her and she kept handing it back to me. The evening was well on its way to being ruined. Nothing was going according to my romantic fantasies. I can still remember Dad saying later that night, after we had taken my date home, "Man, you were going to be generous and loving even if you had to shove all that spaghetti right down her throat!"

Now, of course, I understand what I was doing much better than I did then, but even at that time I had some discomfort in feeling that I had been captured by something I was unaware of. It had been a performance on my part similar to the cartoon of the Boy Scout dragging the little old lady across the street when she does not want to cross—I was determined to "do good." Loving other people, being generous, getting someone else to tell us that our love is okay, is not a "bad" motivation. But it is a capture by a predefined system of thinking or feeling or behaving, and thus blocks real experience. We cannot *be* congruently when we are consumed by doing something else. It does not really matter what that something else is. Good motivations do not prevent the loss of wholeness that comes with a lack of congruence, nor do they prevent us from driving others away by blocking their opportunity fully to be themselves. Even love is only really love when we are not captured. We cannot truly *be* in love unless we are congruently ourselves.

These personal systems probably diminish selfhood more than being captured by cultural systems. A bigot who always goes along with fellow bigots, religious fanatics caught up in their own herd version of the truth, sexists who cannot live in a world of equals are all overtly blocking experience. Their capture is clear to anyone willing to look. Their personal diminishment may well be overshadowed by the additive *cultural* selficide such stances engender, but even these seemingly stereotypic people are originally captured *personally* by their fears, insecurities, and inadequacies. It is out of their original captures that these humans sacrifice their selfbeing to cultural systems.

Being Congruent

It is not easy for humans to be congruent. We are pulled in many different directions, often at the same time. Unfortunately, there is too much truth in what F. Scott Fitzgerald said in *The Crack-Up:* "Like all men who are fundamentally of the group, of the herd, he was incapable of taking a strong stand with the inevitable loneliness that is implied." We are all afraid to be lonely in that sense, and thus have trouble staying congruent. That struggle does not, however, mean that being congruent *causes* loneliness. In many ways, congruence draws others to us as it moves us into relatedness. But we must have the courage to risk the loneliness that we will feel in the moment.

Randy has already been to three different therapists in the past two years. He is now trying a fourth. He does not initially volunteer this information to us, but it comes out over several visits. We naturally ask why, since many people "therapist shop" because they cannot deal with the truth of seeing themselves.

Randy is forty-one years old. He is an articulate, successful contractor who is used to weighing and making decisions on his projects. He cannot, however, answer our question as to why he keeps changing therapists. He says that it is not that the other therapists were not likable or well trained. In truth, Randy is looking for something beyond these ordinary criteria. He is looking for an experience of congruence, and he seeks a therapist who can be with him in that particular way. Experiencing congruence is more important to Randy than what the therapist says, what the technique is, or what the training has been. He wants to be with someone who, when he or she looks at him with what psychotherapist Theodore Reik described as the third eye, looks at him with a strong sense—that is, does not have "blurred" vision. Young children often give us that sense of the third eye immediately, but with adults it is more rare.

Especially as a result of the work of Carl Rogers, congruence—being congruent—has become the term for the prime characteristic of the therapist's *being in the therapy*. That is, the therapist must be in the process congruently in order for the process to work. Certainly, a central task of any therapist is providing a relationship within which the client can move toward greater congruence within him- or herself. As usual, the language of the times develops its own idiomatic words to describe this same essential quality of being. So we work at "getting it together," "having it all together," "getting our shit together," or, in more polite circles, "being centered."

Sylvia, who has been living in one way—having an affair, longing for excitement, wanting to dream—while "living" another—being married, responsible, and down to earth—knows the selficidalness of her lack of congruence. At least she knows it unconsciously, for she seeks a therapist to confront her with it. She is unable to be *all of herself*, as she really is, anywhere. When she is out of the context of her family, she feels the lack of the things she associates with family: respect, closeness, responsibility, and realism. When she is with her family, she feels the lack of the things she associates with her lover: play, sexuality, freedom, and excitement. Nowhere does she feel whole.

We consider the quality of congruence most important in *all* living, not just therapy. This truth is equally applicable to any primary relationship, a parenting relationship, or a friendship. The child does not, for example, ask us to be a perfect parenting machine; he or she does, however, ask that our feelings, words, thoughts, and behaviors go together, that we be congruent. Contrary to much of what is written in the "how to" parenting literature, a child does not even ask that we be consistent, just congruent in the moment. When consistency is compulsive rather than characterological, it seems to do bad things to children. But children do ask that if we are angry, we look angry, say we are angry, and behave in some way that honestly manifests our being an angry person. Children, like lovers, like friends, like all the rest of us, feel more comfortable when their outer world makes sense to their inner world.

Once I (Tom) was seeing a woman named Marlene whose mother was visiting from where she lived across the country. Marlene was depressed, and at the time was going through a difficult separation from her husband. What she was working on with me was a diligent search, for the first time in her life, for some congruence in order to establish a valid basis for her decisions about her life and her participation in her relationships. She was then in her forties.

I concurred in Marlene's request to have her mother come in, and so she came to the next interview. Mother was in her seventies, somewhat retiring but polite, very social in a restrained way. She sat opposite her daughter. Marlene told her mother that she had some questions she wanted to ask her. She wanted to know first if her mother had ever been irritated and angry with her when she was a child.

Mother replied, "Of course not, no; I was never angry with you," and smiled.

Marlene asked, "Did you ever wish that I had never been born?"

"Don't be silly, of course not."

"Did you ever wish I was dead?"

"That's even sillier; of course not. What sort of mother do you think I am?"

"Did you ever wish that I would leave and never come back?"

"Don't be ridiculous."

Marlene then looked directly at her mother. "I ask all of this because I felt every one of those things in you so many times when I was a child, and you always denied them then, too. After years of my feeling them and your denying them, I began to feel kind of crazy. I began to feel that I had a lot of feelings that just were not based in fact. I started to feel like I couldn't trust my feelings as a good basis for making judgments about what went on around me."

We sat in silence for a moment or two. The mother then said to me, "Doctor, would you mind talking to me privately?"

I asked permission from Marlene, and Mother and I went out in the hall outside my office where she asked me, "Do you think I should lie to her and say she was right . . . that I did wish those things?"

I said, "I most certainly do."

"Yes, that might help," she agreed. "It might make her feel better."

We returned to my office and the mother told her daughter, with increasing affect, that indeed she had often been angry and irritated with her. She had often wished that she were somewhere else. Occasionally she had wished that Marlene had never been born, and on just a few occasions she had even wished her dead. "There were even times," she stated emphatically, "when I felt like killing you myself." I do not know of many times in my practice when I have seen a single experience increase the quality of the congruence in a person as much as that one did for Marlene, and, for that matter, for her mother as well.

It is very confusing to children when our eyes are furious but our mouth is smiling and denying the anger. It distorts the child's sense of trust in his own perceptions if we say we are not angry while we are punishing him. It confuses the child if we recoil even slightly in our embrace while we tell her how much we love her. Children intuitively know noncongruence, for it blocks experience. Congruence in one's parents makes the world of other people predictable, makes it a world in which the child can live easily and grow congruently.

Congruence and Daily Living

No one is consistently congruent. What is more important is that we always be *seeking* congruence when relating to other humans. When we sense that we are not, we need to confront our own incongruence as readily as we would that in the other person. We need to develop a sensitive awareness of our disrespect for ourselves—that is, when we misrepresent ourselves to either *ourselves* or *others* in significant areas. The road to experiencing goes through just such confrontation. Developing a "smell" or "taste" of how we are when we are incongruent, we can begin trying to bring all aspects of our selfbeing together as one. When they are congruent, the three aspects of being are fused in such a way that we cannot subjectively sort out any one particular aspect. Nor can another person in interaction with us separate out the parts. When we are incongruent, we can—just as well as the other person—identify the different components by the very fact that they are different; we are acting in a certain way but feeling another way. We *can*, but we seldom *do*. We usually keep ourselves unaware, for our fragmentation is too painful for us to remain conscious of it.

A clear example is seen in Alvis, who is now fifty-seven, father of four children now grown and gone. He relates his experiencing his fragmentation and incongruence—especially in terms of his self-responsibility—as a result of a personal capture.

"I was frazzled last night. I had a rough day and too many things to do at home. Whatever the reason, I forgot to take the dog out. Early this morning, the little mutt tried to tell me. He whimpered next to the bed, scratched the covers, tried to get my attention. But I got up and went through my morning shower and all . . . just like usual. When I got out to the kitchen, he had pissed on the floor. I got furious and punished him. It was only after I whacked him several times in anger that it came to me . . . that I was him."

Now tearful, he finished, "It was just like I always felt when Dad use to yell at me and criticize me for all those things that weren't my fault . . . when I always tried to do my best but it didn't matter."

We can be captured in many ways and live as less than who we really are. Often we do not know we are living selficidally. In confronting ourselves, however, we begin to be available to the experience Alvis eventually came to—knowing who *we* really are. We cannot be how *we* are if we are being who we are at the direction of *someone else*.

As *congruence* means "a coming together," or "a being harmonious," it is clearly a very basic spiritual notion. As the nature of being human is made up of thinking, feeling, and behaving, it is the coming together of these three components in the person that makes him or her live harmoniously in the world. There are, however, too many real-world systemic demands for anyone to exist solely in such a state. Total congruence is, like total grace, a God-like concept.

Sadly, the truth is that we constantly see the lack of such

fusion in humans. There is the sociopath in whom behavior is separated from thinking and feeling. There is the hysteric in whom feeling and behavior are separated from thinking. There is the compulsive with the equally overt preoccupation with behavior and the thinking about it, the compartmentalization of both separate from feeling. Then there is the schizophrenic. Schizophrenia means literally "split by the diaphragm," referring to the early Greeks' belief that thoughts originate in the head and the *pneuma*, while feelings originate in the abdomen or *viscera*. Such people are "split by the diaphragm" which graphically describes the incongruence of thinking and feeling that underlies many of the symptoms of schizophrenia.

To various degrees, all of us demonstrate similar disharmonies. Therapists must continually reinforce congruence and confront incongruence in the clients they see: "Is that really how you feel?" "Why do you smile when you say that?" "I sense that you are sad even though you are talking as if you are happy." "You said, 'maybe.' Don't you know. . . ?" "Do you expect me to believe you weren't angry that he did that?" "Is doing all those things for her any way to let her know how you feel?" "I liked that . . . you looked angry and stated it very well." "You said that beautifully. I knew you were sad, I could see your eyes tearing."

Congruence and Experience

Congruence requires that we have sensitivity to nonverbal experiences. A therapist quickly learns how crucial are spatial seating patterns, eye contact, body posture, and movement. All humans need to become more aware of their ordinary capacities to read that language. We must all have the courage to trust our sensitivity. Unfortunately, as Yeats said in his *Autobiography*, "It is so many years before one can believe enough in what one feels even to know what the feeling is." A good therapist must not only *believe* but must learn to *use* those feelings, and they must be felt, understood (thought), and used (behaved) in a congruent way. The same is true of each of us individually, both with ourselves and in our relationships.

The truth of this need cannot be stressed strongly enough,

nor its difficulty exaggerated. In *The Empathetic Imagination,*
Alfred Margulies writes:

> World views and their inscapes are often dominated by a
> single preoccupation. It can be a symptom, a grief, another
> person, a physical illness, hunger, sexuality, addiction, re-
> venge, a past event, a quest for stimulation and novelty, or
> even an affect. The preoccupation itself becomes larger than
> life and forms the gravitational center of the person's universe.
> Everything attains relevance and meaning with respect to the
> preoccupation; nothing escapes its sway. As it becomes more
> ensconced, the entire world comes within its compass. Clini-
> cally, we use such terms as addiction, compulsion, obsession—
> diseases of the mind. But to the one who endures it, it is the
> hub of existence.

We lose our sensitivity to real feelings, real thoughts, and real
actions—verbal or nonverbal—in our captures by "single preoc-
cupations." We listen to isolated false voices inside us instead of
our congruent real voice. The hub of our existence must become
our congruent sense of self if we are to move to wholeness. And,
furthermore, just as incongruence in the therapist solicits incongruence in the client, incongruence in ourselves solicits incongruence in others. There will be *no experiencing* for either, nor will
there be any change.

There can be no change because the nonexperiencing *is* the
unhealthiness. For therapists to promote change, they must move
into the experience with the client. As psychiatrist Leston Havens
summarized in "The Existential Use of the Self," "Buber's 'imagining the real' or 'making present,' Laing's 'confirmation,' Rogers' 'congruence,' and Raskin's 'getting under the skin' all suppose
the ability to experience something that we and the patient experience as alike."

Only real experience can be *experienced* as alike—can be and
inevitably will be because it is universal, a part of our human
nature, a part of all nature. Such real experience arises from
congruence. In therapy, as Havens says, "Being and staying as
ends in themselves, the commitment to accepting appearances,
translating and extending our shared grasp, 'keeping looking,' the
willingness to confront and change—all these outline a clinical
technique or method." They also outline a way of being in the

world for *anyone* who would allow the experiencing that in turn allows change.

Self-Consciousness and Incongruence

Tammy is thirty-four. She begins therapy anxiously, painfully unsure of herself. She has struggled with anxiety and insecurity at work, at home, and in her relationship with her two children and husband. Tammy worries constantly about how she appears to the *other*. Is what she thinks right? Is what she feels acceptable? Is how she behaves approvable? Tammy is preoccupied with these questions. She watches herself think, feel, and behave. She processes her being, which displaces *being* entirely. When she talks about herself, we see her through *others'* eyes, even though it is her mouth that is speaking. Tammy has little idea who *she* actually is.

The *selficidal* nature of such self-consciousness is fairly obvious. Self-consciousness has nothing to do with being conscious of our *selves*. Instead, it is a preoccupation with or fixation on one aspect of our being. The particular aspect may change from moment to moment, but, at any given moment, one part of our being consumes us. We are, in those moments, what we are thinking, feeling, or behaving. We are never *all of ourselves*. Cut off from the rest of us, the thinking, feeling, or behaving feels no groundedness, no ability to stand on its own. Thus, we become self-conscious. Preoccupied with one part of ourselves, we stop *being* ourselves. We immediately cease to experience. Life the thief who says, "I'm honest except when I'm stealing something," congruence has no meaning one part at a time. An isolated thought, feeling, or behavior can never be harmonious; there are no other parts to harmonize with.

We will be most self-conscious in the most ordinary of acts. Occasionally clients will come in for therapy at a lunchtime or early in the morning and will bring something to eat. This experience is difficult for many people because eating is a basic act and is impossible to disguise or camouflage as something other than what it is. It directly addresses experience and makes real the questions of peerage, dependency, and perhaps most importantly, communion. It is clear in such moments that self-consciousness blocks experience, even the simple experience of tasting the jelly in your peanut-butter-and-jelly sandwich. Congruence operates on just that primitive a level. One will or will not be congruent when eating, sleeping, walking, making love, playing with a child, being with one's God, or talking to one's best friend. In all ways we move away from such congruence, we become less ourselves.

Social Demands and Congruence

Some of the clearest ways we move away from such congruence are found in the push and pull of social demands. Socialization is an undeniably necessary and meaningful part of our living as members of pairs, families, groups, a culture, or an environment. Healthy closeness is required for all of us to function in an ongoing growthful way. But socialization seldom remains so pristinely healthy. It often creates demands, pressures, and life roles which diminish selfbeing and make people less than whole.

Rafael comes to therapy at the suggestion of the employee counselor at his company. He has been having increasing difficulty fitting in at work. He shares with us many examples of the demands he feels are being made on him that are not consistent with his own internal sense of who he is. He often suffers the same alienating struggle with his friends, family, and lover. As he tells his story, we hear a long history of *his* sense that he has always been told what to be, rather than allowed to be what he is.

Rafael represents, in some ways, a caricature of how most of us react to social demands. If we look back to the original experiences which determine congruence and its distortions, we find the phenomenologic child, the child who at first exists simply as a self, and, thus, is naturally congruent. The critical learning that affects congruence happens at the interface between that creative, emergent child/person and his or her early experience with the pressures of society. It is in this interface that the child first consciously experiences the bind of the strong social demands that lead to personal incongruence.

Social demands *guarantee* a certain degree of incongruence

and nonexperience. The only real questions are to what degree, with what message, and by what power. If the degree is too large or the message too distorted, such as a parent's use of conditional love as an enforcer—for example, "I will love you only if you behave as I tell you" (which is often neither conscious nor overtly spoken)—the child will grow up with serious difficulties in being him- or herself fully. Whatever particular manifestation the un-healthiness takes will come out of the child's own biology, the totality of the family's relationships, and the kinds of noncon-gruence that that family consistently engenders. It will be *relationally* formed. *But it will be.* The binds of socialization are real.

Thus, we all give up some of our personal congruence for a communal level of cultural/social congruence. The value of the gift we give is indicated by the hurt and anger we feel when our cultural systems turn out to be neither communal nor congruent. *Healthy* socialization—the moving of the phenomenologic two-year-old to the socially adept five-year-old—is a complex task. Obviously, it begins at birth and goes on actively until death. *Healthy* socialization recognizes that congruence is necessary to experience. It moves humans softly and gently into the ability to choose how to be in any given space and time. Such teaching, however, is neither easy nor common. As a culture, we think we know a great deal about socialization, but actually we know very little.

The fact that we believe we know so much is seen in all the psychological "instruction manuals" being written. Even apart from their questionable validity for the individual, they speak little to the interaction between individual and system. We rarely ask "How do systems work?" or "Why do they capture us?" In dealing with studies such as topology, chaos, synergistics, and general systems theories, we are only now coming to grips with the fact that relationships have pattern and structure, and systems have different patterns and structures from the individuals who make them up.

The fact that we in reality know so little about systems is made fairly clear by the myriad social problems which exist in our society. As lovers, families, groups, and nations, we are all too dysfunctional in our closeness. To have the worst of both worlds, unhealthy closeness *and* a lack of congruence individually, often seems our lot. Margaret Mead wrote in *Male and Female*, "In-evitably, the culture within which we live shapes and limits our imaginations, and by permitting us to do and think and feel in certain ways makes it increasingly unlikely or impossible that we should do or think or feel in ways that are contradictory or tangential to it." It is difficult to be a congruent self in any culture. It is almost impossible in a culture actively antagonistic to such harmony.

Nonfunctional, unhealthy closeness, then, blocks the very new thinking, feeling, and behaving which would allow unhealthy ways of socializing to change. This results in selficide on a cultural level. Naturalist and therapist Niko Tinbergen said in regard to his view on this issue in *Watching and Wondering,* "Because that assessment turns out to be far from optimistic, in fact leads me to the firm belief that *homo sapiens* is losing fitness—is on a course of accelerating disadaption." Our methods of socialization are *not* working, and we are culturally selficidal *and* suicidal.

Collective Man

Failing methods of socialization leave us with *collective man:* we eat alike, sleep alike, talk alike, buy alike, think alike, live alike, die alike—captured by massive systems in order to be consumerized, merchandised, and sanitized, groomed to fit the mass-marketed, mass-advertised, and mass-produced world. Even our rebels are collective rebels, equally as captured and merchandised. The drug business, the vice business, the crime business *are* all *businesses.* Depending on your point of view, television evangelists may provide salvation or satire. Either way, they are still million-dollar businesses. And politics, as shown by the amount of money it takes to get elected, is also a business.

What is frightening is that none of these businesses are interested in the persons who are homogenized by them. Collective man becomes man headed for extinction. A business which functions in such a way that its customers become extinct is a poorly run business. Humans without congruence cannot continue to be human. "Collective man," Jung wrote in *Psychological Reflections,* "is threatening to suffocate the individual, who is absolutely indispensable, for it is on his sense of responsibility that every human achievement is ultimately founded."

Pathetically, we define with catchy terms such large-scale

incongruence: we speak of the bureaucratic mind, the organization man, of yuppies, guppies, and preppies, of the silent majority, the punkers, the religious right, the liberal left. Even being Christian, being Jewish, being Buddhist, being rich, being poor, being middle class become roles with labels. Not only does labeling deprive humans of their full humanity, their unique individuality but people living as labels make themselves helplessly incongruent, and are, therefore, inevitably less than whole. Such humans "live" only when the name on their label is called. They become increasingly deaf to the many other beautiful sounds in the world. They walk without hearing through the world, heeding only the call of their labels. They are alienated from any selfbeing.

I (Tom) remember a wonderful science fiction story about a society that attempted to systematize people so that they would live harmoniously with each other. To bring about this benevolent society, its designers developed a very effective program of training and retraining the citizenry. The training, too, was exceedingly benevolent—there was no harshness, threats, nor punishment. It was a sophisticated psychological program designed to make each citizen a clone of every other citizen. But in order to accomplish this goal, the system had to destroy congruence in its people. The authorities planned to accomplish this destruction by utterly diminishing the presence of feeling in each person's being, so that only behavior and thinking remained. Without feeling, there can be no congruence and thus no real individual identity.

The system was highly successful, except for one man. This particular man repeatedly began to get his feelings back: feelings of anger, feelings of joy, powerful sexual feelings. Each time his congruence returned, the bureaucracy patiently brought him back into the program for retraining. Afterward, not being punitive people, they put him back out into the society, where once again he began to have feelings. It eventually became clear to the bureaucrats that, if left to himself, this one congruent man in this huge society could destroy the whole system. He would disrupt the programmed behavior of anyone with whom he came in contact. There would eventually be thousands, and then hundreds of thousands of people who would become congruent and detach themselves, at least for moments, from the system. By being able to detach and exist as individual beings, they would also be able to look objectively *at* the system, and as a result would respond to it differently. In our real society, we need to do the same. We need to step back from and examine the systems that control so much of our living.

Collective Craziness

When we can look at the "civilized" world and see it in this detached way, we become like the innocent "primitive" in the film *The Gods Must Be Crazy*, who so clearly saw our organized insanity. So much of collective civilization is collective nonexperience, collective self-diminishment. In many ways, modern man is invested in not allowing *anyone* to be congruent. It is as if we are afraid to see too clearly. Perhaps the pain we would feel if we saw what we were missing in our living would be too great for us to bear.

Nicole has anxiously struggled with making decisions ever since she can remember. At thirty-one, she is obsessed with doing what is right—emotionally, morally, pragmatically. There is little joy or growth in such a struggle. Relationally, our indecision tends to make those closest to us doubt our commitment. After all, if we have to go through that much effort to decide questions that involve them—for example, whether to go somewhere with them or share some experience with them—just how committed can we be? In truth, Nicole is highly committed, committed to everything in her life. But she still spends hours trying to figure out how to say the right things, have the right feelings, and act the right way.

Nicole is not indecisive simply in that she appears to be struggling to please or appease others. She is not really struggling for approval from others, nor to appease others at all. She is struggling with herself.

"I've never been free of me," she tells us. "I know that sounds crazy, but it's sort of the way I feel. I can't just go to a party, even with my friends, and have fun. If everybody is together, having a great time, I'll feel not quite a part of it. I just watch, instead of really being there . . . you know what I mean?"

She tells us she cannot *experience* her emotions. "I didn't really even realize it when I got divorced. I knew it in my head, of course, but it wasn't really real, I couldn't taste it. That's the way things always are with me. Then, a long time later, things will catch up with me. A lot of times they catch up with me in my dreams, although I don't always recognize them at first."

The clichéd organization man, the political zealot, the collectivized human, is more clearly distorted than someone like Nicole. Being captured by an external structure is humanistically worse than having an internal structure block one's experience. Such external blocks (bellicose nationalism, class hatred, racism, sexism, religious intolerance) applied mindlessly to other minds—with little thought as to the effect on those minds or the effects that those minds will then have on still others—is the core of much of mankind's misery.

In such systemic cases, the blocking of experience is almost complete, as anyone who has tried to deal with even the less virulent systemization of dehumanized bureaucrats and organizations knows. We are just a number or a bother or irrelevant, and we are clearly made to feel so. People joke about trying to talk to computers about bills or other complaints, but in truth, that is nowhere near as painful as trying to talk to another *human* who is so incongruent that he or she behaves like a machine. The human "computer" is much worse than the electronic one. Human computers may eventually even forget to dream. They do not even have the help that Nicole has. At least her dreams give her a chance.

I (Tom) have found it increasingly difficult over the years to know what to do with clients who work for deadening organizations and who come to me saying, "I can't deal with it anymore. I want to quit. I'm just not like the rest of them." They are often confused when I reply, "Great!" My difficulty has to do with my dual responsibility to do both counseling and therapy. Healthy humans *should* be able to cope. But counseling people on how to cope with being unhealthy seems untherapeutic to me. I grow more and more inclined to push them toward their own internal congruence rather than train them to cope. But the risk is real. People often try to run before they can walk.

The fact that things are not working is even apparent to the system managers themselves. The search for new management strategies, new ways to deal with organizations, new ways to motivate people has quickened and widened in the past few years. Business writer Peter Drucker illustrated the problem well with an anecdote in *The Effective Executive:*

Alfred P. Sloan is reported to have said at a meeting of one of his top committees: "Gentlemen, I take it we are all in complete agreement on the decision here." Everyone around the table nodded assent. "Then," continued Mr. Sloan, "I propose we postpone further discussion of this matter until our next meeting to give ourselves time to develop disagreement and perhaps gain some understanding of what the decision is about."

What Mr. Sloan meant by gaining "some understanding of what the decision is about" is what we mean by experiencing. We can know our experience only if we are detached enough from the system to disagree. We can be congruent only with such detachment. "Detached" does not necessarily mean opposed, antagonistic, or in any way conflictual. It simply signifies the absence of capture. It means having the capacity to move to an uncaptured position in which we can exist as *ourselves* in the world we are in. Such living is not merely internal (which would be unrelated to the experience of what is outside) and is not merely external (which would be unrelated to ourselves). It must be internal/external, a wholeness that comes out of the merging of the two, a synthesis in which wholeness transcends parts.

Incongruence and Gender

Perhaps in no other area do we see the loss of such wholeness as obviously as we do in our views of our maleness and femaleness. Looked at as systems, *being male* or *being female* can completely capture a human being in subtle as well as obvious ways. These are particular systems from which few people can detach themselves. Our stereotypes of gender roles are deeply ingrained and powerful.

The truth is, of course, that these stereotypes *are* stereotypes. We are not saying that male and female are not different. We are saying that both males and females are, *first of all*, persons. That fact is not only more important than their roles, it is more germane. Existence precedes essence. All humans have both masculine and feminine characteristics which must be actualized if they are to be fully human, fully congruent and fully experiencing. If we exist as only part of ourselves, we inevitably will be less than whole. Male and female form a duality in which personhood must transcend gender.

In *The Descent of the Goddess*, therapist Sylvia Perera discusses the patriarchal ego in both men and women as instinct-disciplining, striving, progressive, and heroically active. Reconnection to the self, she says, requires finding as well the matriarchal ego:

> This inner connection is an initiation essential for the modern women in the western world; without it we are not whole. The process requires both a sacrifice of our identity as spiritual daughters of the patriarchy and a descent into the spirit of the goddess, because so much of the power and passion of the feminine has been dormant in the underworld—in exile for five thousand years.

The problem is no different for modern men. Male's alienation from his feminine is currently undoing us as a culture. The separation from the feminine *or* the masculine in any human will always be self-destructive.

I (Pat) have had to struggle with this issue personally with my two children. I have had to recognize that it was much clearer to me that my daughter, Shannon, needed both her masculine and feminine qualities than that my son, Tom, needed the same. I was much clearer that she needed her athletics *and* arts, her academics *and* activities, than I was that he needed the same. This realization came to me slowly over some years, and it surprised me. I knew that I did not consciously feel that way. I have since worked hard to increase my understanding of his needs—not merely to know them intellectually, but to support them functionally. For a parent to want any child to be less than fully human is frightening. It is particularly frightening that capture by systems can be so subtle, so difficult to detect even in ourselves. I now realize that I must remain watchful about my vulnerability to gender stereotypes. We all must.

Centering

Centering is, literally, just that: in order to remain congruent, one must not be captured by either side of any duality—

internal-external, closeness-intimacy, system-individual, masculine-feminine, or any other personal or cultural system. Unhealthiness is *not* the exclusive property of "sick" people. A continuum between health and sickness is present in every individual. None of us is completely free of impulses toward sociopathy, obsessiveness, compulsivity, depression, hysteria, or mania. These ways of not fully being ourselves are the various remnants of the past of each particular biologic child growing up in a particular family in a particular culture. Since we all have a biology and grow up as children in families in a culture, we all have remnants. Some remnants can hospitalize us, some can seriously circumscribe and delimit our lives. Some simply compromise our growth into our full potential as human beings. Growing from this incongruence, this nonexperiential life position, to the congruent-experiencing one is vital to *every* human being. Remnants make us less congruent. As tiny or not so tiny systems, they can capture us.

Here is often the kernel of the nut. Only with repeated experiences of reinforcing congruence and of confronting incongruence—especially when the person can be aware of that incongruence—can a therapist or anyone else move usefully *with* the other toward growth. Confronting a person who is incapable of using that confrontation can be either useless or disastrous. It will be useless if the therapist, congruently aware, is wishfully asking for something prematurely. It will be disastrous if the therapist, incongruent in him- or herself, is *doing* something to the unprepared person. And so it is for us with our lovers, families, and friends. And, *most of all*, so it is for each of us with *ourselves*.

Centering is like a harmonic chord, or a balanced painting, or a complete poem, when everything falls into exactly the natural place. When it happens, it is wonderfully reinforcing. It feels real and exciting both to the centered person and to anyone with whom he or she is being congruent, fully alive. We know the center when we are in it. As Galway Kinnell wrote in "Saint Francis and the Sow":

> For everything flowers, from within, of self-blessing:
> though sometimes it is necessary
> to reteach a thing its loveliness.

9

THE SIXTH WINDOW:
Presence

And I have felt a presence that disturbs me with the joy
of elevated thoughts.

—William Wordsworth

During the first forty-seven years of his life, Howell never imagined that he would find himself in a psychiatrist's office. If the question had arisen, he would have said that he did not think a person should have to rely on someone else's help to solve his own problems. Nevertheless, Howell and his wife, Kay, are now in our office along with their teenaged daughter, Kathy. Kathy's school problems and behavioral difficulties at home have "caused" the family to seek help.

The family's discord is plainly evident. There is, in truth, no real sense of family even present. That is, there is no sense of connection, no shared way of dealing with their problems. The many hidden agendas, readily seen by the therapist, are not seen by the family. They have no conscious sense of how they are blaming each other, no awareness of how alienated they are from each other. After listening to the parents' extended description of the problem, we ask Kathy what she has to say. At first she acts hesitant, but then launches into an elaborate and vociferous explanation of all the ways in which she feels misparented. Like her parents, she, too, goes on for quite some time, justifying her side of the struggle.

"Why don't you tell *them?*" we finally ask her. "It's *them* you're feeling this way about. Why don't you talk to *them?*"

Kathy is quiet for a minute, then (with direct eye contact, something she has not shown until now) she replies, "Why should I talk to them? They're not really here. I'm the only one besides you who's really here." There is a long silence while all three look anywhere but at each other. The conversation dies. The disconnection in the family is both powerful and real.

In a sense, Kathy is correct. Her parents are present only in the sense that they are there as her mother and father. They are carrying out roles, not being persons. In the session, Kathy tells us that they treat her just the way her mother used to treat Howell himself, and we learn that Howell is a "reformed" alcoholic. We learn that Kay had lectured him about his drinking for years. They had each lived their separate roles, Kay being the "good" wife and Howell being the "bad" husband. This *nonrelationship* had not escaped their daughter. Although Kathy was not currently owning *her* own responsibility for *her* behavior, she was at least able to define her parents' lack of presence and to see what that lack did to their relationship with each other and with her. She was living out the truth that educator John Holt described in *How Children Fail*, "Children who depend heavily on adult approval may decide that, if they cannot have total success, their next best bet is to have total failure."

Understanding such approval as *presence* makes sense if we reflect on what it does to the child—what it did to each of us as a child—to have a parent be *really* present. Our parents' enjoyment of being with us, their eyes lighting up when they saw us, their attending to us happily, are the only real definitions of approval that have significance on a deep level. Approval originally meant "to find the other good." Over time, the word unfortunately has taken on judgmental connotations, usually implying that someone has done something as we instructed and desired it to be done, and we, therefore, approve. It would be far healthier to stay with its deepest meaning, "to find the other good." In that way, we could approve even when disappointed.

Real presence provides that steady and sure foundation on which all parenting is based. Presence makes children experience both the joy *and* the responsibility of being themselves. It is, moreover, the most meaningful way any of us can live with *any other person.* One can best understand presence as the outward manifestation of a profound internal congruence.

We too often confuse *presence* with being *present.* We know when others are present without really *being* there. And other people are equally aware of our not being there in their presence. Such relating, if masqueraded as caring, is usually destructive. It produces the feeling so well described here:

> I felt his cold eyes all over me, ignoring me. I wanted to get away from my body that he had touched—to leave it to him. To have one's individuality completely ignored is like being pushed quite out of life, like being blown out as one blows out a light. I began to believe myself invisible.
> —Evelyn Scott, *Revelations: Diaries of Women*

"Being present" has a quality of appeasement: "Here I am, what else do you want?" There is no real commitment in living in that way. To the other person, such appeasement means little, and mostly feels like the rejection it actually is.

Presence means more than making an appearance. From *pre* (before) and *ence* (being) comes the definition of presence as, literally, *being before.* If the other person knows and feels that he or she stands before a *being,* then someone is truly present. When we experience another's real being, we experience being real as well. I am here, now, with you. *Present,* on the other hand, simply means *sent before.* When we are merely present, our child, spouse, lover, or friend must wonder who *sent* us, and for what reason.

Truly being with another person involves more than being in the same place at the same time. Simply here and now is not enough. Only personal presence makes the here and now more than trivial. You are, as psychoanalyst Rollo May says, "bringing all of you to bear on the immediate experience." Each of us clearly feels it when someone is *being* with us in this way. It makes us feel *real.*

A good example is seen in Pete. After struggling with his fourteen-year-old daughter's behavior and isolation for some time and getting nowhere, Pete decides *he* must change, *he* must find some way to truly get with her. He begins to look directly in her eyes, listen intently, really "bring all of himself to bear" when he is with her.

"I knew it was changing," he explains, "when a week ago one of her friends called while we were talking about something and my daughter said, 'Can you call me back later? My dad's talking with me right now.' "

Pete's daughter felt *real* and *approved* in the new relationship. Her behavior reflected that change. No longer would just any excuse do to avoid him—a pattern seen in so many children. She felt his presence and found both joy and herself in it. He, likewise, found joy and himself in the experience of her. Such relatedness is the living manifestation of presence.

Psychology in its broadest sense has never dealt well with either space/time or presence. The notion of space/time seems to be especially elusive when looking at relationships. Human beings live most immediately in space/time, but with few exceptions are usually described by psychologists and psychiatrists as if their behavior is both timeless (transference) and spaceless (the same no matter where they are physically). Presence, in the more intimate sense of which we are now speaking, is seldom dealt with at all.

Some people feel that space is more relevant to their being present than time. "I am here in your personal space" is how they experience presence. Other people feel time is more relevant and feel the experience in more temporal terms: "I am in your present moment." Marshall McLuhan said that "for tribal man space was the uncontrollable mystery. For technological man it is time that occupies the same role." We suspect, however, that real presence has to do with a psychological confluence of time and space. I am in the here and the now and I feel no separation of time and space. When we are present in this way, the other person is moved into the same immediacy of personhood. That is the gift that is given. In the experience of true presence, space and time become indistinguishable for both persons. Presence thus involves real space/time touching. For experience to happen, both the experiencer and the experienced must intimately be in the here and now. The absence of presence, the lack of intimate space/time touching, assures nonexperience, and so self-diminishment. Whereas we may think of *presence* as either temporal or spatial, to be whole we must unify the two because space/time is the basic parameter of experience.

Presence is learned in childhood from the reciprocating and accepting presence of the parents. It is an approval which is neither condoning nor permissive but celebrant and creative. We all were once children, and we all mislearned to some degree. This leaves us with less than whole life positions which we then defend: "I am who I am."

Such impaired life positions are diversions from immediate experiencing. They are not who we are as whole persons. To the extent that it is determined by the past, any experience is depressed. To the extent that it is determined by concern with the future, any experience is anxious.

This point is made beautifully by Spencer Johnson in *The Precious Present:*

> *It is wise for me to think about*
> *the past*
> *and to learn from my past*
>
> *But it is not wise for me*
> *to be in the past*
> *For that is how I lose*
> *my self.*
>
> *It is also wise to think about*
> *the future*
> *and to prepare for my future*
>
> *But it is not wise for me*
> *to be in the future*
> *For that, too, is how I lose*
> *my self.*

Both depression and secondary anxiety are nonexperiential phenomena. One has to *see* the flower, not remember other flowers or use the sight of a flower as a stepping-stone to a better life. Experience is most felt when immediate, when the energies are not diverted by either the past or the future. It is then available and full.

Living in the Past

In *Ghosts*, Ibsen's tragedy about congenital syphilitic madness, Mrs. Alving says:

> I am half inclined to think we are all ghosts . . . they are
> not actually alive in us; but there they are dormant, all the
> same, and we can never be rid of them. Whenever I take up a
> newspaper and read it, I fancy I see ghosts creeping between
> the lines. There must be ghosts all over the world. They must
> be as countless as grains of sand, it seems to me. And we are
> so miserably afraid of the light, all of us.

As Ibsen said, "The ghosts of our past can and do capture all of us to one degree or another." Being afraid of the light, we hide in our pasts from our real presence. When we understand that the ghosts *are* past, that they are bits of real experience but are not changeable, we see how a system of trying to change them, trying to make them come out differently, can so easily capture us. If we felt unaccepted as children, no amount of ingratiating ourselves to others as an adult is going to change that past experience. But we desperately hold on to those pasts, with the fantasy that they may change. To the degree that we are captured in that way, we will be less in the here-and-now, have less presence, and, therefore, be less able to experience. There is no existence in living in the past.

Ann Louise is fifty years old and lives alone. A great deal of her life is spent quietly within herself. She has few close personal relationships, but is well liked by most people who know her because she is an unobtrusive and gentle person. She is an excellent teacher of young learning-disabled children, and her students love her. However, she makes her colleagues uncomfortable. They think of her as somewhat eccentric and do not understand or know how to accept her distancing herself from them.

Ann Louise's preoccupation in life is with her past, not only in terms of her memories but also in terms of her actual present experience, for she often revisits her paternal home in a rural area of the Deep South. Ann Louise's father is dead. Some of her siblings have moved away, but they often return home just as she does. Her mother is still living, but in the throes of a chronic depression, oppressed by her own past. The history of her extended family contains a multiplicity of personal difficulties, relational struggles, and economic problems. In reality, her family life has been almost the opposite of what Ann Louise remembers as always idyllic, a memory she particularly associates with her father. Many of the problems Ann Louise has in her current living, in her relationships with others, in her own economic problems, and in her professional relationships stem from her preoccupation with and distortion of this past and her consequent lack of presence in her current living situation. "Each of us," as Virgil said, "suffers from his own ghosts." Ann Louise has many.

Such nostalgia, whether of positive or negative feelings, does not have the immediacy of experience itself. True, one can *remember* the past and can *reexperience* it, and to do so is a most important part of humanness. Without reexperiencing we do not grow. Healthy reexperiencing does not, however, lead to being captured. In fact, just the opposite happens. Healthy reexperiencing involves being able to deal with the past without capture, being able to deal with it without losing ourselves, being able to maintain our existence in the present while remembering our past. Only in that way do we *learn* from our pasts. *Existence* means "to stand out," or "emerge." We may emerge into the present while remembering, but, like Ann Louise, we cannot emerge into the present while lost in the past.

André grew up as the only son of a demanding alcoholic mother. His father left when André was two years old, and the boy spent his youth trying to please and appease his mother. However, since the source of his mother's displeasure in life was not André in the first place, nothing he ever did was quite enough. He could do nothing that would change *her*. He was a straight-A student, a "good boy" who excelled at almost everything he did. But these accomplishments became burdens as André grew older. He became a compulsively perfectionistic person. He also became chronically depressed. His two basic life positions were his depression and a repressed rage that would occasionally break out around the edges. On one hand, he would get exceedingly angry about other people's imperfections. On the other, he could pout and withdraw when others did not accept his "help." At fifty-one, he came to therapy because a three-year-long relationship with his lover was about to break up.

André tells us, "I don't want the same thing to happen again. My marriage ended this way. She says I'm so controlling and so depressed . . . that I'm no fun. I guess I'm not. I just can't seem to let go, be as free as other people can be. But I'm so damn busy . . . there's so much to do. I don't think she realizes how important all the things I have to do are. Damn it, somebody has to be responsible! Everybody can't just go around doing what they feel like and saying whatever they want to. She says I need to find the pixie in me. What the hell does that mean?"

This last remark is made with both longing and resignation, the latter carrying an undertone of anger. For someone who is not put off by André's chronic anger, his depression, resignation, and longing are poignant. He lives in a long-gone past where he is still unable to be perfect enough, to take care enough, to be *something* enough to make his mother smile. The cost to him is priceless: he does not ever get to be André. That loss, more than anything else, makes him depressed and angry. Only now is he slowly becoming aware of how costly that loss has been for him.

André fights living. He longs for *some* standard he could meet to satisfy "her." He displaces that past longing onto his current living. He displaces it onto his language, his body movements, and his relationships with others. His words seldom say what he actually means. André wishes to avoid those real meanings. They revolve around the old expectations he feels so unable to meet. They speak to his depression, his rage, and his alienation from himself.

In his ghostly world, without permission to be himself, André feels impotent to find whatever it would take to make the *other person* okay. The depression he lives out is very real and very self-diminishing. He is never present in the *presence* sense. He is just not there, whether there is walking in the park, going to dinner, or making love. His lover feels this acutely, and his longtime friends feel it chronically. During the rare times when the real André briefly appears, both lover and friends understand why they care for him. But dealing with the everyday André takes a high toll.

André does not remember the past, he lives in it. In the experiential sense, *he puts his past into his present.* Trying to get him to reexperience the past instead of being captured by it will be one of the first tasks of therapy. Change happens only through experience, and experiencing can only take place when we are in the here and now uncaptured. Then healthy reexperiencing allows us truly to escape the past, not simply forget it, so that we may live and experience in the present.

We also see the loss of presence in *putting ourselves into the past*. Such living in the past is technically named regression. Take the twenty-seven-year-old who has achieved independence, but who, when faced with major stress (for example, he gets in trouble with the law), reverts to the dependency needs of a seventeen-year-old: he wants his parents to get him out of trouble. Or the middle-aged person who runs from his present responsibilities (for example, a marriage, a tough job, or a dying parent), to an adolescent attitude of "I never had enough fun—girlfriends, sex, new cars, adventure, freedom—and I'm going to get mine now."

Regression is present in all of us to some degree. For example, most of us regress when we are physically ill. Such minor displacements in time are fairly normal. But living ordinary life as an ill person will just as surely make us "ill." We cannot put our *selves* back into the past and expect to be able to experience in the here-and-now. There are no H. G. Wellsian time machines. To be *who we are*, we must be able to be *where we are* and *when we are*.

Living in the Future

Gregory is a gifted young musician. Since the age of five, his remarkable talent has been obvious to others. From his unhappy and bitter attitude, however, one has the clear feeling that his difficulties in life stem from his sense of failure that he is not already being wildly applauded at Carnegie Hall. He is not yet world-famous, and it will take him many years to get there, if, indeed, he ever does, but Gregory is so preoccupied with the future that he may delay his success or, tragically, make it impossible. He is never where he is right now. He cannot take his past, marry it to his future, and end up in his present. Instead, he lives in a future that may never exist.

Presence is as easily lost by living in the future as it is by living in the past. When we exist in the here and now we *meet* the future. It comes to us, we do not need to go to it. Going to the future, living in it, and being captured by it all make us less than whole, block real experiencing, and diminish our ability to be fully ourselves. Gregory is living proof of what that can cost. Our future comes to our present. We cannot go to it without depleting our personal presence, energy, and being where we truly reside.

Living in the present does not mean we cannot plan for the future. Indeed, only by truly living in the present is one able to meaningfully *plan* at all. Being *present* does not mean passively awaiting fate; it means actively being part of a moving process. Unfixed to any particular past or future, we open ourselves to the potential of many new ones.

As a young adult of twenty-three, Rose began having "nervous spells." She had quit school to get married, and during the first three years of her marriage things seemed to go well. Her husband, Hal, found a better job and Rose was promoted at the bank where she worked. They made some friends and were fairly active socially. It surprised her, then, when she started to feel anxious about being in new places, being around crowds, or going very far from her house. At first she simply tried to cover over her fears. As time went on, she began dealing with her anxieties by making excuses, becoming ill, or even picking a fight with Hal so they would not go out or participate in activities. After some years of this behavior, her changed personality had greatly affected their life-style. In her late twenties she decided to go into therapy. She finally decided she had to do something to stop her world from completely closing in on her.

Rose tells us, "I don't know why I feel this way. There's no reason for me to be so afraid of going to a new store. I'm even afraid to go on vacation. I get so anxious. I start breathing too fast and my heart starts skipping and I start perspiring. Sometimes I feel like I'm going to come right out of my skin, or faint, or just go to pieces. I've never really told Hal about how I feel because I know he already thinks I'm crazy. It's getting worse. I feel anxious most of the time, but I really don't know what about. I wonder if Hal is going to leave me. Sometimes I worry that I'll get some bad disease and die. Do you think I'm out of my mind?"

Rose is not "out of her mind." She is "out of her present." Living in the future of what might be, could be, should be, she wishes would be, is afraid will be, or needs to be limits Rose's presence in the here-and-now. Hers is a different kind of living in the future from Gregory's—she is afraid more than angry—but she also lives without presence. Without presence, she is experiencing less. She is less able to change and grow, to learn new ways of being Rose. Thus, she feels stuck, unable to do anything to alter her "fate."

Whatever the issues are that displace us into the future, the result will be nonexperience brought on by our lack of presence. What we *could* know—our present—we give up for a preoccupation with what we *cannot* know—what will be in the future—and thus live just the same as we do when preoccupied with futilely trying to change the past. "Putting ourselves in the future" usually manifests itself as anxiety, phobias, or obsessive worrying. In addition, we are more apt to procrastinate by putting ourselves into a rosier future. Everyone knows someone who is always getting ready to live. "I'll find time to be myself next year. This year I'm too busy making money/getting through school/trying to find a mate, etc." Experience—really living—is always going to come about tomorrow.

Samantha is a perfect example. She has been increasingly angry about her sex life for the past four years. She feels her lover is insensitive and unresponsive to her needs. However, Samantha has said nothing to him. She is always *going* to say something. Next time. Of course, next time becomes the next time, and so it has been for four years. When the next time comes, Samantha will not experience her sexuality. She will have already moved on, at least inside herself, to the next time. None of the pleasure of life today will be experienced. Her existence is all in service of what she will be in the future. Samantha is neither intimate nor close. She neither experiences nor reexperiences. Instead, she nonexperiences, and nonexperience in the here-and-now *always* diminishes self.

Human beings are too often like fishermen in time. We cast into the past or the future in hopes of justifying our present. We do not live in what Blake called the "minute particulars." We live this way to attain security. But emotional preparation for future life will inevitably block here-and-now living. We cannot stand outside, a puppet master to ourselves, and expect those selves to experience real life. Those selves have no *presence*. They exist only as dolls on the ends of long strings—long enough to reach into the future or into the past. Or, the strings may reach to other *places*, for we can be *spatially* as well as *temporally* displaced from our presence.

Spatial Displacement: Affect

We may just as easily not be *here* as not be *now*. However, the spatial aspects of our living are less easily seen by most of us. We see ourselves living in a flow of time but are less comfortable seeing our existence also passing through a flow of space. We are so far removed from our hunter-gatherer roots, so far removed from those natural spaces in which we evolved, that it is much easier for us to escape in time than to escape in space. Escaping in space seems too obvious. Escaping to the past or future is so much easier for us to deny, to ourselves *and* others. Perhaps artists, with their "right-brained" life positions, are more adept at seeing our spatial displacements since they more easily see gestalts—the whole as opposed to its parts. A greater part of current civilization is "left-brained" and time-oriented. Those of us who are not busy keeping to some time schedule are apt to be busy rebelling against one. Our common difficulty with presence may reflect this relatively poor functioning of our sense of the *here*.

Few of us have the chance to live in a timeless manner, more involved with the space we are in than with time (schedules, deadlines, etc.). Few of us are able to *allow* ourselves to live in such a way even if afforded the opportunity. The majority of us find, for example, that it is only near the end of a two-week vacation that we really begin to live in the space we are in. That way of life was surely closer to the existence of the evolving hunter-gatherer human. Before clocks and schedules, time must have been a more global concept, like space, and not a dissection of life into nonnatural segments.

Time has been captured by systems to a much greater extent than space. We look at our watches and know what time it is. Right now it is nine o'clock. We know that three years from now, at this moment, it still will be nine o'clock. That predictability gives us a feeling of security, as if we could control time itself. We know that is not true, but it feels that way. On the other hand, if we were to walk outside and look across the darkened space of the sky, or even over a distant hill, we would have no real sense of having any control of those spaces. Of course, we can individually move our chair to the other side of the room or collectively carve a tunnel through a mountain, but generally we feel little control over our spatial lives.

I (Tom) received a special lesson in spatial presence many years ago from one of my daughters. She was six years old and we were having one of those parent-child conversations that are both silly and profound at the same time. We were arguing about which of us was bigger. She said that she was bigger than I was. "Sheila, that's ridiculous," I told her, "You can see by standing up next to me that I'm much bigger than you." She replied, "You don't understand, Dad. I'm ten feet deep." Her remark gave me some "deep" insight into the fact that presence has spatial as well as temporal qualities. For all of us are deep in the here as well as the now. Children know this. Adults can relearn it.

The most frequent spatial displacement that diminishes presence is *affect displacement*. In its most commonly dramatized form (the TV version), a person has a fight with his lover and then goes to work and has a fight with someone there, usually someone of the same sex as his lover. The affect (the emotional response) of the first fight is spatially displaced into the second fight. Outsiders may think, "Well, he is simply taking it out on so-and-so." And that may indeed be so. But that analysis does not describe the lack of *presence* occurring in that person himself. It may describe the behavior he engages in, but it does not describe *his being*. And it is, in fact, his being that is distorted. His lack of presence makes him not only unreal to the displaced object of his anger, but also unreal to himself. Being unreal to ourselves is self-diminishing. I cannot *love* an unreal me. I cannot *enjoy* an unreal me. I cannot *be* an unreal me.

We all occasionally displace affect in this way. Like the proverbial act of being angry at our boss and kicking our dog, we take a feeling arising in one relationship and transfer it to another. It is an all too ordinary part of our living; nonetheless, few of us are aware of living in those ways.

Positive Displacement

Sometimes people speak of positive displacement of affect. That is, we have a good experience with someone at home and so we go to work feeling good. Naming such a concept "displacement" is confusing. It would be better to speak of generalizing our affect. Generalizing joyful affect is a very positive experience, and one which makes the person feel good about both himself and the world. Since both feelings are true *self* experiences, there is no real displacement. Perhaps we made love that morning, so we go to work full of loving feelings, more fully ourselves and more loving with others. Driving along, we find that people in the cars next to us look, smile, and even wave. Our co-workers seem friendlier and more related to us. It is amazing how contagious such generalized affect can become. But we are present as selves in each experience; our being is real.

I (Tom) was recently feeling very happy one mid-morning. I was in a grocery store where I frequently shop. As I moved through the aisles, I whistled, which is not uncommon for me. This particular morning, I must have been whistling some fairly joyful songs, although I am never consciously aware of what they are. I was stopped by a woman with a shopping cart who asked if she could follow me around the store and do her shopping while I whistled. I asked her why. She said, "Well, it helps me. I love whistling. I was here once before when you were whistling and I shopped behind you without your knowing it. When I got home I realized I'd bought a lot of things that ordinarily I wouldn't buy because I'm such a frugal person. You know, like fresh-ground coffee. My husband wondered what had happened to me. He was really pleased with my great spirits. So maybe if I shop with your whistling I'll do it again, and he and I will have a great evening."

This curious experience showed me how powerful is the generalization of affect. It was a very positive experience for me as well. When we live in that way, we know the joy in us and we own it. We claim our feelings, thoughts, and behaviors as our own. We carry our presence with us through space, much as I did in the grocery store. Why call this a displacement?

When the affect experience is negative, it is more properly termed a displacement. The person who kicks the dog instead of his boss often consciously believes that it is the dog he is mad at. Such behavior is incongruent. The person is displacing, *living out* his affect somewhere else as if it really belonged there. Conversely, for us to make love and then go to work more fully loving of others, is to own our sexuality. Owning our sexuality is very different from living it out with substitutes at work. The latter very often is a self-diminishing displacement of affect. Office affairs are not manifestations of our loving nature.

In our current stressful culture, displacements frequently occur. We get hurt, angry, or afraid at work and then take those feelings home to our family. It is a very common experience with couples and families, and it is becoming even more frequent because of the enormous increase in the number of families in which both parents work. The complexity of feeling shared in the first hour or so home together can be frightening. Often, as the poet Robert Bly says, we end up sharing only our temperaments with each other, not our persons.

Even children—since they too come home from a stressful and systemized atmosphere at school where restraints on their expression are considerable—are often guilty of the same kind of negative displacement when they arrive back in a safe place. Sometimes a bizarre nonpresence of the entire family occurs. For example, while the family is at dinner, one child, hurt from a fight at school, is picking on another. The mother, harassed at work, is angrily complaining to both children about their not helping around the house. The father, who feels somehow inadequate, first at his job and then at home with his family, tries to get everyone to be quiet. No one is living in the here-and-now of their shared lives.

These can be upsetting and frightening experiences. Each person may feel that some other person is "doing something" to him or her. Worse, family members frequently interpret this interaction incorrectly, as if it defined their real relationships: "How you are with me now tells me how you feel about me." Such mislearning is often carried further, particularly when it is the parents who are displacing negative feelings onto the children. Sadly, children may then go on to feel, "And how you feel about me tells me who I am." This internalization of a displaced feeling is, of course, not based on the truth. How one person feels about you does not define you. It can, however, create confusion and pain, and can make the regaining of congruence and presence within the family system difficult. Even more sadly, the mislearnings of children can stay with them for a lifetime.

The way you are with me tells me who *you* are, not who I am. It frequently also gives me some very helpful *information*, not definition, about who I am. That is what is so important about presence. By your presence I know the real you. And knowing the real you as you interact with me gives me vital information about the real me. Not because you have verbalized that information, but because in responding to the real you I begin to feel the real me. That is relational presence.

Two people with a true connection are often described in books and songs as if they feel each other's presence. This capacity is usually presented as mystical or extrasensory, but we would suggest that, quite the contrary, it is simply natural. Humans, if they would only be themselves, would indeed feel presence as a tangible thing. The only mysterious aspect of it is why we have so abandoned it as a way of living. Our real presence is our availability to our universe, our God-ness manifest.

Spatial Displacement: Context

My (Pat) wife teaches drama. Along with many other professionals, I have come to believe that theater has much to teach psychotherapists. Actors learn that they need to have *presence* on stage, and that presence is clearly something akin to the window to experience we are describing. It is *a way of being, a way of being capable of conveying to the other the realness of ourselves.* It is irrelevant that an actor's realness is not real—that the movements and dialogue were written by a playwright—as long as it *is* real in the contextual sense. Watching an actress learn to convey reality in her own context makes clear to me that presence has a *context* component, as well as an *affect* component. Watching Elaine teach children acting makes clear to me that *being* precedes *doing* in learning presence. She has a long list of situations—little minidramas that call for certain roles—that require students to experience the presence of some particular character who finds him- or herself in those situations. She teaches by reflecting back her emotional response to that presence.

Many of us lose presence not through *affect* displacement but through *context* displacement. Here is a simple example of context displacement: a couple go out, relate to each other well in the social context of a party or business meeting, then return home and continue to relate to each other just as if they were still in the formal social situation. As a result, there will be no real experience at home for either of them. What they are living will not be what they *are*.

Such displacement can sometimes become a problem in therapy. A couple, perhaps an entire family, will come in for a session. They become very real with each other, saying directly what they feel, want, need, and experience. They then return to the world of everyday living and continue this way of being in their everyday context. One might ask, "Is this behavior a problem? Shouldn't we always be totally real, say directly what we feel, want, need and experience?" No. Context matters. The police officer giving us a ticket will have little interest in our notions of the unfairness of the judicial system *or* how he or she, much like the authority figures in our earlier years, seems to be taking some pleasure in having caught us. The police officer may not only have little interest, he or she also may respond quite negatively in a way that is not good for us. Our boss may be very upset about a contract the company just lost and may not respond favorably to the fact that we have just decided we need a vacation. Our lover, grieving the loss of a parent, may not be able to deal with our sharing our experience that the deceased parent had always been basically demanding and uncaring anyway. Being fully present is *not* the same as the current notion of letting it all hang out.

In all these situations, it is not that we should fail to be ourselves. Instead, we need to find the *particular* us to be. *Presence is contextual.* There is a *you* of real presence that can *be* in each case.

If we are chaperoning a group of teenagers, we can become playfully teenlike without being displaced from our adult judgment. If we are playing a competitive game with our child, we can be "not so good" at it without being condescending or inattentive. At work, we can know better without having to be a know-it-all. We can suspend our particular needs in any given situation in order to be most fully the person we are in those situations.

Recognizing the context of presence is not the same as saying that presence is conditional. Like "conditional love," "conditional presence" is essentially a contradiction in terms. *Conditional* is systemic and controlling. It diminishes self. Contextually is dyadic and mutually explanatory. We exist relationally, so there *must* be a context to our living. We must find a presence to be, in each and any context, that allows us to be our most real and healthy selves in that context.

Attention

Happy the man, and happy he alone
He who can call today his own;
He who, secure within, can say,
Tomorrow, do thy worst, for I have lived today.

—JOHN DRYDEN, *Imitation of Horace*

Presence gets people's attention. That is one of the straightforward lessons we can all learn from theater. It attracts us not in the attention-grabbing sense, but in the more profound grabbing-the-inside-of-us sense.

Ed, a huge man, comes from the mountains of Tennessee. He is in his late sixties, a war hero, and still carries scars both physically and emotionally. Over the years, episodically he has come in to therapy sessions with me (Tom), as his anxieties and depression return. He now returns once again, bringing with him a brown paper bag full of apples he has picked from his own trees. He gives the bag to me, and, taking the bag, I thank him. There is silence.

"Well, don't you want to eat one?" Ed asks.

I take a few bites of a large red apple and say it is very good. Ed sits wordlessly for a while and then says, "Well, eat some more." While eating the rest of the apple, I ask what brings Ed back to visit.

"I started getting nervous again. So I went to this doctor and he gave me some pills to take." Ed speaks with a deep, raspy voice that matches his large frame. He fills the entire easy chair, and leans toward me as he sits. His eyes are clear, and he looks directly at me when he speaks.

"Did you take them?" I asked.

"I did for a few days, but then I threw them away," Ed replied with a smile.

"Why?" I inquired. I knew that this was not the first time Ed had been given medicine by other doctors, but I also knew that he had never taken any medication regularly.

"Well, they cut down on the sunshine," Ed replied. "I decided I'd rather come down here and watch you eat them apples."

"Cutting down the sunshine" was Ed's way of saying that

the pills emptied him of presence. He could feel how he was changed by the medication: he was not the person he normally was. Those around him could feel it, too. Our drug-abusing culture has reached the point where symptom relief (medically speaking) or escape (nonmedically speaking) is more valuable to us than presence. Ed's presence attracted attention. It made him known to the therapist. It also was more valuable to him than comfort. That choice is not easy for many of us to make. Nevertheless, taking that freedom *and* responsibility, we know that we are never inappropriate to ourselves.

We have all met an Ed at some time and place. He or she was perhaps a relative, a camp counselor, a schoolteacher, a friend, or, if we were lucky, one of our parents. That person was someone who was always *present* with us—so full of presence that our attention was riveted, not in a doting, but in a passionately attentive way. We felt alive and real inside us, knowing for the moment that we *were*, that we truly existed. Presence, in that way, is truly contagious.

Being real and present does not mean that we will not have, like Ed, our anxieties, hurts, fears, or angers. We will. Being real and present does mean that each of us takes responsibility for knowing how the choices we make affect whether we will be more or less whole. All ways of escaping, avoiding, or distorting our personhood move us further from wholeness.

Absence

Absence is one of the most common complaints we hear from couples in therapy. "He's never *there*." "I feel nothing from her." "I feel like I'm trying to see through some sort of glass case around him." "There's no real person in there."

While we know that these individuals' complaints are only half the story (since each has his or her own role in what is happening in the relationship), their sense of an absence in the relationship is, nonetheless, very real. Relationships often break down because one person demands to feel the reality of the other person. Or perhaps more sadly, relationships die *as relationships*, even if the two humans remain together, when the experience of being a person with each other is abandoned entirely.

A popular narrative about giving up on selfhood is the classic Christmas movie *It's a Wonderful Life*. While Capra's ostensible plot is that the protagonist learns what life would have been like had he not been born, what the angel actually shows him is what life would have been like *without his presence*. Jimmy Stewart's self-denial, seen early in the film, is acceptable only as it is a manifestation of who he really is. His presence *is* real. That presence is what allowed him to make such a difference in other people's lives. The extraordinary popularity of this film is an indication of how vitally concerned people are with the concept of presence in their lives.

At work, school, church, government, or volunteer functions, think what happens when, usually quite by accident, a group of people get together who meld to form a group presence with each other. Think of the communal spark that occurs. It is like what happens in good theater. The group uses that energy and experience to *do*. Powerful doing comes out of powerful being and, just as important, makes possible further powerful being. Presence evokes creativity. The power of healthy presence to transform our family or other groups is awesome.

Compare such power with the listless inefficiency of systemic groups which we so often become a part of. Committees have become a running joke in our culture. Most such groups (whether in government, school, business, church, or elsewhere) get nothing done. How many times have we sat in a group simply waiting to be somewhere else, asking ourselves what are we doing there, and being angry about the waste of our time?

What is much more difficult for us to realize is that we live exactly that way *with ourselves* much of the time. A committee just makes our individual inauthenticity public and visible. Group selficide is much easier for most of us to see than the ways in which we commit selficide ourselves. We seem to sense much more clearly in groups that living without *being* is a choice, and that we could do otherwise. We must heed what Marcus Aurelius advised long ago: "Remember that the sole life which a man can lose is that which he is living at the moment." Without being alive in the moment, we have no life. Thus is presence a vast window to experience. There is no wholeness for any of us without being alive in the moment.

10

THE SEVENTH WINDOW:
Freedom/Free Choice

Freedom and constraint are two aspects of the same necessity, which is to be what one is and no other.

—Antoine de Saint-Exupéry

Elizabeth and Norman are forty-one years down the path of a marriage that has been both a haven of strength and a battleground. In their sixties, they are on the verge of their retirement years and wonder where the path will now take them. Faced with the reality of constantly being around each other, they have become more aware of all the ways in which they do not know *how* to be with each other. Their children are grown and gone, no longer buffers between them. There is a deep sense within both of them that they would like to find a way of not needing a buffer, a desire truly to be with each other as they really are, despite the anxiety they feel.

In therapy, Elizabeth describes Norman as a "reluctant dragon," a passive captive who has agreed to come to therapy with her under the guise of reasonableness. I (Pat), however, have a different feeling. I sense that Norman is glad to be here, in some deep way hungry to change. The two of them agree that Elizabeth is the one who was enthusiastic to begin therapy, but I am not so sure. There is in her a certain sense of timidity, a hint of anxiety, a reluctance of spirit that seems to tell me, "I am eager for things to change but afraid about what my part in that change may be."

Norman is a quiet, compulsive man. He has been a successful businessman, more involved over the years with his business than with his marriage or family. He lives in a world of behavior and thinking, fairly alienated from his feelings, especially when he is around those whom he loves most. Although he has deep feelings, they usually go unexpressed and unshared in his relationships. He has been aware for some time of his wife and children's anger at his refusal to share himself, but he has never known what to do about it. He has felt completely trapped in his sense of responsibility, his need to be serious about life.

Elizabeth is very different from Norman. Living mostly in her feelings, she seldom refrains from expressing them, in the relationship and elsewhere. She has always been the communicator, the emotional expresser, for the marriage and the family. Although Norman has often viewed his wife as disorganized and irresponsible, he realizes that she has in many ways been the stabilizing influence in the family. Like many women of her generation, Elizabeth—left to parent and homemake essentially on her own—become overidentified with her mothering. This has been a source of resentment for Norman and, subsequently, a source of resentment in Elizabeth about his attitude toward family and marital issues. After the children left home, Elizabeth returned to school and then found a job selling real estate. She now has an active life of her own outside their home.

I liked this couple. I particularly liked the feeling I had that Norman was glad to be there; it seemed like a good omen of things to come. In one session, they were telling me about a recent benefit they had attended, a party for a charitable cause. Norman was describing the gathering with a great deal of genuine laughter, coming out of what seemed to be sincere delight on his part. He was describing how Elizabeth had been dancing, insisting that he had never seen her dance so freely before. He was telling me about a particular dance in which no one had danced with a partner, but rather solo, to some rock music. Norman said that she was absolutely *astonishing*. While looking gratified, Elizabeth was a bit taken aback by this. She said she did not quite understand why he was so surprised, that she had always secretly felt he knew that uninhibited part of her. But Norman immediately denied having *ever* seen her be that *free*.

At first Elizabeth looked hurt, then she said to me, "Perhaps I *can* understand that, because I've never been that free with him." When I asked, "Why not?" she explained, "Well, when he . . . I don't know if you've ever met anyone like this, Pat Malone . . . he counts 'one-two-three-four, one-two-three-four, one-two-three-four.' He's been doing that for all our years together and I've *never* been able to feel the kind of freedom to do what I did by myself the other night. And God knows I don't know if I would have been able to do it if I had known he was watching so closely."

I said with a smile, "Norman, is that true?" He was quiet for a few moments and then said, "Yes, it's true . . . but I wonder, I really wonder, how it would have been if she had just moved away and done some of the things around me that she was doing on the floor that night. Maybe years ago I would have stopped *counting*. I guess I haven't been able to be free all these years either. . . . Hell, I've counted everything . . . and she hasn't felt free enough to tell me to go to hell."

"Freedom," said Nietzsche, "is the will to be responsible to ourselves." In that sense, neither Norman nor Elizabeth have been free. They both have waited all these years for the other to set them free. Unfortunately, "freedom is not something that anybody can be given," as James Baldwin said in *Nobody Knows My Name*, "freedom is something people take and people are as free as they want to be." Norman and Elizabeth's wait has been long and the experiences missed have been many.

Freedom

There are few subjects in our society so much discussed yet so little understood as freedom. The notion of freedom elicits strong cultural, social, and personal reactions. However, a response is not the same as *understanding* freedom, and it is miles away from feeling or being free. In personal terms, being free means that we have to learn to choose. If our being with another person is dictated by that *other person* or by our concern with the response of that *other*, then we are not free. What determines *our* freedom is whether *we* choose it.

Mary and Phillip have been married for nearly thirty years.

Both are capable, responsible, and good people. When I (Tom) first met them, they were in their late forties. Phillip was a typical Westernized male, competent in most areas outside his family, but in his family life basically dependent. Unlike many men, however, he was not a particularly resentful dependent. Phillip was more placid than resentful; he just went along. Mary was a domineering and controlling woman who was usually correct about the issue at hand, but who, correct or not, dictated to both her children and her husband "the right way" in everything they did. This couple had come to therapy because of a surprising depression in Phillip. It may have been a surprise to them, but it was no puzzle to me.

They told me about the following episode: one evening they were going to dinner at a friend's house, driving through an old area of town with many circling streets. Phillip was driving, and they were late. Coming to a crossroads, he started to turn left. Mary said, "Good God, what are you turning left for, don't you know that's the wrong way? Turn right. We're already late!" Phillip had been listening to her controlling orders for many years, and suddenly he could bitterly taste the fact that for many years before that he had listened to his mother's orders. He stopped the car, and just sat there for a moment. "I need to think about this," he said to himself. So, pulling over to the side of the street and parking, he leaned his head on the steering wheel, closed his eyes, and thought.

His internal dialogue was the opening of a window for him, a movement into wholeness: "She's right. If I go to the left, it's much farther. If I go right, it *will* be faster. But then I'll just be doing what she told me to do, and that's what I've been doing all my life . . . and I know I'll be resentful about it and my stomach will burn for the rest of the evening. On the other hand, if I go ahead to the left, I'll be making a fool of myself just to avoid doing what she says, and I'll be resentful the rest of the night about *that* and not have a good time. What the hell should I do?"

Phillip said that suddenly something happened inside him that had never happened before. "I chose. It sounds almost ridiculous to be saying it, but I said to myself inside, 'You know it's silly to go to the left, when I can choose, regardless of her, to go to the right and get there much faster.' " With that, he said he felt wonderful. "I started the car, I backed up, and I started going to the right, and had not driven more than a quarter mile before

Mary said very angrily, 'Are you making fun of me?' I never will forget it. As stupid as it sounds, it was a turning point in my life. And part of what made it so important was I *knew* I hadn't done it to make fun of Mary. I'd finally just done what I wanted to do."

How do we choose to be ourselves in the world as it is? Free choice is the real issue in freedom. Freedom is not always getting our own way or always getting to do what we want to do. There could be no healthy closeness, no family, no society, no culture, under those conditions. Freedom is choosing to be us in the way that best allows us to be ourselves in each given circumstance. We must live as Thomas Merton described in *No Man Is an Island:* "We must make the choices that enable us to fulfill the deepest capacities of our real selves."

Freedom as Process

The history of the word *freedom* tells us much regarding what we have forgotten about the concept, for it most directly reflects *process*. Civilized man seems much more interested in end points than in process, usually to his own detriment. When we confuse end points and process, we lose track of meaningful choice.

For example, there is a real difference between making love and simply having sex. The same kind of difference exists between having a business and simply making money. We find another powerful example in our politics. When we allow the government to say, "Trust us, we'll take care of it," we live in a world of end points. "They" is no longer part of "us." And as we have seen so often over the past years, the methodology chosen to reach those end points (Watergate, Iran-Contra, etc.) is destructive of the very process that our government is supposed to be protecting. Freedom is most easily lost when we accept end points as justifications. What is true of us as a nation is just as true for each of us as individuals. When we search for end points to make ourselves secure, we end up undoing our ability to be free.

I (Tom) have a pet expression which some of my clients make fun of—as do some of my friends and family. I say that if you do not enjoy going to Cincinnati, there's absolutely no way you can enjoy being in Cincinnati. This aphorism essentially means that if we are not involved in the process, but simply in the end point, then we are not involved in life. We are not involved in being. If in driving to Cincinnati, we fight every time we stop to go to the bathroom because it will delay us, or we argue about where we are going to eat and then hurry our eating in order to get to our destination on time, if generally we spend the whole trip in psychological disarray with each other in the car, we would be foolish to expect that when we get to Cincinnati, we will enjoy the two days we are planning to spend there together. There is no way that we will not be, at the end of our journey, as we were along the way. There is no *choice* in such "end point" living.

The Definition of Free

The misfortune which befalls man from his once having been a child is that his liberty was at first concealed from him, and all his life he will retain the nostalgia for a time when he was ignorant of its exigencies.

—SIMONE DE BEAUVOIR, *For a Morality of Ambiguity*

The word *free* comes to us through old Celtic roots, meaning "dear." The blood kin of the master of the house were considered *dear* or *free*, as opposed to slaves. Since *choice* started out meaning "try," a *free choice* would be a "dear try." Thinking of a free choice as a dear try can help us understand why we must freely choose in order to experience. Experiencing requires a risking with faith. Risking with faith is in many ways a dear try. Without risking or faith there is no experiencing, only stasis.

Infants begin making dear tries at birth. Each new movement, every attempt to communicate, is a free choice. The organism moves to the natural expression of itself. It experiences the world and allows the world to experience it. Freedom is at first only the outward expression of our nature. Since movement and control are so large a part of the first developmental tasks, mobility becomes our first synonym for freedom. Free to move: "Don't fence me in." Sadly, many people never really grow to a more mature notion of freedom. As adults, we become anxious at having to choose to be free. We long for the time when it seemed natural. We forget that children also *choose*.

A good metaphor for this lack of growth in our culture is the traffic jam. We sit in our "mobility machines" unable to go anywhere. The perceived loss of freedom causes anger, frustration, hostility, impulsivity, even violence. I (Tom) had a revealing experience of this unhealthiness this past year. I drive to work on a busy thoroughfare. People routinely exceed the speed limit by twenty-five or thirty miles an hour. I generally drive just a little above the speed limit, and frequently stop to let people in from the sides, at shopping centers or apartment complexes. I've often noticed that my behavior makes some other drivers angry.

On this particular day, a man driving behind me obviously became very exasperated with my sedate speed. He kept blowing his horn, and when we had to stop at a light he pulled up behind me, got out of his car, came up to my window and said, "Why don't you get your ass in gear!" I replied, not being particularly upset, "Why don't you get a gear in your ass." He looked becalmed, puzzled, and as if something had happened that had never happened to him before. He walked back to his car scratching his head, got in, and when the light changed drove fairly calmly and at normal speeds behind me. I wonder. Perhaps he got in touch with the fact that he did have a choice—that he actually could enjoy driving to work. Of course, he may have just thought I was a kook, and that he would be wise to keep his distance.

Like a child physically pinned down, we struggle to break free. But such metaphors are not meant to be lived literally. Growth means increasingly being able to incorporate the complexity of closeness, family, tribe, society, and culture into ourselves without losing innate intimacy, the natural freedom we are born with. Sadly, we so often see the freedom of intimacy as a loss of control. But it is true that, as the character Zorba said in *Zorba the Greek*, "A man needs a little madness, or else . . . he never dares cut the rope and be free."

Taken literally, of course, Zorba's attitude would lead to chaos. If it were true that freedom was only mad license, no civilization would be possible among free humans. But taken metaphorically, it leads to healthy experience, to our giving up our *selficidal* ways of living. Unlike madness, true freedom is not license at all; it is the capacity to choose. Its pleasure is the empowerment choice brings.

The free choice of infancy is relearned in adolescence when the natural concept of freedom as mobility, present in the developing child, and given up in latency, is reinherited in adolescence as free choice. This reexperiencing of freedom as our own *choosing* to be how we are and who we are is an absolutely necessary step toward being adult. Natural freedom is transformed into disciplined free choice. Free choice is still the dear try, but it now exists contextually. That is, it recognizes *self* as existing in a relational world, a world of closeness as well as intimacy. In the healthy reexperiencing of adolescence, choosing comes to be valued above mobility.

Confusion about this transition is why so many of us currently feel a lost sense of freedom. The true loss is our inability to be the *chooser* in our own lives. The freedom of being the chooser is precisely why Phillip, as he made the right turn, felt so elated and real. In choosing, he had without anger negated Mary's control. That negation was what made her so angry: "Are you making fun of me?" She had been choosing for him for years. She experienced anger both at losing that control *and* at her having had to be his chooser for so long.

Sadly, a literal inability to choose is imposed on far too many humans. Political prisoners, the oppressed, the ill, those in war zones, those starving or so poor that survival is tenuous are not free to make many of the choices in their lives that are taken for granted by others. Their choice is essentially narrowed down to life or death. But most of us, far more fortunate, willfully renounce the role on our own. In ordinary living, we give away choice in hopes of getting something else. The something else is usually a passive security, as it was with Phillip. The loss is real, but the gain imaginary. Most important, our sense of the loss of freedom that accompanies our refusal to be the chooser in our own lives is terrifying—terrifying to humans who feel no freedom, and terrifying to all who fear for humanity in general.

The desire for mobility will always remain real on a primitive level. We *do* feel freer hiking in the Rockies than sitting in a traffic jam in Chicago. Mobility, as in the hunter-gatherer tradition, is undoubtedly an integral part of our unconscious. Closeness, which is to say our communal living, requires the transformation of our sense of freedom. Civilization itself forces the transition. By the institution of homes, cities, property, possessions, and systems, we have made a maturing transformation necessary. To return to the metaphor of the traffic jam, we must learn that we have a choice even if we cannot move. The dear try must be reclaimed. We have to experience our choosing even in our least mobile moments.

Commitment and Freedom

Abe has had difficulties in relationships with women for many years. Starting in his adolescence, he has not been able to maintain a long-term relationship. Whenever the issue of commitment arose, Abe would move on. As a teenager, he was not really conscious that this feeling was determining the pattern of his dating. He had reasons for why each experience turned out the way it did. But now, as he is approaching his thirtieth birthday, he is much more aware of his anxiety and fear.

Abe experiences being committed to someone else as a loss of freedom. He feels as if he is somehow not free to be himself, not free to choose what he would choose, not free to go where and when he wants because he is bound to a primary relationship. A low-grade chronic anger accompanies these feelings and turns his relationships from joyful ones to ugly, painful ones. Abe ends up blaming each successive woman for his internal sense of constriction and deadness, as well as the lack of joy, play, and, eventually, failed sexuality that he feels.

He tells us: "I just end up feeling like I've been living *her* life all the time. Taking care of *her* feelings, meeting *her* needs. I burn out. They all say, 'I never asked you to take care of me. As a matter of fact, you're so angry and cold that I feel like I have to go around appeasing you all the time. If that isn't taking care of somebody, I don't know what is.' But that's not how it is to me. Somehow it always seems like a woman is like a child. I mean . . . I feel responsible for them most of the time."

He tells us: "Women say to me, 'You never seem to enjoy being with me. I feel so lonely inside, like I'm not worth your loving. Sometimes you make me feel like there's something wrong with me.' I don't mean to make them feel that way."

He tells us: "It's like I'm always holding up the world. I feel so responsible for everything I have anything to do with. In a silly kind of way women are no different from my job or paying bills. . . . I don't mean that badly . . . I just mean everything ties me down. I can't have any fun. I can't feel turned on when I feel tied down. I don't feel free, and that ruins it."

In his reflections, Abe is beginning a journey which will, if successful, allow him to regain free choice in his life. *Commitment is not the opposite of freedom* despite the fact that many of us live as if it is. *Commitment is a choice,* an expression of our freedom. Commitment means choice; it literally means to "put oneself with." To do so is to make a choice very different from that of being captured or imprisoned. Equating commitment with capture can leave us diminished as persons, as Abe diminished himself in his relationships. Abe says *he* feels responsible, but he lives with women as if they force him to be that way. He lives *irresponsibly.* He lives as if commitment makes him behave as he does.

In truth, Abe uses commitment to bind himself to his own past. He misuses the here-and-now in order to be somewhere else when he is with women. To do so is painful. It is a self-inflicted closing of our windows, and it makes any of us less than whole. In contrast, true commitment in the here-and-now is a free choice that brings affirmation to the chooser. That is always the power of the dear try. It allows us to expand ourselves. Every time a plant sends out a new shoot, every time a baby tries a new movement, every time you or I make a choice, growth happens. And happening is what choosing is all about.

When Elizabeth dared to dance so freely by herself, by herself but not alone and lonely, she sent out a runner to Norman. It wrapped itself around his feet. He *felt,* which is exactly what is difficult for such a thinking, behaving person as he was. He was excited, delighted, and aroused. He grew. He knew, in that moment, that the feeling meant he had married the right person. It was her dear try. He responded. They were in that moment intimately related. Because she had been freer and he more real, both were more congruent and present. Such growth is the whole purpose of relationship.

Choosing as an Active Art

I (Tom) became quite concerned a few years ago when those bumper stickers that said "shit happens" were popular. It was not that shit does not happen, because, of course, it does. But the slogan represented to me the trap we have fallen into culturally, the attitude that *life happens to us*. I was reminded of the time when my daughter Kareen, then eight, came home all dirty and scuffed-up. She had a long walk home from school and had just walked up the driveway looking quite disheveled. I asked her, "What happened to you?" She looked at me with exasperation and said, "Daddy, nothing happens to me, I happen to everything." Her remark represents a crucial phenomenological truth: *I am the chooser in my own life*. My response years later, when I saw the bumper stickers, was to have a few of my own made up. They were green on a white background and said, "I happen."

"Choosing" was something I (Pat) had to relearn in my adolescence. Dad used to say, "I actively choose to go to work each day" and I would say to myself, "Sure, just like I choose to go to school every day." He would explain to me that he made a point of asking himself each day if he would go to work. I would say that as far as I understood it, I did not have any real choice about going to school. He said he thought my choice about school was no different from his choice about work. This exchange came to a head in my senior year of high school. I got into the habit of turning my alarm off in the morning to get a few extra minutes of sleep. I would wait for Dad to come to my door and yell for me to get up—we rode together in one car in the mornings. Then I would hurriedly get ready.

One morning he came in my room and quietly told me, "This is the last time I'm going to come to wake you up. The car leaves at seven-thirty every morning. You can choose to go to school or not." I chose to go, that morning, and from then on. It took a while for me to realize that it had been the choosing that was my task, not the getting up early in the morning. Whenever I see his "I happen" sticker now, it brings that experience back to me with a smile.

Robert Frost said, "Caution is security. 'Bold' is freedom— the breaking thing. . . . Freedom lies in being bold." Being bold means actively choosing in our own lives. We cannot, of course, be bold all the time, for that would be capture just as surely as the refusal to risk is capture for the cautious and other-oriented, but we can risk ourselves enough of the time to keep us enlivened. "Be careless, intrusive, irreverent, and irrelevant" has been my (Tom's) advice to all of my careful, compulsive clients. It has also been my commitment when I see them in therapy. If I am careful, social, too respectful, and logical, they die as people in my care.

As one of his careful compulsives, I (Pat) have for years struggled over the issue with Dad. About school grades, he would say, "Make A's or B's or make F's, do it and enjoy it or don't do it and enjoy that, but don't bring me any damn C's or D's." I always sensed in his admonition to be careless and irreverent the same message. There is growth in such playful risking. Being careless, intrusive, or irreverent in a way that is either self-diminishing or goal-directed, is, on the other hand, at best self-destructive, and often overtly dangerous.

Risking is necessary to living as a whole person. It is the experience of choice. We forgo it only at great danger of self-diminishment. Not choosing shutters the window. In small individual moments (for example, not really letting the other person know what we would like to do tonight), our unwillingness may not seem particularly destructive. But as a way of life, not choosing is selficidal. If we never have a choice about where to go or what to do, we do not exist.

Carla is thirty-six, a sales representative for a leasing company, married for nine years and the mother of two. She comes into therapy "to talk about what I need to do about my marriage." Even in my (Pat) first moments of listening to her it is clear to me that Carla has long ago *chosen* to get out of the marriage. Her decision is tangible. Intellectually, she talks of non-communication, coldness, lack of touching, as if there were still something to be done, but her body and soul have already chosen. Like most of us, she more readily sees her husband's part in all the pain than she does her own. Therefore, she sees the failure *un-healthily*, as if it is *his* instead of *theirs*. She says she is trying to make up her mind whether to stay, but it is clear that she "moved out" years ago. Carla insists, however, on living as if she has not chosen. For years she has lived a life *that is not of her own choosing*. There is no way such a life can go well, either for her or for her family.

In our ordinary relational living, we can be sure we will get what we want, even if we have no idea what that is. Even if we loudly deny that what we ended up with is what we wanted, it is. We got it. We own it. We *chose* it. We have only to choose a better way to get what we want without diminishing ourselves. Being depressed or anxious or phobic is painful to us: it is also painful to others who care about us. If our depression is a way of being angry or dependent, it would be healthier to go ahead and honestly be angry or dependent. At least from that real position, that chosen position, we could learn something and change.

Physical, Behavioral, and Emotional Choosing

> We know in our practice of psychoanalysis that lack of freedom is shown in all aspects of the patient's organism. It is shown in his body (muscular inhibitions) and in what is called unconscious experience (repression) and in his social relationships (he is unaware of others to the extent he is unaware of himself). We also know experientially that as this person gains freedom in psychotherapy, he becomes less inhibited in bodily movements, freer in his dreams, and more spontaneous in his unthought out, involuntary relations with other people. This means that autonomy and freedom cannot be the domain of a special part of the organism, but must be a quality of the total self—the thinking-feeling-choosing-acting organism.
>
> —ROLLO MAY, Love and Will

Choosing is a whole-self activity. "I happen" means that as a total self I choose to be myself in the world. I choose it physically, behaviorally, emotionally, not just intellectually. Freedom is a congruent activity. A true dear try comes out of a congruence of all parts of ourselves. *Freely choosing is always a process event*, whereas end points (*security* in its myriad disguises) are antiprocess. The nonexperiential nature of security is clear. We do not experience while trying to stay the same. By its nature, experience makes us different. To choose freedom is always to risk the new.

Given that it must be a total organism that chooses, we are forced into dealing with the difference between *inner* and *outer* freedom. We frequently confuse the "I can do what I want" concept of outer freedom with the "I can be who I am" concept of inner freedom, as if the same rules did not apply to both. It is easy to lose contact with the process nature of both and forget that *as processes* they are the same.

Rollo May again, this time in *Man's Search for Himself*, said: "It requires greater courage to preserve inner freedom, to move on in one's inward journey into new realms, than to stand defiantly for outer freedom." It seems to us, however, that the very fact that we have come in some ways to see inner and outer freedoms as different is a manifestation of our problem. We create a dichotomy between the more primitive mobility (outer freedom in its various forms) and internal free choosing. Whether we see outer freedom in terms of defiance, heroism, martyrdom, or non-conformity, and inner freedom as free will, spirituality, reflectiveness, or self-definition, makes no difference. The fundamental nature of the *process of freedom* is the same. If the outer is easier than the inner, it is so because it is more closely connected to the mobility of the child. Moving is something you *do*. Internal freedom is how you *are*. Ours is a *doing* and not a *being* culture, so we see life more easily in that way.

By age twenty-nine, April has already had three different careers. She cannot seem to find what she wants to do or be. Her closest relationships are still with her family. At home, her parents do not understand her. They want her to settle down in some way, although they are respectful of her right to be herself. She is not a loner or an isolated individual, not a misfit or strange person. In truth, she is quite likable. But she does not understand herself any better than her parents do.

April tells us: "I've always known I really didn't like to get into a rut. You can use up years getting lost in just doing the same thing. You get tied down. Look at all the people that do it. I've always liked to get away. I go camping or hiking or maybe just traveling whenever I can. Those parts of me don't bother me. What's started to bother me is my relations with people. I don't seem to be able to stay connected for very long."

She tells us: "I've got lots of friends. I'm pretty sure they like me . . . but it's hard for me to get close, to hang around too long. I guess that's especially true with men, though I do have men friends. I never feel really comfortable, like I can let go and relax. I find myself needing to move on. I just don't feel free. I used to think maybe I didn't like people or was afraid of them, but that's not so. I like people. Whatever the problem is, it's in me."

April is in many ways like Phillip, in his car at the intersection, his head despairingly on the wheel, deciding whether or not to *be*. It *is* in April to choose wholeness, just as it is in any of us. While that may be difficult to accept, it also is a real gift to know.

Freedom and Being a Self

Diana is now forty-two. Married, mother of two children, she struggled with alcoholism for fifteen years before seeking help. The last two years have seen periods of sobriety with occasional slips, but she has remained unable to deal with how others will perceive her "being alcoholic." Consequently, she especially fears social situations and avoids them whenever possible. She does not want to have to say, "I don't drink." Invited to a party at her husband's employer's house, she feels she must go. Diana drinks club soda from a wineglass for the first half of the evening, but then is confronted by her host with an open wine bottle.

"Here, you need a little of this," he says pouring the wine into her glass while he speaks.

By the end of the evening, Diana is quite intoxicated. It is only later that she realizes how much the experience felt exactly like the times her uncle had abused her as a child.

Having a choice means we are free to change. We are free, if we will choose, to become our whole selves. If we face the shadow side of ourselves, we can become free. The most crucial issue in freedom is this reciprocal nature of selfbeing and free choice. We need to make free choices to learn to become our real selves. As we increasingly know our real selves, we have fewer choices of how to be. When we are totally ourselves, we have no more choice, because we are totally free.

There is a freedom in not just responding to others outside us. There is a freedom in not just responding to inner messages. But there is no freedom in not being our *selves*. There is only *selficide*, being less than whole humans. Free choice about our response to others means that our personalities are subject to our free choice, our free will. Some of us sense that this capacity is within us. Others of us disclaim even this level of self-responsibility. We can choose, for example, as to how we attend to others. We can choose how we are close. We can choose how we use or do not use reexperience for learning.

A good example of our power to change can be seen in Gary. At twenty-seven, confronted by his lover, Ben, about his perfectionism and judgmental postures, Gary decides he indeed does live in those ways and needs to change. He exercises his right and responsibility to choose. It is not easy at first, but with time he begins to catch himself when behaving in those ways. Then he learns to identify the mood that goes along with such moments. Eventually, he comes to know the feelings even before he has spoken, and with that knowledge comes the insight that the problem is his own needs, not other people's imperfections. He can then make a choice. For example, he can share his frustrations with his own perfectionism, or his fears of things being out of control, or any other more whole part of himself. He has experienced the freedom to become more him*self*—not to be confined by the personality that he has before always fostered.

Our internal character is also subject to choice, although fewer of us sense this truth because we see character as cast in stone. Indeed, "etched in stone" is pretty much what character actually means. And character *is* more difficult to change. The choice and the change must be profound. They will have to shake the foundations—not in the sense of being loud or violent, but in the sense of being deep and meaningful. Other people usually see such changes in us as being spiritual. We use the word *spiritual* here in its largest sense, meaning "of the spirit," whether traditionally religious or not.

A famous literary example of such spiritual change is the transformation of Ebenezer Scrooge in Dickens's *A Christmas Carol*. His change is total and real. His internal imprint has been altered. He has chosen to be a different person. Many of us, reading this story or watching an adaptation of it, will have tears in our eyes at the end and may attribute them to sentimentality or emotionality. We suggest that they more directly represent our innate response to a natural truth which, for the most part, we have lost contact with: *it is possible to choose character*. It is not easy, but the possibility is both joyful and frightening to us.

In contrast to personality and character, *self* is not choosable. It is only attainable. We can choose ways to be less than our *selves*, that is exactly what *selficide* is, but we cannot choose to be more than ourselves, better than ourselves, or someone other than ourselves. *Self* is our reality. Like having skin, needing to breathe, being part of what we eat, or existing in relationship to our environment, self is not choosable. *There is no freedom in not being ourselves.*

We assist the development of life by moving toward wholeness as a human being. Freedom is used to enlarge our selfbeing, not to run from our responsibilities. *Freedom is not license.* Not having to do something is not freedom—not having to go to school would not make me (Pat) free, not having to go to work would not make me (Tom) free. Most often the truly free person is a doer; he or she does what their selfbeing, what the enhancement of that selfbeing, requires them to do. *They choose to be themselves.* That may sound strange, but it is simply the underlying expression of individual choices. "I choose to go to work every day," or "I choose to be married to this person I am married to," or "I choose to believe in this spiritual path." Whereas wild license shackles us, "wild liberty breeds iron conscience" as Emerson wrote in *The Conduct of Life.* "Natures with great impulses have great resources, and return from far." Choosing empowers us.

Not Choosing as Choosing

There is an old cliché: "Not choosing is making a choice." Many who work in the large systems of business, government, or the military would admit that that is exactly the way most choices *are* made. As a culture, we have learned to fear responsibility and thus avoid choosing, as choosing makes us feel insecure.

A perfect example of this running from the responsibility of choice is seen in the way our institutions of higher learning have come to rely on standardized tests in making decisions about which students to admit into their programs. "I did not choose these people, they chose themselves by the scores they made," is the refuge of those who are unwilling to choose to choose. The policy is having profound effects on what kind of people we are educating to be our leaders. That process of selection then "trickles down" to affect what our cultural mores become. This happens despite the fact that we ourselves are unconvinced that our souls, bodies, or minds are best led by, or entrusted to, those who can "put up the best numbers."

Paralleling our cultural avoidance of responsibility, we attempt personally to avoid having to be active choosers. Entwined in our own private systems, we want our own numbers, our proofs, our assurances before we declare ourselves. We want to know we will get the job before we try for it; we want to know someone will love us before we risk loving her or him. We want to be secure at any price. But there is no one to take our "money," no guarantees to be bought, and we are still choosing *something* in our not choosing. As with our educational system, we are on a road to somewhere, complaining the whole way that it is not where we want to go, but unwilling to do what it would take not to go there.

Vern comes in to our office the first time to talk about whether he should come in. He cannot decide whether he needs help to figure out why he cannot make decisions and choices in his life. His behavior might be humorous except for the fact that it affects him at home, at work, and in his relationships with friends. At forty-two Vern cannot decide whether to stay with the job he has or do something else. He cannot decide whether to stay in the relationship he is in or get out. He cannot decide whether he drinks too much or not. Vern is not being silly; his pain is genuine and real. He perceives himself as being caught in a dilemma. "If only I had enough information, or knew how A or B would go, then I could decide." In short, Vern cannot choose. He cannot choose how he will be himself.

Vern's inability or refusal to choose is a choice in itself. It is a choice to not be himself. Perhaps he still hopes that some loving, all-knowing parent will decide for him, or that the same parent will not hold him responsible for any consequences of the choices he makes. By default, Vern makes a self-diminishing choice. Trying to stay secure keeps him from experiencing his own reality. Alice Miller speaks directly to this issue in *The Drama of the Gifted Child*:

> The inner necessity to constantly build up new illusions and denials, in order to avoid the experience of our own reality, disappears once this reality has been faced and experienced. We then realize that all our lives we have feared and struggled to ward off something that really cannot happen any longer: it has already happened, happened at the very beginning of our lives while we were completely dependent.

Sometimes we choose not to choose. But to elect not to choose is an *active* process, involving the work of choosing freely and the responsibility taken for accepting the outcome. Choosing is hard work. As Camus said in *The Fall:*

> Freedom is not a reward or a decoration that is celebrated with champagne. Nor yet a gift, a box of dainties designed to make you lick your chops. Oh, no! It's a chore, on the contrary, and a long-distance race, quite solitary and very exhausting.

Freedom does not come from outside us, either as gift or earned credit. Each of us individually must find in the depths of our being our own choices, our own dear tries. We must struggle through the maze of needs, desires, fears, hurts, angers, lusts, shames, sadnesses, and loves to choose those which most represent who we are. Doing so is a great deal of work. It is also solitary, because no one else can choose for us. "Everything that is really great and inspiring," Einstein said, "is created by the individual who can labor in freedom." We must labor; we must risk; we must choose.

Allowing a choice process to run its course requires one to risk. We must then have the self-responsibility to accept the outcome. This risk is often seen and felt most acutely in parenting, but it is no more real or prevalent in parenting than in the rest of life. If we reflect on our own childhood, we may remember distinctly when our parents took a risk, *by choice*, with us. It may have happened frequently or only once or twice, but it is a very unique and specific experience, and, often, remembered as a profound one.

Larry and Celia sent their oldest son, Darrell, off to college a year ago with some trepidation. They were unsure of his maturity and had doubts that he was ready to go a thousand miles away and live essentially on his own. They discussed it with each other and then together with Darrell, and actively decided to allow the process of Darrell's life to continue on the course he was choosing. It was a rough first year. Normally an A student, Darrell made C's both terms. It was a struggle for him to make friends, and he had problems coping with the alcohol and drug use which he found pervasive there. Darrell ended the year depressed and with his self-image hurting. Larry and Celia set up six therapy sessions for the family during the summer months.

"We all made this decision together," Celia said, "so we'll all deal with it together."

The family not only grew closer and stronger through the experience, but Darrell went back to the same school the following year and did much better. His dear try had worked in the long run. He had risked, and he had grown. He had chosen, and in the long run that choice had empowered him. His family had done the same.

In making dear tries in order to experience, we accept the consequences of those free choices. We surrender to the outcome of our living in the world as it really is. In doing so, we realize that the hoped-for security of trying to control outcomes before they happen is only a code word for nonexperience. The selficidal results are apparent in those who make default choices. They try to avoid the risk, the responsibility, and, therefore, the consequences of choice. Instead, they end up avoiding experience. Darrell will be okay. He will learn and grow because he and his family are living in the real world. They may stumble, and may even fall, but if they continue to choose freely, they will be as fully themselves as they are capable of being. That is what freedom is really about.

We can all fall, as Camus was so well aware. However, we can also soar, as he said in *Resistance, Rebellion, and Death*:

> When one knows of what man is capable, for better and for worse, one also knows that it is not the human being who must be protected but the possibilities he has within him—in other words, his freedom.

If we learn our limitations too soon and too well, we never learn our possibilities.

11

THE EIGHTH WINDOW:
Making Do/
Personal Surrender

Love is an attempt at penetrating another being, but it can only succeed if the surrender is mutual.

—OCTAVIO PAZ

The phrase "making do" has an idiomatic or slang usage that defines a wide and profound window to human experience. In essence, it means: "I've been all I can be and done all I can do. This is what there is, so I will make the best of the situation that exists." Making do, as we are using the phrase, carries this meaning without any sense of resignation and without any feeling of despair. True *making do* means that in this moment, in this immediate here-and-now, *this particular reality* is what exists, and my wholeness resides in my being able to be myself healthily while I make do with it. We never recognize this juncture beforehand. When we have done all we can, we can only decide at some point that we accept an end to trying and may then have the experience that is available. This quality of *openness* to the experience *available* is a matter of personal surrender.

Personal surrender is one of the foundations of any healthy closeness. Our awareness of the other person or thing enables us to accommodate in our own feelings and behavior to affirm those of the other. Living in this way we accept, and make the best of,

217

realities that are not exactly the realities we wanted or needed. We let go of our way to find *a* way to gain maximal experience and selfbeing from the reality we are faced with.

"Make the best of" does not mean giving up, or giving in. It does not mean we lose our own feelings or sense of ourselves. In fact, just the opposite occurs. We become more fully ourselves by *surrendering to ourselves*. We live with our feelings, knowing them for what they are, accepting them and ourselves for having them. Out of that self-acceptance comes the ability to allow our concern to be, for the moment, with the being of the other person or thing. This accommodating is not done out of guilt or fear. It is not done out of a sense of being social or proper. It is a chosen emotional and behavioral response, a way of being in our world in which we can give over to the other.

> *"Let me light my lamp"*
> *says the star*
> *"and never debate*
> *if it will help remove the darkness."*
>
> —RABINDRANATH TAGORE,
> "Fireflies"

The Inability to Make Do

At any given point in our lives, each of us appears to have some fairly consistent capacity to accommodate and personally surrender some percentage of the time. We then seem to need to get our own way or have our own needs met the rest of the time. It is important to differentiate the latter need from being intimate. We can be very confused about that distinction. Too many of us believe that it is necessary to get our way in order to be ourselves. It is not. In being intimate we do not *get our way* or *have our needs met*. Instead, *we are ourselves*.

Intimacy tends to last for only short periods of time, usually moments, and seldom more than hours. It is not the nature of intimacy to be a *maintained* position; it is always changing. In contrast, the healthy closeness represented in making do with a particular part of our life may last for days, weeks, or even longer in difficult circumstances. Most of our time living is spent in closeness, and we are whole only by choosing to live in *healthy* closeness. Choosing to surrender personally allows us to experience maximally and most fully be ourselves in the situation that exists. It is the *foundation* of healthy closeness. "To serve is beautiful," wrote Pearl Buck in *Men and Women,* "but only if it is done with joy and a whole heart and a free mind."

Bev always feels as if she is "serving," and, worse, that she has no choice about it. She spends most of her time moving back and forth between a chronic hurt and an equally painful chronic anger. They are her ways of relating to her world. When her husband, Nick, is late coming home from work, she is initially wounded and then explodes with rage. Whenever he is supposed to do something, in her mind he never does it correctly. If he buys her a gift, it is never exactly what she wanted. And when he makes love, it is never in the right place, at the right time, or in the right way.

Bev's struggle is not merely with her marriage. Her two children also live with her painful inability to accept life as it is. If her daughter does not get the role in the school play that Bev thinks she should get, Bev becomes so upset that neither she nor her daughter enjoy the play at all. Her eighteen-year-old son is forever strained by her insistence that he is dating the wrong girl. He seems unable to please his mother. It feels to him as if he cannot even *earn* his mother's love.

When they go on vacations, Bev complains about the location or decor of the hotel. This disappointment ruins the whole trip for her, as well as then ruining it for the rest of the family. Nick spends most of his time scrambling to keep her from being upset or from finding anything to become upset about. This in turn evokes anger and resentment in him, and he moves further away from any intimate relating to her.

Nick understands that Bev is insecure, that she takes all the things that "go wrong" as meaning that she is inadequate as a wife, mother, or person. Nick understands that on a deeper level she feels that if she were a good enough wife, he would get home on time, he would make love to her more often. He *understands* this, but is losing his ability to deal with her. He retreats into passive caretaking and thus loses his actual caring. What he cannot understand is why Bev cannot accept the world as it is and enjoy her life, herself, her children, and her husband. Nick, in his own way, however, can no more personally surrender than can Bev. He is simply quieter about it.

Learning to personally surrender means giving up *our* needs. Just as Bev must give up her need for her world to constantly affirm that she is lovable, Nick must give up his need for his world to tell him that his love is worthwhile. Working together, they may be able to learn mutually how to make do with the *world that is*. If not, and if the relationship is going to survive, one will need to find the courage to surrender on his or her own. Out of that surrender, the other may finally learn to become more whole also.

At twenty-six, Ralph goes to stay with his parents while recuperating from surgery. He is healing fairly well when he returns as scheduled to see the doctor for a follow-up. After some cleaning of his wounds, Ralph comes home nauseated with a migraine headache and during the day vomits several times. He calls the doctor, who tells him that the reaction is fairly normal, things are okay, and that he just needs to rest. Ralph tries to rest, but his mother insists on feeding him. She comes into his bedroom every half hour or so with something different, "one of your favorites," on a tray. He keeps refusing the food, but his mother persists. It is as if she does not hear him, as if he does not really exist.

Ralph remembers that it has always been this way. He can feel the young boy inside him trembling with frustration. "You don't see me. You don't know how much I love you. Everything I do is wrong." They are old and strong feelings. Sadly, she cannot see him as the person he is, cannot let him be himself as he is. Her own needs override what is outside her, override the needs of the other person. The distortion in their relationship multiplies; she feels rejected once more, and Ralph forgets, as he has for so many years, how, as a child, he would love, and give, and touch joyfully before he gave in to just reacting to her.

I (Tom) had a couple in my office not too long ago, a man and woman in their thirties who had a painfully conflicted relationship in which both felt unloved and uncared for. Their intercourse—on all levels—had degenerated to open hostility. On this particular day they brought along their youngest child, Bobby, who was five years old. They had been unable to arrange for a baby-sitter and while they were warming up by blaming each other for that mix-up, Bobby sat on the floor with an activities book and began coloring a rabbit orange. I sat silently in the chair between Bobby's parents. After a few minutes of their quarreling, Bobby said while continuing to color, "You guys don't hafta fight today. I'm here." He intuitively knew more about surrendering than either adult. He was simply asking, "Why don't you two just be here, too?" He was more than willing to give up *his* needs.

The Capacity to Make Do

I (Tom) have felt for years that when I have an experience where I have failed to be intimate when I really needed to be, and instead have chosen to be close, I am subsequently quite aware that something is wrong. I feel a disquietude about myself, and have a vague dissatisfaction in my memory of the experience with the other person. I feel in some profound way that I have violated my personal aesthetic code. I feel a little bit of disrespect for myself. Having had this feeling on numerous occasions has helped me increasingly to attend to my subjective sense of my *choice* to be close or be intimate. When I desire to create something new and different from what is presently in the relationship, I must not choose closeness. Creating the new only occurs when one is truly intimate in relationship. Intimacy provides a relationship with new dimensions and energies.

I (Pat) feel a similar disquietude in the choice between *healthy* closeness (making do, pursuing healthy needs) and *unhealthy* closeness (pursuing my own security needs, my own agenda). When I do not personally surrender and accommodate to the other in situations in which what I really wanted was to strengthen my relatedness to them, that same sense of self-violation is present.

I had an enlightening lesson about that struggle a few years ago. My seventeen-year-old daughter, Shannon, came home one evening after I had arrived home from work and was already in the family room writing. My wife, Elaine, was working late at the theater at school, so I had been home alone. Shannon walked by the door to the family room and, with a short "hi," went upstairs to her room. I continued writing, but, after a while, I wondered why she had not come back down. It was unlike her not to be downstairs talking or doing things. After another half hour, I found myself worried and wondering. "She's seemed a little down lately. Maybe I should go up and make sure she's not depressed or having a problem."

But then another voice in me spoke up. "If you always go up and help or interfere, she'll never learn to work through things on her own. It gives her the message that she can't take care of herself. So don't go up there." The two voices in me continued to debate. Gradually it became clear to me that if I went upstairs at that moment I would be responding to my own internal needs, not Shannon's. Later on she came downstairs smiling; she had been talking to one of her friends on the telephone. I was glad that I was *intimately* aware of her but had healthily chosen to *let her be.*

The capacity to make do—to choose healthy closeness over unhealthy closeness—and then to make a self-enhancing choice between being close in that way or being intimate, is an essential quality in healthy living. It is essential to our wholeness. I (Pat) grew by surrendering, by confronting my own insecurities, and in so doing gave Shannon room to grow. If a person is growing, this capacity for making do will increase. There will be fewer instances where having our own way seems vital to our sense of our own worth. We will be able to accommodate more easily to realities outside us while remaining in touch with ourselves. A capacity for total surrender, a total openness to experience, might have been possible for Jesus, Buddha, or other God-level beings, but as ordinary humans, we can only grow toward that spiritual state as we increase our capacity to choose to personally surrender.

Making Do

Many years ago, I (Tom) was a psychiatric consultant for Atlanta's police department. I was called one day to see a man in his late sixties who had been arrested. I was usually summoned for serious and violent cases, so I asked the sergeant what this man was in jail for. He said he had been arrested for vagrancy. Somewhat baffled, I went to the jail and was told that the man was in the large holding cell where they usually kept fifteen or twenty prisoners awaiting disposition. When I arrived, this particular prisoner was, indeed, in the cellblock, but they had removed all of the other prisoners. He was seated on the closed commode, fully dressed. He had a full head of white hair and looked elderly, but strong and fit. He wore clothes that looked expensive in origin but were now worn and old—including a vest that made him look like an old banker down on his luck. Seated around him on the floor in a semicircle, just like students, were six policemen of all ages. They were all talking with him.

I went in and introduced myself. No one said anything in particular to me, and the policemen did not move, so I sat down on the floor with them. I mostly listened. They talked intimately to the man, and he responded. They told him about themselves and their lives—their families, marriages, loves, fears, and desires. They asked him about his life—about what he had learned and how he might share those things with them. After a while I could understand why they were talking so personally, so intimately. He gave himself over to them completely. Each one he spoke with felt *personally* attended, even though he spoke to all. This man's very being was an invitation. He could surrender his own need to the other so completely that it was tangible.

I remember one moment of that meeting which may, at least as a metaphor, convey to you the quality of these interactions. One of the policemen smoked. A man who was seated near him also smoked but did not have any cigarettes. He asked the first policeman for a cigarette. The policeman took his pack out and bumped it on his hand until one cigarette emerged, and then he pushed the others in so there was one cigarette protruding from the rest. He pointed the package at the other policeman who took the one cigarette and lit it and began to smoke.

Later the same policeman asked him for another cigarette. The man with the pack was seated right next to the old man on the commode. Our prisoner reached over, picked up the pack of cigarettes, reached across to the man who had asked for them, lifted the man's hand, put the pack in it, and closed it. Then he straightened back up on the commode. Not a word was said. No one laughed. I do not think in his presence that anyone consciously thought anything about it. It did not need to be commented on, and it certainly did not need to be explained.

The story is simple, but the experience was profound. The man made do with the world as he found it, and did so in a way that empowered others. He allowed others to be as they were. He communicated with his being what it meant to give over to the other person. The cigarettes were not important; the message of surrender was.

After sitting there for a while, I had to leave. The old man walked with me to the door and said that if I were concerned about him, he would give me a number to call. It was the office of his son in New York. He said the call might relieve any worries I might have. I spoke to the administrator at the jail and found out they had called me because they did not understand why this wonderful man was a vagrant, and wanted me to try to get him safely home. The following day I called New York and talked to his son. I told him I was calling to inform him that his dad had been arrested for vagrancy and was in jail. The son laughed. He said, "Well, that should be an interesting experience for Dad. I don't think he's ever been in jail before." The son did not seem concerned, but at the same time I had the feeling that if there was any way he could help me, he would be delighted to. I also had the feeling that he did not feel his father needed any help. He did tell me that his father was a successful businessman who had retired some three years previously, after his wife died, and that he now spent most of his time walking about the country. Presently, he was walking from New York to Florida, and had made it as far as Atlanta.

I went back to these group meetings in the holding cell for the next few days. I do not know when I have learned as much about human relationships, without knowing consciously what I was learning, as I did in those visits to the bullring in that Atlanta jailhouse. After a few days, I was informed by the sergeant that the man was no longer there. When I asked where he was, the sergeant smiled and replied, "Probably spending the weekend with the chief." I never saw the old man again, but I have never forgotten him. This man convinced me of the truth of the fact that the more one is capable of making do, the more one is capable of being intimate. He chose to accommodate his being to others, while never losing his own direction. He was full of selfbeing.

Self-full and Selfish

There is probably nowhere a greater confusion in our perceptions of human relations than in understanding the difference between being *self-full* and *selfish*. Nowhere does this distinction become clearer than around the issue of personal surrender or making do.

We usually think of personal surrender as giving in or letting others have their way. Perhaps we see it as placative, as in losing an argument. We may console ourselves by calling our surrender a noble gesture, but it never quite loses its connotation of defeat. Likewise, making do is often seen at best as toleration. Even more often, however, we think of it as just getting by, or as accepting second best. Again, the connotation is negative even if the alleged motivation is in some way supposed to be positive. Such split responses are all too common in most of us. We are taught that we are supposed to be good even when we do not want to be. And, of course, this is part of the reason why we then do not want to be good. We end up thinking that to be selfish is bad, but so is surrendering. What are we to do? We do not know because we are not taught what Sophocles wrote in *Oedipus at Colonus:* "The good befriend themselves."

Being good when we do not want to be is not being good at all, and it certainly is not being healthy. Being good because you *should* be contains no gift either to self or to other. We feel no empathy for other people when we resent letting them have their way. We learn nothing new from them, or about them, or about ourselves. We simply feel our resentment over and over. We remain the same.

In just that way, it is not in one's *self-full* interest to be *selfish.* The two concepts are exact opposites. Many classic stories, such as George Eliot's *Silas Marner*, show how the route to self-fullness actually may be the overcoming of selfishness. Such growth is a traditional theme in literature, folklore, and mythology. The path of the heroes teaches us that by letting go of *our* need, we may learn from the other person's need. We give the gift of our accommodation, and, in return, we gain the chance to learn, change, and grow.

Personal surrender, in this sense then, is not *giving in;* it is *giving over*. It is the recognition that our being fully ourselves includes our willingness to allow the other the relational opportunity to be herself, himself, or itself with us. The old man in jail lived out that truth, a volitional giving over to the other's insistent and immediate need to share himself with you. Such giving over is not passivity, placation, or losing. It is an active, chosen, personal response that sets aside our own personal agenda and invites sharing. It is a *being with*, which is reciprocal to *being*. It is the other face of life.

Making do is the recognition that the experience of the given moment is the maximal experience available to us at that particular moment. It is the real world manifestation of presence. If we are doing what we are doing, doing it at the time and place we are doing it, and doing it with the other we are doing it with—that is, if we are honestly in the here-and-now as ourselves—we can do no more. We can do no better at that moment, given who we are at that moment, where we are at that moment, with whom we are at that moment, than to be who we are. Experience always peaks; that is the nature of real experience. To analyze or comment about what might have been felt, done, or thought is simplistic and a denial of the inherent nature of experience. Experience, if nothing else, is ordinary.

Thus, personal surrender is neither a toleration of the other, nor subjugation to or defeat by the other person. It is, instead, a recognition of being a fellow traveler. We exist only in relationship. To have relationship there must be another. To have real relationship that other must be real, not just to us but to him- or herself. When we are healthy, we try to maximize how we are with that other, *and* maximize how that other is with us. We will *give over* to that other person for our own growth and joy.

Our growing means recognizing that we need both the close *and* the intimate experience. Healthy closeness is reciprocal with intimacy. Neither has any meaning without the existence of the other. Making do and personal surrender are the cornerstones of healthy closeness, just as acceptance and naturalness are the cornerstones of true intimacy. Being whole requires both.

Living in the Real World

In the film *Some Like It Hot*, Marilyn Monroe says to Tony Curtis, "I always get the fuzzy end of the lollipop." Her remark sums up a typical adolescent philosophy of life. The first response of the child having to moderate his or her natural impulses in order to live in the outside world may well be to feel that he or she is getting less than a fair share ("the fuzzy end of the lollipop"). But to become a healthy adult, we must grow beyond that feeling.

The major thrust of parenting in the child's years from six to thirteen is to foster this process of socialization in the external world. The confined socialization of the earlier years in the immediate family is replaced by the need to deal in and with larger and less controllable external systems. We, as parents, can control how we react to our child at home but have little control over how a teacher, a peer's parent, or other outside adults will do so. This thrust in parenting coincides with the movement of the child into the literal world of others, away from the home. Involved in this change is an inevitable blunting of the intimate instincts of the natural child. What is crucial, however, in the development of the *healthy* human, is that the socialization be done in some way that does not diminish the child's *self*.

The only way such healthy socialization can occur is through the child's learning personal surrender and gaining the openness to experience that comes with the ability to make do. An example can be seen in a mother's responding to her child's question. The mother says to her four-year-old son who is talking on and on, "I'm glad to listen to what you are telling me about cars because it's interesting. But you started out by asking me to tell you why the car had to go into the shop. I can't tell you until you *want* to listen." Allowing the child to learn to surrender his own needs in a way which does not diminish his self is helping to build the whole person. Confirming the child's personhood in this way is far different from interrupting him with, "If you don't want an answer, don't ask"—or its many emotional equivalents.

As children move into adolescence, the consolidation and refinement of such socialization takes place. Some of us will learn to make do, to personally surrender and be healthily close. Sadly, some become distorted, having instead been taught appeasement, placation, intimidation, angry toleration, or unhealthy dependence. In the latter cases, the unhealthy closeness will become increasingly manifest in our behaviors as we reach adulthood. Equally destructive is a rebellious independence, which is also reflective of an unhealthy closeness. There are few meaningful differences between the self-sacrificing appeaser and the self-destructive rebel. Neither knows how to be *himself*. That lack of knowledge can be crucial for our adulthood. Adolescence is both the trying ground and the proving ground for *how* we will live in the real world, *how* we will make do.

The healthy human needs an increasingly profound awareness of the other, whether that other is a great teacher, a hostile person, or a corporate policy. Such awareness will be an integral part of the decisions we make. "Courage is required not only in a person's occasional crucial decision for his own freedom," writes Rollo May in *Man's Search for Himself*, "but in the little hour to hour decisions which place the bricks in the structure of his building of himself into a person who acts with freedom and responsibility." Awareness of others is half the foundation of our building, the companion of awareness of ourselves.

The Cult of Personhood

Freedom and responsibility are in many ways synonyms for intimacy and closeness. The whole person has both. They are not opposites, but a pair that exists meaningfully only as a pair: awareness of self, awareness of other. It is unfortunate that many current attacks, particularly by those writing about psychology, have blamed selfhood for selfishness. Such writers have begun decrying the cult of "self" or "personhood" as the villain in the breakdown of marriage, family, morality, and social systems in contemporary society. Identifying obsessions with "self" and the emphasis on "personhood" as the culprit in our downfall, they see the lack of commitment, community, and personal integrity as the result of the search for "personal fulfillment."

What an unfortunate choice of words. We could not agree more with such woeful appraisals of our current society, or even with these authors' sense that there are *personal* reasons for what is happening. But we disagree vehemently with their choice of words. The cult of "self" has nothing to do with *self* at all. What they mean is the cult of "me," as in "Let me have my way," or "Give it all to me." The cult of "personhood" has nothing to do with *personhood* at all; it is the cult of "I," as in "I want to get my way," or, "I demand to get what I want." These ways of living have nothing to do with being a whole person, that is, being a *self-full* person. Quite the contrary. They are destructive of personhood, of selfbeing, of healthily being in the world. Neither hedonism nor narcissism lead to selfbeing. Selfishness is nonexperiential. It diminishes us as persons. It is *not* the case that our current cultural problems exist because we have too many fully actualized, *self-full* persons.

Our problems exist because we are oversystematized, overcontrolled, and overly close in an unhealthy way. Too many of us are neither truly close nor intimate. We are more interested in selling ourselves as persons than in finding or being ourselves as persons. There is in contemporary society little interest in or inspiration for moving into *self, personhood,* or *personal fulfillment.* We misuse these words to describe the unhealthily close, co-opted person's dependence or rebellion. Either is a secure life position. It avoids the hard work and painful honesty that real self, real personhood, and real personal fulfillment require. It avoids the truth that selfishness is never self-full, greed is not part of being an actualized person, and a lack of ethics, morals, and commitment can never lead to personal fulfillment, any more than thinking we have a corner on ethics, morals, and total commitment can ever lead to personal fulfillment. These are all *captured* life positions.

Betty is a thirty-year-old woman who works as a sales representative in a small but growing local corporation. Several years ago she met Walt, and they have now lived together for two years. His career as an accountant has also gone well. They both work at least fifty hours a week, but still frequently eat out and go to concerts and plays. The rest of their leisure time is spent exercising at a health club and entertaining their friends. Their combined incomes afford them all the creature comforts. It would seem an enviable life.

Nevertheless, Betty shows up in our office without telling Walt she has made the appointment. She says, "I feel foolish even being here. I don't have anything to complain about. I mean, I've got everything I could want." After a moment of silence, her face begins changing, the tears start coming, and she chokes out, "So why do I feel so bad? Why am I so unhappy?" The tears begin in earnest as her long concealed hurt starts surfacing. After a few minutes, she composes herself and whispers, "I'm sorry, I don't know where that came from."

Betty feels that her life has no real meaning. As she talks, she shares her fear that if somehow she let Walt know this feeling, he would stop loving her, as if in some way it would tell him that *he* is meaningless. She is successful, she is intelligent, she is comfortable, but she feels no real connection in her life. She does not feel *related* to Walt, nor to anyone or anything else. As fulfilled as she appears to be in her life, she does *not* have an obsession with *self*, *personhood*, or *personal fulfillment* in any real sense. She has, in fact, a deficit of all three. It is her very search for a way to be the real person she is that has brought her to therapy.

Betty is not selfish, nor is she lacking in morals or commitment. People who are frankly hedonistic or narcissistic are almost completely alienated from self and personhood. They seldom ask for help and even less often are able to see their own roles in what is wrong in their lives. Betty is simply lost. She has enough personhood to know that she is lost, and to hurt with the feeling, and to know that it is the part of her that needs growing and expanding. Neither "me" nor "I" is a substitute for self. Most of us know that truth in our souls, but many of us are afraid to face it.

Golden Rules

What real *self* and *personhood* entails is the clear experience that we are, as humans, more alike than different. Who we are exists in a relationship to others *of which we are a part*. Our basic need to be free to be ourselves is mirrored in the other's need to be him- or herself. Our basic need for acceptance is mirrored in the other person's need for acceptance. The same goes for choice, freedom, time, and space, and all the other requirements of being.

The simplest statements of this truth of being human are the golden rules:

> CONFUCIUS in 500 B.C.: What you do not want done to yourself, do not do to others.

> ARISTOTLE in 350 B.C.: We should behave to our friends as we would wish our friends to behave to us.

> JESUS CHRIST: Therefore all things whatsoever ye would that men should do to you, do ye even so to them.

There are many other formulations of the same principle in the literature of humanity. They reflect the fact that we are all of the same cloth. For all of us, intimacy and closeness are names for halves of an inseparable whole. Closeness without intimacy is not healthy closeness. It is unchosen dependency, or rebellious independence, and is always a false search for security. This is why in *healthy* closeness, we cannot give away our own selfbeing.

Kevin comes to therapy seriously contemplating divorce but unable to comprehend any reason for it. He has been married for five years and has a two-year-old son. He wants to know why he would wish to divorce a woman who worships him:

"My wife adores me. She was becoming a concert violinist when we married. She has given that up for me. When I spoke of divorce, she said she would do everything she could to make *my* life better and more fulfilling. I was afraid to leave home that day. I thought she might commit suicide before I returned."

Kevin's wife is not being intimate or loving with her adoration. Nor is she personally surrendering in her relationship to Kevin. By giving herself away as a person, she gives no gift to anyone else. Such pseudointimacy—"I love you so much that I will give my life over to you"—is neither making do nor an openness to experience in the relationship. It is a life position driven by neediness—dependency and fear—not wholeness.

Intimacy without closeness, that is, *pseudointimacy*, is an escape. It bears no resemblance to the reality of love. We are not personally surrendering by sacrificing ourselves to others. On the contrary, truly making do *includes* our own selfbeing. A wholeness of personhood comes only out of such a wholeness of experience, and that requires being ourselves *and* supporting the selfbeing of the other. True intimacy supports *being with* the other. It empowers *both* people.

Actualizing and Being With

Out of our ability to experience our likeness to others comes our ability to actualize ourselves as persons. Learning to give over to the other person's need to be a self allows us to experience our own similar needs. Making do with the here-and-now as presented to us allows us to experience ourselves living in that here-and-now. We make do or surrender in order to experience fully who we are, to maximize our own persons and our own growth.

Actualizing ourselves, becoming fully who we really are, is only possible in the context of our relatedness to others. Selfishly bending the world to ourselves, in any form, guarantees nonexperience. Such bending distorts the other, and the act of so distorting the other distorts us.

> But ceremony never did conceal
> Save to the silly eye, which all allows,
> How much we are the woods we wander in.
>
> —RICHARD WILBUR, "Ceremony"

We must be intimate and close within ourselves as well. The same dynamics that produce a healthy balance of intimacy and closeness with another are necessary for the balance of intimate moments and moments of closeness within ourselves. The intimate moment may involve experiencing some new feeling, new awareness, and a sense of new being, different from our usual selves. Such an experience happens not uncommonly in our dreams. It is equally true that at other times while awake and alone, we feel a loving and accepting delight in ourselves as we are. We feel no sense of need or of having to be different, but simply a full-souled acceptance of who we presently are. *We make do with ourselves in our world.* That experience is one of closeness to ourselves.

In both instances we have a sense of relating to ourselves as another. That particular feeling is very difficult to describe. It is not at all like self-alienated ways of looking at ourselves. We must distinguish between such *nonexperiences*, which are unhealthy and prevent our being close and intimate with ourselves, and healthy self-relating. Obsessing, giving ourselves pep talks, false reassurance, negative self-talk, rationalizations, self-pity, and other such nonexperiences wherein we make objects of ourselves, do not lead to wholeness.

Vail is forty years old, a manager in a large local firm, on track to become one of the company's executives. She is aggressive and driven and comes into therapy only because her husband is threatening to leave her.

"He says I don't care anything about him or the kids, but I do. Actually, what he says is that I put work first. That's true. Hell, I don't know what he wants. He says I'm more interested in money and getting to the top than in being with him. But I'm doing it for us. What does he really want?"

She tells us: "If you don't keep at it . . . well, only a few get to the top. Then you can slow down and do other things. He was furious last month because I couldn't go on vacation with them. We had set up a trip to go to Disney World . . . but I had a big project come up. I told him to go ahead, that he and the kids could have a good time. He was furious. It's like he doesn't understand what's important. I can go to Florida anytime."

Vail's way of living in the world is much like her way of dealing with her family. The notion of giving over to the other, of surrendering her own needs, is totally foreign to her, whether the relationship is with her husband, her children, her friends, or people at work. She is much the same with her possessions; she fights with them all. She drives as if her car and its machinery are her adversaries, becoming furious with anything that does not work as it should. She needs to impose her sense of the world on all her others, not directly as a dictator, but compulsively, frenetically, aggressively, as an unhealthy human. She never can make do with the situation she finds. She must bend it to her needs. She never relaxes and allows herself to be part of a process.

Consequently, Vail *experiences* little. She misses the reality of her growing children and their playful loving of her. She misses the reality of her husband's desperate desire to touch and be touched. She misses the reality of her friends, home, and neighborhood; she misses it all. In like fashion, she misses being Vail. She feels she is *giving* in all her drivenness, but does not understand that she is selficidally *giving herself away* as a person instead of *giving over* in a growthful way. She is not actualized as a person. She has no awareness of her real self, her real life, her real world. She does not know how to *be*.

The Plains Indians of "precivilized" America had the spiritual concept that humans were first energy-beings who, God-like, knew everything—except one. They did not know limitation. So they came to earth in human form to learn limitation, or, as we would put it, to learn personal surrender, to learn how to make do, to learn that being fully who we are requires that we participate in the world in a way that *healthily* allows the other to be who they are. Healthy allowance does not mean accepting murder, crime, injustice, debasement, or cruelty. They are *not* what we are talking about. Full experiential humanness recognizes full being in any other, and *just as easily* recognizes what is nonexperiential, inhuman, and destructive of life and growth. Limitation may mean joyfully learning to walk as slowly as our child. It never means learning to allow someone to hurt our child.

We are not talking about issues of criminal or sick behavior but about how each of us adapts in our relatedness to the ordinary situations in our lives: for example, the child who has some problem or disability (such as a birth defect or limitation) which we ourselves then allow to diminish our experience with that child; or the spouse or lover who has needs we respond to by becoming less present; or the job that does not go as we wish so that we turn off, doze off, or run off; or the situation that will not be as we wanted, so we will not be as we perceive the situation wants us to be; or even the rainy day that we will not enjoy because we had wished for a sunny one. To be able to give over, to make do, *is* a very difficult adaptation for most of us to make.

That adaptation is most difficult at the very times when it is most profoundly needed. Can one personally surrender in the case of a spouse with a serious illness, the death of a child, or falling into acute poverty? Yes. We can realize, for example, that we can sit with our spouse who is dying, holding her body next to our own, and surrender our need for her to live so that she may deal with her dying in the fullness of her own personhood. It is during such terrible moments in life that the power of personal surrender is most manifest. If we remember that giving over is not giving in, then we will see how surrendering our personal needs empowers us. The person giving over never stops caring or trying. Being the healthiest self we can be in those moments, being grounded in the reality of our world even if it is terribly painful, is the best response available. There is no meaningful alternative to being ourselves. The question in any situation—even the most devastating—is always *how* we will be ourselves. The openness to experience found in personal surrender maximizes our wholeness and thus is the best adaptation possible.

Duty and Courage

Understanding personal surrender, giving over, in terms of actualizing oneself and maximizing the experience one has in life, brings us to a different understanding of what duty and courage are. Instead of "doing what you should do" (duty) and "facing what you are afraid to face" (courage), we would redefine duty as "being who you are" and courage as "doing what you are."

Healthy duty ceases to be owed conduct. In any situation, the maximal us possible may be found in chosen duty. *But it must always be chosen.* Blind duty has caused untold horrors and suffering. Chosen duty is part of the basis for healthy closeness in a constructive system, regardless of whether the system is a marriage, a family, a community, or a nation.

What does it take to live out such healthy closeness? It takes healthy courage. In *Letters to a Young Poet,* Rilke spoke of this type of courage:

> We must assume our existence as broadly as we in any
> way can; everything, even the unheard of, must be possible in
> it. That is at bottom the only courage that is demanded of us:
> to have courage for the most extraordinary, the most singular,
> and the most inexplicable that we may encounter.

To *"assume our existence broadly"* is fully to be what we are, and courage allows us to live in that way. The old man who had been arrested for vagrancy had the courage to be himself in the world he found. He was courageous in that *being* sense.

Experiential courage has nothing to do with bravado or machismo. If anything, it is a gentle phenomenon. The mother and father caring for their sick child, the lover facing the death of a loved one, humans who quietly live up to their duty to community and world—it is these people who exemplify real courage. "Courage is the best slayer," Nietzsche wrote, "courage which attacketh: for in every attack there is the sound of triumph." Personal surrender and making do are active/attacking ways of being in the world, an insertion of *self* into the here-and-now, a participation which, regardless of the outcome, will always contain the sound of triumph.

Originally, it may be difficult for people like Betty or Vail, or for you or me, to see ourselves as lacking courage in our living. We tend to look at courage in terms of facing *death*, as in battle or illness, rather than in terms of facing *life*. But in truth, *it takes more courage to live.* To live as one's self in one's ordinary life is the most courageous of acts. I (Tom) find courage easier when I am in jeopardy; it is much more available then than when I am bored. To be what we are, in any and all ways, is to live in that highest form of courage. The simple acts of playing with a child, comforting a distraught friend, enjoying the game we are losing, singing even though we cannot carry a tune, saying how we feel even though we are not eloquent—these deeds are deeply courageous in the human sense.

With courage, we can live in the ordinary world in which any experience at any given time is worth something. In *any experience*, we do not include the horrors of physical or mental violence—being victimized, brutalized, mistreated, abused, deprived, or any of the many other ways in which humans are dehumanized, for these are externally imposed, and, therefore, nonexperiences in the existential sense. We mean, rather, that in ordinary experience there is always something for us if we will but participate. There is always a way to be maximally the *self* we can be in that situation, and that is our job. Moving away from the realms of control and dependence, righteousness and judgment, prejudgment and irresponsibility, we can *be with* the other, *give over* to the other, *make do* and participate in the process.

Competition

Does giving over mean we should not compete? No. The word *competition* first meant "to seek along *with* another." But it has lost its context of seeking *with* and now invariably means to "seek *against* another." We see this clearly in our systems and behaviors. Athletic events are not games, they are battles, massacres, routs. We have hostile corporate mergers. Religious sects and creeds vie for believers and power, and have sometimes openly slain their competitors. We see this same sense of competition in ourselves as individuals. We fight traffic to get home first. We struggle with finances to pay for a bigger car or bigger house. We climb over the backs of co-workers to rise in the corporate, government, church, or institutional structure. We are all against each other; there is very little *seeking with*. Is such competition good for business, good for our character, good for us?

In *No Contest: The Case Against Competition*, psychologist Alfie Kohn points out that most scientific studies have shown that for one person's success to depend on another's failure actually makes for less productivity, less success, and less superior performance. In many studies, there has been found an *inverse* relationship between competitiveness and achievement. In business, the arts, and education, competition *diminishes* performance. Not only will the vast majority of humans choose *cooperation* over *competition* as a way of dealing with others, but they will also do much better under those circumstances. One of the most powerful motivators of humans is a sense of accountability to other people.

Competition is, however, a fact of evolution and of natural life. We see this as we watch the weeds and the grass struggle with each other in our front yards. But in natural life, competition, too, is natural. That is, it is an outgrowth or result of things simply being what they are. A weed grows to become fully itself. It has no concept of being against a blade of grass. In order to compete, the weed does not become distracted, distorted, or diminished from what it is. The case is clearly, and sadly, different in humans. Instead of such natural competition—a celebration of each individual simply being the best he or she can be—we have nine-year-olds trying to win the championship so their parents will love them. We have so-called adults trying to wipe out their friends on the tennis court, or beat out their office mates for accounts or the boss's favor.

There is no giving over in such living, no attempt to maximize the other, no making do with the here-and-now. Rather than healthily competing by being the most us we can be, we expend energy trying to be more than the other or even make the other less. We do not understand that this feeling and behavior lessens *us*. We confuse self-aggrandizement with selfbeing.

Empathy

The missing element in this *against* method of living is *empathy*. Empathy entails an awareness that we are more alike than we are different, that we are all responsible for ourselves, that we all live and exist only relationally, and that we maximize our experience as humans when we maximize the experience of others. "Putting one's own consciousness into another," the simple definition of empathy, requires a recognition of enough alikeness to make the experience meaningful. Personal surrender might be seen as empathy in which the unconscious as well as the conscious is given over to the other. Over the years, each of us has met someone like the old man in jail, someone who had that kind of total empathy. We have also met many who have very little empathy—even with those closest to them.

Bonnie has many complaints in life, but her loudest is that her children do not come to visit her. Now fifty-seven, she is mother to three grown children who live in the same area. Since she and the children's father, Alvin, divorced five years ago, she has seen less and less of her daughters and her son. There is no open quarreling, but there is little connection or involvement either, and Bonnie feels increasingly lonely. She comes in to see a therapist reluctantly, and mostly to complain about her children.

"It doesn't seem to make much difference that I took care of them all those years. They all have some of Alvin in them. He never appreciated me either. Part of why I divorced him, besides his drinking—he was an alcoholic, you know—was because he was so unappreciative."

Bonnie continues to tell us what her children think, do, feel, and want, but she says little about what goes on inside herself. "You'd think children would retain something from how they were brought up. I taught them to think of others. But they don't. They all just go off and live their own lives. Almost like I wasn't even here."

For a therapist, someone like Bonnie, who speaks always of how the other person is doing something to her, presents a problem. She must be accepted as she is (including her blaming others), for no change is possible without that acceptance. At the same time, however, the therapist knows that the blaming must eventually be confronted, and the person returned to her own self-responsibility. It makes no real difference whether what the other is doing to them is behavioral, emotional, or intellectual, or even whether it is accurate. For despite the fact that being hit physically, for example, and being yelled at or ignored are very different things and require very different responses, our own self-responsibility remains the same. It is not dependent on things outside us. The only thing *we* can do something about in the internal sense is *us*.

Seeing things *only from our own perspective*—always blaming the other, as Bonnie does—is the simplest form of lack of empathy in life. As Bonnie's story unfolds, we see that a lack of empathy has been a long-term problem for her. She hurt *for* her children, not *with* them. She needed them to do well in school so she could feel okay. She was chronically angry at Alvin for what his drinking did to her, rather than what he was doing to himself. In seeing this, it is important, of course, for us to remember that Alvin and the children are part of what has gone on over the years as well. In a family, everyone participates. No one is without responsibility for themselves.

It is not that Bonnie does not have a right to hurt for her kids, or to be angry with Alvin for what he does to her, or to bask in some reflection of her offsprings' glory. She does. But that is not enough; her lack of empathy leaves her less than a full person. It is self-diminishing in that it keeps her from the fullness of life that real selfbeing offers.

Personal surrender does not block us from being ourselves; it is, instead, the onset of the task of being ourselves. As Alfred Margulies wrote in *The Empathetic Imagination*, "Invariably in searching for the other in an active fashion, we come to our own reflection, the fundamental projective nature of empathy, and the dialectical quality of finding and creating meaning."

We must learn personally to surrender in our relationships with others. We must be willing to give over our needs, our knowings, all our prearranged internal sets and stages that block experience. We must creatively entertain the new possibilities that are forever occurring outside of us. True empathy is living *with* the world instead of *against* it. It is recognizing that life is process, not stasis that can be lived and defined at the same time. To define life, or any process, restrains it. Definition leads to some understanding, but to understanding of a static life, life frozen in a moment. Empathy is connection to the process of moving life. It creates knowledge in another way.

Such individual change in each of us is necessary in order for our culture to change. For example, nations persuade armies to kill by persuading the fighters that their enemies are *not like them*—that they are subhuman, alien, animals. This shuts off empathy, giving us permission to kill. We do the same with the homeless so we can ignore them and the destitute so that we can feel more comfortable with our success in life. We can convince ourselves that our smoking is more important than someone else's breathing, our rush to get somewhere more important than someone else's safety on the road, our power production more important than someone else's trees, lakes, and ecology. We must come to a point of giving over on a cultural level if we are to survive.

In *Contingency, irony, and solidarity*, philosopher Richard Rorty speaks to our need to change:

> This process of coming to see other human beings as "one of us" rather than as "them" is a matter of detailed description of what unfamiliar people are like and a redescription of what we ourselves are like.

We must give over our mislearnings and preknown ways of seeing others and our world. We must surrender to the truth that we are all more alike than different.

Just like closeness and intimacy, which they obviously reflect, understanding and empathy form a dyad. Both are necessary. Personal surrender, the ultimate act of healthy closeness, leads to intimacy. In the same way, complete naturalness, the ultimate act of healthy intimacy, *naturally* leads to closeness. Nature is not perverse. It is we who pervert the process.

12

THE NINTH WINDOW:
Environmental Nourishment of Self/Attentiveness

You have to study a great deal to know a little.
—Charles de Secondao

I (Tom) first met Veronica many years ago. I had initially been her husband Dom's therapist. He had come to see me for depression. Coming in had been something he did against his wife's advice. Making this choice was one of the few times in twenty-five years of marriage that Dom had actually *decided* to do something. The decision was made because he felt he had to do something about himself. He was increasingly both sad and angry about his relationship to his wife. Knowing that history, I knew that seeing Dom without her might be necessary, although if I *could* include her from the beginning, it would not only be helpful to him, but perhaps also to her, and thus helpful to the ever-present third party, their marriage.

After seeing Dom alone a few times, I suggested that he ask Veronica if she would mind coming to the next appointment. To both of our surprise, she came in. Her choice showed great courage on her part. She was in her late forties, immaculately dressed, polite, yet honest and straightforward in what she said. She told me about her very difficult childhood. She, her sister, and her mother had been abandoned by her father when she was a small child. The mother had been a quiet, withdrawn, noncomplaining person who had provided for her two children by unending hard work: she did housework for a number of families and held a second job. She managed to send both of her children through college, but died in her early fifties.

Her impoverished upbringing had left its scars on Veronica. She had a powerful need to be in control and to be secure. She was far removed from any awareness of the pleasures of spontaneity, of what William Congreve described in *Love for Love:* "Uncertainty and expectation are the joys of life. Security is an insipid thing, and the overtaking and processing of a wish, discovers the folly of the chase." Veronica's early uncertainty and fears, in the absence of a warm parental support, had, instead, left her feeling the need always to be in control of her life. She never wanted to be deprived again, or without money or things, or lacking full control over what happened around her.

Veronica spoke of *her* house, *her* children, *her* plans, and *her* intentions. She kept an immaculate house, decided what her husband and children would wear, and at times would even remove clothing from them if she did not approve of it. She did not quite command Dom to finish everything on his plate, but she did insist that the children do so. Both children had left home early. They were now living on their own, not coincidentally in distant cities.

There was no doubt that Veronica was a deeply compulsive person. She never negotiated her rightness or her correctness, she simply lived it. Her controlling was not done arrogantly, hostilely, or aggressively. It was done as if she genuinely felt that her way was correct, and was not only good for her but for others as well, whatever their feelings about it might be. Most of the time, Veronica did not seem to have any sense of her husband's or children's resentment and discontent. In our sessions, she seemed genuinely surprised when Dom would mention some past event about which he was still angry.

According to Dom, one habit of Veronica's nicely summed up her whole manner of relating: after he poured his morning coffee on the weekends, he would walk around his house, while he shaved, read the newspaper, or just puttered around. Veronica would follow him (more specifically, follow his cup of coffee) around with a folded paper towel. Whenever he put down the cup, she would place the towel under it, after carefully wiping the surface underneath. She would then get the coffee pot and refill the cup. None of her behavior seemed to have any connection to what he either felt or wanted. She was not angry or hostile, just totally out of touch.

After seeing me a few times, Veronica began to do the same sort of thing with me. My office is an untidy place, filled with piled-up books and papers, paintings hanging askew, and memorabilia scattered about in chairs and under chairs and on top of books. She began spending the first two or three minutes when she came into my office straightening out the more obvious things. I smoked a pipe back then, and she would empty my ashtrays and wipe them clean. She would rearrange whatever seemed to be near the edge of shelves. She would remove dirty coffee cups. Then, finally, she would sit down. In the meantime, Dom and I would be talking.

As time went on, she began to clean house *during* our sessions. I often take my shoes off and put my feet up on the hassock while I work. One time she came over, picked up my shoes, and looked at the soles. She told me that she thought I really needed to get them resoled soon or I was going to lose the stitching. I thanked her. When I thanked her, her husband looked at me, somewhat puzzled. Dom could not understand why her behavior did not make me as angry as it made him.

Veronica became something of a legend with the clinic staff. She was helpful to everyone, and always without any sense of hostility or criticism. She simply believed that if you just relaxed and listened to her, she would tell you how to live, and, as a result, you would be much better off. I would like to brag about how much Veronica changed in therapy, but I cannot. I would like to say that she is now attentive to others in her life, but I cannot. She and Dom are still married, and as a result of better communication their relationship is somewhat improved. But she is only slowly learning to "attend with" Dom: to be receptive to his person instead of being driven by her interpretation of his needs. Veronica still does not really understand why he was depressed or why her children moved away.

People who help or do for others cannot be described as attending to others if they are driven by their own internal needs. We tend to think of people who cannot attend to others as not being helpful, but we can as easily fail to attend to others in our helpfulness. Taking care of others, being considerate of others, and thinking about others are not in themselves ways of attending to others. Attending to others is a *way of being*, not a behavior or a thought.

I (Tom) have a sign someone painted for me many years ago that I have always prized. It says, "Every time I think, I get sick." Last year a good friend—a man who has become considerably less compulsive than he was in the past—gave me a T-shirt with the same message printed in bright red. I dreamed recently that I was wearing it as I read Thomas Aquinas's *Summa Theologica*, while trying not to think.

I (Pat) think Dad can dream such dreams because thinking does not really make him sick. A more useful sign would say, "Thinking, Feeling, or Behaving Instead of Being Makes Us All Sick." Being requires more than just our own thoughts and ideas, feelings, and behavior. We must be fed by the thoughts, ideas, feelings, and actions of others. In other words, our being is very much related to the being of others. Veronica's total involvement in her own feelings, behaviors, and thoughts blocked her from nourishing her personhood, and thus from changing. She was not even very much aware of just how painful such alienation is.

Listening

Mason has been divorced for five years. He dates, but also is still involved with his ex-wife. She, too, has never remarried. Mason is another compulsive and driven person but, unlike Veronica, he is a sensitive one. He has been depressed on and off over the past six years, for which he has been in and out of therapy. He usually comes in a few times, begins to feel better, then leaves with the inner issues still unresolved. He is always embarrassed to come back, as if it is a surprise to him that his depression has returned.

Mason has now appeared again and is speaking about an insight he had while driving to the clinic. "The problem is, I never listen. I don't mean this in a bad way, but I've never even listened to you. I never listen to anybody. Not that I don't care about anybody else, or think I'm the only one that's important. Because I'm not really like that. But I'm always thinking and I'm always processing everything so much that I never hear what's really been said. I guess that's true about everything in my life. Even when I ask something, like I do in here, and I really want an answer, I just can't really listen to it. So I never change."

Mason begins to cry a little as he reclines further back in the chair, until he is speaking to the ceiling, or to the room, or, more likely, to himself. "I'm scared to listen, but it feels so lonely in here all by myself. Everybody else thinks I'm strong and everything's in control, but inside I feel like this little boy who really does wish somebody would help him." Then he sits back up a little, and half smiles. "What's the matter? Am I crazy or something?" Mason, like so many of us, sees his real *self* as dangerous, embarrassing, or possibly even crazy. What a sad predicament in which to go through life.

We could say to Mason, "No, you're not crazy. As a matter of fact, you have come to a tremendously beautiful insight, one that may change your life." We could, but we will not say that, not right now. Now *we need to listen*, for listening is what this moment is about.

I (Pat) watch the Special Olympics and often find myself in quiet tears. The power of attending to others—the ways the coaches and staff support, encourage, and celebrate the participants—can be seen there in its full beauty. I also feel tears for the foolishness of how we humans, conversely, live with each other in most of our ordinary interactions. These "special" humans *all* get hugs for being the best they can be. *Everybody is a winner just for being.* But in the "real" world, the supposedly unhandicapped world, seldom does anyone get a hug, and even winners feel mostly that they are winners because they have beaten someone else.

Perhaps even more important, those who are hugging these "special" humans get to experience *their* full being. In attending to the other they nourish themselves. One can usually see this phenomenon quite clearly by simply watching people helping others. In hospitals, in wars, during natural disasters, during industrial accidents, or when family crises arise, we frequently observe humans rise to a powerful wholeness. Most of the time, however, we do not nourish ourselves in such ways. Humans often seem, instead, almost to be trying to destroy themselves. As William James said in *The Energies of Men*, "Compared with what we ought to be, we are only half awake."

In listening to Mason, we attend to him. We participate in his own struggle to learn to attend. He is starving, starving for nourishment from his environment. Like the Ancient Mariner, he has people, people everywhere, but not a soul gets in.

As he says: "I'm not dumb. I know when other people aren't there for me. My friends do the same thing to me. I can be telling them something, but I know they're not hearing it at all. They're too worried, or maybe too mad, or something. Sometimes I think I know how Sally felt being married to me. I always argued with her when we'd fight about my inattention, but now I think I understand . . . because nobody listened to me when I was growing up. . . . What a mess."

Attending to Others

> When the Pleiades and the wind in the grass are no longer a part of the human spirit, a part of the very flesh and bone, man becomes, as it were, a kind of cosmic outlaw, having neither the completeness and integrity of the animal nor the birthright of a true humanity.
>
> —HENRY BESTON, The Outermost House

When the self is deprived of environmental nourishment, humans wither and the process of self-diminishment begins. Unable to listen to others, we not only are unable to listen to ourselves, we also find ourselves steadily shrinking and dying. We take in nothing from outside, so we literally starve emotionally and intellectually. It is not merely that we are cut off from other humans. We starve in our inability to attend to the rest of nature and the world. The result is the tragic ways we misuse and mistreat other species, our land, and our seas.

If making do and personal surrender are the underpinnings of healthy closeness, then attentiveness is how healthy closeness manifests itself to the outer world. We exist in relationship—there is no other existence available. Whether it be to our air, our food, our water, our lover, or our child, we exist in an environment from which we derive our sustaining nourishment. Life is not the one-way street on which so many humans try to live. The other person, the other species, the sea, the land, also requires attending. If we want healthy closeness, we will attend to others in ways that allow us to continue being who we are and them to continue being who they are. Ultimately, we will find that such healthy closeness actually maximizes our ability to be who we are. It increases our level of intimacy.

Attend means literally "to turn one's mind to," just as listen means "to lean toward." In both these etymologies, we see the experiential task made literal: to turn one's mind and lean toward others. Both are necessary for living as a whole person. We cannot be intimate if we cannot attend to the other. It takes more than a willingness to share who we are in order to manifest ourselves. We must also allow others to share themselves. We must be willing to suspend our inner agenda and listen to the other person. Only then can we nourish ourselves, can we take that *other* in as he, she, or it is. It makes no difference if the other is a person, or a sunset, or a tree, or a poem; the same truth applies. *Self's* appetite is itself dependent on its constant feeding. Unfed, self's beautiful hunger goes away. *Self* dies, and either *I* or *Me* comes out of the grave, not *I and me*. *Self* thrives only on a varied diet.

Endless examples of self-starvation can be seen in the superficial interactions among people in their day-to-day lives. Our society's decline in polite manners—in so far as they generate consideration and gentleness—is a glaring manifestation of the inability of so many of us to attend to others, to nourish ourselves through the world we live in. That inability is why we see the concomitant increase in greed, in "me-ism," and in selfishness. We know we need nourishment; we simply mistake its source. Starving people will eat anything. Too many people mistake material things, status, or power for soul food. The best soul food is other souls—the souls of the dust particles moving in the sunlit window, of butterflies, azaleas, bright stars, strangers, as well as other ones. Spiritual anorexia is a widespread and devastating illness.

In meaningful personal relationships, our difficulty is equally real and usually much more painful. The rates for divorce, abuse, drug and alcohol use, and general unhappiness all attest to how little attended to most people feel. It is not a question of whether any one of us *deserves* attention. We are all humans. We all need to remember what Arthur Miller wrote of Willy Loman in *Death of a Salesman*:

> I don't say he's a great man. Willy Loman never made a lot of money. His name was never in the paper. He's not the finest character that ever lived. But he's a human being, and a

terrible thing is happening to him. So attention must be paid. He's not to be allowed to fall into his grave like an old dog. Attention, attention must be paid to such a person.

We are all human, and must both attend and be attended. Everyone needs a hug and everyone needs to hug. We all need nourishment.

Needing the New

We attend or listen to others not for their benefit but *for the benefit of our selves.* That means literally that to continue to survive and grow, our *selves* need the nourishment they get from outside. A large part of nourishment is change, the ongoing introduction of the new and different into the self, into our personhood. The necessity of continual exposure to the new comes directly out of the way our brains work. The need for newness is real: "To fall into habit," wrote Miguel de Unamuno in *The Tragic Sense of Life*, "is to begin to cease to be." Habit blocks new experience, and new experience is necessary to being.

Over the last quarter century, neuropsychological research on how the brain functions has increasingly pointed out that we are not born totally amorphous. While we may have precious little data as newborns, our filing system is to some degree already in place in our brains. We have structures that are ready to receive grammar, colors, and spatial concepts. People will universally pick out the reddest red, even those who have no word for red. These structures may not be what we might call hardware. They may, for example, be more like stable states in a neural net. But the systems are there, and they powerfully affect how we are as humans.

Writer Charles de Secondao said that, "if triangles had a god, he would have three sides." Just so: the brain tends to see the external world in the same patterns that it itself contains. For example, since our brain is itself patterned, we impose similar patterns on what we see in our world. This trait is enormously useful and evolutionarily successful—to a point. But it has, as we are increasingly learning, certain vulnerabilities wherein system begins to override being. The brain, metaphorically, creates systems in its own image, and those systems then sustain that image. To our detriment, we become shut off from the new. The brain, and therefore the person, has an ingrained tendency to accept only incoming sensory information that agrees with what it already knows. Security needs displace the true safety found in continual renewal, continual evolution and growth.

Complex systems have properties that transcend their individual parts. The weather, for example, is more than just clouds, humidity, temperature, and other simple components. It is a process—a wholeness—that *happens*. This paradigm is also true for our internal systems. We might call those complex level properties our *selves*. If we think of it that way, then the idea of stable states in a neural net—or whatever other metaphor for this complex state turns out to be scientifically correct—can be most helpful in understanding how we live and function, as well as in grasping the importance of new input.

Complex systems will demonstrate stable behavior around a known pattern. We see this in our brain function: it seeks the known pattern, often seeing things in ways determined by that pattern. It will take slightly different input and make it familiar, make it fit the pattern. For example, many divergent shapes can be seen as cups if they fit the pattern for cup. In past times, prior to urbanization or industrialization and perhaps prior to agriculturalization, humans lived experientially. Knowledge was based on our experience of being in our world. The pace of change was slow enough that the brain did not have to maintain stability by simply latching on to the known.

In the past three millennia, however, the rate of change has grown exponentially—*not just the change, but the rate of change.* The transience of fixed states has made us very time-oriented. We are increasingly left-brained, increasingly clock conscious. The diminished or even lost spatial, right-brained components are sorely missed. Much of our nonexperientialness arises from this loss. We struggle to hold on to experience, instead of enjoying the ride. We not only hold on instead of enjoying, we short-circuit the real experience. It is as if on a roller coaster we begin visualizing the end of the ride before we even go over the first dip.

The change from living out of our experience to holding on to experience became more pronounced with the advent of the printed word. Reading about life replaced experiencing it. Now we are involved in a video revolution in which watching life replaces living it. The video "life" does not even require the imagination that a reading life does. We are moving farther and farther away from our natural patterns of living, including the natural ways we modify our patterns. "Pythagoras and Plato knew that pattern was fundamental to all mind and ideation," Gregory and Mary Bateson wrote in *Angels Fear,* "but this wisdom was thrust away and lost in the mists of the supposedly indescribable mystery called 'mind.' "

We have become *commentators on,* in lieu of being *participants in,* our own living. As such, our brains have become increasingly inclined to hold on to the known for security and stability. Such living is *not* secure or stable, however, for it blocks experience. It is nonnatural, nonevolving, and nongrowing. A stable state stagnates without sufficient new experience *to change* the stable state. Our blood sugar has a stable state range it remains in, despite significant differences in input. But it also has the capacity to change states when necessary, when conditions basically change. Our brain also needs both properties: it must be able to change its stable states as well as maintain them. Unfortunately, in our current overloaded condition, we have tried to balance the rapid changing outside by limiting change inside.

What changes stable states is new experience. In fact, the two concepts are inseparable. An experience *is* a change in the state of the brain—the state of the brain as complex system, not just as a collection of individual parts. The complex level involves changes in the relationship between things, not just sending impulses down nerves. It is as we hear in the "Sutra of Hui Neng" (W. Chan, *A Source Book in Chinese Philosophy*):

> From the point of view of ordinary folks, the component parts of a personality and factors of consciousness are two separate things: But enlightened men understand that they are not dual in nature. Buddha-nature is non-duality.

Inattentive Attention

Many of us confuse attending to others with paying attention to others. The two not only have little in common, they are in many ways antithetical. "Paying attention to others" involves *them*. It derives from our security needs, or fear, and thus displaces our being ourselves. "Attending to others" involves *us*, coming from our feelings of love, care, connection, and acceptance. It maximizes our being ourselves. The clearest example of this difference is found in those ways of interacting that are traditionally seen as being paranoid.

Riva is forty-seven and works at a local manufacturing plant. She has undergone several major changes in her life in the past ten years. She and her husband divorced after many years of conflict. Her children grew up and pursued their own lives of school and work. Her father died five years ago, and two years later Riva left her old job, where she had been for many years, to take the new one at the manufacturing plant. She says she changed jobs because the new company offered better benefits and retirement, and claims that, at the time, she was happy with the change.

However, in the past three years Riva has gradually grown more depressed and more suspicious of others. She worries what others are doing and why, who is against her, who is trying to take her money, who is trying to do her in. Her attention to other people, events, and things is total. Her children no longer want to be around her; her friends are drifting away. In truth, she is very difficult for anyone to be with. For despite all the outward *attention* she pays to others, she *attends* to no one. It is painful to be reacted to as an object rather than experienced as a person.

I (Tom) remember years ago hearing a national safety campaign slogan for safer driving: "Watch out for the other guy." It serves nicely to show the difference between attending to others and paying attention to others. As any ex-ballplayer can tell you, watching out for the other guy, as opposed to doing what you are doing well, is about the best possible way to get hurt. You cannot remove yourself from the flow of things without paying a price. It would indeed be a terrible travesty if "watching out for the other guy" turned out to be the basis of many motor-vehicle accidents. I would feel much safer with a driver who was paying primary attention to his own driving experience, his car, his speed, his control, his being in his environment because then he *would* be truly attending to others. He would be maximizing his *self* safety, and thus maximizing mine.

Removed from the source of nourishment, self starves and is unable to grow. *The lack of growth*, as with any living thing, is the clearest indicator of nonexperience—*living* organisms are always changing. These changes are not necessarily major, but they are constantly renewing and evolving, and prevent capture and stasis. Paranoia is a blatant example of capture and stasis. Paying attention to others is its garden-variety presentation. There are, however, many others much more subtle—such as unhealthy marriages.

Marriage and Self-Nourishment

Along with our species' reproductive functions, mutual self-nourishing is the major basis of long-term permanent relationships in humans. Marriage here is used to signify such relationships and their commitments. Many such pairings nowadays are not officially marriages, but exist, nevertheless, as permanent or long-term relationships. In such committed relationships, we can observe attending to others, or its lack, in its most basic form.

In that sense, a marriage is the relationship that provides the deepest assurance of continued self-growth of both persons. The family grows, and so do the people in it, if the marriage grows. The marriage fails when one or both persons in it do not grow and change. If one partner grows because of outside healthy relationships, that one often leaves the marriage. Generally, if neither grows, the two stay unhealthily together and die as a couple together. Or perhaps, one partner gets too anxious, and the various forms of unhealthiness supported by the culture—affairs, overwork, alcohol and drug use, etc.—do not contain that anxiety. That partner leaves, to seek another human who can assure growth and so marriage. Anxiety is, after all, a *stalled* effort to grow and change.

I (Tom) was sitting one day with a couple I had been seeing in therapy for some time. They were what I have come to think of as badminton players. I sat in the middle. They sat in chairs to my right and left, hitting back and forth volleys of wrongs, hurts, accusations, and defenses. The best I could do, if I had had any interest in doing it, would have been to keep score.

One day they were playing this game so determinedly that it was pathetic, in the sense that I felt the pathos of their denial of life. Yet they seemed really to care about each other, so their situation was not entirely hopeless. I asked them to excuse me a moment. With only a brief glance at me, they went right on with their arguing. I returned from the reception area with a yellow legal pad. As they played their badminton, I wrote the following:

To stay married we have to . . .

1. Realize that marriage is ongoing hard work. There is no other way to be married.

2. Understand that we marry the missing parts, the rest of us. Being married to oneself would not only be a bore, but would almost guarantee our premature demise as a person.

3. Realize that we have to learn from the ways in which we differ. This task is a significant portion of our motivation for marrying this particular person.

4. Decide that we are going to stay in the marriage. It is astonishing how few people ever decide that.

5. Realize that we are responsible for our own happiness and unhappiness.

6. Know that if our spouse is having a bad time, we have something to do with it even though we may not be "responsible" for it.

7. Bring something new of our person into the relationship *every day*. Our living together healthily involves a constant renewal.

8. Know without any reservations that the greatest gift we can give our spouse is our genuine love of ourselves. The greatest gift we can give to our children is our love of each other.

9. Know that if we want something, we must give it. If we want our spouse to tell us about himself or herself, we must tell them about ourselves. If we want our spouse to listen, we must listen to our spouse.

10. Accept the fact that despite being male and female, both of us are both masculine and feminine.

11. Realize that play makes marriages. Without joy and laughter, marriage is simply an incessant dying.

I asked them if they wanted to help their marriage or if they were, instead, looking for a judge. Like almost all couples, they said they wanted the marriage to work—although again, like so many couples, they really wanted a judge. I showed them my list of what they were getting themselves into and waited. After a few moments of silence—the first silence that had occurred in the session—both asked if I would make them a copy of my list. Although work lists will not make a marriage work, that couple was at least willing to try.

Few people accept the self-responsibility needed for true marriage in these ways. Instead of seeing the other as a source of self-nourishment, we see them as causal, controlling, to blame, or at fault. We marry with a fantasy of marriage. It usually takes five or more years to give up the fantasy and live, and so grow with the reality of each other. If we are lucky we can let go of the fantasy, but the process is frequently sad and painful. It is then that we begin to be really married. But many of us do not or will not let go. The hidden enemy of the marriage then becomes the persistent fantasies that distort and destroy the realities of the relationship. For example, we may see the other as a good parent we never had, as a lover who will make us feel adequate in our loving, or as a source of energy and excitement in our lives. Unable to see the other as who they are, we cannot attend them. Unable to attend the other, we cannot nourish ourselves. We are captured by the marriage as a system, instead of participating in it as a loving, growing experience.

We not only hear these failed fallacies about marriage lived out in our offices, we hear them celebrated in our rituals: "the two shall become one," "they lived happily ever after," and so on. These are not descriptions of real life, not ways in which real people live or experience life. Becoming one with someone else is selficidal for both. Becoming two—joyfully, healthily, responsibly—would be a much better goal. An experiential family cannot be founded on a nonexperiential relationship, any more than real castles can be built on sand. Being unaware of the other as "not us" is guaranteed to prevent our attending to them.

John Jay Chapman spoke of such unawareness in *Memories and Milestones:*

It is a very rare matter when any of us at any time in life sees things as they are at the moment. This happens at times . . . that we become aware of what is going on about us and of the infinite great worlds of force, of feeling and of idea in which we live, and in the midst of which we have always been living. These worlds are really in progress all the time; and the difference between one man and another, or the difference in the same man at different times, is the difference in his aware-ness of what is happening.

So many humans, married or not, live unaware. Unawareness in this sense is *not attending to others*. In committed relationships, we see it crucially in how we do not attend to spouses, lovers, and families. In other areas of our living, we may not attend to other people or our environment. "Seeing things as they are" must start with seeing things at all, or hearing, touching, and feeling things. That is, to be in our world aware, we must attend to the other.

Lack of awareness can be even more devastating when we see our intimate partner only as a projection of ourselves, only as a copy of us. Fortunately, most of us tend to choose people for mates on whom it is difficult to project because they are very unlike us—they are Jung's shadows, the rest of ourselves. Be-cause of this, pairing between humans is an experience which offers us the best chance to grow toward our wholeness as human beings. But such growth occurs only when we attend to the other.

Learning and Attentiveness

In order to attend to the other, and thus nourish ourselves, we must be able to allow the other freedom to be. Perhaps even more profoundly, we must *celebrate* the other in being what he, she, or it is. The only way we can learn more is to have more real experience. *We become free by freeing the other.* Many of us find it difficult to accept that fact. When we do finally accept it, we find that celebrating the other empowers them and, in turn, empowers us.

Charlene comes to the office alone on the first visit, essen-tially to tell the therapist how to respond when her lover comes in with her. She does not say so directly, but this message is quite clear. She is very afraid her lover will not understand why she feels the way she does. Charlene is frightened of almost everything in her life. What she has difficulty seeing is the connection between her way of being in the world and her unhappiness, emptiness, and painful sense of not really being alive.

She confesses to unhappiness but makes judgments about both herself and others. "I wish I could be like everybody else. They all seem so happy. They just don't seem aware of what's really going on . . . so they don't have to worry about it or take care of it, I guess." As the interview proceeds, we find out that Charlene is bulimic and struggles with depression, as well as her fear: "I feel so disconnected, so all by myself . . . I just want somebody to love me."

It is not the case that Charlene is overly aware, as she tries to suggest. Quite the reverse. She is unaware. When reality is controlled ("taken care of") as she is always trying to do, it is not reality. Charlene is unaware of the others in her life *as they are*, and feels the emptiness of the resulting lack of self-nourishment. She sees them only *as she is* and only through her own need to control. As with her bulimia, she takes things in not as what they are, but as what she uses them for. Like the food she eats, then regurgitates, they are of no intrinsic use to her. They do not nourish her *self* and are thus pushed out as the something else she takes them to be. She never learns, for nothing gets inside as what it is, and she is never what she is. She has no real experience. The jailer is as caught as the prisoner.

If we are unreceptive to our present, we cannot learn. Many humans cannot learn from the past or future either. Frequently, it is only at the time of their dying that people will fully open themselves to past, present, and future, and become truly aware. At that time and place they attend to others and take strength from others' being what they are. Similarly, and equally sadly, we too often attend to others only when *they* are dying. We finally accept them, their fears, feelings, needs, and dreams, without demanding that they be different. In so doing, we are also sustained and, without knowing it, become much more who we are.

I (Tom) had a particularly significant and moving experience with such a revelation. When I was about thirty years old, I decided that I needed to talk to my father. He was a somewhat dependent man, passive, but enormously creative, sensitive, and caring. He might have been an artist if he had followed his natural inclinations. Instead, he became a brewmaster. On this occasion, I traveled from Georgia to where my father lived in Pennsylvania and spent six hours talking with him. I insisted on my mother's absence. I had decided before I went that I would not get involved with his responses. I had decided that I would stay committed only to my willingness to share with him what I felt, what I thought, and what I remembered, and that I would accept his responses as they were. He responded much as I had expected he would: "I don't know why you felt that way," "That's not what I meant," "I don't know why this means so much to you." I felt that all his statements indicated a lack of awareness on his part of the depth of feeling that was involved in my coming to talk to him. I left, pleased that I had shared myself and heard him, but disappointed with his responses.

Twenty-five years later, my father was dying and I was at his bedside. During the intervening years, he had never spoken of our intense conversation, although I had been with him on many subsequent occasions. The day before he died, he called me over with a gesture; he had had two strokes and could speak only with great difficulty. I went to his bed, and he motioned me to lean over to hear him better. All he said was, "Thanks for talking."

It is difficult to express how much that simple sharing has meant to me personally. In a profound way, I am certain that in the twenty-five years that elapsed between my original conversation and his final response, my father *had been talking with me.* That twenty-five-year conversation has made an enormous difference to me, not only in my memory of my father, but also in the role that my father, as I have internalized him in my person, currently plays in my life now that I am a seventy-year-old person.

Our lack of attending to the past has always been self-destructive. Americans in particular fail to attend to the past, agreeing with Henry Ford that "history is bunk." Our cultural lack of attending means we learn little from past mistakes. We are like trees cut off from their roots. We are not nourished by our past, neither our "precivilized" or our "postcivilized" past, and, thus, are unable to learn the important lessons of both.

Lack of attending to the future is more difficult for most of us to conceptualize. How can one not attend to what is yet to be? But, like Dickens's Scrooge, we are unable to allow the unfolding of the infinite possibilities of what the future may hold. Instead, we limit possibilities in an attempt to be secure. Living that way, we deprive ourselves of the nourishment that exists in the infinite all. That may at first sound esoteric, but if we stand out under a clear autumn night sky, looking out into *our* universe, all of us instinctively feel its truth.

Healthy Closeness

For years, I (Pat) would come home from work and "have to" listen to whatever my wife, Elaine, had been dealing with that day. I felt this as a burden because I had it in my head that she was looking to me for answers to those things which bothered and upset her, and that it was incumbent upon me to meet those needs. I would feel this obligation regardless of the fact that she never said she wanted my answers. Since I felt obligated to be there, listen, and fix things, I also felt the concomitant resentment that such obligatory living always causes. I would be further irritated when she was annoyed by, or dismissive of, or shot holes in my perfectly good solutions, and would get even more peeved when she eventually disclosed that she had already decided what she was going to do anyway. I felt that I was being mistreated, although I would never admit to it.

As I grew over the years, I began to notice that, in reality, Elaine seemed to do very well with her problems and her answers to them . . . at least as well as I did with my own. I slowly came to realize that "obligation" and "fixing" were *my* issues. She simply wanted *attending*, not fixing, taking care of, or solving. It is now much easier for me to relax and enjoy being with her, because I can now be with her instead of being only with me.

A therapist colleague of ours says that he and his wife spent the first third of their marriage each absolutely sure they were right and could tell the other exactly what to do, think, feel, and be. After "the big fight"—the turning point crisis that happens in most pairings where the two people decide whether to stay together or not—he and she began to have some begrudging respect for each other. Each still felt they were mostly right, but both could now give the other some credit and space. Only in the last third of their marriage have they come to *celebrate* each other.

They see each other as the nourishment they really are for themselves. They solicit and enjoy the differences and diversities of relationship. They attend to each other.

Such attentiveness is the outer framework on which all *healthy* closeness is based. The reexperience gained in such relating provides the feeding that each new seedling, each new experience, requires in order to become functionally a part of how we live. Growing requires letting the outside in, attending to the unknown, appreciating variation, because growing requires something new in order to happen. That is what nourishment of *self* really is: the taking in of what is outside us in order to grow.

Unfortunately, most of us end up fearing the unknown and constructing defenses against it. These defenses usually involve our not attending to others out of our own needs and distortions, as was the case with my (Pat) reaction to Elaine's "demands." We may be controlling, dependent, depressed, angry, paranoid, or anxious, and any of those life positions can prevent us from listening to the other. When we cannot attend, we cannot be healthily close. The same is equally true for our ability to receive ideas, poems, flowers, and dreams. We do not take them in as they are and so allow ourselves to grow. Instead, we reject, distort, homogenize, or ignore them so we can securely remain the same. Taking in nothing new, we die as persons.

Why our peculiar propensity for death and nothingness? Perhaps if we could understand this addictiveness to habit, we could better understand our drug problems—both the identified and advertised problems of pot, crack, speed, heroin, and cocaine, and the far more common but less commonly attacked problems of alcohol and tranquilizers, antidepressants, and painkillers.

Our defenses against life also take cultural and social forms. The current states of journalism and news as entertainment, sports and religion as marketing, and music and art as advertising are examples of this homogenization of difference and flight from the new and unknown. We see this very clearly in the loss of individuality of our towns—the stores are the same, the fast food the same, the experiences available the same. We give up the positive of individual experience for the security of systemic consistency. Manipulation of people is easier when life is consistent everywhere. It is more secure than allowing individual experience.

In just this way, society operates out of the idea that allowing individuality is in some way a threat to "our way of life." Closeness based on the notion that humans are inherently dangerous or sinful produces, as religious scholar Elaine Pagels discussed in *Adam and Eve and the Serpent*, dangerous closeness:

> Finally, we have seen how Christian views of freedom changed as Christianity, no longer a persecuted movement, became the religion of the emperors. Augustine not only read into the messages of Jesus and Paul his own aversion to "the flesh," but also claimed to find in Genesis his theory of original sin. In his final battle against the Pelagians, Augustine succeeded in persuading many bishops and several Christian emperors to help drive out of the churches as "heretics" those who held to earlier traditions of Christian freedom. From the fifth century on, Augustine's pessimistic views of sexuality, politics, and human nature would become the dominant influence on Western culture, Christian or not, ever since. Thus Adam, Eve, and the serpent—our ancestral story—would continue, often in some version of its Augustinian form, to affect our lives to the present day.

Christianity is obviously not the only religion to see humans in this way. Most systematic religions are themselves system-captured and cease to view human individuals as sources of environmental nourishment, worthy of positive attentiveness instead of negatively defined attention. Rather than protecting *ways of life*, they foster *ways of death*.

Too much of organized religion is in this way probably the greatest example of our capture by unhealthy closeness, our inability to nourish ourselves from others. It surely has caused more destruction, stagnation, and death than any other form of cultural defense. The spiritual concepts of receiving and accepting are displaced by the "religious" concepts of judging, blaming, and rejecting. Just as with personal defenses, the end result is selficidal: nonexperience and a lack of nourishment for the soul. True religion, as mentioned before, is about *retying*, not separating. True religion is another name for healthy closeness, just as spirituality is another name for healthy intimacy.

True religion is about the reexperiencing of the growth brought about through spirituality. It is *based on* attending to the other. We cannot retie to what we cannot receive. With most of

what claims to be religion in our current world, there is no receiving. Telling others what to think, say, believe, and do is much
more common an approach. Such "religion" completely prevents
attending to others. We cannot listen when we are always talking.

Religion is joined as a defense against the unknown by other
large systems—technologic, economic, political, or scientific. Government or administration in its many forms can equally prevent
attentiveness. They can and do institutionalize social inattention.
Our current homeless and mental health crises are prime examples. "Scientificism" can block attending as well. For example,
many studies are but justifications of cultural biases. Like "religion," such "scientificism" has little to do with real science. Real
science attends tremendously to the other. Such attentiveness is
its entire basis.

Defending against the unknown is self-diminishing, for it
makes us something other than a connected part of our world.
Unlike a healthy wariness, unlike a curiosity mixed with wisdom,
unlike a playfulness guided by learned rules, *defending* against
the unknown makes us unable to experience it. We are too busy
looking for some power to protect us (that never relinquished
hope for the perfect parent).

> I believe that to some extent people respond to power as if it
> were truth . . . the fact that there is something lacking in our
> assessment of the world of expanded possibilities puts us at the
> mercy of the world we have struggled to escape; and we are
> ruled by people who know much less than we do.
>
> —GEORGE W. S. TROW, "The Third Parent"

While escaping from the risk of taking our own responsibility and
taking in others, we escape from ourselves. Attending to others,
participating in healthy closeness, and being ourselves are inseparable.

As therapists, we spend most of our time making people
unhappy. That is actually our biggest job—to make them unhappy with their unhappiness. Most humans dance a terrible
dance of death, frightening because it appears so driven and inevitable. Watching it, we often feel as if we are useless and helpless. It is painful to be unable to make people realize that their
lives need not be so wrenching. Most of us seem unhappy about

262   THE WINDOWS OF EXPERIENCE

our unhappiness only in retrospect. When not dancing, we seem separated from the other by the length of the ballroom. We wait, then wander aimlessly around the large room looking for what or who we need and want, occasionally bumping into each other. Delightedly, we begin to dance. All too soon, however, we become serious, we cease attending to the other, cease being ourselves, and, instead, devote our energies to trying to *change* the other.

We cannot *be* without being part of our world. Attending to the other, taking the other into ourselves *as they are*, is the only nourishing way to be in our world. While it may be easiest for us to see our self-defeating behavior in how we do not notice the world around us—do not see a mountain or hear a poem because we are so consumed with our own agenda—it is the loss of nourishment from not attending to other humans that costs us most dearly.

13

THE TENTH WINDOW:
Play/Engagement

Well, I've wrestled with reality for thirty-five years, doctor, and I'm happy to state I finally won out over it.
—Jimmy Stewart as Elwood P. Dowd, *Harvey*

Lee loves baseball. He is forty years old, and his enthusiasm for the game is just as intense as it was when he was a teenager. His wife, Rachel, however, considers baseball boring, and her refusal, as Lee sees it, to enjoy the games with him makes Lee unhappy. Lee gets tickets to a big holiday game. Full of anticipation and excitement, he invites Rachel to go with him. Rachel does go with him, but she takes along a book to read. "I know she's going for me . . . and she's not in a bad mood or anything . . . but it just ruins it for me. I don't have any fun."

Lee has forgotten how children persuade other children to play with them. He has lost that notion of positive seduction with which children are so facile. He has no concept of creating a space and letting Rachel be in it as herself, of enjoying her choice to be with him while she reads, instead of staying home to read by herself. If he could only go on being himself, having all the fun that is in him, living his excitement and joy, she might look up from her book one day and wonder what it is that is so enjoyable, and why she is missing out on it. And, in truth, that is the *only* way she will ever "get into the game."

Lucy signs up for drawing lessons to "get more in touch with the other side of myself." Usually overresponsible and overcontrolled, she wishes to be more playful and free. She starts classes with nervous energy and hope. Soon, however, she is struggling. Drawing a stack of boxes, Lucy finds she draws them "like they are" but that they do not "look like they look." She knows one side of a box is longer than another and draws it that way even though that is not how they look if she could indeed just look. Lucy trusts what she knows more than what she experiences. She will not let the other side of herself emerge.

Herb works about sixty hours a week. He seldom gets home before seven o'clock at night. His lover, Christine, resents his absence and his unwillingness, in her terms, to have any fun in life. These issues have been the source of many long struggles between them. On Christine's birthday, Herb gets excited with the idea of doing something spontaneous. On his way home from work, he stops to buy her gifts, a cake, and a gourmet take-out meal. Arriving home at seven-thirty, he is furious to find that Christine has already eaten, as she usually has, and has opened the presents some friends had brought by. He feels betrayed, and has no understanding of how he gives away his joy for his anger, how he chooses what he needs over what he wants, nor why Christine might resent his anger.

Sara has felt driven to move up in her firm from the first day she walked through the door. She puts in extra hours on weekends and evenings, volunteers for committee assignments, and can always be depended on for special functions or activities. What time off Sara does have, she spends seeing a physical therapist for her chronic back and neck pain. The tension she always feels is armored into her muscles and becomes her constant companion. Even if she does end up one of the youngest partners the firm has ever had, her body may well be old before its time. "Everybody tells me to take it easy. But I don't have time to slow down."

Mick stays anxious so much of the time that his body rebels. His constant gastrointestinal problems are frightening reminders of how he is always trying to remain in control. He clamps down on his feelings just as he clamps down on his intestines. He is forever caught in the middle, between his wife and children, between his wife and parents, between work and home. He feels the tension and says, "I can't relax anymore. I've lost the playfulness I used to have. You wouldn't believe the good times I had when I was young."

He tells us: "I'm trying. I realized that I always drive whenever we go anywhere . . . and I'm always uptight and angry when I do it. So the other day I asked Betty to drive. It almost drove me crazy. There's nothing wrong with how she drives, but it was like I couldn't turn off. I had to watch, think, and worry for her . . . like I'm responsible for the world. How do I turn myself off?"

Paradoxically, it is the fact that Mick's self *is* turned off that causes him so much pain. His attempts to make himself relax or let go simply increase his tension. Playing or living playfully is a natural phenomenon. We must surrender to it for it to happen. If we surrender all our needs, agendas, and intentions, we will *naturally* live in playful ways.

Playing

"Mama, I'm going out to play." "I was just playing up the street, I didn't realize it was getting dark." "Daddy, wanna play cars? I'll let you pump the gas." Listening to and looking at small children, it would seem that *playing* is an easy and simple activity. And, of course, for them it is. Playing is simple and easy for children because it is natural. Animals in the wild also play. That is how they learn. Play is nature's permanent classroom. Children intuitively understand that it is in play that they learn on the deepest level how to be a person. In play, they learn to walk and talk, to be with others, to read how other people really feel, to imagine, to feel good about themselves even when they lose. We all *learn* about the most important experiences of life through play. Then we go to school, sit in stiff chairs, are ordered to be quiet and listen, and we are *taught.* And yet we wonder why once school starts we learn so much less in so much more time, and why we lose that joy of learning that is so obvious in the young child. And, of course, in most families the same transition occurs at home, too.

For most adults, play has become an elusive dream, a longed-for way of being, remembered in the past but always just slightly out of reach in the present. Many of us remember play in our past, plan to play in our future, but never quite manage to play in our present. We are alienated from that marvelous feeling of freely being ourselves. We even have difficulty understanding what play really is. We adults tend to see play as childish and frivolous. However, play is not frivolous. Nor is it childish; it is *childlike*. Play is the basic way in which we all learn. Cut off from playing, we are cut off from learning. Deprived of learning, we do not have the facilities for changing. We cease to grow.

Such damage to growth is easily seen in the children of alcoholics. Alcoholic parents are too often unavailable to their children, and playfulness is a foreign feeling for children with emotionally absent parents. We see that truth in Irene. Irene spent most of the first seventeen years of her life with two parents whose drinking was out of control. Not surprisingly, she left home early to get married. But by the age of twenty-two, she was divorced and on her own. Her husband had been looking for a mother, and Irene was already disillusioned with taking care of other people.

However, Irene did not enjoy being alone. Her loneliness put her painfully back in touch with how desolate her family had always felt. By age twenty-six she was married again, this time to an older man who seemed gentle to her. Yet as the years passed, Irene found herself more and more anxious. She was caught between her need to have everything right on the one hand, and her fear of hurting anyone's feelings on the other. Irene was exceedingly fastidious both at work and at home. The towels could be folded only in a certain way, and the stacks in the linen closet had to be straight and aligned. The same orderliness she imposed on the utility room and kitchen, she demanded of her children and husband. Irene was always angry, even though she did not want to be angry. She never had time to play with, or even be with her children. There was always too much to do. Their father took them places or joined in their games while Irene worked in the house.

She tells us: "I guess I was oblivious until he had already drifted far away from me. . . . I guess I drove him away. But I didn't mean to. That's not what I wanted. It's just so hard for me to let go of all the things that pull at me. It's not any fun being this way."

It is no fun living in any nonexperiencing way. Unable to live playfully, we die as selves. In our adultness we consider playing a luxury instead of a necessity. Like Irene, we forget that play is the most natural manifestation of being. Although that truth is difficult for us to realize in our unplayful society, it is directly visible in other cultures. In *Flash of the Spirit*, art historian Robert Farris Thompson describes such a culture:

> At the core of the Ejagham artistic phenomenon we find men and women involved in continuous, intensely spirited, brilliant play. The propelling force of the culture—hidden by some of the densest forest in West Africa—is a conscious choice to create objects and sequences of human motion through the playful application of vision and intelligence. In all the arts and rituals the Ejagham play for the sake of formal excellence, transcending, like the Greeks, their material existence through acts of aesthetic intensity and perfection.

How unlike the Ejagham we are. Our rituals, like Irene's, are often painful instead of playful, and we remain convinced that excellence is the product of work, not play. Those convictions mean we seldom transcend our material existence, confusing business with being.

Play

The word *play* comes to us from Old English, and means "activity for amusement or recreation." But play has other important roots that contribute to its meaning in ways we easily forget. The frolicking aspect of play, its nonintentionality, is the one adults most easily lose. Adults also tend to ignore how play involves paying attention. Such paying attention is not quite the same as attending to others but instead can be summarized as *engagement*, a total involvement in the present experience. In our adult search for recreation, we are so full of goals and intentions, and have so many things to "pay attention to," that true play is neglected.

Such engagement—true play—is the only way of being part of something that allows a person to remain a *self*. That is, play is the only *doing* that allows us to avoid being captured by whatever system we are *doing* in. It is for that reason that play is the *natural* vehicle for learning. It is nature's way of allowing a knowledge of systems to be gained without the complete loss of unique individuality. That uniqueness is necessary, for it provides the essential thrust to new growth, change, and evolution that life itself is based on. We cannot live, either as individuals or as a community, without it. It is increasingly clear that play is as important a part of our health as our nutrition, exercise, and social contact.

One of the ways in which play is important is that it keeps us in touch with the fact that there are no answers and explanations to life; living is a process that unfolds as we live. We are not separate observers who watch life but participants in the making of the process. We are authors in our own books and our lives are the stories we write, the tales of our being, and our not being, ourselves. Stories are the only truths we have about persons. We are all stories or, if you will, we all have our stories, and playing allows us to stay in touch with our own individual narratives.

We easily forget that other people, too, are their own stories. We incorporate them into ours as if they have no narratives of their own. Usually we return to the struggling stories of our parents, to their lives or their marriages, and we insist that the persons with whom we are currently relating be actors in those old stories. They, of course, resist. They do not know the lines or script, and to live in the roles we give them would mean giving up their own personhood—their own stories. No one can do that. Our continuing insistence only makes them angry.

Since they will not be in our story as we wish, we blame them. We see them as the cause, and ourselves as the effect, in our lives. We are miserable because they do not love us, or will not save us, or will not make all our pain go away. Meanwhile, just as insistently, they are putting us into their parents' story, they are seeing us as the cause and themselves as the effect, and blaming us. Alienated from our own real stories, we have no real knowledge of ourselves, of our others, or of the world around us.

Play, as the direct connection to the story of our lives, is indispensable to safe living. Play is a primary pathway to being ourselves in the world in good faith, to being whole. Sadly, it is a pathway lost to most adults—*sadly* in both senses, because joy is the energy of that faith, the clearest manifestation of true play.

The Cutting Edge

At fifteen, Eileen is deeply depressed, beyond a normal teenaged "I hate the world" moodiness. Her continuing withdrawal has become a real concern to her mother, as well it should. In a society where one or more out of every ten teens is going to try to kill him- or herself at some point, she should be concerned. The unplayfulness of our current culture, and its resultant stresses, is a large part of why the world of modern teens is a very dangerous one.

Eileen is the older of two children in a single-parent family. Her mother and father divorced when she was five; she has not seen her father in the years since, except on rare visits. He lives two thousand miles away, and money is a problem. Outwardly, both parents have tried to deal fairly with the difficulties their problems have caused the children: there is little overt combat, but there is little joyful or playful living either. The stresses are still there and have accumulated in Eileen. She has always been an overachiever in school and an overly docile child at home.

Eileen, her mother, and her younger brother came to see me (Pat) just one time. I did not see any of them again for ten more months, at which point the mother came in by herself. "I don't know whether to be here or not. I mean, I don't know whether to be glad or worried. Since we came that time, Eileen has changed a lot. She's really come out of her shell. She's playing soccer, she got involved in the school student council, and she's started playing the piano again. They're doing a musical at school and she wants to be in that. Maybe a bigger difference, if you can believe it, is at home. She's joking, cutting up, plays with her brother, kids me. She's like a different person. Do you think she's okay?"

Several issues were clear. First, one family meeting with me did not cure Eileen. She simply found something in that meeting that she needed to restart her own natural growth. The process of therapy, when it is working, is like play. It is nonintentional, and, since it has no intent, it is impossible to define what in particular it was that allowed Eileen to change. It is a *story*, not an *explanation*, that contains this information. Eileen was the only one who could tell that particular story and she was not present this time.

Second, the mother did not come in to ask me if Eileen was okay. She came in to see me about herself. Eileen's natural return to play, her rediscovery of a powerful engagement in life, had left her mother acutely, although not consciously, aware of her own lack of play and joy in life. It was this hurt that she really wanted to talk about. Given half a chance, children will play and learn, but, too frequently, we adults give ourselves no chance at all to play or learn. It is selficidal to miss the *experience* that such playful engagement brings.

Experience always moves to the new, the novel, the never-before-experienced. *Experience will always abandon a goal for more experience.* The opposite of curious experience is boredom, and the hallmark of boredom is the familiar. The clearest form of the familiar is *work:* the reattainment of previously attained goals. Such reexperience, done healthily, is necessary, but is different from experience itself. More than anything else, real experience depends on an evolving creative and novel engagement in the world. That way of being is *play.*

The necessity for play does not mean that work is unhealthy. But work that is driven by needs—unhealthy needs that are not chosen and represent a form of repeating past struggles—is unhealthy, a form of unhealthy closeness. It does not matter if it is compulsively doing yard work, trying to be attractive, trying to be the best bowler in the league, or staying with a job we detest. They all diminish us. However, work that is truly reexperiencing is a part of healthy closeness. The reexperiencing contains the kernel of the new, the acute edge of the growth that the new experience brought. None of us can work healthily at all times, but we can begin to move in those directions. As we play more, we "work through" what we have learned in play and make it part of us. Play, in that way, is always the cutting edge of our personhood. Play is always up front, where *being* is happening.

Without play, we miss that cutting edge. Many of us experience this lack as a deficit of adventure, risk, and freedom. And so it is. Without play, without the intimate engagement in life that play represents, we do not risk, we are not curious, and we do not freely venture. We do not experience, so we diminish ourselves. We are not curiously involved in our world, so we do not explore it. We are not curious about either ourselves or the world in which we live. We lose track of what Robert Lynd described in *Solomon in All His Glory:*

There are two sorts of curiosity—the momentary is concerned with the odd appearance on the surface of things. The permanent is attracted by the amazing and consecutive life that flows on beneath the surface of things.

That amazing life is our world, and that permanent curiosity is our playful engagement in it. Watching a child for a day can show us just how real such play is. Like Eileen, when children are unblocked, they live on the cutting edge.

Risking Re-creation

Jerry spends his weekends jumping off mountains. He is approaching middle age, and has come to feel that his life is stagnant, that his wife and children are boring, and that excitement is sorely missing from his life. He jumps off mountains while flying in hang gliders or rappels down mountains while rock climbing. He does both in search of excitement. Like many humans, he mistakenly believes that taking risks can replace the risking of play. It cannot.

Play is any activity we engage in that has no intention and no goal. It is activity simply for the experience of being active and actively being. Seen as such, we can easily understand how so little play occurs in our society. We are full of intentions and goals. Visiting fitness centers to get in shape, going to night spots to meet someone, coaching Little League to recapture our youth, playing tennis to win the division championship are not ways of playing. They are, instead, examples of the many ways we cannot let ourselves enjoy our selfbeing.

We cannot force ourselves to play, nor can we coerce ourselves into engagement. Putting ourselves at risk does not mean we are playing. Albert Einstein once said, "It is a very grave mistake to think that the enjoyment of seeing and searching can be promoted by means of coercion and a sense of duty." Such seeing and searching, whether by a physicist searching for a new particle or a child searching for a four-leaf clover, will be playful only if it is real. The true explorer is the playful wanderer, not the man on a mission. Play is always nonintentional. "Trying to," like "having to," makes it something else. We have to risk finding the new in order to be renewed.

That truth accounts for the increasing desperation that therapists find in the Jerrys of our time. Frantic to find the passion and adventure we miss, we frenetically search for something *to do*. We run further and harder, jump off higher mountains, go faster, deeper, and longer. But none of it works. We forget that filling up leisure time, exhausting ourselves, and external risk-taking are not playing. Playing is *re-creation*, an experience of *self*. We must confront the monster we fear most—ourselves.

We are *re-created* each time we play. That is the true risk, since we are risking whatever new us will appear each time. We risk the changes. We risk being reborn. Engagement makes us be real in our world, and in realness we always change. We risk our past to be *here*. We risk our future to be *now*. Only experiencing in the here-and-now leads to selfbeing.

Understanding that play is the fundamental learning context has tremendous implications for our educational system. Sadly, that system now seems very out of touch with *learning* as opposed to *informing*. All teaching that is not grounded in play simply informs. We do not mean "simply" to be negative. Being informed can be quite important. But meaningful informing is possible only when previous learning has created a place for that information to exist. Learning creates a context for information to make sense. Informing then becomes the re-experiencing of the previous learning. It becomes a confirming enhancement of what is already known. The process is innate. Natural curiosity is the basis of learning.

Unimpeded, all humans will play. And while playing we will learn. We *can* trust that process if we would. The risk, of course, is that everyone would then be different. Humans would not fit into neat little boxes so they could be stacked, moved, and exchanged easily. Play is a dangerous activity. To see that, we only have to watch how serious life is in a totalitarian state. Repress play and we repress learning. Repress play and we repress growth, curiosity, and risking. Repress play and we live among mass man. Those same costs are incurred individually when we repress play in ourselves. Selficide is inevitable without play.

Trust is the real risk. It is the platform for risking engagement in our world as a part of it. The risk of *being*. Education, freedom, growth, adventure, intimacy, and eventually healthy closeness all begin in the play experience. It is as the Chinese philosopher Mencius said, "The great man is he who does not lose his child's heart."

Renewal

Backward, turn backward, O time, in your
      flight,
Make me a child again just for tonight!

—ELIZABETH AKERS ALLEN,
      "Rock Me to Sleep"

Where then are we left as adults? Play obviously occurs in children. It is clearly natural. Children learn, are re-created, are intimate with their world. Play by definition is what is new, re-creating, and energizing. It is the experience of our yet-to-be. Playing is always a new experience, even if we have done it before. As soon as it is no longer new, it is no longer play. Children live in the novel, instinctively rebirthing themselves, needing no instructions, needing no plan. How do we as adults renew ourselves? What do we do to ensure constant rebirthing?

In the child, play is free. As socialization proceeds, the child becomes more responsible. Unfortunately, as we become more responsible, we begin to lose our ability to play. We feel as if we have no choice: we can either be playful or be responsible, but we cannot be both. This feeling, which has been ingrained in most adults, is the ultimate lie. It lurks in the cores of our souls, gnawing at us. "I cannot play and be responsible at the same time. But if I choose . . . if I am foolish enough to choose . . . I lose either way." We begin to play resentfully and rebelliously. That is, we work at playing. We begin to be responsible and to work without pleasure, work ourselves to death long before we die. Nature's truth is lost. We never learn that we can playfully be responsible or responsibly be playful, and in so being, be not a workhorse, but a horse running free.

In adolescence, this window to experience is presented as precisely this choice: Can we learn to play in the context of our responsibilities as an adult? In our culture, we do a very poor job of helping adolescents with this developmental task. Few adolescents solve it by learning to be both playful *and* responsible. Instead, most teenagers mislearn to repress play in order to try to be responsible, while some fewer mislearn to repress responsibility in order to try to be playful. Few learn that being really responsible is a necessary element in play. Playing requires being responsive to the world around us. We engage our world in such play and become more able to respond.

This unhealthy way of being is evinced in all kinds of symptoms, from use of alcohol and drugs (we even talk of *recreational* drug use!) to various personality and character disorders— passive-dependency, passive-aggressiveness, or sociopathy are only a few examples. The majority of us, however, simply end up being unenergized, unhappening, and uncreative. Like Jerry, we miss the adventure, excitement, risk, and renewal that we nostalgically remember from childhood. We usually associate the memories with things we *did*, and miss the point that, in actuality, it was a way we *were*.

Thinking erroneously that renewal came out of the things we *did*, we look for things to do now that will recapture those moments. We usually call these activities games or hobbies. But they are seldom playful. They do not engage us in our world or help us relate to it so much as they set us up to compete with it. We try to *better* our golf, to *win* at tennis, *improve* our bridge, collect *more* antiques, swim *faster*, travel *farther*. In *Prophetic Voices*, George W. Morgan said:

> Our social fabric militates against relation. Competitiveness pervades everything we do and is taught from the time we are small children. Work and play are conceived of as contest and race. . . . We seize on the half-truth that competition forces everyone to do his best (half-truth, because his best is by no means always the best in human terms) and completely ignore what this does to human meeting. Our fundamental stance is not to respond to others, but to outdo them, vie with them, beat them.

Renewal as a self will never come out of such competition. By definition, competitive living cannot be nonintentional, so it can never truly be play. It blocks experience because it is not intimate. It does not allow us to be ourselves while we accept the other person fully. Many of us even live competitively with our loved ones. Like two tennis players, we head out to the court to have fun and be with each other. One would think we would be interested in the *rally*, keeping the ball in play as long as possible, helping each other participate, learn, and grow. Instead, we begin playing *against each other*: we smash overheads, hit directly at the other person, and try to tick the lines. We become *intentional*. Our intent is to win. Play is forgotten. Experientially, there can be no playing *against*, only playing *with*. It is not a question of how hard we play, but of our intent.

In *Finite and Infinite Games: A Vision of Life as Play and Possibility*, theologian James Carse talks about the difference between such forced play and free play:

> If the goal of finite play is to win titles for their timelessness, and thus eternal life for oneself, the essence of infinite play is the paradoxical engagement with temporality that Meister Eckhart called "eternal birth."

Infinite play, or engagement, is the play that renews, recreates, and energizes. It is the only thing humans can *do* about their *being*. It is the way we become the poets in our own lives. It is the most direct window to selfbeing, and its closure the surest route to selficide. Without "eternal birth" we are destined to "eternal death." We must be infinite players to be reborn, mothering and fathering each new self toward fuller selfbeing.

Sexuality

John and Mindy had been married twenty-two years when they first came to see me (Pat). They had three children, the youngest of whom was fifteen, and that many years had passed since there had been any sexual relations between them. Both were good people, and their close relationship was tense but not ugly. The increasing strain of their lack of touching was taking its toll, however. But nevertheless their complaints about their closeness were what had brought them to therapy.

In this couple, there was a long history of an almost total inability to be playful with each other. As best as I could tell, they engaged in no teasing, no silliness, no private jokes, no playful ways of being with each other at all. Both were quite aware of this lack and would talk about it freely. They seemed clearly to understand what the lack of playing with each other was doing to their relationship. They could not, however, talk about their sexuality at all, much less freely. It was like pulling teeth to try to get them to recognize that the two subjects, play and sexuality, were one and the same.

One session, Mindy came in alone and told me about how she had faked orgasms in the early years of their marriage. The insanity of faking pleasure in being yourself reminded me of what Umberto Eco said in *Travels in Hyperreality*:

> This is the reason for this journey into hyperreality, in search of the instances where the American imagination demands the real thing and, to attain it, must fabricate the absolute fake; where the boundaries between game and illusion are blurred. . . .

It was as if the "real thing"—Mindy's fantasy of how she and her relationship should be—was more important than the reality of Mindy herself. Mindy said that she had never enjoyed sex and it was very clear to her that John did not enjoy sex with her. She was so serious about the matter that I decided that if sex really was what she was struggling with, she would probably be correct to avoid it completely.

Soon afterward, John also came in alone, and my interaction with him was not too different from that with Mindy. Just as she had faked her orgasms, he had faked his interest in her. The sad thing to me was that it felt as if they really loved each other. They simply had no idea how to be themselves. It seemed very clear that their lack of sexual knowledge was a direct result of their inability to play. They could not be sexual because they could not safely be childlike. Whatever the past hurts and injuries in their childhoods, the resulting fear blocked them from simply playing with each other.

The most direct example of play for adults is sexuality. The failure of real sexuality, an almost universal complaint in our culture, is a direct manifestation of the inability to play. It is probably also the clearest example of the self-diminishing results of that inability. It is a painful dilemma. I (Tom) once saw a woman who immediately began talking to me about her sexual frustration and unhappiness. As she paused, I asked her if she was orgasmic. She replied, "Sure, I can come . . . but I don't. I always stop myself when I feel I'm about to come. I don't want to give that s.o.b. the satisfaction of knowing he could ever satisfy me."

That is about as unplayful as a human being can be. Obviously, this woman's "sexual" experience with her partner was not sexual. Nor was she being loving. She was simply using the sexual relationship as a platform to express other feelings and to fight about other issues. There was no play involved. Her behavior was loaded with intention, as was clear in her response to my question.

Such behavior is not uncommon. So many of us use our "sexuality" to express a variety of feelings quite apart from our actual sexuality. Tenderness, pleasure, play—all of the *being with* behaviors that are part of true sexuality—are missing in intentionality. The growing, creative, and evolving nature of true sexuality is found only in engagement, not in entrapment or entanglement.

The sexual experience in our culture has most commonly become a contextual relationship in which both men and women act out not their playfulness or sensuality, but a variety of other feelings and needs, most of which are unhealthy. Aggressive dominance, passive manipulation, and proving one's worth as a man or as a woman are some of the games that are played out in the name of sexuality. None of these behaviors are sexual. Using the other person as an object is not sexual. Nor is using him or her as a way to masturbate ourselves. There is no playfulness in such encounters.

One of my (Tom) clients came to a session ecstatic. He said to me triumphantly, "Last weekend my girlfriend had multiple orgasms." He had struggled for years with the feeling that he could not satisfy women. Of course, I congratulated him. But with a smile, I asked him how many orgasms *he* had experienced.

"None," he said.

Performing is not making love. And doing something to someone else is not experiencing the sexuality of our bodies. We have such difficult getting back to ourselves that we lose track of what our *sexuality* is.

It is instructive to note how many of the sexual fantasies of both men and women are with anonymous partners. Is excitement possible simply because of the relief from shame and guilt, and the escape from our mechanistic and moralistic concepts of sex? Those issues are certainly part of the reason. But there is another issue as well. I (Pat) saw a woman whose first successful orgasm occurred during an anonymous fantasy, after many lurid fantasies with recognizable partners had failed. "It was like I didn't have to pay so much attention to what he was or felt . . . I could really pay attention to what I was doing and what I felt." We cannot play when we are not being ourselves. In true intimacy, we experience our selfbeing. We do not take care of the other person.

The most common difficulty experienced with sexuality is that of experiencing close personal love while at the same time experiencing passionate sexual love. When we are being sexual, we are being intimate if that sexuality is real, passionate, and fulfilling. When we are being personally close, we are paying more attention to the feelings of the other person than we are to our own. In so doing, we are no longer sexual. Our common difficulty lies in being unable to make the transition back and forth.

Foreplay involves true closeness and a meaningful awareness of the other person. As foreplay proceeds, there is a gradual and gentle shift from the enjoyment of the closeness to an enjoyment of the more intimate sexual passion within each person. In the continuing relationship, that passion is shared. But it is shared differently than in foreplay. At a certain point, our awareness shifts to the feelings within us rather than the feelings of the other person.

The transition is one of moving from personal closeness, as experienced in foreplay, to the intimate experience in both persons as experienced in intercourse. Orgasm, which is a total awareness of self, is the experience of being able to have that self-awareness expressively in the immediate presence of another. With the recession of passion and intimacy, there is a beautiful return to the tenderness and the security of personal closeness. While this description portrays sexual relations, it also describes the prototype of what all experiences between two caring people can be, whether sexual or not. Playing with one another is just as healthy when we are talking together, walking together, or simply being with each other.

Familiarity

Unhealthy closeness, closeness which captures and entraps, blocks such play and engagement. And nowhere is this diminishment of self more clearly seen than in our loss of sexuality. Trapped by the known, the familiar, we are unable to explore, unable to play, unable to experience passion. Passionless sex is just that: nonexploring, noncreative, and nonplayful. The loss of passionate sexuality is likely the most common complaint of adults, because adults in relationships are most commonly separated from their playfulness and thus from their sexuality. They cannot be nonintentional, and there is no passion—sexual or otherwise—with intention.

The serious person is apt to demonstrate this truth well. Unable to distinguish the difference between the *important*—how we and others feel and think—and the *serious*—those few moments in life when what we do right now makes some real difference—they live everyday life as if it were an ongoing crisis. Consequently, they cannot frolic. Some are aware and regret the lost ability to play; others are unaware and inflict themselves on all they come in contract with. In either case, the damaged ability to experience will have major effects on how the person lives his or her life.

Hal is twenty-nine and five years into a relationship that he is now considering leaving. He comes in to share these thoughts with someone who "knows about these things." With me (Pat), he is just as serious as he evidently is at home and at work. He is determined to advance in his career and to "make the most of his chances in life." There is no humor, no laughter, not even a smile. He is strictly somber:

"I'm certainly not very happy. Abby is a good person . . . but a lot like a child . . . she goes through life without any real understanding of what's going on. You can look at how she deals with money or the house and see she has no real grown-up idea of what the world is about."

He tells me: "I end up having to take care of everything myself. . . . I have to make all the decisions. It's a lot of work and it's tiring. That, and the headaches I constantly get, really drag me down. I'm just wondering if I'd better put an end to it."

Abby may indeed be childish; she is certainly responsible for her half of whatever is going on in their relationship, but she is not Hal's problem. Hal is Hal's problem. He is slowly but inextricably shrinking his selfbeing by his inability to play, to engage in his own living. His headaches tell him that, his tiredness tells him that, and his relationship tells him that, but he does not listen.

Over time, I discovered that Hal's sex life was also telling him of his premature death—the death of his personhood. More correctly, his lack of a sex life communicated this message. The serious person, the person who lives in the world as if in crisis, can never be sexual. We cannot make love waiting for the ceiling to cave in on us. Sexuality in its meaningful sense requires playful being. One can exercise power, control, manipulation, or dependency while genitally "working," but one cannot be *sexual* without being *playful*. We do not need to conduct in-depth research studies to discover just how few people are currently living playfully, that is, sexually, in their relationships. We only have to listen and watch.

Playful Work

The damage done by seriousness is seen in all areas of our lives, including our work. I (Tom) for some time saw a man who ran a sheet-metal company. Ned and his wife had come to me with marital problems, but over time I naturally learned about his problems with his work as well. A story Ned shared with me is very instructive as to the importance of play.

In the annual trade publication, Ned's company always came in second in productivity, profitability, and whatever other statistics were compiled in that journal. They were always second to another small company located in New England. Over the years, Ned grew curious as to why this was so. One day he called and asked the other owner if he would object to his coming up for a visit. The older man met him at the airport, took him to the plant, and proudly showed Ned around. This man was full of life, talking and laughing over the machine noise with his employees, touching and hugging them, and sharing in their private jokes. He was alive and enlivening, and Ned could feel the energy he carried whenever he went.

During dinner that night at the owner's house, sitting with this man and his wife, Ned said, "You really enjoy what you do, don't you?" The old man laughed and replied, "Yeah, it sure beats the hell out of working." At that moment Ned understood why he always came in second to this man. It is something we could all learn from. The profit motive is certainly no proof against self-diminishment. A *joy* motive, a *wholeness* motive, might better serve us.

The same confusion is blatantly evident in our educational systems, our governmental systems, our health care systems, our legal systems—indeed, in all of our *systems*. Systems capture, and if not balanced by dyadic being, very effectively block play. Therefore, they obstruct learning, communal participation, healthiness, and natural orderliness. Play is the only way we can deal with systems without a loss of self. It is the only *doing* thing that completely allows *being*. Play is nature's conscious window to the unconscious, a nondiminishing way to work on ourselves.

I (Pat) have over the years worked in several different psychiatric hospitals. I have no doubt in my mind that the best ones have been those with the most playful staffs. Not the best-trained staff, not the best-paid staff, not, certainly, the most serious staff, but the staff which is capable of full engagement. It is they who create the healthiest environment for humans who are hurting. "Patients" grow only in an environment in which *everyone* is growing. We can no more teach someone to grow than we can pay someone to love us. I do not mean to discount professionalism, training, and teaching; they are all important, necessary, and can and do help. However, they are not sufficient unto themselves. It takes more. It takes the intimate ability playfully to be with someone to heal them, just as it takes that ability at school, in court, at home, or in corporate offices in order to nurture growth.

We so easily become confused about growth. Growth occurs naturally. That is, the act of growing in humans, just as in trees, is naturally given and naturally driven. As the process is *natural*, it will occur as long as we do not block it. We can thus *allow* it, but we cannot *make it happen*. We can feed a tree, water it, prune it, give it more light, and give it more space, but we cannot teach it to grow. Trees innately know how to do that. People are no different. Humans must learn to experience on their own.

The Dance of Life

One should dance because the soul dances. Indeed, when one thinks of it, what are any real things but dances? I mean the only realities—moments of joy, acts of pleasure, deeds of kindness. Even the long silences, the deep quietness of serene souls, are dances; that is why they seem so motionless. When the top dances most perfectly it seems most still; just as the apparently still earth is dancing round itself and round the sun; just as the stars dance in the night.

—HOLBROOK JACKSON, *Southward Ho!*

Teilhard de Chardin said that "Joy is the most infallible sign of the presence of God." Regardless of whether we see God as deity, nature, communal reality, or universal unconscious, this idea must be valid. Joy is the sign of the divinity of life. The newborn child enters life and engages his or her world playfully. He or she proceeds nonintentionally to suck, pull, and tug at what is near, to grasp, taste, and examine all within reach, to listen, smell, talk to, and move with all the rest of what is. He or she playfully enters the dance of life. Whatever selfbeing the child will later have, and whether he or she will live in self-diminishing ways, will in large part depend on how the child learns to dance.

Most of us cannot remember our dancing. As adults, we are too often left sitting on the sidelines watching. We long for the freedom of moving but are afraid. In our fear, we miss out on our being. We all are most perfectly ourselves in our true playing, our true engagement in our world. At those times, we seem still in our being even while active in our doing. We grow, we learn something new, we are changed. We spin more perfectly with each new experience.

14

THE ELEVENTH WINDOW:
Aesthetic Morality/ Moralness

If you do not tell the truth about yourself you cannot tell it about other people.

—VIRGINIA WOOLF, *The Moment and Other Essays*

Pearl lives in an apartment overlooking a park in Atlanta. She has been increasingly perturbed by the homeless people who have been gathering in the park over the past few years. She is not disquieted in the sense of simply wanting them to go away, but in the inner sense of not knowing how to deal with them within herself. When she walks across the park, she is afraid to look directly at anyone for fear of locking eyes with another person who could make her feel guilty about having enough to eat or enjoying the cozy warmth of her own living room. At sixty-one, Pearl does not know how to deal with someone in that position. She does not know whether she should give them money, become socially active to help them, or try to get them to others who could help them. She cares, but she does not know *how* to care. She shares with me (Pat) her pain and confusion.

"I feel like I need to do something, but I'm afraid . . . or maybe ashamed. I'm not sure exactly what it is. I know I wouldn't want to be living like that, and I know they don't either. It upsets me that I don't know how to deal with it. No . . . I take that back. It bothers me that I don't know how to deal with myself about it."

I asked Pearl what she *wanted* to do, what would make her feel good about herself. She told me that she had always been a simple person—that people were more important to her than things—and that she liked just to talk with people and be helpful to others in any way she could. She said that she had always derived part of her self-esteem from being a giving person. I asked her why she did not do just that. I knew that there was a family history affecting her struggle. She had lately become caretaker of an older brother, and had taken care of her parents for many years prior to that. She did have difficulty separating caring from caretaking, but she was willing to wrestle with her issues. There was no question that the issue being raised was significant to her.

I suggested to Pearl that she might try doing what she wanted to do. Talk to the homeless and be as helpful as she might. It seemed to me that if nothing else, she would learn more about what she was trying to deal with.

She replied, "But what will I ask them? I can't just say, 'How did you get here?' or things like that. What will I talk to them about?"

"Why don't you talk about you," I responded. "Or talk about something you like. Then you'll at least know you're being you and not somebody else, which seems to be part of what you're fighting with yourself about."

I did not see Pearl for several months after that, which was not an unusual pattern for her. When she returned to see me, she was much less anxious and much more alive. Responding to her smile, I said, "Well, I assume you solved your problem about the homeless people." She had indeed.

Pearl had become a participant in the life that was happening around her. She had decided to talk to the people in the park, and had done so. She mostly talked about philosophy, since it interested her, and she had discovered that there was philosophy to be found in the park. She cooked soup for the homeless, because that was what she liked to do, and she discovered that friends could be found in the park as well. But the most beautiful thing that had happened was that she had discovered Pearl in the park. She had found how to live in a way that made her feel moral to *herself*, instead of to *others*.

Ethics and Morals

The ancient Greek word *ethos* meant "character." Our word *ethics* originally came from that concept: from the belief that how we lived in our lives was connected with our character, our inner being. The Roman concept of *mores*, "principles of behavior" (their translation of *ethos*), became our word *moral*. Morals concern the *mores* of the society, the customs of our tribe as opposed to the customs of another tribe. Ethics and morals have become generally indistinguishable in present everyday usage. There is, however, a basic and meaningful difference between them: Where does behavioral control lie? Is it internal (ethos), or external (mores)?

The word *aesthetics* contains the *ethos* root, and in many ways remains connected to its original Greek meaning. Beauty, as an *intrinsic quality*, seems closer to concepts of character than social custom. Let us consider then the phrase *aesthetic morality* as a way of describing how humans might decide how to live in the world, as themselves, within their tribes.

Peter is an intelligent and capable man in his early forties. He came in to see me (Tom) reluctantly, at the urging of his wife, Renee. He said he felt like a captive in my office, that he did not feel he needed any help and did not want to be there. Peter felt that people in the "professional helping business" were unrealistic and should go out and find real jobs. He did not view as a marital problem the fact that he was having intermittent love affairs of some consequence. He considered himself a thoughtful person and, at least consciously, an honest man.

Despite my "unreal" profession, Peter spoke to me as if I were a fellow businessman, discussing his relationship with his wife and children in a manner that suggested we were going to make a deal or a merger, or perhaps buy someone out. He accounted for all the difficulties in terms of Renee's problems. He was angry with her and clear that if she would "just get her head straight," everything would be okay. I think he was slowly warming up to the notion that getting Renee's head straight was something he and I could manage.

As we have seen, such blaming is not uncommon in relationships. To some degree, all of us blame our others. It is a subtle trap hidden in life's underbrush, waiting to snare us whenever we judge others because we are not whole within ourselves. But Peter's problem was not simply that he was blaming and defensive, or even that he thought his way through life instead of living it. The major problem with Peter was that he had no connection to the real issues in his life—his relationships with his wife and children, and his own selfbeing. In many ways, he was wandering around in the dark.

Renee had been raised in a wealthy family, but essentially she had no parents. She had been cared for by nannies and had that unbondedness seen in those who are not lovingly touched by their parents when young. The unbonded are those humans who, like vulnerable trees, are not firmly rooted in the ground substance of life. But Renee had evidently been fortunate enough to have someone among her caretakers who had reached her intimately, for some sense of what is important in life had been given to her on a deep level. She had at least kept living. She had lived in a dependent, maternal, accommodating relationship to Peter for the first fifteen years of their married life. She had stayed home, living with and through her children, and was always there whenever Peter chose to be there with her.

A few years before they came to see me, however, Renee had begun to change. She had seen a pastoral counselor at her church, and that relationship had been very helpful in her growth. She began to think of being herself as a separate yet caring human being. She had continued on that pilgrimage to the point where she was more independent. She became more assertive and expressive and was less accommodating to Peter. After years of being unhealthily close, she had developed an initial capacity for being herself in an intimate way. Unfortunately, this new intimacy was seen by Peter as her not caring, not relating, and not being close to him. It made *him* feel less secure. He sensed an increasing ambivalence in her, and, in that feeling, he was probably correct. She had grown ambivalent about mothering him and living dependently with him.

Aesthetic Morality

Peter and Renee were at the point of either living together in a better way or separating. Renee was drawn, deep inside herself, to separating. What compelled her toward leaving was her feeling that Peter had absolutely no sense of the absence of beauty in their relationship. He, in contrast, was simply confused by her feeling this way. He felt that by any standards their relationship had always been a workable one, and, as he said, "Certainly better than most people's." He did not understand her desire for an inner morality in him (his integrity), even while he felt guilty about his lack of external morality (his affairs). He was not connected to her enough to know that she could forgive the latter, but could not live with the former.

It was precisely Peter's lack of any sense of the aesthetic aspects of himself and their relationship, not his external moral failures, that was driving Renee away. She could only vaguely articulate the feeling. It is not easy to describe such internal states even if one can overcome the anxiety of being so personally real. Her position was clear to me, however, from listening to her. It was also clear to me that if Peter could sense her feelings, look inside himself and know who he really was, and then share with her his own hurts and dissatisfactions with himself, she would stay.

The aesthetic morality we feel in our relationships largely reflects our sense of self-worth and self-esteem. Peter had little of either, in any meaningful sense, and thus had little that was meaningful to share with Renee. He was successful in terms of earning money, but failing in terms of being a person. He was drifting away from his wholeness as a human being.

If we are to understand human living, healthy and unhealthy, we must deal with the questions of values, ethics, and morality. We must deal with them not so much to be the complete philosopher as to try to come to a *real* conception of how the relational human exists. Morality, in this sense, is a wide window to being fully human. And, since the *relational human* is the *experiencing self*, any ideas about wholeness, selfbeing, or selfbeing's diminishment—selficide—must deal with the values, ethics, and morals which define the primary form of how humans relate.

We tend to forget that experiencing is itself a *moral* act. Not moral by legal, societal, or dogmatic religious definitions, but in the internal spiritual sense, in the sense of inner integrity. We tend to be so caught up in our moral fanaticism, whether religious, economic, or political, that we forget that life has a morality of its own. Experiencing has the morality which all of nature possesses naturally. "Nature," Joseph Cornell wrote in *Listening to Nature*, "is an expression of God; or, if you prefer, of the creative force and intelligence in the universe." Nature is innately moral.

Our own inner morality, then, arises from our existing in a *natural* state, from our being congruent and living with innocence. It cannot be negotiated, modulated, or traded. It is not a system concept and is not amenable to systemic rules. It forms the basis for our self-respect, our self-worth, and our self-esteem. Inner morality involves how we see ourselves, not how others see us; how we love ourselves, not how others love us.

Experience and Morality

We are all ultimately our own punishments. Not in some obscure philosophical sense but in the pragmatic sense that real experience requires an internal morality in order to happen. Self-being is thus sacrificed in any and all ways we lack such moral capacity. Experience, in terms of its fullness, is sensitively attuned to external judgments of right and wrong. Perhaps nothing except the overt lack of self-love circumscribes experience more seriously than exterior judgment. It makes no difference whether this judgment is expressed interpersonally, culturally, or as internal threatening introjects (such as an internalized critical parent). In all three cases, the judgment is exterior.

Experience is most full when it judges itself, and is significantly lessened when it submits to any external judgments. Experience increases when the judgment becomes internal and maximizes when *judgment* gives way to *aesthetic discrimination*. That is, there is less truth, less love, less reality, and less beauty in nonexperience. When experience is wrong it is *less* experience, when it is right it is, nevertheless, still *less* experience. When experience is ugly it is *more* experience, and when experience becomes beautiful it is *most* experience. An aesthetic internal morality characterizes all true experience.

It is disturbing for many of us to conceptualize morality as a personal much less an aesthetic choice. So much of humanity is consumed by the notion that there must be structure and rules imposed from outside. Millions have been burned, hanged, and slaughtered for the sake of moral creeds. One can always depend on a large segment of humanity to distrust *humanity* itself. But we would disagree, feeling as did Charlotte Brontë when she said, "Conventionality is not morality, self-righteousness is not religion. To attack the first is not to assail the last."

We *can* deal with real world issues without judging others. We *can* accept differences as ugly or beautiful, without being captured by labels of right and wrong. We *can* understand the question Jesus posed to the men ready to stone the woman for adultery: "He that is without sin among you, let him first cast a stone at her." What he asked is the *important* question: *How will each of us be with ourselves if we do this, how will we be internally within ourselves? Will our behavior be beautiful to ourselves?* And that, of course, is the real question for all of us about all our behavior.

Although it is not always easy to do, one can retain a sense of humor about our society's hypocrisy over such life issues. In his *Intimate Journals*, poet Charles Baudelaire relates a vignette that succeeds in doing so:

> All these imbecile bourgeois who ceaselessly utter the words: immoral, immorality, morality in art and other idiotic phrases, make me think of Louise Villedieu, the five-franc whore, who, having accompanied me one day to the Louvre, where she had never been before, began blushing and covering her face with her hands. And as we stood before the immortal statutes and pictures she kept plucking me by the sleeve and asking how they could exhibit such indecencies in public.

Despite the worries of those who believe that humans need controlling, the *only* control possible on the experiencing level is *self*-control. Aesthetic morality is our window to seeing our own behavior for what it is. It is participatory, internal, and amenable only to self control.

This dilemma—that the only control possible on the experiencing level is *self*-control—is precisely the shared difficulty of Peter and Renee. Participation in relationship produces a sense of beauty or ugliness, an aesthetic dimension. The nonparticipation that is necessary to make objective judgments does not allow the aesthetic dimension; it cuts us off from the experience. Most of us are too out of touch with each other to know if our experience is either beautiful or ugly. Either feeling would be more relational and participatory than what one might call "reasonable judgment, complacently shared." Aesthetic participation is what Renee hungers for, even if at first it is only an awareness in Peter of the ugly in her. And vice versa. Instead, rationality is what Peter shares: his reasonable and controlled assessment of their relationship. It is an exterior judgment as opposed to a participation. She, he, and their relationship all become objects in his predefined world. It is not even actually rational, for Peter's thinking ignores many truths he himself knows, but will not let himself know—the truths of how he feels and who he most deeply is.

Morality and Therapy

Nowhere does the issue of internal morality arise more clearly and directly than in the event of psychotherapy. Arnold is twenty-seven, referred to us from the probation office, and no pleasure for anyone to deal with. He is sarcastic, passive-aggressive, and demanding. Arnold's difficult history goes back to his early childhood. He was always in trouble, could not follow the rules in school, did not get along with others, and was constantly fighting authority. He has incurred many minor legal offenses, was asked to leave the Army, has been let go from many jobs, and is now on probation for trying to shoot a neighbor's dog with a handgun.

He tells us: "Look, Doc, I don't want to be here any more than you do . . . ha-ha. They're full of shit. That damn dog was driving me crazy barking. I bet everybody in the neighborhood would've liked to shoot it. They oughtta give me a medal."

Does the responsible therapist, or any responsible person relating to another, confront Arnold's values, ethics, or morality? It is easy to dislike Arnold, and easy to see how he is socially wrong, but that judgmental response avoids the question. It is clear that no one changes without acceptance, so seeing Arnold as wrong and disliking him does more than not answer the question. It perpetuates the problem. As in our ordinary relating, judging guarantees defensiveness. The more difficult question remains: Does a therapist, or anyone, confront the values, ethics, and morality of the other person?

All therapists experience the conscience of the person who shares him- or herself with them, and the experiential response of a therapist, over a period of time, will quite likely modify that conscience. What is the therapist's conscious responsibility? Is there a difference between morals, particularly morals based on religion, and personal morality? Outside of the obvious unconscious effect that any one human will have on any other when the two are in meaningful relationship, what is the role of a therapist in a person's changing internal moral states?

Does the *secular* therapist have the right, or even the obligation, to confront the values, ethics, and morals of a client? If he or she does, as with Arnold, then does he or she have the right or obligation to impose his or her own value/ethic/moral system on the person? That question is particularly pertinent when the therapist sincerely believes that his or her value/ethic/moral system is the best and most congruent of all possible systems. But the issue of acceptance always returns. Even though we may recognize what is wrong with a person, to confront that wrongness immediately and suggest to the person alternative and logically better (that is, more workable) feelings, thoughts, and behaviors is simply another way of depriving the person of his or her basic right to be him- or herself. As such, we provide at best no more than a benevolent recapitulation of the original controlling parent, society, or culture. At worst, it is a direct violation of the other's personhood.

This violation is especially present when we attempt to substitute our own values, ethics, and morals for those of the client. Acceptance is of vital importance. Without accepting people where they are, a therapist—just like any of us in our ordinary relationships—can never help them become more, come to be what they themselves, not others, want them to be. Part of that acceptance, a most basic part of it, is the genuine acceptance of a person's religious beliefs, ethical convictions, and spiritual stances as the parameters within which the other person—therapist or not—then works.

A person's value systems, ethical convictions, and religious beliefs are areas that a therapist confronts only under very special circumstances. Otherwise, therapy becomes a frightening, proselytizing, propagandizing endeavor. Humanity is *never* the exclusive property of the liberal or the conservative, the religious or the secular, the Christian or the humanist, the Buddhist or the atheist, the sinner or the saint, the educated or the ignorant. It is certainly not the exclusive property of any given therapist. It is not even the exclusive property of the sick or the well, the healthy or unhealthy, the mature or immature, the sane or the insane. We are all human—the superstitious and mystified primitive as well as the pragmatic and sophisticated urbanite. Circumstances must be special to invite such incursion.

"Illness" Versus Nonexperience

What then are these special circumstances? What if a value of another person, an ethical stance, or a religious conviction is part and parcel of that person's "illness"? What if the sociopath, much like Arnold, conveys to you his value/ethic/moral conviction that the end justifies the means? What if he dresses this dishonesty up? ("I'm embezzling money from my employer to pay for this therapy I so desperately need.") To take another instance, how do we deal with the more subtle self-diminishment and self-denial of the dependent, depressed minister who is jeopardizing his marriage and family with a self-destructive sacrifice of himself to his parishioners? One cannot doubt that his parishioners need him. The world is full of need. His self-denial has real and recognizable benefits to others, even though on a deeper level it teaches them to be unhealthily themselves.

Such behavior models the selficidal practice of *giving self away* rather than the self-enhancing living of *giving over* to the other. A lawyer or plumber could serve the same example if they lived their lives in similar ways. Conversely, what if clients' value systems are money-based, success-based, or power-based? Are these the special circumstances under which a therapist must become confrontive?

What about the hypomaniac person who with eager generosity gives all her savings away to a deserving human charity, to the great detriment of her own family's future? Or the hysterically oriented person who sees sexual freedom as his right to do whatever he wants as long as his action does not seem harmful to others, including his lover or spouse? Where do we draw the line?

The dilemma is even greater when the value/ethic/moral is part of a systematized, ethically definitive, religious tradition. For example, years ago I (Tom) had a client named Sissy. Sissy came to me with two major problems: she was very overweight and she was very depressed. The onset of both problems followed her divorce. It seemed clear to me from the start that Sissy's weight gain was a defense against her sexuality, just as her depression was partly a reflection of the loss of that sexuality. She hid from relationships with men who were available to her, for her religious convictions prohibited sexual experiences outside of marriage and, even more specifically, forbade marriage with any man not of her religious faith. The pain of being caught between her needs and her convictions had led her to shut the system down. She had become obese and depressed.

As a therapist, do I confront those religious convictions in Sissy? I know that unless I do confront them as being a real and substantive defense against her sexuality, she will probably remain obese and depressed. Sissy came to me when I first began as a therapist. I did not confront her religious beliefs, and she went away just as forlornly overweight as when she had first seen me. Would it have been different had I been different?

I(Pat) would say yes, although I suppose that depends on what "it" means. *Something* would certainly have been different, if only the fact that Sissy would have/would not have given up on therapy. My own struggle with this issue has often left me uncertain, and I have often chosen wrongly. I am not convinced that there is *anything* in a person that is off-limits in therapy. I have little patience for those people who say, "Don't anybody expose me to any different ideas, or challenge my faith, or ask me tough questions, because that's personal." If our faith, ethics, values, and morals cannot withstand the tough questions, exposure to difference, and challenge, then they do not really exist in any real way. They are just defenses against life.

Any life stance or belief that blocks experience must be dealt with in therapy if that therapy is to have any real meaning. Seeing the *nonexperiencing* in clients instead of seeing them judgmentally as being "ill" allows a therapist to accept and confront at the same time. In *The Spirit of Chinese Philosophy*, philosopher Fung Yu-Lan spoke to this dual possibility:

> Every creature cannot but regard himself as right, and
> those things which are different from him as wrong. This also
> is natural in every case; and from the viewpoint of the Tao this

is inevitable, and the creature is to be let alone to do this. The result is that the man who has reached "the axis of the wheel" does not need to discard the ordinary man's interpretation or argue over right and wrong. The only thing is that he "does not follow them, but views things in the light of heaven." This, then, is not destroying but transcending . . . this is why a sage harmonizes the different systems of right and wrong, and rests in the revolving of nature.

The "axis of the wheel" is selfbeing, based on an internal, aesthetic morality. The "revolving of nature" is the natural process in which that selfbeing is found.

These same questions arise in the ordinary relationships any of us have. Do we confront the values/ethics/morals of those we love? Do we try to impose our own values/ethics/morals on them? When do we engage our others around such issues? When do we challenge the religious belief systems that they profess? Clearly, the only reference point that is not judgmental is the internal one. Does the value/ethic/moral/religious system make the other person more beautifully—wholly—himself or not? Or does the belief, conviction, or stance block experience, push the person further away from his or her wholeness as a human being?

Confrontation and challenge are often conceptualized as *harsh* interactions in our culture. That is not the context in which we use these words. Therapists can encourage others to examine their belief systems as they try not to sell them their own. Clients have often bought a package, but never opened it to examine what is inside. Too many of us believe something just because our mother or father told us to—a subtle form of ancestor worship.

But, many ask, what is the alternative? Even if aesthetic morality determines self-esteem, they worry, will it control external behavior? Can we maintain a functional society based on how we feel about ourselves?

Inner Morality

To answer those questions we must deal with the issue of just what the control mechanisms in humans are. Obviously there are laws, rules, and customs that *define* behavior. But what controls behavior *within the person*, that is, within the person relating to their world and the others in it? Such controls seem to fall generally into one of three categories.

First there is external control, wherein the person's feelings about self are dependent on the response, the approval or disapproval, of significant others (and later the manifestation of others as systems—religious or otherwise). An example: Rafael expresses his anger at his lover's humiliation of him at a party. His lover responds that it is hard to see why Rafael is upset, given that everyone else at the party also felt that he was making a fool of himself, and that if he does not think that is true, he should call any of them and they will be glad to tell him so. Rafael retreats to a depressive, apologetic, and self-deprecating posture. He allows others to be his judge. His morality is external and dependent.

Second there is external control which has been internalized. Here the internalized introject—the voice of conscience, the parental voice modified by subsequent parents, the systems of belief accepted—tells the person how to feel about self. Rafael shares his anger with his lover's humiliation of him at a party. However, he feels strangely apologetic while he expresses his anger, which is actually well justified. His lover appears surprised, stunned, and hurt by the confrontation. Rafael, feeling guilty and inappropriate, says, "I'm sorry, I didn't mean that. That was wrong of me." This morality also comes from the outside, even though it has now become part of Rafael. He has not grown past his fear of expressing anger or his need to appease the parent figure. The voices may be inside him, but they are still other people's voices.

Third, there is authentic internal control wherein the determining experience in how the person feels about self depends on whether his or her thinking, feeling, and behaving are congruent with each other and congruent with an already present sense of self and how the current behavior then makes him or her feel about him- or herself. Rafael shares his anger with his lover's humiliation of him at a party. He says, "I need to talk. I'm very angry with you, which I don't enjoy being, and I do not want to go around all day feeling like this." And when his lover responds by saying everyone at the party also thought he was making a fool of himself, Rafael says, "I will be responsible for dealing with them. For now, I want to deal with *our* relationship."

There are really only three ways to teach morality or ethics to people, and these three forms of control track the examples outlined above. First is force. While we usually think of force as authoritarian or even punitive, it also includes the force of our personality, the force of parental concern, the force of love. Nevertheless, it is an outside voice that defines which thoughts, feelings, and behaviors will be acceptable and enforces them. We have an external standard. For example, our parent approves of being careful about appearances in life, so we find ourselves being careful people.

Second is information. As the answer to questions about how we will live our lives—how we will be ourselves—information is necessary but not sufficient. Even after it is internalized, information will still carry the flavor and nuance of those who imparted it to us in the first place. It is impossible to tell anyone anything without the intrusion of such metafeelings. We then have an internal standard that contains external definitions and feelings. For example, a favorite teacher exposes us to the concept of scholastic integrity and intellectual honesty, so we find ourselves living out that creed. As a creed, such integrity may be useful, but it nevertheless contains the flavor of that teacher, her feelings and expectations. It is not yet fully our own. A transition—some *self*-experience—is required for it to become part of our selfbeing.

Third is example. Teaching by example allows the other person to learn as he or she will. What they then decide will be *of them* and not *of the teacher*. The metafeelings will not have to be internalized. Such teaching is experiential in nature and is how natural learning occurs. Talking, smiling, relating, and participating in the family are all learned this way. It is the most potent form of learning: that is why dysfunctional families produce dysfunctionality. It is also, thankfully, our way back to health and wholeness. We can get back in touch with our internal sense of self, our inner morality, by learning as ourselves.

In a person who lives out of an internal aesthetic sense, behavior control will be directly connected to selfbeing. The person will live in ways that maximize wholeness. The behaviors and actions that make the person feel more beautifully and fully him- or herself will be the ones chosen. We all intuitively know this truth. We feel that unique "best us" when we live up to the best of our inner self. The feeling empowers us. We not only feel more real, we feel more alive.

Values, Ethics, and Religious Beliefs

All the ways in which we allow our behavior to block experience diminish us and damage our self-esteem. They are apt to be the core issues which arise either in therapy or in our ordinary relationships and are central to our growth. Values, ethics, and religious beliefs all fall into this area, but our inner morality is the central issue.

Our inner aesthetic morality must be defined separately from what we traditionally mean by values, ethics, and religious convictions. These aspects of our persons are tremendously important and meaningful, but they alone do not contain the wholeness of our persons. At their healthiest, they move from being internal judges to being integral parts of ourselves. However, they are not the same as our inner voices. We must realize that inner morality *is* different. This difference is crucial to understanding the role of a therapist with a client, or each of us with a significant other, or even each of us with ourselves in struggling with these issues.

Ethics and morals deal with the manner of our living with each other, but they are system concepts. That is, any given society sets up systems of ethics and morals for its own security. They are rules about closeness that are externally determined. Morals are the surface rules of the society—how people are with others in the ways they behave in their public living and interactions. Ethics are the forms of the deeper structure—how people behave in their private living and interactions. That is why it is more threatening for members of a society to be unethical; it jeopardizes the society to a greater extent. Religious beliefs are codified systems used to institute such rules. But none of these concepts are actually internal or intimate. They speak first to how we will be with others, not how we will be with ourselves. That truth does not make them any less valuable, just different. They are codes of conduct, not windows to experience.

Inner morality speaks to the issue of subjective guilt, whereas values, ethics, conventional morality, and religious convictions speak to the issue of objective guilt. For example, most all of us would agree that a murderer is objectively guilty. On the other hand, he or she may or may not be subjectively guilty, i.e., feel guilty or remorseful. It is the latter guilt that deals with aesthetic and inner morality. Inner morality involves those experiences that make us feel good about ourselves or bad about ourselves, that are conducive to selfbeing or conducive to self-diminishment. The ultimate issue becomes whether, in response to our behavior, we like or dislike ourselves, or, more deeply, love or hate ourselves.

How do we feel about how we behave apart from how society feels about how we behave? Our inner moral response depends on how we feel about our behavior when our feelings are stripped of dependent considerations. Apart from what others think or feel, how do we feel about what we are *being?* This question is simply another way of asking how our reflections on our own behaviors affect our sense of self-worth. Our self-esteem in this way directly reflects our inner morality. If I dislike myself for my behavior, apart from how society feels about my behavior, my self-esteem suffers accordingly. If I like myself for my behavior, even if my behavior is disapproved of by society, my self-esteem is enhanced. Inner morality becomes increasingly a matter of self-esteem.

Many will ask: "Does that not mean then that the person who feels good about his bad behavior will continue it? That our punitive systems have no corrective power if they do not cause the individual to confront *himself?* What do you do with the street kid whose self-esteem and social standing are enhanced by his drug dealing, robbing, and blowing people away? Isn't the problem that social approbation affects self-esteem profoundly, even to the extent that it is impossible to isolate self-esteem's determination?" We would say no. Social standing and the "self-esteem" that comes with it—regardless of social level, regardless of whether positive or negative (for we could ask the same question about the successful corporate raider)—are aspects of security, not true *self*-esteem. No normal human feels more him- or herself out of such behavior. It can, and sadly does, however, make many humans more secure. That is why such behavior—both in "positive" and "negative" forms—becomes more and more prevalent.

Contrary to popular belief, self-esteem is not a constant, just as maturity or immaturity are not constants. Self-esteem changes. As a feeling, it waxes and wanes depending on life experience. The variations are usually minor, but sometimes changes can be drastic, especially when we dishonor our *selves* (as with Peter and his affairs). More than anything, a healthy inner moral sense assures a maximum self-esteem. It assures that we will generally, al-

though not always, avoid experiences that lead us to devalue ourselves. It assures that we will try to live in a way that maximizes
our selfbeing.

Inner morality constitutes the essential control mechanism
in humans that, when healthy, enhances experience instead of
blocking it. The quality of this control is extraordinarily important in mediating the self in its environment. Perhaps more than
any other structure in the psychological universe, inner morality
will determine the amount of real experience people *allow* themselves.

Beauty and Ugliness, Goodness and Evil

The distinction between inner and outer morality is important because it goes to the heart of aesthetic morality, that is, to
the question of whether beauty and morality are connected. It is,
of course, the foundation of the Platonic ethic that to know the
good is to do the good, and that, as Socrates took as a given, the
good is beautiful. If, however, beauty is seen as external appreciation and morality as external approval, then they certainly are
not connected. In "Goodness Knows Nothing of Beauty," novelist
William Gass spoke to this connection. While he spoke to the
formal qualities of artifacts—art—we feel that the point is also
useful in looking at human experience.

> Artistic quality depends upon a work's internal, formal,
> organic character, upon its inner system of relations, upon its
> structure and its style, and not upon the morality it is pre-
> sumed to recommend, or upon the benevolence of its author,
> or its emblematic character, when it is seen as especially rep-
> resentative of some situation or society.

Applying the point to human experience, we would agree.
The problem with most of external morality is precisely its disconnection from inner systems of relations. Inner morality is a
manifestation of "isness," internal formal character, and relatedness. It is an ecological concept. If we see beauty as likewise an
ecological event, a manifestation of "isness" and not an external
objective appraisal, it is clearer in just what manner the two are

related. Artist Marc Chagall said, "When I judge art, I take my painting and put it next to a God-made object like a tree or flower. If it clashes, it's not art." In just that way can inner morality be evaluated. It is the manifest connection between aesthetics and inner morality.

Gass lists as human goals truth, goodness, beauty, happiness, and salvation. He sees them as different, equal, and independent. We would agree that they are different and equal, but feel they are independent only externally. Internally, on the *self* level, we believe goodness does know something of beauty, and truth, and happiness, and salvation. But it is only the goodness of inner morality (or inner beauty, or inner truth, or inner happiness, or inner salvation) that is so connected. As Gass says, in the world of politics, power, economics, and righteous religion, what we would call the world of systems, goodness knows nothing of beauty, nor of its siblings.

In response to Gass, fellow novelist Robert Stone wrote in "The Reason for Stories":

> Life matters, lives matter, because earthly human history is the arena in which the universe acts out its consciousness of itself, displaying its nature as creation. . . . Above all, what I wish to argue is that the laws of both language and art impose choices that are unavoidably moral. The first law of heaven is that nothing is free. This is the law that requires the artist to constantly make decisions, to choose between symmetry and asymmetry, restraint and excess, balance and imbalance.

The laws of art and language are the laws of real experiencing. The connection between inner morality and beauty is a *pattern-based* connection, a direct manifestation of what is. It is a *self*, not a *system* event.

On the *self* level, the child learns to see beauty as good and goodness as beautiful. Conversely, the child learns to see evil as ugly and ugliness as evil. This beauty is not the attractiveness of the Hollywood starlet; this goodness is not the donation of the philanthropist. This ugliness is not the face and body of the Elephant Man; this evil is not in the boss who secretly uses company funds to buy a second house. We are speaking, instead, in the context of the relationship of these qualities to ecological states. Is or is not a human being living as who he or she is in the world that is? Does or does not a human move that process forward in any given moment? In this sense, selficide is evil and ugly, selfbeing good and beautiful. Wholeness is an *aesthetic* concept.

There are critical periods in childhood in which such connections are made. The psychoecology of the developing child is the realm where controlling parameters will determine the form of the child's inner morality. Will the child learn by example and develop an inner morality, or will he or she be taught an external one? In adolescence, as the child separates from the parents, these choices are exercised and practiced. Does the young person live only out of external controls, or are there inner self controls? Is the developing adult left with the resentment that dependency—doing what others want us to do because we need them—always brings, or can he or she live in the world unangrily by living out of internal choice and internal morals? *The actual behavioral choice in most of us will, most of the time, be the same,* whether our morals come from outside us or inside us. But it makes a tremendous difference in the person and how she lives as a self whether the behavior—the way of being in the world—is *chosen* or not. One way blocks experience, the other enhances it.

We are not saying that external systems are not useful and important. Socialization and acculturation clearly comprise half of how we live as persons. But they are only half. We misuse them because we are imbalanced into unhealthy closeness and captured by our systems. Instead of remaining healthy parts of reexperiencing, they become stumbling blocks to real experiencing. Captured by them, we live in self-diminishing ways. External codes alone limit our capacities as humans.

Philosopher Bernard Bosanquet, in *Some Suggestions in Ethics*, spoke of these capacities:

> Values are the development of capacities. It takes the whole system of values to draw out the whole capacity of man; it takes the whole capacity of man to be the basis of a perfect system of values. If in any community there are underdeveloped capacities, so far the system of values is strained and obstructed.

That community is the human ecology, and the underdeveloped capacities are our ability fully to be *selves* in it.

Self-Determined Versus Selfish

Inner aesthetic morality is self-determined but not selfish. It is energized not to *gain* but to *become*. There is a tremendous difference between the two goals. Gain, whether it is seen as gaining truth, money, power, salvation, or any of the other names we have given to security, is a drive toward some fixed end point, some externally defined goal. As such, the drive inevitably blocks experience. It is selfish in that it tries to define the world in the interest of the "self." But this is not the *self* of connection, it is the pseudo "self"—the false self—of nonexperience. Becoming, on the other hand, is open-ended, having no goal other than more becoming. It invites us to new places, new feelings, new thoughts, new actions. In other words, it invites us to experience.

There is a potent confusion here. Many people associate self-sacrifice with goodness or morality, as if in being one's self a human would not be good or moral. That is a devastating way of seeing ourselves. Philosopher Judith Farr Tormey replies to such thinking:

> But one need not be caught in the false dilemma which requires a choice between self-sacrifice and egoism. . . . To be unselfish one need only give the interests of others their proper weight.

"Giving the interests of others their proper weight" is a *natural* part of true self. *Self* recognizes that it enhances itself by enhancing the other. In a dyad, both grow or both diminish. Nature knows no winners, only growing and stasis. In growing we *become*, we increase selfbeing. In stasis we cease becoming, we are selficidal. And *we* are responsible, for, as Teilhard de Chardin said in *Divine Milieu*, "One makes his own soul."

Vi is thirty-one and has lived in a primary relationship for the past three years. She and her lover are polite and close, but there is little joy or intimacy. The relationship is increasingly strained and Vi is frightened. She worries that her lover will leave, and this worry, not any desire to change herself, brings her to therapy.

"I don't know what to do. I don't want to be alone. I can't be all that bad." Vi says that her lover feels that she is a selfish individual, that she is determined to have her own way in life whether that way is material, emotional, intellectual, or behavioral. It is not that Vi is a "bad" person. It is more that Vi's life appears to be predefined and constructed around needs for which she does not take responsibility. In Vi's world the other tells her whether she is worth loving. She therefore has a powerful need to construct that world in a way that will allow her to feel secure. Her lover feels that she is manipulated by Vi, always put in a position in which she is supposed to be some way so that Vi can feel all right.

Vi devotes her energy and time to ensuring that her needs are met. She does this despite an awareness that in many ways it pushes her lover further away from her. Vi forgoes her own becoming, which means that she forgoes relating to her lover. Both live in stasis, mutually self-diminishing in *fixed* ways of relating. Vi has little capacity to "give the interests of others their proper weight," and that fact is clear to her lover.

Many of us have the same difficulty. Like Vi, our inability diminishes us as persons. We have difficulty understanding "giving the interest of others their proper weight" as an internal aesthetic aspect of self, instead of as an external action directed toward those others. When we lack that knowledge, our window to growing and changing remains shuttered.

Vi says she wants to change, but no change occurs. She has yet to understand that the problem is not her behavior, or what she thinks, or even what she feels. The problem is her lack of inner morality. She is not living in a way that enables her to love herself. Psychotherapist Sheldon Kopp reminded us of this malady in *If You Meet the Buddha on the Road, Kill Him:*

> Patients in therapy all begin by protesting, "I want to be good." If they cannot accomplish this, it is only because they are "inadequate," cannot control themselves, are too anxious, or suffer from unconscious impulses. Being neurotic is being able to act badly without feeling responsible for what you do. The therapist must try to help the patient see that he is exactly wrong, that is, that he is lying when he says he wants to be good. He really wants to be bad. Morality is an empirical issue. Worse yet, he wants to be bad but to have an excuse for his irresponsibility. To be able to say "but I can't help it." His only way out is to see that his pilgrimage to the heavenly city

must be undertaken along the road through hell. When we lay claim to the evil in ourselves, we no longer need fear it occurring outside of our control.

If we understand "good" and "bad" in terms of inner or aesthetic morality instead of externally defined control systems, then the value of the "road through hell" is clear. The evil in us is our lack of aesthetic inner morality. It is the ways in which we are selficidal and diminish our selfbeing. The "heavenly city" is living in the world in full selfbeing. It is not easy. We will not get much cultural support for such living. But it is eminently worthwhile. An inner aesthetic morality is the only guidepost by which any of us can live. It is the only constant reference point we have on our journey in life. Moving away from that interior conscience is always *self*-destructive, regardless of the pain of living with and by it.

15

THE TWELFTH WINDOW:
Connectedness/ Reciprocity

Mark has been in the hospital for four days, undergoing detoxification from alcohol dependence. At forty-two, he has been divorced for many years and currently lives with his mother. He is sitting on his bed in a semiprivate room. When his roommate's wife is ready to leave at the end of visiting hours, she kisses her husband good-bye and then comes over and kisses Mark lightly on the top of his head. "Good luck," she says, "and take care of yourself." As she leaves the room, silent tears roll down Mark's face. He does not feel worthy of being touched.

Mark feels unconnected to anyone in life, and finds it difficult to accept that this woman could care about him. His sense of alienation is profound (although not complete, as he is emotionally touched by her gesture). He is a walking example of the truth Goethe stated: "To be loved for what one is, is the greatest exception. The great majority love in another only what they lend him, their own selves, their version of him." Mark feels that other's version of him must be unlovable. Most painful, he feels this way even in the face of his loving others. He sees no reciprocity to his loving in his ordinary relationships.

Mark's ordinary relationship is mainly with his mother. After his father's death, he moved in with her, but their relationship has always been strained. She is consistently critical of him. He does not go to bed when he should, reads the wrong books and magazines, does not eat properly, and cannot even make a decent cup of tea. Her chastising is always addressed to him in the plural: "We should lose weight. We've already had too much to drink today, haven't we?" Even when what she says is correct, Mark feels judged. He feels tremendous anger toward her, but says nothing because he does not wish to hurt her feelings. But he dreads hearing her footsteps coming down the hall at night, and turns off his light so she will think he is asleep. He wonders why she does not understand that he, too, has feelings.

Mark closes his eyes when tender or poignant moments occur on TV or in the movies, for he cannot stand how they make him feel. His sense of longing for *and* fear of such touching overwhelms him. On one of his rare dates, he was aware of how angry he was that the woman he was with asked questions during the movie. He was embarrassed by her talking, but later felt ashamed of his critical feelings. When confronted by his therapist about his negative sense of self—so different from how the therapist experiences him—Mark replies that he remembers a quote from somewhere: "Entrenched beliefs are not changed by facts." He finds it almost impossible to believe that someone could find him lovable.

For Mark, as for many of us, there is a tremendous inertia against becoming alive. It feels as if we are at the bottom of a steep mountain and cannot climb it, so we simply stay there, discouraged, without even making an attempt. Change seems overwhelming, if not impossible. We feel utterly alone in our pain. The small voice inside us says, "Why doesn't anyone know I'm here, realize that I'm tender and passionate? Why won't anyone touch me?" We feel no connection, and without that, we see no way to grow. We forget that we *are* somebody.

In the classic film version of *Gone with the Wind*, Rhett says to Scarlett as he is leaving, "It seems we've been at cross purposes, doesn't it?" There are so many humans who could say the same of their relationships. They always seem to be at cross purposes to those closest to them, to those they love *most* if not *best*. Given how often relationships end up in that situation, we could almost believe that it was a natural part of being or, perhaps, that humans are simply perverse and undirected by any common sense.

Common means ordinary, but it also means communal. What is common involves both me and you, as well as others. Sense means, first of all, a feeling and awareness of the other. So common sense literally means a feeling and awareness of one another. Exactly what is missing in those like Scarlett and Rhett, who are at cross purposes in a relationship? We see people every day who are at cross purposes and who appear to lack common sense. They are good and intelligent people who were never taught by example the beautiful simplicity of common sense—that is, feeling and knowing each other. They are left out of touch, with no connections except their ambiguous words, distancing behaviors, and painful memories. Are they simply perverse?

There is another possibility. Humans may at times be perverse and, indeed, frequently do show a lack of common sense, in that they do not live their lives in a way designed to make those lives joyful. But their being at cross purposes comes more from their failure to participate in life as a reciprocal process than from any willful perversity. Being at cross purposes is not natural. It is, in fact, just the opposite. Nature reciprocates. It does not confound merely for the sake of being perverse. When the wind snaps a tree trunk, there is no accusation or defense. The wind and the tree are reciprocal aspects of nature. It is part of their natural relationship. Vindictiveness, blaming, and being at cross purposes are strictly human creations, although we have clearly taught them to some domesticated animals. All of nature is connected, recursive, and reciprocal. In their search for security, their flight from real experience, humans withdraw from this process selfi- cidally, and shutter the window to nature's wisdom.

> It is only crying about myself
> that comes to me in song.
>
> —THE TUNGIT INDIANS,
> "Song of the Poet"

Reciprocal Living

Otto and Gayle are two years into a relationship that has all the earmarks of a déjà vu experience. Both were married previously, then they found each other at the local bowling alley. Each seemed to the other to be the answer to their relational prayers. Each seemed so different from the other's previous spouse. It was a chance to *be* in all the ways that they had been unable to be for years past. The first year of their dating was exciting, romantic, and fun. It seemed as if it would go on forever. In their second year together, forever seemed to come in smaller bits, a few moments at a time. Soon, it was not coming even in small bits, and they were no longer having much fun at all.

She says: "It's hard for me to believe he's changed so much. He used to be considerate and affectionate. Now he's just like my ex used to be . . . doesn't think of anybody else. Sometimes I don't believe he thinks at all. He never asks me anything anymore, doesn't even talk to me. It's like he feels that I'm *making* him relate to me or something. I spent over twelve years with my first husband dealing with that stuff. I don't need any more of it. The thing that really irritates me is that he's not responsible. He says he'll be places at certain times, but he isn't. He says he'll do something I asked and then he forgets. . . . He doesn't really listen in the first place."

He says: "She stays mad all the time now. Our first year, she was easy and seemed to like me . . . we relaxed with each other. I enjoyed talking to her. Now it's like everything has to be her way or she loses it. Sometimes I think she's really nuts. Maybe it's just the way women are. My ex-wife was the same way. You couldn't please her. It feels to me like it's her way or no way. Well, I don't need that. That's why I got divorced before."

Gayle and Otto certainly seem at cross purposes and may even sound perverse in these encapsulations of their life positions. But they are not stupid or perverse people. Gayle is thirty-seven, intelligent, and considered a sensitive person by her friends and co-workers. Otto is forty-two, also intelligent, and also seen as caring by those who know him. Yet these two good people have found a way to be at cross purposes with each other that is much like their previous relationships. Sadly, they did not continue to live in those new *ways of being* with each other they both enjoyed when they first met.

The recapitulation of earlier failures, in second or even third long-term relationships, is very common. Indeed, many of us can trace our tendency to re-create our past back to dating in adolescence. Most of us can also remember one relationship that was somehow different; we usually leave that one with some sense of confusion. But for the most part, our new relationships turn out to be much the same as our old relationships, as we relive our old beliefs and experiences.

Almost all of us want to love and be loved. But having begun our love affairs as mutual *explorations*, we frequently turn them into mutual *exploitations* as we repeatedly struggle with the same issues. We do not relate as who we are to others as who they are. Instead, we rehash what has already been rehashed: we agonize over our fear of loving, our failure to carry our caring over to intimate relating from which we could learn and grow. Equally common is our fear of being loved. We flee the *self-revelation* that true love forces upon us. Or we struggle over particular issues of our childhood, insisting that our partner play his or her part in our scenario, insisting on recapitulating our past hurts in the fantasy that they will come out differently this time. In all of these cases, we are left at cross purposes. We agree to forgo being who we are with each other in order to fight about who we were, could be, might have been, or should have been. Why do we do this?

The most obvious answer is simply that we learned nothing from our earlier failures that makes a significant difference in our subsequent choice of partners. In a strange way, if our second pairing is a success it would mean our first was not a total failure, for we would have learned and grown from the experience of the first. Usually, we merely reconstitute our earlier choices in new packaging, eventually to suffer the same pains, problems, and impasses we suffered before. And most of us will do so with absolutely no realization that we are making the same choices and that we have learned nothing from past experience.

Reproducing old relationships is a manifestation of the lack of wholeness with which we live—living with shuttered windows, if you will. We will painfully end one relationship and search assiduously and with apparent forethought for someone who is different. But somehow we find ourselves once again in a nonexperiential struggle with the same kind of person, having the same dreary arguments. Usually our motivations are completely unconscious. The arguments may appear different on the surface, but, as we saw with Otto and Gayle, underneath they are the same old issues.

When confronted with how we have repackaged the past, we deny, blame, feel sorry for ourselves, and present ourselves as victims of fate. Or we claim we were deceived by the other person. We seldom see the reciprocity of our relationships, the connection between ourselves and our others, or our self-responsibility for our part of that connection. We do not understand that we are *in* the dance of life, instead remaining with the stagnation—but security—of living "death."

Some years ago, I (Tom) saw a thirty-eight-year-old woman named Carol who had been divorced twice, both times from men who had physically abused her. Prior to her first marriage, she had felt a gut sense that the man might be abusive, but he seemed such a wonderful person, and their sex life was so exciting, that she married him anyway. After several years of being periodically punched and shoved around, she divorced the man and, within a year, married someone who showed no signs of a violent disposition. At least Carol had matured, for this man only had to beat her once before she left. She divorced him and came to see me, wondering what was going on in her life.

A few months later, Carol developed a relationship with an older man and dropped out of therapy. This man was in his fifties, quiet and kind, comfortable with others. Carol was sure she had made a rational choice this time. Three years later she returned to see me. She told me that in the past few months her husband had begun hurting her physically, first in their sexual encounters, then at other times as well. She was now in the process of leaving him. She wanted to know why she was so *unfortunate* as to have married these abusive men. Carol had an almost complete lack of awareness of the reciprocity of *her being* with *their being*. It took her several years to come fully to grips with her involvement. The issue was not that she was making these men abusive, was asking for it, or was in any way responsible for their reprehensible behavior. She was not. But she was responsible for *her* behavior, for *her* choices, and for *her* participation.

Carol was responsible for choosing angry men and needing them to love her enough to give up their anger. She participated in their unresolved anger, relating to them in many ways through that part of their persons. Carol had to open a window to experience in order to learn. To make her life different, she had to

311 CONNECTEDNESS/RECIPROCITY

realize that we all live in a reciprocal world. There is no other real world to live in. There is only the dance. And once we have honestly danced, we know about reciprocity.

Relational being is always simultaneous. How you are with me and how I am with you will always come, in the moment, out of our individual and shared being. Existence happens simultaneously; it is not cause and effect. Mutuality, reciprocity, recursion, and complementarity are the hallmarks of existence. We share equally in *being* with each other. Each of us is responsible for our participation in the relationship. As feminist reformer Lucretia Mott wrote long ago, "In the marriage union, the independence of the husband and wife will be equal, their dependence mutual, and their obligations reciprocal." That truth must be the truth of all relationships. There is no other way of living possible if we are to have real experience and be whole humans.

Reciprocity Versus Fault

It seems difficult for us to develop a germinal sense of the reciprocity of life. As therapists, we continually watch couples spend months accusing each other and defending themselves. Just as frequently, we see individuals who relate to their absent others with the same offense/defense approach. It is a common interaction in therapy.

We ask him: "Why do you blame her?"

He replies: "Because she's wrong."

We ask her: "Why do you defend yourself?"

She replies: "Because he's wrong, and attacking me."

We ask her: "If you feel the lack of care and love in attacking, why do you attack him?"

She replies: "Because he's wrong."

We ask him: "Why do you defend yourself?"

He replies: "Because she's wrong, and attacking me."

An endless cycle. One that is as easily, and as often, carried on in our minds alone as it is between two of us together. In both cases, we are righteous, certain that we are correct and that the other is at fault. We equate responsibility with blame and punishment, and end up with self-diminishment.

No-Fault Relationship

Fault creates more impasses in a relationship than almost any other feeling. We fault each other and argue both as judge and accused, switching roles as it is our turn to talk. To be rid of this defensive and endless pattern of denial, we must realize that the fault is *in the relationship*, not in *either one* of us. That is what reciprocity means: we dance together. When we accept a relational life, we realize that it is not in *either* of us—it is in *both* of us. We are then connected, and able to live life together without blaming or defensiveness. When problems occur, we can look at our own participation in how the relationship is not functioning healthily instead of simply accusing the other. Such connection applies in our relationships to friends, parents, and children, as well as lovers.

It is difficult for us to accept that life is not happening *to* us. So often it seems as if it is. In a nonordinary world—a world of disasters, war, terrorism, and other forms of cultural insanity—life often does impose itself on us. We are caught up in history. But in our relational world, life does not happen to us. We participate in it, and we are responsible for that participation. Gayle and Otto—the couple who found each other at the bowling alley and then lost each other in their relationship—chose each other exactly *because* they reciprocally related in the very ways they now complain about and hurt with.

It is not that the complaints and hurts are not real. In terms of factual *information*, each person in a meaningful relationship is almost always correct about the other person. That is, unless we have some reason to believe that the other person would deliberately misreport *their experience* of us, then what they have to say about us is likely to be experientially correct. If one lover tells another that when he is with her he is angry, distancing, and does not accept her, and that when he makes love he always withholds part of himself, she is very likely to be perceiving something true about him. But her interpretation of what that experience means about him will almost always be wrong. Who we are and why we do what we do happens inside *us*. In our example, when she says that he is angry *because he does not love her*, that he is withdrawn *because he does not care*, she is attributing her own feelings and issues to him. In fact, *he* lives the ways *he* lives because of *his own issues* within himself. Motivation and definition are provinces of the self and are self-determined. Others can report their experience of us, and they will be sharing real information, but they cannot tell us *who we are*.

This confusion in our intercourse between ourselves and our significant others forms the basis of our blaming and defending. One lover says to another, "You are never the sexual initiator between us, you hold back and judge me . . . waiting for me to act. You don't love me. You're not capable of loving anybody." The first two statements are most likely true. They are a report of one human's experience. It is equally likely that the second two statements are not true. They are judgments of motivation and definition. As wise humans, we learn to accept the report and discard the judgments. We learn to use the information to grow, and neither defend nor counterattack the judgment. But this is far from easy to do, since we are so accustomed to reacting and living out our reaction to the other.

We live and act simultaneously out of our own being or, so often, our nonbeing. We are neither created nor generated by the other person. Mark's mother, with her critical controlling, does not cause him to be as he is, any more than Mark, with his passive dependence, causes her to be as she is. Mark and his mother are connected and reciprocally related; they are in the world in those ways together. The same is true for Gayle and Otto, or any of us in our ordinary relationships.

Change

To change a relationship only requires one person to change. This concept is hard for most of us to understand or accept. We tend instead to get into bargaining positions, replete with threats and inducements: "You'd better change your ways or I'm leaving," or "I'll change if you'll change," or "I've already done more than my share," or "This is all your fault," or "Why should *I* change?"

None of these positions represents the truth of relationship. They are only our old nemesis, security, rearing its ugly head in one more form. Relationships *must* change when one person changes, precisely because *they are relationships*. Profound change occurs when one of us begins honestly *being*, expressing who we really are in the relationship regardless of the responses, or lack of responses, from the other person. We come to understand that in loving ourselves, *being who we are honestly and wholly*, we find our real love for the other. As Alice Miller said in *The Drama of the Gifted Child*: "A little reflection soon shows how inconceivable it is really to love others (not merely to need them), if one cannot love oneself as one really is."

Life is a contagious process. Depression is contagious, paranoia is contagious, and compulsive judgmentalism is contagious. Just as surely, excitement, acceptance, and love are contagious. *All affect is contagious.* Once we understand that truth, we have both more reason and more courage to act unilaterally in the relationships that are important to us. (In other cases—such as that of Carol and her abusive husbands—the change in ourselves would be to share our healthier affect and sense of self with someone else.) However, people resist change. It makes them feel insecure. It takes courage to risk selfbeing. Even though in the immediate moment we may not get the response we want, over time we will begin to find the responses that we have hoped for. Such living, however, is not easy. "No one can be good for long," Bertolt Brecht observed in *The Good Woman of Setzuan*, "if goodness is not in demand." Still, we must try to have the courage to live what we want and to risk what we may receive in return.

It is clearly true that if we want something, the best way to get it is to *give* it. This is not news. Homer said it: "The sort of thing you say is the thing that will be said to you." Plutarch said it: "Evidence of trust begets trust, and love is reciprocated by love." Mencius said it: "He who respects others is constantly respected by them." Jesus and Confucius said it. If we want someone to listen to us, we must listen to them. If we want someone to talk to us about themselves honestly, we must talk to them about ourselves honestly. If we want someone to be quiet, we must be quiet ourselves. If we want someone to be accepting at a difficult time, we must be accepting of their difficult nonacceptance. Whatever we want, we must give.

Such relating is the best way for any of us to find what we want in the other person. To say so is simply to reiterate, in a recursive way, the importance of reciprocity. However, it is also a statement about the reality of unilaterality: we can continue to honor our own selfbeing without any ostensible cooperation from the other person in the relationship, and find that so *being* can alter the relationship in ways that meet our needs.

Seeing people in therapy year after year leads to some basic ideas about psychological realities. We listen to people in their nonreciprocal courtroomlike battles. Their accusations and defenses are almost always factual: "Last Friday, after I told you I'd be home early, you weren't there. You were off with some of your friends." The inference is made that because you were off with your friends, you care more for them than you do for me, or that you are irresponsible and uncaring. Or another example: "You knew that my meeting had been scheduled for weeks. It ran late. That's what held me up. I assumed you'd understand that." The implication is that the other person is forgetful and insensitive, judgmental and stupid.

We grow to realize finally that facts are simply implements we use to facilitate our unhealthiness. The relational truth always seems to have little to do with facts. A turning point occurs when we finally give up our preoccupation with facts and counterfacts, and begin to deal with relationship, reciprocity, and experience.

I (Pat) sat with a particular couple, listening to their verbal Ping-Pong. Their basic exchange was one in which the man would say that he wondered why the woman was so unendingly defensive. He would then document this accusation with a number of facts—for example, that she never listened to him and never credited his opinions. She, in turn, would respond to his confrontation by saying that she was defensive because he was so unendingly offensive, and then she would document her accusation with a number of facts—for example, that he was always yelling at her and trying to tell her what to do. I'm sure that all these facts, on both sides, were entirely accurate. But I wondered why I was sitting there with them. They did not seem to need me to do what they were doing. Whatever was going on was strictly between them. What made them think that I would know which of them was right, or that the "loser" would accept my verdict?

One day as they were involved in this to-and-fro accusing and defending, at a certain point the woman hesitated and was silent for a moment after the man had just offensively attacked her. I took the opportunity to say to her, "Why don't you tell him what you just felt?" She told him in a low voice, "I was afraid of you, and it made me hate you for scaring me." He began to cry

316 THE WINDOWS OF EXPERIENCE

and said, "I never wanted you to feel like that." From that moment on, the relationship became significantly different. They had suddenly realized that they were connected.

To see that one person can change a relationship is to recognize the reciprocity of life. If we learn to listen, attend to the information we get from the other, and then find motivational and definitional reason in ourselves, literally in our *selves*, to change, we will do so. The relationship will then change automatically. We cannot change the other, but we are sure to change the relationship if we change. It becomes a powerful idea if we realize that *all* of existence is *relationship*. Upon receiving his Nobel prize, Albert Schweitzer reminded us, "You don't live in a world all alone, your brothers are here too." When we realize that our brothers (and sisters) are *everything that is*, the importance of connectiveness and reciprocity to selfbeing and wholeness becomes clear.

Open and Closed Systems

There is a direct connection between our ability to empathize with others and our ability to be whole. Psychoanalyst Heinz Kohut has written about both the failure of empathy in parenting, which he feels leads to nonexperience in children (and thus unhealthiness in adults), and the failure of empathy in therapists, which leads to such unhealthiness remaining unchanged. If empathy is seen as the living recognition of reciprocity, its power can be more easily understood. Reciprocity is the giving back and forth that all true empathy embraces. Only in the recognition of the connection between us that such giving back and forth implies, can we build a complete human being from the pieces of our living.

Most of us are aware that we do not live in a vacuum. What is more difficult, however, is for us to take a defined experience in which we set the boundaries—an experience in which we both relate to another and perceive the experience (which is the truth of all experience for humans)—and still know that life is reciprocal. We are much more likely to see the latter case as a closed system, a system of linear causes and effects, and believe that we understand it. (That is, since we *constructed it*—perceived it—we believe we understand it.)

Being trapped in this way is precisely the life position of couples like Gayle and Otto. Since they each have defined the truth (the boundaries) of their relationship, just as they did in their previous marriages (that is, by the same internal needs), they live in a closed system. Closed systems are neither reciprocal nor connected, and they lead to nonexperience. Believing that someone else causes us to be the way we are is self-diminishing. Others can make us *do* things—we all have to pay our taxes—but no one else can make us *be* anything at all. No one can make us love, hate, fear, be angry, care, or believe. Those *being* things we have to *be* ourselves.

In the open system—as in the ecosystem or psychoecosystem that life itself is—reciprocity and connection are the norms. In relationship, we happen *with* each other, not *to* each other. When we begin to judge, blame, and accuse, we not only challenge the other person to be defensive, we also lose the sense of our own responsibility for how we are being. As a space/time phenomena, human relating is neither linear nor cause and effect. Gayle and Otto re-create their previous relationships because they insist on living in the closed system of past causes and past effects, rather than in the open-ended system of the here-and-now. As a result, their experience remains the same old experience, which is to say nonexperience. It is just a big security loop, not a living and growing being in the world in good faith.

Projection for Protection

By judging and blaming, we project our experience out onto others so that it becomes nonexperience to us. The problem is personal *and* cultural. Carl Jung said of such projection in *The Undiscovered Self*:

> It is in the nature of political bodies always to see the evil in the opposite group, just as the individual has an ineradicable tendency to get rid of everything he does not know and does not want to know about himself by foisting it off on somebody else.

We lose information about ourselves because we insist it is about others. As a result, we impede our ability to grow.

Just as national or racial or religious blaming and judging stop the growth of understanding and peace, personal blaming and judging stop the growth of closeness and intimacy. No information is spread because no experience is had. Since no information is spread, there is no change. Therapists Paul Watzlawick, Richard Fisch, and John Weakland, in a book titled *Change*, pinpoint our difficulty. In relationships, they say:

> . . . it is of secondary importance to ascertain the "true facts." For one thing, it is nearly impossible. More importantly, to whatever extent the accused is indeed engaged in some form of unacceptable behavior, the accuser's method of dealing with it can only perpetuate and exacerbate the problem. Even if the accused is really behaving rather well, how can he convince the accuser, who "knows" differently?

The answer, of course, is that the accused cannot. For those who live in the world of cause and effect, it is always the *other's* fault. To those who live in a reciprocal world, however, it is no one's *fault*. Instead, it is everyone's *responsibility*. Searching for security by projecting our fears, hurts, needs, or struggles onto others simply guarantees we will not be ourselves. There are no "true facts" about relationship other than the reciprocity in which we live.

One of our colleagues in the clinic has a young grandson who aptly illustrated this point about reciprocity. He was telling his mother about a dream he had in which an animal appeared. His mother asked, "Did you notice what kind of animal that was in your dream?" The child, living in a naturally connected world, assumed she had seen it too and replied, "No, what kind was it?" It may be only synchronistically true that we exist reciprocally even on the unconscious level of dreams, but it is operationally true that we exist reciprocally in our conscious and preconscious living.

Around 350 B.C., Chinese philosopher Chuang-tze was describing the Ottos and Gayles of the world:

> Suppose you and I argue. If you beat me instead of my beating you, are you really right and am I really wrong? If I

beat you instead of your beating me, am I really right and are you really wrong? Or are we both partly right and partly wrong? Or are we both wholly right and wholly wrong? Since between us neither you nor I know which is right, others are naturally in the dark . . . thus among you, me, and others, none knows which is right. Shall we wait for still others? The great variety of sounds are relative to each other just as much as they are not relative to each other. To harmonize them in the functioning of nature (the revolving process of nature) and leave them in the process of infinite evolution is the way to complete our lifetime.

It is this understanding that physicist Fritjof Capra explored in *The Tao of Physics*: "In the Eastern view then, as in the view of modern physics, everything in the universe is connected to everything else and no part of it is fundamental. The properties of any part are determined not by some fundamental law but by the properties of all the other parts." Whatever God or the ground substance is, it is a connected *process*, not an abstracted, observational dictum.

The "revolving process of nature" is a reciprocal process. In relationship, no one is fundamentally the law, the definer of truth. When we live as if *we* were, we live selfidically, diminishing our selfbeing by blocking "the process of infinite evolution," that is, blocking experience. We try to protect ourselves by projecting our inside struggles onto the other person. In truth, we undo our *selves* by putting ourselves into the nonexperiencing world.

Difference and Connection

Harold has made, then not kept, two therapy appointments. He arrives at our office this time somewhat apologetic, but mostly justifying himself with explanations as to why he had not been able to keep his earlier dates. He tells us, "I tried to get here, but I just couldn't. Some important things came up. As usual, I got stuck with them. You know how it is: if you want anything done, or at least done right, you have to do it yourself." His *courtship* with the therapist, as our friend and fellow therapist Carl Whitaker defines it, began before the first phone call and continues into the office today. We will *participate* in this courtship, for therapy is foremost a reciprocal process.

Harold is vice-president of a small company of which his father, Al, is president. Over the years, the conflict between the two has grown steadily. Now it has come to affect not only work, but home life and the relationships among others in the extended family system as well. The rest of the family cannot help but see how alike Harold and his father are. Both are bright, strong-willed, and, in their own ways, very stubborn men. Yet despite their similarities, or perhaps because of them, they choose to live in the world of their differences. They live unconnected and un-reciprocal, out of touch with each other and the truth of their lives. Their anger is the only channel through which they relate.

It is as if these two men know how much alike they are, but instead of this being a bond it has become a barrier. Each asks of the other, "Why can't *you* be different?" What this question really means is, "Why can't you be as I want you to be?" Neither seems able to ask the real question: "Why can't *I* be different . . . softer, less compelled to be right, more giving and less stubborn, more willing to fold into the relationship and feel loved and warm without fearing I've given up being captain of my own ship?"

It is painful to watch two people hurt each other, two people who care for and love each other as these two do, but who will not allow that love into their relationship. Because of their obsession with similarities that they cannot abide, and differences they can-not bridge, Harold and Al touch little and learn even less. Neither seems able or willing to dance with the other.

Harold: "Dad's got no respect for me. He thinks he's the only one who knows how to do things. He's rigid, stuck in his ways. They may have worked okay back then, but not today. He drives me crazy. He's always interfering with everything. He's always got to be in control."

Why is it so difficult for Harold to understand that if he warmly let Al be in control, not as a ploy but as an expression of love and acceptance, it would surely eventuate in Al's insistence that Harold take over. Without the distraction of his fight with Harold, Al might realize that always being in control year after year is a pain, and that he has had enough of it. In a way, since he has had enough, he may then be able to let go of always fighting to get his *share* and give over to *sharing* his space.

We hear nothing from Harold of his role in their relationship, not even how similar he sounds to his descriptions of his father. We especially hear nothing of how Harold is *with* his father and how Harold is *with* himself. He behaves as if he has no understanding that they live relationally in a connected world, one in which Al no more causes Harold to feel, think, and act as he does than Harold causes Al to feel, think, and act as he does. The truth is, they live in those ways together, both simultaneously and by choice, whether they are aware of it or not. As we see in so many people, their lack of reciprocity is manifested in their *living in their differences*—in reality, their *dying* in their differences.

Living in differences is a common relational impasse. In families, couples, or individuals, differences often become the paramount feature of the relationship. The result is we miss the fact that we could grow with each other if we were to forgo our differences while celebrating our commonalities. We forget that we could learn to accept difference as an opportunity to grow, instead of as a challenge to defend.

I (Pat) obviously work with Dad not just as professional colleagues at the clinic but also in our writing together. With pleasure, I have also worked with him over the years on building cabinets, pouring patios, fixing appliances, and painting pictures. We have very different personalities and characters. But with all our difference, we are 99.99 percent alike. In that alikeness, we share an even greater communality, we are connected, we live in the real world together, we are equally real and valid pieces of "Godstuff." Knowing we live connected, *knowing that there is no other way we can live* opens the window for us to experience both self and other for what they really are. I know Dad best, I know myself best, when I know we are reciprocals, *not causes or effects* of each other.

Another father and son speak to this same point:

The father, American philosopher Henry James, Sr., in one of his letters:

> It is no doubt very tolerable finite or creaturely love to love one's own in another, to love another for his conformity to one's self: But nothing can be in more flagrant contrast with the creative love, all whose tenderness *ex vi termini* must be reserved only for what intrinsically is most bitterly hostile and negative to itself.

His son William James, the founder of American psychology, in *Talks to Teachers*:

> In God's eyes the differences of social position, of intellect, of culture, of cleanliness, of dress, which different men exhibit, and all the other rarities and exceptions on which they so fantastically pin their pride, must be so small as practically quite to vanish; and all that should remain is the common fact that here we are, a countless multitude of vessels of life, each of us pent in to peculiar difficulties, with which we must severally struggle by using whatever of fortitude and goodness we can summon up.

Both "creative love" and "fortitude and goodness" are experiential products of living as *self* in a reciprocal world. When we retreat to our worlds of difference, of separation, of alienation, of disconnection, we lose them. And, as with Harold and Al and all those close to them, the price is high. There is no security in being disconnected from the real. There is only hiding.

> *Thus let your streams o'erfill your springs,*
> *Till eyes and tears be the same things:*
> *And each the other's difference bears;*
> *These weeping eyes, those seeing tears.*

> —ANDREW MARVELL, "Eyes and Tears"

Alienation Versus Connection

"Love," wrote John Yeats to his son William Butler Yeats, "is the instinctive movement of personality." Such instinctive movement can take place only if there is a connection between the lover and the loved. By its nature, movement is relational and involves connection. Without reciprocity we may have compatibility, adoration, lust, or need, but we will not have love. There is an alienation, an unloved and unlovingness to all nonreciprocal living. If two things are not real, are not existing in the same real world, they cannot connect and therefore cannot love.

Alienation is our estrangement from self. As Erich Fromm and R. D. Laing say, it is the word we use for the nonexperience that comes from not living in the world reciprocally. Most of us, like Gayle and Otto or Harold and Al, are angry, judging, accusing, and blaming. It would appear on the surface that we are very much involved with and connected to our world. But we are not. Underneath the noise is the pain, the pain of alienation, of living alone in a world of our own, of feeling no connection to others.

We see it happen every day. Humans forget that they happen *with* each other in ordinary life. Certainly someone could rob, beat, or even kill us. But if we are fortunate enough not to live in a war, or under an oppressive government, or as a mistreated minority, that is not the ordinary process of life. We would even suggest that the lack of connection, the lack of being in the world aware of its reciprocity, is a large part of why such special behavior (muggings, rapes, murders, oppression, mistreatment) is getting more and more common.

As experiencing persons, we know that we cannot change the other, we can only change ourselves. We *can* nurture our growing selves, which will then reciprocally influence others by the very fact that we are connected to them. We *can* be a presence in our world. But we will always be a part of what happens in our relationships in that world. Trying to avoid that truth diminishes our selfbeing. It makes us less than what we fully are.

Connectedness

We rediscover connectedness as adults. The natural reciprocity of the child is usually lost in the alienation of adolescence. Feeling apart and being treated as apart leaves too many adolescents convinced not only that their world is not reciprocal, but that it is actively alien and alienating. The suicide rate in adolescents, the teen pregnancy rate, the school dropout rate, and the drug abuse rate all point to just how alienated our adolescents have come to feel.

A gaunt young man wanders around the waiting room of the clinic. He looks hollow and afraid. He stays over near the corner, away from other people who are sitting in the chairs reading and occasionally talking to one another. Rick is eighteen, a freshman at a local college. He is a bright and sensitive young man who feels disconnected from his world, alone and alienated. He responds to his name with a glance, but walks into the office with his eyes cast down. There is little feeling of contact; he is surrounded by an aura of pain that keeps others away.

While we most commonly see our lack of reciprocity in our fighting and struggling, our blaming and judging, it can present itself in much quieter ways—like Rick's. Loud or quiet, however, a lack of reciprocity is just as evident in how we relate to our world in general as it is in how we relate to those close to us. Rick's alienation is such that he feels no connectedness to anything in his world, not his parents, friends, school, or even life itself.

Rick tells us: "I'd say I wasn't a very happy person. I like to read, and I like movies, still, most of the time, well, this world is not for me. I don't really have any friends, and my family would just as soon not have to deal with me. Sometimes I'd like to know what it would feel like to be like other people."

Rick feels no going-back-and-forth between himself and others. He has no sense of his empowerment, of his capacity to be part of his world. He has lost the natural feeling of affecting and being affected by others. He feels little healthy closeness and no healthy intimacy. He has no healthy reexperience, because he has no healthy *experiences*. He is rapidly, selficidally cutting himself off from his own living. The first job of the therapist will be to make connection with Rick. Only slowly, gently, and experientially—that is, in the experience of the relationship with the therapist—will Rick refind his connection to life. With that window open, he may then begin to grow.

As adults, we all must rediscover reciprocal living. Since we exist only in relationship, we must be intimately and closely a part of all we do. Without being connected in this way, without unshuttering the window of reciprocity, we cannot be in the world in good faith.

Henry James, William's brother, wrote in his novel *The Ambassadors*:

> Live all you can; it's a mistake not to. It doesn't so much matter what you do in particular, so long as you have had your life. If you haven't had that, what have you had?

16

THE THIRTEENTH WINDOW:
Physical Experience/ Risking

Our own physical body possesses a wisdom which we who inhabit the body lack. We give it orders which make no sense.

—HENRY MILLER

In *The Social Contract*, Rousseau says, "We always want our own well-being, but we do not always see what that is." In no area is our lack of insight more visible than in our blindness to our need for risking. Our withdrawal from our physicalness—that is, our tendency to avoid living in the world as the part of nature we really are—in an attempt to stay secure, effectively shuts us off from a great deal of experience. Unwilling to risk being truly alive in our world, we miss much of what that world has to offer us.

Albert is now fifty-eight. Only late in his life has he come consciously to recognize what unconsciously has controlled so much of his living for so long. He is unable to live directly and passionately as the person he is. He feels he is outside his experience, always looking in at his own life. He laments missing the real feelings.

He tells us: "At my mother's funeral, everyone else was crying, really feeling sad. Somehow it was like I was inside, behind my own eyes, just watching. I knew I was sad but I couldn't *feel* sad or cry like they were."

He tells us: "I've got this low level of anger inside me that just won't go away. I didn't know it was there until I got older . . . other people knew, but I didn't. I'd always spent so much time trying to be a good person and make everybody happy that I didn't notice how angry it was making me. It always felt like I had done everything I should do, so why didn't anybody love me? I've always wanted somebody to be good to me, be nice to me. I guess I've never really felt that anybody loves me."

Many of us are like Albert, with our own similar ways of not really *living*. We are unwilling to take the risk of really feeling our feelings, following our thoughts, or empowering our behavior. We may be afraid that the experience will overwhelm or consume us—that some secure, fixed life position would be challenged by the experience. Perhaps we are managing our image, or trying to get others to take care of us by holding back. Regardless, we are living "secure," once removed from the true force of our physical being. We do not take the risk required to experience fully.

Risking

"Get out of my face! I'm going to do what I want to do . . . and I don't care what you think. I'm going to make my own decisions."

The Halsey family is seated around the office. The rest of the family and the therapist listen as the older son, eighteen-year-old Hans, explodes. "I've never been able to do what I wanted—never!"

Hans's outburst is directed at his father, Rolf, but his fifteen-year-old sister, Kim, his eleven-year-old brother, Rudy, and his mother, Pam, all feel the heat of his anger.

The father reacts: "Well, damn it, do you think I get to go around doing only what I want to do all the time? You think you should be special in some way, get special privileges? Just who the hell do you think you are? Yeah, you can make your own decisions . . . when you can support yourself. I'm the one who takes all the risks around here. So I'm the one who makes the decisions."

Rolf is forty-two years old, intelligent, uptight, and locked in

327 PHYSICAL EXPERIENCE/RISKING

a powerful struggle with his son. His own anger is obvious, as well as a deep hurt he seems unable to articulate.

Pam gets up from her chair and walks over to sit on the couch next to Rudy. She hugs him, trying to comfort his anxiety at the anger so strongly present in the room. One can sense Pam's own anger at both Rolf and Hans for "hurting" everybody else. She says nothing, but continues to hold Rudy. Rudy, for his part, is not particularly comforted. He feels he is being put in the middle. It is as if he lets her comfort him in order to comfort herself.

The daughter, Kim, looking around the room, says softly, "Sometimes I don't like being a member of this family. Sometimes I think none of us has the guts to be any different. We just keep doing the same things over and over again."

Kim is all too right. Her family is, indeed, addicted to the habitual repetition of the same old conflicts and struggles. What is familiar is safe and secure. What is different is precarious, unknown, and unpredictable. Taking a risk, as Kim did when she said, "none of us have the guts to be any different," is rare in the family. And since such risking is the open door to change and aliveness, the Halsey family never changes. The same hurts keep hurting. The same wounds remain unhealed. There is no wholeness.

The Halseys want to change. They came to therapy because they were not functioning well as a family. When their pediatrician told them that Rudy had the beginnings of an ulcer and that, at just under twelve, he was rather young to be having that kind of stress, she referred them for family therapy. The Halseys are just beginning to identify and deal with their dysfunctional ways of living. Perhaps now they will change because they are taking the risk of opening themselves to each other.

Risking Versus Putting Self at Risk

One approach to understanding the role risk taking plays in healthy and unhealthy ways of living is to look at who is actually *risking* in this family. Is Hans risking by demanding his freedom and the right to decide? Is Rolf risking by his constant caretaking, compulsive working, and ever-present controlling? Is Pam risking by protecting Rudy from someone else's feelings? Is Rudy risking by allowing himself to be the answer to someone else's needs?

We would suggest that the only one who is *healthily* risking in this family is Kim. The others may well be putting themselves at risk, but they are not risking in the experiential sense. We use *risk* in its etymological sense—"to cut or cut off." Kim cuts to the truth at hand, cuts off the nonexperience cluttering her living space, and cuts herself off from the security of the known. In doing so, she *risks*. She risks the insecurity of not knowing what the *other* really is or will do. Without the imprisoning preconceptions that we so often call real life, real experience becomes more likely. *True risking is an internal openness to experience.* Just as acceptance occurs when we risk taking the other into ourselves, physical risking occurs when we allow our real selves to be experienced by the other.

In this instance, Kim risks what we all risk when we are being honest, expressive, and openly intimate, but are uncertain about the strength of the closeness in our relationship. Being our real selves when we are insecure about the other is a risk. Probably the most important risking that human beings do is sharing in this simple way. Kim must have felt secure enough in the family session to take the risk, but doing so required courage, as such sharing was uncommon in her family. To say what she said revealed an enormous and admirable willingness to expose herself. She lived as the real person she was in that moment.

The value of such risking resides not only in what it might accomplish in terms of family change, nor, perhaps, in how it might help the parents to see their son Rolf differently. More important, it makes a difference in Kim's own life. She grows into an increased willingness to expand her own experience in relationships by risking being herself. By learning to be ourselves in our families, by taking the risk in a supportive environment, we most easily learn fully to be ourselves outside our families.

Such risking is the opposite of putting ourselves at risk—bravery and bravado—in its popular usage. Courage is more than an adrenaline rush. In truth, many of us seek the high and the rush of excitement *because* there is so little real risking in our lives and in our culture. We look to the artificial thrill only to find how quickly it, too, becomes nonexperience. We then feel compelled to move on to something else. Real risking ensures a *new* experience each time, and assures *energizing* and *revitalizing* experiencing.

Therefore, risking is a core component of experiencing. There is no experience without *peril*, and peril comes with risking. It is an early childhood awareness which we as adults must relearn. To the child, all risking is a physical part of being in the world. Reaching, trying to crawl, falling down at first steps, banging and being banged by our world, putting our world in our mouths, all are very physical experiences. They are also, in the wholeness of the child's interaction with his or her world, spiritual experiences. The true risking necessary for experiencing is rooted in that deep physicalness. It is grounded in having a *body/soul*. Only as adults do we selficidally move to body *and* soul, failing to heed what the writer John Galsworthy warned against: "The body and soul are one for the purpose of all real evolution, and regrettable is any term suggestive of divorce between them."

Physicalness

> The greatest poverty is not to live
> In a physical world, to feel that one's desire
> Is too difficult to tell from despair.
>
> —WALLACE STEVENS, *"Esthétique du Mal"*

Without physical experience, we all live poorly. Our bodies speak loudly and directly to our close and ongoing relationship to our evolutionary past. In evolution, the risking is to *grow*, to become more, not just to *do*. Plants and animals experientially push, stretch, lean, reach, pull, grasp, fly, run, and crawl to be more of what they are, not to secure outside opinion. The flower attracts the bee out of and for its own evolution. In return, it participates in the bee's evolution. Together they live in a world ecology, a connected habitat of communal risking. Humans too easily forget that they live in that same world, in that same Darwinian struggle for existence.

The physical experience of risking is the infrastructure of spiritual and vital existence. Growth, the essence of existence, always involves risk because it represents change. One can never know for certain beforehand the result of any change, any growth. Peril is thus an intrinsic part of the process. But without change there is *no* life. Stasis is the same as death.

People come to therapy, listen, and begin to learn. They develop insight about their problems and themselves. Then they say, "I understand. I know what's wrong with me. I even know how it came to be. So what? I'm still the same. I don't know how to be different. Can you help me with that?" The real issue for all of us, whether in therapy or not, is "How can I change?"

Therapists listen to body language. Clients may say they understand, that they need and want to change, but their bodies draw up into hiding, defiant, or inaccessible postures—tense, hunched over, cringing in ostensible fear, retreating as if beaten and rejected. Or frightened postures—watchful, tension mostly hidden, with ready-to-flare anger. Or nervous postures—trembling, tugging on tufts of hair, nail biting, foot twitching, fingers strumming, tongue clicking. The body belies the avowed understanding and willingness to change. The body, that is, at least one part of our *being*, does *not* understand. It announces this lack of understanding in its postures.

When we are in such defensive postures, we are not being perverse. We are frightened. We are addicted to the world of the secure, and our bodies carry that commitment faithfully. Some call it body armor, but it goes much deeper than armor. It is the nonexperiential decision to stop risking growth. It is defensiveness made manifest on a cellular level—not abstractly, but concretely, as our health care statistics so directly show. It is selficide.

Body armor manifests our stress level. As such it probably announces more clearly than any other index, including most mental indices, the immediacy of our susceptibility to disease and death. It is much more than a metaphor—in fact, it is very real. Using our bodies to defend rather than to risk results in their breaking down and becoming ill. As modern man grows increasingly aloof and removed from living physically and naturally in his world, the level of body armoring rises. And so does the price paid.

Body Being

Stress is the result of neglecting our *selves*. It is a tension, the result and measure of the distance we are removed from being who we really are. It is a loss of integrity and wholeness, made evident by and in our bodies. We might well define the reality of our cellular nonexperiencing as a lack of *body being*. Many of us are far out of touch with the experiential reality of our physicalness, out of touch with the reality of this body being and the immediacy of it to our personal being. In *All Is Grist*, G. K. Chesterton said:

> The old ceremonial gestures of the human body are necessary to the health of the human soul: The gesture that pledged the guest in the goblet; that strewed flowers upon the grave; that drew the sword for the salute or set up the candle before the shrine. In that sense a man can actually think with his muscles; he can love with his muscles and lament with his muscles.

There is no doubt that we not only remember with our cortex, but also, more primitively, with our muscles. Our bodies are tense before we first become anxious just as often as we become anxious and then tense, because bodies and minds are not separate entities. Our feelings and motivations may antecede our behavior, but, just as frequently, our feelings can emerge out of our behavior.

The difference is expressed clearly in an example: we can be feeling angry and then begin behaving angrily. Conversely, we may behave angrily before we begin to feel angry. Both happen in human relationships. In some instances, we feel angry and, therefore, behave in an angry fashion. In other instances, we simply respond in an aggressive way to some provocation, and the feeling of anger comes after the behavior rather than prior to it. Our physicalness is not simply an afterthought to our minds.

I (Tom) treated a young woman who suffered anxiety attacks at work and so was referred to me by her employer. After getting to know her and her past history, it became clear to me that her anxiety was directly connected to the physical abuse she had experienced with her father when she was a child. She had so memorized the muscle tensions, body postures, and facial-muscle movements that preceded her father's outbursts that she could still unconsciously recognize them. Whenever her current boss was angry, which he evidently often was, she would read his muscles and have an anxiety attack in her own muscles—the same anxiety she had experienced so long before.

I (Pat) have seen muscle memory in action when dealing with people who have been sexually abused. Often they will curl up in childlike body postures, or hide in fearful body positions, or even return to the exact body poses in which the abuse took place. Their body/soul is searching for a way back to and then out of the shattering trauma. I remember one woman who had an explosion of memory—the pain, hurt, fear, loathing, shame, and all the other feelings that accompany such invasion of personhood— while she was working around her home one evening and in a particular moment happened to assume a body posture identical to one she had been in when abused as a child. There is no question our bodies remember just as well as our minds.

So we would rephrase Chesterton's insight—that we can experience with our muscles—to say that we *must* experience with our muscles. There is *no* experience without physicalness, without risking, without body being. Body being, as a full partner in body/soul being, is basic to being in the world in good faith. Blocked from freely expressing and experiencing, our muscles turn to stress, and all the resultant problems that accompany it. And the stressed-out person is all too common. The best-selling medicines in our culture are for ulcers, hypertension, and nerves.

Stress can be said to be the lack of synergism—the healthy connection and working together—between soul and body. The most common word used to describe this disunity is *psychosomatic.* In psychosomatic illness, there is an overt lack of synergism between the psyche (the mind) and the soma (the body). It is the absence of synergism that creates the "illness" in the soma. Most of us are much clearer about that truth than we are of its corollary. The same absence of synergism, in which the soma is not friendly to the psyche, also creates affective, behavioral, and mental dysfunctions.

A preoccupation with dualism—dividing mind and body into two separate entities—is a hallmark of our culture. In our scientific pursuit of empirical facts, we often miss the holistic truths. At some point self and cell become one; at some point, chemistry and psyche become one. In the whole person, body and mind are totally integrated.

To our loss, we persist in seeing the human being dualistically. Separating mind and body leads us not only to individual illnesses but also to many of our social disasters. Our failure to recognize the effect of the human psyche on chronic illnesses— cancer or cardiovascular disease, for example—often causes premature death. Conversely, our failure to realize the effect of our dietary intake or our air and water quality on our thinking, feeling, behavior, relationships, and even family, is both distressing and dangerous.

The fact that many of us spend hours each week training our bodies to wellness by jogging, aerobics, or tennis is highly commendable. But if, when we return to our home life, we seldom talk to our spouse, or we are with our children only when they are watching television, then we are not being whole. Our failure to pay as much attention to our emotional and spiritual life as we do to our physical bodies is destructive to selfbeing. Many of us have the opposite imbalance. We start counseling or therapy, spend hours reading self-help books in order to understand our relational struggles, seek out healthful and rejuvenating spiritual experience, but then virtually ignore taking care of our physicalness and exercising our body being. Neither extreme leads to wholeness.

We have lost touch with our body/soul being, which largely accounts for our current stress epidemic. Physical nonexperience *is* stress. To deal with how we feel, we turn to medicines, legal or illegal. If, however, we listened to the Gullah-speaking people of the coastal islands off South Carolina and Georgia, they would tell us that the trees are medicine; the plants are medicine; the oceans, lakes, and streams are medicine. The traditional mythology of American Indians would tell us the same. Perhaps those who are more closely connected to nature are more directly in touch with body/soul being. Estrangement from our natural surroundings— alienation in its most basic form—*is* making us ill. This malady cannot be treated with pills.

Many have noted this increasing alienation from our physicality. In *Male and Female*, anthropologist Margaret Mead wrote, "Talking about our bodies is a complex and difficult matter. We are so used to covering them up, to referring to them obliquely. . . ." Morris Berman, in *Coming to Our Senses*, said:

We have inherited a civilization in which the things that really matter in human life exist at the margin of our culture. What matters? How birthing takes place matters; how infants are raised matters; having a rich and active dream life matters. Animals matter, and so does ontological security and the magic of personal interaction and healthy and passionate sexual expression. Career and prestige and putting a good face on it and the newest fashion in art or science do not matter. Coming to our senses means sorting this out once and for all. It also means becoming embodied. And the two ultimately amount to the same thing.

The psychological division between appetite and transcendence is the movement into nonexperience, the self-diminishing decision. We live with secure desire and end up with a lack of wholeness. Heartiness of appetite for life, gusto living, is not the glorification of external risks that advertisers would sell us. It is not drinking or eating ourselves to death, or engaging in aggressive behaviors. It is, instead, a real and committed way of being in the world, a risking way that engages life in its ordinariness, not the specialized thrill of climbing a mountain or driving a car at high speed. Packaged highs are sublimated yearnings for the empowerment of real self-experience. Such sublimation is not gusto, it is the direct result of our lack of physicality and risking in our ordinary day-to-day living.

Body as Soul
and Soul as Body

Body/soul living—the acceptance of life as an ongoing reality in which our wholeness participates—would lead us *naturally* to much healthier living. This change would not be insignificant. According to the latest statistics, *over 50 percent* of all current American deaths and illnesses are unnecessary or premature. The price is staggering—of alcohol and drug abuse, of smoking, injuries, unintended pregnancies, unwanted children, neglect, abuse, overstress, and a general inability to relax and play. The "risks" we take in our unwillingness to live in a naturally engaged way are enormous, and overtly selficidal.

All those individual personal tragedies add up to significant social tragedy. If we add to them our ecological insanity—our denial of our physical relation to our planet (the *one* world we have) through pollution, nuclear proliferation, poor land and resource management, and all the other damage we humans inflict in our arrogant supremacy, the toil is frightening. We live in our world as if we have no fear at all of our ultimate self-destruction as a species.

There is an entire theme in literature that addresses the issue of risking and body/soul unity. That area is the quest genre. A quest is really an allegory for our search for self. The physical dimensions, the geography of the stories, the tasks, the trials, the endurance, the tribulations of heroes like Odysseus or Jason, clearly reflect the direct relationship between risking and being. In most such stories, the protagonist finds him- or her*self* on the journey *in the very acts undertaken.* Often, literal physical transformations are part of the spiritual transformations. A quest is all of us or none of us. Either body/soul, or neither body nor soul, emerges.

These stories always involve romance elements—symbolic landscapes, fantastical creatures, mysteriously meaningful maps. They have narratives of exotic characters, as in J. R. R. Tolkien's *Lord of the Rings;* exotic powers, as in Ursula Le Guin's *Wizard of EarthSea Trilogy;* or exotic actions, as in Robert Heinlein's *Glory Road.* These exotic components speak to the newness and strangeness that are always features of risking. Quest mythology appears throughout all cultures. Heroic myths, which have such a significant effect on our development as a species, are reflected in an endless parade of embodiments by the toy and movie heroic figures, from Superman to Batman to Princess Leia. They fundamentally represent an unfolding story of risking, both physical and spiritual. They represent the experience of body/soul as one.

Experiencing, by definition, is participation in the new. Risking involves allowing the new to happen. Exotic sea voyages or assaults on dragons, however, are not necessary. Questing occurs in our ordinary day-to-day world. Spiritual unfolding occurs anytime it is allowed to. It can happen when we must knock on the door of our own home because we happen to have forgotten our key. Those inside suddenly become real people to us in that moment, not just appendages to ourselves. It can happen when we are talking with a friend, more friend than we know, who hesitates in what he is saying because we are momentarily looking into each other's eyes. Such unfolding is ordinary *and* spiritual.

I (Pat) noticed that Nigel was withdrawn inside his own body the first time I saw him sitting in the waiting room. His personal space was pulled right up to his skin, and he obviously avoided any touch from the outside. He had flunked out of the prestigious university to which he had devoted much of his adolescence securing admittance and was finally experiencing the depression that had been part of him for many years.

Nigel is so quiet and unobtrusive in the waiting room of the clinic that the receptionist frequently does not know he is there. He enters and sits in my office with much the same quiet. He lives in the world as if he might break it, or, perhaps, as if it might break him. But his is not the softness of gentle strength; it is the quietness of intimidation and fear, the isolation of depression. Nigel is aware that he is lonely, that he feels broken, and that he is missing out on much of life. He has no lover, for he has no passion. He has no passion, for he takes no risks. He sits, watches, and waits. And waits and waits. What is he waiting for?

He tells me: "I wish I knew how to get involved. I wish I wasn't so scared. It isn't like I enjoy being this way. I'm glad I'm intelligent and like the things I like and have the values I have. But I would like to be more involved in things, to feel some excitement, to have a relationship. Sometimes when I realize how lonely and depressed I am, I get terrified. I wonder if I can go on."

Nigel waits for permission to live, which he will never receive. No one else can tell him how to live as his body/soul.

The Loss of Self in Fear

Nigel has little trust or faith in life. He takes the physicalness out of his living, thus diminishing himself. He tries to live as if living were not a contact sport. Not "contact" in the overly brutal way that we see in so much of our athletics currently—sports encouraged as a reaction to the lack of physicalness in our normal living—but contact in the more ordinary sense of touching. Contact with our world must be real for us to be real. Fear that blocks touching will block experience and selfbeing.

Probably the most important single formative relational experience that a human being has is the bonding that occurs between that person as an infant and his or her mother. It is well known, from studies done years ago, that the absence of this experience of bonding can result in severe damage to the child, even death. Such bonding, which Nigel never fully experienced, involves the true creation of a space for the other's personhood.

This bonding, which is the experience of being continually touched in ways that make one feel safe and cared for, involves other areas besides physical touching: the sounds that are made by the mothering parent around the child, the responsiveness of the parent to the child's sounds and cries, the mutual eye contact, and the recognition of scents. All these ways of touching develop a *weltgeist* in the infant—*weltgeist* being "a feeling about the world around us." Is that world friendly? Is it warm? Is it related? The absence of such touching (and thus bonding) creates an enormous psychological emptiness and confusion in the child. It will not necessarily mean that she will feel the world as hostile; it may simply mean that she has no basis on which to feel that her world is supportive. Trust and faith will not develop. There will be little development of a sense of her world as positive and receptive instead of negative and rejecting. Trust and faith are formative developmental experiences and fundamental bases for wholeness.

Children who lack such physical bonding grow into unbonded adults. Lack of bonding is an integral part of many psychological illnesses. It is an issue in those who are prone to depression, in those who are loners, in those who distrust others, and in those who are paranoid. It is most clearly a part of what went wrong in the development of borderline and narcissistic personalities. Some humans *are* wounded. Does that mean they are doomed? No. One's life, one's being, *is* one's own creation and responsibility. We *can* change ourselves. Yet infancy and childhood relations *are* the formative experiences of adult psychological states—as when the lack of bonding leads to trust and faith not developing.

What is the pathway out of this dilemma? What is Nigel's way back? One must learn in adulthood what one missed in childhood, relearn the natural selfbeing of the undistorted child still present inside oneself—in short, unshutter one's closed windows. We have everything we need in our unconscious; we only lack the experiences by which we learn to be a wholeness as a self. We *can* reclaim our personhood if we will risk having those experiences. For those more wounded it is more difficult, but not impossible.

The capacity to grow *is* the process of life. Nigel has a chance if he will take it.

Most of us fear the demise of our false self—the nonexperiencing self. As we can see in those who, when things are going well in their being, seem driven to return to having problems, the hurt child inside equates giving up the old conflicts with giving up his or her existence. We hang on to our hurts and defenses as if they were our *identity*. We keep our windows shuttered, fearing the light that will come in and let us truly see ourselves. We fail to understand that we need not change the past nor change our experience of the other. We need only the experience of self that we are missing. For example, we do not need to experience our parents' love, but we must experience our own lovability if we are to be whole. Our real identity lies in our real selfbeing, and *our* experience is what we need to move toward that wholeness.

Courage

Most of us maintain some degree of low-grade apprehension in life because we feel we lack relational information. We do not know we are lovable; we do not know our love is worthwhile. We are not so much confused as we are uncertain. Because of these feelings, we limit our risking. Our passion is too often confined, whether it be in our play or in our sexuality. We tend to be careful and circumspect in our relationships and in our language. We are usually good people, hoping to be loved. But we carry an undercurrent of dissatisfaction, relational hunger, and low-grade anger. The anger is not overt and is seldom claimed. It is more a disgruntlement, a dissatisfaction, and a feeling of having been cheated.

The most poignant example I (Tom) remember of adult pain resulting from a lack of early physical bonding was in a man who came to see me because of his dissatisfaction with his profession. He was a successful lawyer, but he was constantly looking for something else to be. A consultant. A bookstore owner. A businessman. During the time he was seeing me, he and his wife had a child, their first, and after her birth the three came in together. His wife sat with the baby. Her hands were constantly caressing and touching, playing gently, and drawing pictures on the baby's skin. The mother's sounds were those of a satisfied animal, a human purr. Meanwhile, her husband sat across the room talking to me, but watching them. Gradually he ceased to speak. In the silence, he simply stared at his wife and baby. After a few minutes his eyes welled with tears.

He turned back to me and said very softly, "You know, that never happened to me."

Many of us feel as if that never happened to us enough. We feel a lack of something that leaves us with a hunger for a more perfect wholeness. Unfortunately, that deficit causes us to fear, and our fear blocks us from the very ways of being which would increase our wholeness. The fears cause us to shutter our windows and retreat from full selfbeing.

We cannot be present in the here-and-now, or congruent, if we are afraid. We could fear *and* be congruent if the fear and its object were actually in the here-and-now (if a bear was chasing us, for example), but that is not the case with most of our fears. The baseball player Satchel Paige supposedly once said, "Don't look back, something might be gaining on you." That is how most of us live our lives. Our fear is usually from "back there," and we run away from ourselves. But we cannot really escape. Instead of escaping, we are captured, captured by our running and hiding, captured in our room with shuttered windows.

Such fear and capture are nonrational and thus not amenable to rational solution. As Paul Williams said in *Das Energi*:

> The nature of fear is that it feeds on itself. Under proper conditions, it feeds itself incredibly quickly. Reason is not fast enough to stamp out fear. That is the mistake most of us make. Do not argue with fear. Wipe it from your mind the instant you recognize it . . . fear is the greatest enemy of awareness. It leaves shame and guilt far behind. Fear is the force that holds us back.

Courage is required for change to occur. Courage allows one to return to physicalness, to risk fully being, to risk touching the real. It allows us to participate in a *living* process. Innovative being, which contains both passion and relationship, is living unafraid. Such being contacts the world at all interfaces, freely and flexibly.

Order and Disorder

In the past decade, the interdependent problems of complex systems, such as the weather and ecosystems, have been illuminated by the increasingly understood new theories of chaos. For centuries, we have dealt with our complex systems as linear systems, that is, systems in which a small change in input at any point leads to a small change in the system as a whole. However, in complex systems this rule does not hold true. In complex systems, a small change in input at one point can cause huge changes in the system as a whole, or, conversely, no changes at all.

Clearly, life is a complex system. It follows the rules of disorder more closely than the rules of order. The rules of order apply to small segments of life that we "fix," usually to allow us to be socialized or to accomplish a specific task—for example, parliamentary rules for meetings, manners and social conventions, or the traditional Western scientific model. Creating rules-of-order is a useful ability for generating all of our technology and engineering, but one cannot count reality. There is no one-to-one correspondence between our ordering and the complex system that life is.

Writer and teacher O. B. Hardison, Jr., wrote about our dilemma in *Disappearing Through the Skylight*:

> Wallace Stevens calls the games the mind plays with the world "necessary fictions." The mind cannot get along with them, but it cannot get along without them either. They organize experience just as religion, mythology, and tradition organize it, they are the preconditions of knowledge. This is frustrating and man forever struggles against it by seeking a supreme truth or, as Stevens has it, a supreme fiction. . . . We know nothing that has not been invested with ourselves. . . . Nature is infinitely complicated and variable. It can only be approximated. . . . This is another way of saying that nature per se is invisible. We have to be satisfied with facsimiles and facsimiles are human artifacts.

Believing that there are real *answers*, we become captured. We stop living physically in our world and become *reifiers*, that is, namers of life. There is no risk in that kind of living and, there-

fore, there is no experience. Fear of the unknown leaves us ignorant. Fear makes us withdraw from reality. Attempting to be
secure by controlling life, we withdraw from our selfbeing.

The Risk of Love

Although it may seem academic and even obtuse when we
talk about it, the withdrawal from our physicalness has profound
effects on our living. We can trace the changes easily just by
studying our language. The time from the past—when language
was more verb-oriented, relational, participatory, and linguis-
tic—up to the present, where language as used is more noun-
oriented, denotative, reifying, separating, and logical—has been
but a short journey on the evolutionary scale. Linguistically, we
have been increasingly captured by a system of seeing *things*
instead of *patterns* and *processes*. The *integration* of experience
has given way to the *collection* of experience.

We make lists, and time-sequence our living. We print, cal-
culate, Xerox, fax, and file. We are more interested in labels than
we are in experiencing the things labeled or even the experience of
labeling. Our designer clothes, designer possessions, and designer
lives all point out how surface-oriented our living has become.
The sports industry, the entertainment industry, and the political
industry are larger examples of our constant labeling. The advertising industry and much of the business it promotes are nothing
but labeling. The essence of life becomes the mass-produced "in-
timacies" of celebrities—the gossip of others—not the experiences of our own living. Life winds up being watched on a screen
instead of being lived.

We have moved from a language of imagining to a language
of defining. The former is musical, like a symphony; it *presents*
what is. For example, saying something like "tears have a taste of
their own, but do not bring our mothers back" conveys a different
experience than a specific description of how we went to our
mother's funeral and how much we will miss her. The latter is
descriptive, *telling about* what was: for example, on the simplest
level we might say, "I cried when my mother died." Both ways of
speaking are necessary—language must translate as well as communicate—but the languages are different and the differences are

important. Imaginative language has to do with interdependent existence, ideas, precepts, connotative meanings, and relationships. It is more space-oriented. One learns *from* it. Definitive language has to do with separate existence, thoughts, concepts, denotative meanings, and things. It is more time-oriented. One learns *about* it. The best of our language contains both. For example, good poetry is one of the most powerful languages we have, being both imaginative and descriptive.

In *The Reenchantment of the World,* Morris Berman wrote about the price we pay for separating our languages:

> . . . my primary focus in this book is the transformations of the human mind. This emphasis stems from my conviction that the fundamental issues confronted by any civilization in its history, or by any person in his or her life, are issues of meaning. And historically, our loss of meaning in an ultimate philosophical or religious sense [is] the split between fact and value which characterizes the modern age. . . . That mode can best be described as disenchantment, nonparticipation, for it insists on a rigid distinction between observer and observed. Scientific consciousness is alienated consciousness: there is no ecstatic merger with nature, but rather total separation from it. Subject and object are always seen in opposition to each other. I am not my experiences, and thus not really a part of the world around me. The logical end point of this world view is a feeling of total reification: everything is an object, alien, not-me; and I am ultimately an object too, an alienated "thing" in a world of other, equally meaningless things. This world is not of my own making; the cosmos cares nothing for me, and I do not really feel a sense of belonging to it. What I feel, in fact, is a sickness in the soul.

Capture by the rational aspects, the naming aspects of language, has increased in modern history, modern on the *natural* scale, for such capture has been an integral part of agricultural-ization, urbanization, and nonnomadic living. One needs names for possessions, specific thoughts for fixed plans, conceptions and definitions for the implements of civilization, and a time schedule to organize and order civilized living. And, indeed, rational language accomplishes these things well, as can be seen in the tremendous advances in science and technology our civilization has made. But we have paid a price. The imbalance between imagining and defining traps us. The capture has brought us to that separate *observer* way of living. Our civilization counts as a way of life: counts money, possessions, and the score. Observers make better scores on tests, but participants have more experiences taking tests. That is why they may score lower: they savor experience, the allotted time passes, and their scores go down. We may score higher as we pay more attention to time limits, but we live less as people.

This observer separation isolates us from our others, from the natural world, the ecology of which we are really a part. We thus learn nothing from those others. We learn nothing about ourselves because we have lost physical, risking contact with the rest of what is. Instead, we develop a sense of difference and righteousness which easily leads to judgment and blaming, to a loss of acceptance and innocence, and to the ultimate denunciation of faith. In the end, we are less able to love.

Love is the ability to allow other people to be who they are, not simply to name or count them. The language of love is a language of relationship and a language of relationships must contain both imagining and defining ways of seeing the other. When our mate arrives home early from work we must be able to say, "It sure feels good to have you home early" as well as "You look tired." Love, like truth and beauty, is a participation in life on the *wholeness* level. It contains both sides of the various dualities that seem to trap humans so easily. We can understand wholeness only when we see that it is only the *union* of these dualities which forms what is real. Being an observer may help us to count, name, and understand, but we do so safely only if we avoid being captured by the notion that the counting or naming is *something* in and of itself. Our brains clearly have both capacities, and that dual nature is both our strength and our vulnerability. We must use our brains to forge a marriage of the two. Doing so is being in the world in good faith. We must live forever in the unresolved tension between two states. We must stay in the *process*.

To do so is to risk. There is nothing *fixed* at love's level of being. The absence of answers on this level is precisely why risking is so vital to selfbeing, and yet we are frightened of that ambiguity, by the tension of not knowing. The love risk most difficult for us to take is the risk of faith. If there is no name or label, no answer, we become anxious. When there is only process, we are unsure. But that is the true nature of life. Around the sixth century B.C., Chinese poet Lao-tzu wrote about the folly/futility of our struggle with not knowing:

The Tao that can be told of is not the
    Eternal Tao;
The name that can be named is not the eternal name.
The nameless is the origin of heaven and earth;
The named is the mother of all things.
Therefore let there always be non-being, so we may see their subtlety,
And let there always be being, so we may see their outcome.

"Not knowing" may sound very mystically Oriental, but it is also a core concept of Western science. We must come to recognize that we are a complex system, living as part of a complex system, which in itself is living as part of a complex system, and so on forever. Reality is recursive and we are part of it. Life grows no less complex and no less recursive regardless of how *we* try to stop it and define it. In so doing, we simply shutter our windows and drop out of the process.

Physical Living

In *The Bending of the Bough*, George Moore wrote, "The difficulty in life is the choice." It is precisely the choice of what risks to take that makes life difficult. Choosing to make choices is the paramount choice, even if poor choices lead us off in self-diminishing directions. Love in its ultimate meaning is a choice to risk our being in order to grow. But our fears frequently block such understanding. In *Kiss Sleeping Beauty Good-Bye*, feminist Madonna Kolbenschlag speaks to this issue in women. It is no different, however, for any human, female or male:

A woman who has unwrapped herself, who has unfurled her wholeness, who has emerged from what Kierkegaard calls "the despair of not willing to be oneself"—a woman, in short, who has come to love herself—is unafraid of loving others.

The physical choice to unfurl and emerge requires courage and faith. It is the ultimate physical risk. We must be true to our hearts *and* minds. We must trust and have faith that our real world contains what our hearts and minds need and want. In just that way do we love ourselves and others. In so doing, we become fully in contact, fully touching all our others, all our world. It sounds so big a task and seems so hard a chore for most adults. It is, however, the same thing infants do naturally, so naturally that pediatricians, child therapists, and others who have intimate involvement with the very young know that a child has problems if he or she is not so risking and touching. Love—the faith and trust to risk being ourselves in our world—is a natural part of health and naturally part of healthily being in the world.

Camile spends so much of her time living in the world of might-have-been that she does not enjoy what is. She is not one of those people who overtly moan and groan about what might have been, but she *lives* as if joy or happiness might have been if only something else had happened instead of what did. For example, a long awaited vacation with her lover is ruined because he forgot to bring the camera. It is not simply that Camile will be denied the happiness of taking pictures; Camile will have no happiness at all. She will not, in the sense we are discussing, *physically* be there on the trip. She will not risk letting go of her anger, her past, her nonexperiencing. She will continue to insist on how happy the trip *might* have been, instead of experiencing the happiness that is available. There is almost always a camera missing in our lives, something going wrong for each of us at any given moment. But to be whole, we must risk letting go of needing perfect control.

We so often have the phenomenological experience but miss the story—the natural experience. Only in physical being, in risking self, can we approach that real experience. When we do, we make contact with our whole insides, our unconscious immensity, not just the consciousness of our own small corner of life.

The very "experience of many generations," as T. S. Eliot called it, is the point of our being in the world physically, of our risking to enlarge self. We have learned that we can learn without capture. We can grow with not-knowing. We can be balanced humans in a community of life. Camile can learn to experience her happiness whenever and wherever she can. She can learn that her happiness is her experience of being in the world, her connection to the "experience of many generations," her meaning in life. In short, Camile can discover that happiness is *happening* as a person. It is our natural right, as Rousseau reminded us in *The Social Contract*: "Every man has the right to risk his own life in order to save it."

17

THE LAST WINDOW:
Death and Growth/ Creativity

A dream which is not understood is like a letter which is not opened.

—The Talmud

James was almost sixty years old when he first came to see me (Pat). He lived alone up in the mountains of north Georgia, where he was in the process of working his twelve-step AA program. After years of drinking heavily, James had been sober now for eighteen months and wanted to start therapy to work on his spiritual and family issues. He had led a rough and colorful life, and this past was etched on his face and his character. His understanding for, and insight into, other humans had been hard-won.

The first time James came in, he talked about a painful relationship with his abusive father and how his father had frequently made him feel cowardly and shameful. His hurt was so deep that any affirmation of his worth, such as the support he had received at AA, often brought him to tears. The memory of this father-son conflict had become increasingly meaningful to him since his recovery had begun because of a struggle James felt within himself between God and Jesus.

One evening, while he was still in the treatment center,

347

sitting quietly in his room reading a book, James felt what he called the "presence of God." He said that the sensation was not visual or auditory, but a glowing feeling which erased his guilt while it buried his past. He felt empowered. He told me that this feeling lasted for about eight months. During that time, he felt different, as if he were in a direct relationship with God. About six months before coming to see me, however, James began "to struggle with Jesus."

James explained to me that he had begun to think about what his relationship to Jesus was, and what it was he was supposed to *do*. This struggle had displaced his feeling of connection with God, and he had become depressed and troubled. In a dream, he saw the path back to God blocked by a wall. He knew he could walk around the wall, but refused to do so. He was afraid to step off the path, even though it was necessary in order for him to continue his journey.

James came back in to see me about a month later, and then returned for a third time after a five-week hiatus. I was glad to see him again, since I enjoyed him as a person and felt that I could learn a great deal from him. For a therapist to learn is important, not only for the therapist, but for the therapy itself. Actual learning is mutual when it occurs, and is most potent when it approaches equivalence. James's positive choice—his determination to risk and grow—was contagious. Playing it safe as a therapist, being unwilling to learn, guarantees the same stasis in the client.

After that visit, I did not see James again for over three months. I was not worried, for he had clearly chosen his own direction and was working on his own schedule. When he returned, however, he told me that he had been in the hospital with a heart attack. He looked gaunt and worn out, but his internal strength, if anything, seemed greater. He wanted to talk to me about what had happened when he "almost died."

This is what he described: "There weren't any lights like people talk about. It was dark and simple. I was real conscious of that . . . nothing was complex there. And it was clear to me that it was my choice to live or die.

"I knew I couldn't take forever to decide, that my body was slowly deteriorating back there. It wasn't a pressure or anything, just a choice I had to make. It was strange, too, because for some reason I remember that going left was going back to life, going right was death. But death wasn't a bad thing . . . it felt like peace, but different from being alive.

"I could feel a whole lot of love from somewhere outside pulling me back. Even then, I figured it was the living people calling me back . . . but it was like I had to make up my own mind. While I was thinking, God spoke to me. Not in a voice, it was just something that came to my mind and said that I had to know that the only condition for going back was to give love without needing anything in return. I knew then what I'd been fighting about with Jesus, what the wall really was. I hadn't realized that I was already like God. I didn't have to do anything but just be what I really was."

Death and Growth

We can see why people have assumed the answer to the human condition would be to avoid death entirely. As I. D. Yalom writes in *Existential Psychiatry* and Ernst Becker in *The Denial of Death*, fear of death is our primal anxiety. Historically, fleeing death has been our search, a desperate search for immortality through religion, art, science, transcendence, and denial. But in many ways, as seen so often in our myths and literature, our search leads us in the opposite direction from the one we intend. The search for immortality is the search for security. It is the prime mover in the loss of selfbeing. "The moment one is on the side of life," said Henry Miller, " 'peace and security' drop out of consciousness. The only peace, the only security, is in fulfillment."

As James directly experienced during his heart attack, dying is a central component of living—not simply the end of a life, but a part of living. In truth, we must learn to accept death as a part of life, not merely as the *unavoidable* part it is, but as a *necessary* part. We must learn to accept death not fatalistically but as part of the life-giving and creative process. We must choose as James chose, and make our choice an understanding that life and death are part of the same condition.

The art and craft of being a person—our intimacy and closeness—are grounded in the continuum of making conscious more and more of what is unconscious. This unfolding of our whole nature—our unconscious being made conscious—is the essence of experience and reexperience. However, it requires our consciousness to make room for the new. Some of *what has been* must stop being, so that what has not been can come into being. Growth requires death.

I (Pat) believe that it is easy to fall into thinking of this connection between creativity and death as being heavy and serious. However, I am helped in my understanding by my own "light" experience of it by my wife, Elaine. I collect things that interest me, from matchbooks to model trains, and have a difficult time throwing anything away that might be somehow useful in the future. I am clearly not cut out for the disposable society. Elaine often points out to me, as I take another load to the basement, that I need to get rid of some of the old stuff so I can have some room for saving more of it. She says it humorously, but that does not make it any less true.

That same process of letting go—of letting things die and be done with—is important to the ongoing life process. The object surrendered, be it a thing, an idea, or a feeling, is less important than the process of life in which we give up the security of what is known, and go on to the new and unknown. The object taken to the basement may not be an old rug or a sputtering electric razor. It may instead be an idea, a belief, a bias, an expectation, a feeling, a memory, a goal, a plan, a dream, a relationship, an anger, a desired person, a hated place, or a conflicted past. When we can let them die, we have more energy for growth and more room for the new. All attachments demand energy. New energy becomes available when old attachments are abandoned. And new patterns can form which generate even more energy.

Paradoxically, energy is further enhanced by the exhilaration and excitement of our having the courage to let something important go. We allow our enjoyment of the vibrant colors of autumn to fade, and become excited with the smell of snow in early winter. How much more gratifying this is than to resent winter's intrusion on autumn, to be disappointed with spring because it is not as glorious as we wished, to be bored because summer always seems the same, or to resent autumn for ending our summer. Such nonexperiential living leaves us with little chance of becoming a person for all seasons. We may understand this truth in its poetic or abstract sense, but we seem to have difficulty applying the notion that *learning something new* always involves the *demise of something old.*

A few years ago, I (Tom) was given an award at the annual meeting of a professional society for contributions in the area of psychotherapy. After I gave a short acceptance speech, someone in the audience asked me what I considered to be the major accomplishment, professionally and intellectually, of my years as a psychotherapist. I said I thought my greatest achievement was the fact that at my present age, which was seventy, I knew considerably less than I'd known when I was thirty years old. I believe that this attitude reflects healthy dying.

Most humans fight this process of dying as if it were bad or threatening. That distortion is part of the price we pay for living in a propertied civilization. Before we had permanent residences and an accumulation of objects, land, domesticated animals, domesticated plants, and the accouterments of the same, there was little property to hold on to. What *things* there were, were artistic and craftful: songs and arrowheads, pictures and satchels, ideas and dreams, stories and relationships, experience and experience made manifest in reexperience. We held on to each other and the folklore of our past with each other.

One's being was not so strongly held hostage to possessions, literal or metaphorical, that had to be protected, kept alive, or made immortal. One's possessions, whatever they consisted of, were manifestations of one's being. The man or woman *literally* made the clothes, instead of the clothes making the man or woman. None of this description is meant *romantically*, since hunter-gatherers were probably as much in search of security in their own way as we are today. But they lived and searched in a real world, and their metaphors for living, the patterns of life they traced, were real metaphors.

Holding on to "Life"

Habit is a second nature which prevents us from knowing the first, of which it has neither the cruelties nor the enchantments.

—MARCEL PROUST, *Remembrance of Things Past*

Most of us currently live *propertied lives,* not only in the materialistic sense but also in terms of our feelings, thoughts, and behaviors. We are captured by the unfinished past—our unfinished feelings, unfinished thoughts, and unfinished behaviors. This dilemma describes the classic loss of wholeness: most of us are liable to spend our lives vainly attempting to finish old experiences. In that futile effort, we compulsively repeat what kept us from finishing them in the first place instead of letting them die in order to keep growing. We block current real experience by our attachment to old experience. As Carl Whitaker said in *Midnight Musings of a Family Therapist:*

> The panic of the dialectic eventually fades into the limbo of what I call "metaliving." The essential component in psychotherapy and the challenge we all struggle with endlessly is that most of us live a fragmented life: we are either preoccupied with the horrors or the glories of the past, or we are preoccupied with the horrors and the glories of the future. We don't live; we just use our left brains to endlessly think abut living. This kind of metaliving is just like metacommunication—the disease that plagues all psychotherapists. We spend our lives dealing in a framework in which we talk about talking and many times never say anything. And if we're not careful, that process (or non-process) contaminates the rest of our living and the rest of our talking.

We are so afraid of death we prolong the past, eventually elongating it into the future. When we cannot accept death, we remain fastened to propertied space and time, so we never can be truly present or congruent in space/time. We lose faith in becoming because we cling to what has been. Thus, we cannot experience, cannot learn, and cannot change.

Marty has been in therapy for some time, but has changed little. He understands himself more clearly, but he still *lives* the same way. He says he would like to be more playful in his relationships, more spontaneous, more in touch with his feelings, more who he is. But every time a spontaneous idea comes to him, he forgets it. Every time a real feeling arises, he negates it. Every time he has a chance to be who he really is, he avoids it. Marty is frightened of doing anything, lest he change anything that might upset the status quo. He is afraid of dying and being reborn. He does not understand dying as a part of living. Marty has yet to give up his habits.

Marty is propertied with his old conflicts. The angers, fears, and hurts of his past remain his companions. He defends and protects them as if they were valuable possessions not to be lost, especially not to be *taken away by another person*. Marty lives, as many of us do, in the world of theft and deprivation, not growth and death. He mistakes his possessions for his identity, his connection, and his faith, thus dying the death of stasis in the false world he has created. He will not *forsake* his past for the *sake* of his present.

It is as if we are on guard duty, defending our fort against attack. With tremendous cost of energy and time, we are constantly defending. We are out of touch with the truth that the fort is now a National Historic Trust, empty of all but memories, and that the only attackers are tourists. While tourists can be annoying and troublesome, for the most part, they just visit. Our adult selves could save all the energy and time spent defending if only we could let the past die.

I (Pat) once saw a patient whose good faith had been revived after many years of struggle. However, after a visit with his parents, he came in to me and said, "I don't want to be well and happy. I'm not through being angry with my parents. I feel as if being happy would be forgiving them. I'm not ready to do that. I want everyone to know what they did to me. The only way I can do that is by staying angry. My anger is so deep that I'd rather give up my happiness than forgive them. Children deserve to be loved."

But happily, a few weeks after his pronouncement, he did give up his anger at his parents. He had dreamed about giving birth to himself, and knew, out of his dream, that the old must be parent to the new. *He let it die.* And so he really began to live.

Our desired world of security would exclude death, but in so doing would exclude life and love as well. We cannot stop the world without paying the price. As Faust and Daniel Webster learned, the price is always much greater than we think it will be. Blaming our parents for who and how we are is a way of trying to stop time. It never works. Creative being is the only alternative to being locked into stasis.

Clark Moustakas said, in *Creativity and Conformity*, that "Creativity . . . always involves a solemn compact between one's self and others or between one's self and the raw materials of nature and life. It is a pure form of self-other relatedness." Creative growth requires participation in the process of nature as it really *is*—the nature of life *and* death. Imagine the horror of having only one thought, only one feeling, only one behavior for the rest of our lives, of being certain that what is now is what will be forever. To live in an eternal summer would be hell.

Dying to Live
and Living to Die

It would be easy to deal with the idea that *we have to die to live* as a purely spiritual or philosophical notion. Conversely, it would also be easy to deal with the same idea purely in practical terms, as in "If you're going to build a new house there, of course you're going to have to tear down that old one that's on the same site." But more to the point of our own growth, we must remember that letting things die is giving up our closeness for the moment in order to allow intimacy. That is, we must stop reexperiencing the old so we may experience the new in our living. The duality of intimacy and closeness, experience and reexperience, can quickly capture us. We easily are seduced into grasping one or the other in the pursuit of security. However, we must try to stay in the fusion of the duality, and address as an *ordinary* aspect of living the reality of moving back and forth—of having to die in order to live.

Children know intuitively that the death of one thing makes room for the birth of another. They do it naturally all the time. They learn, grow, and change so quickly in their development that there is much less sense of fixed living than we see in ourselves as adults. These constantly repeated little deaths—letting go of a favorite toy, changing a prior belief, giving up crawling for walking, leaving the breast for the cup, moving to abstraction from concreteness, allowing omniscience to become participation—all are part of the process of growing and creating the new reality of self.

Children accept that little growths come from little deaths, and realize that the big death lies in *staying the same*. As adults, however, we are apt to avoid change. We are hesitant to let anything we are secure with die. We need to learn from children their comfort with little deaths. They do not actually anticipate changing overnight in big ways as adults seem to expect, although they do have such fantasies. Children seem to realize innately that beginnings require endings and so big changes would require big deaths. Perhaps their ability to be playful about the big deaths—to let go of their own identities and take on new ones in their play, for example—makes them more comfortable with the little ones.

In this strange way, children seem to know the difference between fantasy and real life much more clearly than adults. Even when wounded and battered by life, and living in fantasy as an escape, on some deep level children appear honestly able to distinguish between fact and fiction. As adults, we are more likely to believe that our imaginary world is the real world, and tend to fight being honest with ourselves. In so doing, we are living to die instead of dying to live. Unlike an injured child who, given the chance, will go out to play, we keep ourselves locked in our shuttered prisons, licking our wounds. We are passing time until we come to our end in the world of non-experience. Afraid to die, we live dead. "Those most like the dead," wrote La Fontaine in his *Fables*, "are those most loath to die."

There is no escape. In Robert Anderson's play *I Never Sang for My Father*, the son opens and closes the story by saying, "Death brings an end to life but not to relationship." Dishonesty in adults makes us inclined to forget that truth. The relationship of life goes on even after we deaden ourselves. We cannot avoid the truth of living, only hide from it. That paradox is the source or our own internal pain and hunger as well as the hurt and fear of those who love us. It is the most direct manifestation of our self-diminishment. Rigidified by our fear of death, we cannot live.

Theologian Paul Tillich wrote in *The Courage to Be*: "Only in the continuous encounter with other persons does the person become and remain a person." He went on to say that "if the self participates in the power of being itself, it receives itself back. For the power of being acts through the power of the individual selves." Such participation and encountering requires *creative* living, including the willingness to allow the old to die so that the new may live. Otherwise, our encountering will be neither real nor continuous.

I (Tom) remember a couple who came to see me at the

insistence of their family doctor. They were both in their fifties, well-to-do, physically healthy, and quite depressed. He was apathetic, unfeeling, and unliving. She was angry, unhappy, and complaining. I asked them to tell me about their long marriage. Both said, with a conscious certainty, "Our marriage is fine; we are very happy with each other." I could only say to them that that was at least a start. I was not being sarcastic. I meant what I said. It was a start. To me, it was also startling. When our security captures us so completely that we cannot see, our windows are completely shuttered.

Unhealthy Living

The night is the mother of the day
The winter of the spring
And even upon old decay
The greenest mosses cling.

—JOHN GREENLEAF WHITTIER,
"A Dream of Summer"

In our unhealthy living we will not allow night to give birth to day, or winter to spring. We will not give birth or be born. We know nothing of *resurrection*, and the very idea of it both confuses and terrifies us. What we are familiar with and committed to is *redemption*. We spend our lives redeeming. *Redeem* means literally, "to buy back." Since life is free, it is ludicrous to think it can be either bought *or* bought back. The fear of resurrection comes from our deepest fear, which is our paralyzing horror of death and dying. We are petrified by the paradox writer George MacDonald described in *What's Mine's Mine:* "You will be dead so long as you refuse to die." We have little or no faith, no faith in life that arises from death. The core of our repetition compulsion is our insistence on trying to redeem our life by repeating our failures. We are unwilling to let them be, to let them go, to let them die.

In our unhealthiness, we cannot be creative. We are unwilling to allow new parts of our unconscious to be born, unwilling to allow them to become conscious. We try to escape everything unknown, even our own unconscious. Since we fear our unconscious, we have trouble remembering our dreams. The whole person experiences her unconsciousness as a creative part of the human engine, and remembers her dreams. Her conscious and unconscious are good friends. Only in such internal friendship, such wholeness, can we find real peace and the privacy of being safe within ourselves. And it is especially important not to be "self-intrusive"—not to have fragments of our personhoods that block our own wholeness—when we live in a world which intrudes on our persons almost constantly.

Many of us do struggle with such self-intrusions. Cassy constantly returns to her little-girl role with men. She persists in trying to please in a desperate attempt to appease a father whose chronic anger and displeasure actually had nothing to do with her in the first place. Of course, along with the appeasing comes the resentment, hurt, and fear. Emotional abuse, just like physical abuse, almost always produces nonexperience in those abused. Unable to face the shame of our experience, which then must become nonexperience, we cannot let it die and thus cannot free ourselves. We fear the intrusion of what some part of us already knows. Therefore, therapists often struggle with "the family secret," which frequently has become the family legacy and heritage. Letting it die seems to family members like letting our self die. But real *self* is not "living dead." Real self is *not* "not living." The false self in which we see our identity as the unfinished business of our lives is a sure way to be less than whole. It is that self that must die for resurrection to take place.

Not living is not the answer to the problems of living. Problems are solved by evolving and creative growth, not by the nonexperience that stasis brings. In *On Becoming a Person*, Carl Rogers said that the curative force in psychotherapy is *"man's tendency to actualize himself, to become his potentialities.* By this I mean the directional trend which is evident in all organic and human life—the urge to expand, extend, develop, mature— the tendency to express and activate all the capacities of the organism, or the self."

Actualizing is a creative act. It creates more selfbeing and is thus the counterpoint to selficide. A new state of being can arise, phoenixlike, from the ashes of nonbeing or even from previous states of being. Rather than regret and resist the demise of the old, we should celebrate the arrival of the new. It is not merely exchange. It is renewal. It is resurrection. As Hesse's Siddhartha said, everything is necessary. We do not throw out the old as if abandoning an old friend. Instead, we enlarge the friendship to include more of ourselves and the other, to make it *something different from what it was.* We allow an old way of being to die so that we may be born into a new way of being.

The Ambivalence of Creativity

Death, and the growth that springs from its fertilization of life, is the basis of all creativity. The word *create* comes from the Latin *creare* which means "to produce" or "cause to grow." It was originally an agricultural term, as in growing potatoes or onions, and hence basically meant "to come into existence." *To come into existence and grow* is a beautiful description of a person becoming the most he or she can be in living and in relationships.

Risking, with faith that the new will produce and grow and become more alive, is an essential way of life for farmers, but it is increasingly foreign to modern man. In that connection, it is illuminating to observe how many of the basic words that form our experiential vocabulary arise out of rustic, agrarian ways of life. *Crazy* is such a word, and provides us with an interesting illustration of the ambivalence we feel about the risks involved in letting something die in order to create something new.

Crazy is frequently used to describe someone who is not in touch with reality; it is in this context synonymous with madness. Both words are used ambivalently. We also use the word crazy to tell someone how much we love them and enjoy them: "I'm really *crazy* about you." Or we may say, "You're crazy!" using the term not as a condemnation, but in an excited and admiring sense. Madness has the same kind of ambivalence. If I say, "I'm mad *at* you," you will be distanced and offended but will not assume I am insane. However, "I'm mad *about* you," is similar to "I'm crazy about you."

The word *crazy* comes from the Old German *krazen*, which referred to the pecking away at the shell that birds do in order to come out into life and be born and grow. It meant "cracking the shell" in order to be alive and free in the world. There is a positive aspect to the death of the egg, for it leads to the birth of the chick.

On the other hand, the word *mad* reflects the darker side of our ambivalence. *Mad* originally meant "to cut up or commit mayhem." So when I say, "I'm mad about you" I may be sharing with you the negative part of my ambivalence about caring so much for you. The risk of loving frightens most of us.

Love is not always seen as desirable. It is not always easily accepted, readily enjoyed, or joyfully embraced. For many people, love is a feeling fraught with concern and anxiety, considered dangerous to both oneself and the loved one. It demands the death of the old to make room for its birth. This fear must be grown through before we can learn through experience what real *loving* is. The combination of fear and faith may account for the negative resonance of "I am mad about you," just as the combination of hope and faith may account for the positive ambivalence of "I am crazy about you." Love is simply another name for the creative force. In that sense, we fear creativity when we fear love. Love makes us new; it *creates*. Creativity not only unshutters windows, it swings them wide open.

Creativity

> . . . *animals are inquisitive, they have an urge to manipulate, explore, to look what's inside, which is independent from such biological drives as hunger, sex, and fear . . . novelty, surprisingness, or puzzlement are as real incentives to learning as pellets of food dropped into the Skinner box.*
>
> —ARTHUR KOESTLER, *The Act of Creation*

We must have creativity to grow, to evolve, and to love. We must have creativity to be part of the real world, for the real world is constantly creating. Creativity and stabilization form the basis of all living processes, the cycle of death and birth. In humans, the exploratory drive may well be *the* primary need.

Dennis is an articulate, competent man in his late thirties. He spends much of his time away from home on business. Although he is not aware of it (and would deny it if confronted), he behaves as if his family should be there at home for him at his convenience and present no particular demands or problems for him after his tedious and stressful business hours. He never consciously admits those expectations, but that is *how he lives*. His children always feel they are somehow bothering him with their questions or requests for his time. His unspoken assumption is that someone else should be maintaining his living space and providing for his basic needs.

Dennis is married to a woman who at first accommodated these needs. Essentially, Alice acted as mother both for him and their two sons. A few years prior to my (Tom) seeing them, she had begun to develop somewhat as a "nonmother," as an adult and a person in her own right. This metamorphosis in her had become the source of enormous tension in their relationship, as Alice no longer maintained Dennis's wardrobe, living space, or personal care needs. She ceased to live her life according to his schedule and desires. Dennis felt betrayed, misunderstood, and mistreated by her. He believed that he had been misrepresented to others as being unfeeling and selfish. He also began to feel that Alice was brainwashing their children to see him the same way she herself saw him.

After a year of psychotherapy, Dennis remained much as he had been in the beginning: a resentful participant. He was judgmental, righteous, and defensive. By this time, Alice had decided to get a divorce. In their interview with me subsequent to her announcing her decision, Dennis was very upset. He was angry that "we" had not come up with some rational plan to salvage their relationship. He felt that he had not learned anything that was useful to him despite a year of thinking through the personal dilemma in which he found himself. I asked him if he thought he could amend his situation by thinking. He said he did not know of any other adult, reasonable way to do it. He said he thought the whole point of being mature was to be able to think clearly and correctly in order to solve one's own problems.

I told him that I considered thinking, by itself, very much like the steering wheel of a car. It reminded me of the times when as a child I had sat in a car turning the steering wheel and making a noise to pretend I had the motor going while I played that I was going somewhere. I shared with him my feeling that this behavior was similar to how he was living his life.

He was put off at first, and stuck with his anger for a moment; then he relaxed a little and asked me what I thought the motor stood for—what the real motor was. My response was that the motor was the real experience that he and I and his wife had together. Thoughts are not enough; experience has to be with all of our personhood. Precisely to the extent that he could relate in the fullness of his person, to that extent could what he found in therapy be transferred to his home life and his relationship with his Alice. We cannot think experience. Experience, however, can significantly alter our thinking.

Dennis phoned me the following day. "For the first time in our relationship," he said, "I really need to talk to you." I told him that I would be glad to see him as soon as I could arrange a time. He repeated, "That's really what I mean, I really need to see you." When something creatively changes in a person, something real and different can happen. Growth begins. Later, Dennis was able to say, "Tom, I really need to talk *with* you." This position was significantly different from his original request to talk *to* me. He had been talking *to* others most of his life. He seldom talked *with* anyone. He was finally *creating* himself as a person, creating the whole person he really was. Dennis has stayed in therapy and has changed. Although he and Alice separated, they have continued to come in together occasionally, and may yet make it. Whether they do or not depends on whether they let the old marriage die and create a new one in which they both can live as the whole persons they are—the whole persons they are creating in their living.

We must all be about the business of creating ourselves as persons. The push to make more of the unconscious conscious is the engine that drives the evolution of man. This is true not just of humans; it is a way of looking at and understanding all of life. In her *Journals,* the writer Katherine Butler Hathaway said:

> Then and there I invented this rule for myself to be applied to every decision I might have to make in the future. I would sort out all the arguments and see which belonged to fear and which to creativeness, and other things being equal I would make the decision which had the larger number of creative reasons on its side. I think it must be a rule something like this that makes jonquils and crocuses come pushing through the cold mud.

That same rule pushes selfbeing through the cold mud of unhealthy tranquility and stasis. Creativity is the birthing process of wholeness.

Creative Living

Love is not a fixed condition of the soul but its motion:
Returned or not, it is a directed impulse outward into life,
into ever richer renewal of meeting.

—LINDSEY CLARKE, *Chymical Wedding*

Why is it so difficult for us to be like flowers and "blossom" as persons? The answer lies in our fear. Unwilling to let go of where we are, however painful that place is, we are unable to go on to anywhere else. We continue to be miserable in our dogged pursuit of happiness. We continue to be insecure in our desperate search for security. We fear the risking and forgo the joy. We fear the death of the "I," our false self, our defended fortress. We know that there is a real risk in starting something, in changing, for at some point the change takes hold and *takes over*. We lose control. We find then that there is no ultimate control in life, no immortality. There is simply being and becoming.

Too easily, we lose awareness of the truth that being and becoming go together. In *Order Out of Chaos,* Ilya Prigogine and Isabelle Stengers write that, "being and becoming are not to be opposed one to the other: they express two related aspects of reality." There is no immortality in *only* being, there is merely stasis. There is no becoming without the little deaths in our being. Life flows, or it is not life at all.

We often hear this struggle within the words of people who are trying to grow. They say, "I don't know how to make it happen" or "Tell me what I need to do." That approach will not work. We can only "make" what we already know. At its healthiest, *making* is a craft, a form of reexperiencing, a practicing of what is good. But more frequently, for most of us, it is the repetition of unhealthy behavior, with which we only make ourselves more unhealthy. We must, instead, come to *letting it happen*. Such *allowing* creates a space for the new, the different, and the changed. It allows something which did not exist before to come into being. We seldom allow change, because we hold on to the past as if we did not want to be absent from it in case our old fantasies should happen to come true. We are afraid to let the old die.

In our modern civilization, we forget how life was experienced up until only a few centuries ago. Going back only as far as the colonists or the pioneers heading west, in leaving the old life one ran the risk of letting it truly die. One went on to the new without telephone calls or easy return visits. Many of our forefathers and foremothers *really* went on to the new, letting life take over and be what it was. In this sense, they lived life instead of tying to control it. They literally took the risk of letting the old go. Risking to grow was a tangible act, a part of everyday living.

Perhaps it is easier to see this point in the arts. Art is the closest description of real experience we have. True art does not judge, nor does it preach. It simply describes reality in its detailed beauty. "Art does not reproduce the visible," wrote Paul Klee in *The Inward Vision*, "rather, it makes visible."

As artists, we struggle with the prototypical issues of living. When we verse a poem, brush paint to a picture, sound notes for a symphony, chisel stone or wood, or give birth to characters in a novel, we take a big risk. If it is real art, the risk will be real, for we can *start* a work of art, but the work will finish itself. If it is a real poem, symphony, picture, or novel, it will be what it is, not what we want it to be. It will blossom into what it would become, not what we are. The true artist, like the true lover, encourages and rejoices in this birthing even though it means the death of his or her own preconceived idea. But such freedom in love or art takes more courage than most of us usually live with.

The Creative Alternative

Scott and Marybeth are six years into a marriage that has often seemed more a joint struggle than a joint venture. Both work full time and there seems little time or energy left for each other. They are pressured by conflicting feelings about their goals in life. Marybeth would like to have children, and has strong feelings about not working after a child is born. Scott is unsure that he wants to be a father—he feels he might be unable to deal with the demands of parenthood—and is worried about finances. The idea of Marybeth's not working upsets him. He does not want to feel responsible for her. Their painful conflict has now continued through six years of living together and has not changed appreciably over that time. They have no *creative* life with each other.

Scott complains, "She doesn't understand me. She thinks I'm selfish and says that I think she is trying to use me. But she is always asking me to 'talk about it' and to tell her how I feel. I can't win. She's obsessed with her own feelings. She thinks there's only one way to live."

Marybeth, of course, sees life quite differently. "Scott refuses to talk to me in any real way. He never says what he really feels. He tells me he is willing to have an open mind and to discuss things, but he always comes back to the same position. He's made up his mind already but he won't admit it. And when I tell him that, it's like . . . 'here she goes again.' "

Neither speech is helpful, although both contain tremendously valuable *information* for the other if they were creatively listened to. If Scott and Marybeth could step into the other's shoes and creatively imagine themselves as the other sees and experiences them, they might learn. It they do not, they will never inherit their wholeness as individuals, whether they stay together or whether they have children or not. Only in being able to creatively and passionately be our *full* selves with each other do we form meaningful relationships. Creativity is always available to us, but we must choose to live that way.

Dreaming

> For we have in the dream forsaken our allegiance to the organizing, controlling and rectifying forces of the world, the Universal Conscience. We have sworn fealty to the wild, incalculable, creative forces, the imagination of the universe.
>
> —ISAK DINESEN, *Shadows on the Grass*

Like all of us at times, Scott and Marybeth will not allow the old to die so that a creative new may be born. They do not dare to dream. Dreaming, in the creative sense, is probably the clearest example of how the unconscious lives. In dreams, death and growth are paired polarities: ideas, people, and even selves die, are reborn, are changed—are metamorphosed.

When we are too unaware of such dreaming and too separated from our unconscious, we do not learn. Rollo May in *Man's
Search for Himself* said:

> All through the ages . . . people have regarded their
> dreams as sources of wisdom, guidance, and insight. But most
> of us today think of our dreams as odd episodes, as foreign as
> some strange ceremonial dance in Tibet. This results in the
> cutting off of an exceedingly great and significant portion of
> the self. We are then no longer able to use much of the wisdom
> and power of the unconscious.

The wisdom available to us is then avoided, the changes proposed
either derided or sheepishly repressed. We forget that the dream
is as real as what we securely call reality. In truth, the dream is
more real, for our dreams are connected to the cycle of death and
growth, while our conscious selves blindly persist in our search
for immortality.

In *The Forgotten Language,* Erich Fromm spoke to the reality of our dreaming:

> There is no "as if" in the dream. The dream is present,
> real experience, so much so indeed, that it suggests two ques-
> tions: What is reality? How do we know that what we dream
> is unreal and what we experience in our waking life is real? A
> Chinese poet has expressed this aptly: "I don't know whether
> I am a man who dreamt he was a butterfly, or perhaps a
> butterfly who dreams now he is a man."

If we do not dream—daydream, night dream, personally dream,
dream for our families, and universally dream—we do not risk
not knowing. We do not wish to let the new, like a poem or a
symphony, take over and change us. We are afraid.

I (Tom) had a very Kurt Vonnegut–like dream about a man
who had the power of telekinesis. He would appear at any place in
the universe he thought of. Unfortunately, he kept thinking all
the time and was therefore constantly everywhere. In the dream,
he asked me how it was that I managed to stay in just one place.
The dream seemed to me a perfect description of the difficulty we
have in finding a balance between intimacy and closeness, experience and reexperience, as well as a reminder that we need that

balance in order to be whole. Certainly most of us, like myself in the dream, are stuck in one place, unable to move. But the space traveler was no better off. We need both—the stability of our being and the dream of our becoming.

Dad's dream reminds me (Pat) of the dreams of our childhood. The memories of such dreams—or, if we are fortunate, such current free and passionate dreams—put us in touch, if only for a moment, with the dreamer inside ourselves. We all have that dreaming child within us, that natural child who is full of being and passionately going about the process of becoming. Most of us have lost that naturalness and freedom to some degree, but inside us both the dreamer and the dream remain alive. Unshuttering our windows allows each of us to return to that wholeness within ourselves.

In dreams, we can lose our fear of allowing life to take us over. We can accept that the poem writes itself, the symphony plays itself, the statue carves itself, and the characters write their own story. We can accept the dying of one "I" so that another "I" can become. We can know the truth of what Tillich called the existential portrait of man: "Man creates what he is. Nothing is given to him to determine his creativity. The essence of his being—the 'should be,' the 'ought to be'—is not something which he finds; he makes it." We *are* free to become, in our dreaming and in our living. It merely requires letting go of our old being.

Creativity is a gift. In many ways, it is *the gift of life*. But creativity is a cycle of life, not a static portrait. The cycle is one of beginning and endings, starts and finishes, growth and death. It is always becoming. In the cycle, we are all connected. We are all both the dreamer and the dream.

18
Experiencing Life

One must not always think so much about what one
should do, but rather what one should be.

—Meister Eckhart

I (Tom) work in an office with a full window overlooking a small
garden that I find very beautiful. It has many colors, some small
trees, vines, rocks, heavy wooden railway ties, and a handmade
fountain. People coming into the clinic walk the length of this
garden. As I sit, talking and listening to clients, I frequently watch
those walking past the garden. It amazes me how often the same
pattern appears. Families come with small children and, as they
walk by, the children inevitably stop at the fountain. They dip
their hands in the water or play with the spray, or go sit on the
old wooden bench. The parents usually walk straight ahead. When
they get to the other end of the garden, they turn and gesture, irritated with their children. Then they hurry them into the
clinic.

I will see the same family come by many times, without
their being conscious of my watching them. Over a period of
time, I notice that the parents begin to gesture in a more loving
way. Then they will begin to pause halfway down the walk near
the fountain for a few moments while their children play. Even-

tually, most of them will sit on the bench while the children play among the flowers or with the water. These people are learning something about living with their natural connection to the real world. I see the same progression in single adults who initially look as if they have been *sentenced* to therapy as they march down the walk. Gradually, as the months go by, they slow down and begin to see, and perhaps even smell, the garden. Finally, they will sit or bend over and touch the water.

When I am asked by clients how I myself would like to live, I tell them that I have always wanted to get to the point where I was always where I was, for the time I was being there, with whoever else was there, doing whatever we were doing *with* one another. Or if alone, that I could fully be and do at that time, and in that space, whatever I was being and doing. Such living implies the absence of any wish to be somewhere else, or with someone else, or in some other time. Living like that implies being fully connected to my world. I would like to live how that garden teaches people to live. I would like to grow out of selficide into selfbeing.

There are certain windows to wholeness that allow us to grow toward our full capacity as human beings. These windows into our real selves—the ones we have described—are simply ways of returning to the truth of our own experience. They do not exhaust or preclude other windows to selfbeing. However, they seem *the most direct pathways* to enabling us to reach our full potential. They suggest that the healthy, growing person has a greater capacity for new experience than the fixed, stuck person. Not only are healthy people's lives characterized by this increased capacity for experience, they also grow and change out of that increased capacity throughout their lifetimes.

A positive anxiety accompanies opening those windows: anxiety about risking, about using our own inner world as the primary basis for living, about being fully present, about nonintentionally playing, about making free choices. The same anxiety is felt when we begin to live with, accept, and enjoy someone who differs from us. We experience that anxiety again when we develop a personal moral system that differs from the external code that has been imprinted on us. And that anxiety accompanies our becoming congruent, as we learn not only to feel what we feel, but to behave in ways which express those feelings, thus openly revealing ourselves.

In contrast, unhealthy people have limited capacities for real or new experience. They tend to reexperience in preprogrammed ways over and over until the reexperience becomes *nonexperience*. Their living becomes robotized and mechanical. Such people prefer the security that comes from the familiar, even if the familiar envelops them in a living death. They cling to their certainties rather than risk any anxiety about their living.

Unhealthiness

Who are these unhealthy people? Are they only people with unusual and acute problems? No. Are those who come to therapy a select, circumscribed segment of the population? No. The majority of people who come to therapy are very ordinary, functioning humans. You and I. In fact, their seeking help often means that they are more alive, more willing to risk than most of us. Coming to therapy represents a desire for new experiences in order to live more fully as human beings in community.

There are, of course, humans who are so severely crippled by their unhealthiness that they cannot effectively interact with others. Some of these people are ill, psychotic or psychopathic, and thus unable to live as whole humans in community. The vast majority of us, however, are *intermittently* unhealthy. Nevertheless, we live effectively in our society. We are productive, responsible, and stable. We are not too aware of our unhealth. Most of us do not seek out psychotherapy simply to increase the quality of our lives and our experience in those lives. We are doing fine—or at least all right. We are stable in our shuttered rooms, avoiding those positive anxieties.

We stay hidden to stay secure, but, in doing so, we block real experience. In *On Becoming a Person*, Carl Rogers summarized the necessity of real experience to our selfbeing:

Experience is, for me, the highest authority. The touchstone of validity is my own experience. No other person's ideas, and none of my own ideas, are as authoritative as my experience. It is to experience that I must return again and again, to discover a closer approximation to truth as it is in the process of becoming in me.

Each of us probably diminishes our *self* in small ways dozens of times every day. We procrastinate, we default on choices, we make righteous judgments, we run from risks. Those actions are very different from the need to block experience when responding to stimuli that momentarily overwhelm us. For example, if, as we are walking quietly down the street, we see someone run over by a car, there is no way we can fully respond immediately to that overpowering stimulus. What happens, for healthy adults, is that we process the experience in small, ordinary ways after the fact. We talk to our colleagues when we finally arrive at the office. We tell them what we have seen. When we go home that evening, we remember what we saw, and drive more carefully. We talk about it with our family. We are more loving of our children that night, and maybe for some nights to come. We even dream of it. Finally, the experience becomes a memory. The slow reexperiencing of the original experience allows us to deal safely with the trauma over time, and that helps prevent it from becoming a nightmare.

For children, the problem is different. Without adult ego structures and resources—and without colleagues, spouses, and children of their own to help them process the trauma—they are in a much more vulnerable position—a dependent position. For that reason, they need parents who can move the same process forward for *and* with them. It is not difficult, then, to understand why, when parents do not provide such support, or, even more clearly, when they are the *source* of the trauma, that children cannot prevent the nightmares.

The purpose of naturally spreading out a traumatic experience over time is to allow us to respond to it in little pieces until we have responded enough to take it out of our current experience and make it a memory. Reexperience reduces overwhelming experience to memory. We repeat the processing until we are no longer possessed by the hurt, fear, anxiety, anger, or sadness. When we cannot continue that processing, we end up stuck—frozen into states of nonbeing.

Unfortunately, most of us hold on to even nonacute hurts and traumas in the same way. We carry the hurts and deprivations of our childhoods as unhealed scars. We experience walking into a room full of strangers as if we were walking into the gas chamber. We take a social slight like the loss of a limb. Our pasts, our childhoods, our parents, and our parents' relationship are not reexperienced and allowed to become memories in the healthy sense. Instead, they become ever present reoccurrences—unresolved memories. We want all the old problems solved; we want the good stuff that we did not get. But the past cannot be changed.

We therefore compulsively repeat experiences in the hope that we will eventually respond adequately or get an adequate response from the other. For example, we pursue beautiful lovers to repair our old sense of inadequacy, and, in so doing, pass over those with whom we might have beautiful relationships. These unhealthy repetitions may last months, years, or even a lifetime. The fixed patterns do not usually stem from some single trauma but, instead, from thousands of relational experiences early in life. However, we often search for a trauma to explain (even to justify) our current unhappiness. We rummage the past for instances of neglect, abuse, conflict. Or we repeat bad experiences over and over (dating the same type of person, seeking the same escapes) but never succeed in making the pattern simply a memory. It is no longer a reexperience; it has become *nonexperience*. We move to the secure world of repeating our pasts and avoiding new experience. We hold on in the hope of being fixed.

Of course, that approach does not work. We all know that truth from our own lives. We never get *fixed*. Some people try therapy to help them solve their problems. Those who come to therapy, however, do not stay in therapy until all of their problems are solved. Indeed, if they grow, they soon learn that they are not even in therapy for problem-solving. They are there to increase their capacity to learn on their own. They intuitively understand what Brecht meant in *The Mother* when he said, "What you yourself don't learn, you don't know." One can sense in another person when she reaches the point at which she has developed a sufficient momental growth to continue growing the rest of her life. That change does not mean that she does not struggle. It does not mean that she will not retreat intermittently to unhealthiness. It means that *she will not stay there;* she will not hide in the shuttered room again. Such people are *being in the world in good faith*.

Being

What are the particular windows to human experience that are primarily responsible for assuring our being? Simple *existing* is not being. *Being* means that although we live in a large and complicated world, we *exist* individually. We exist in a way that transcends any and all of our roles. We have an identity separate from the parts we play in all of our systems—our families, jobs, communities, nations, races, genders. We are unique. Full *individual being* is internal integrity.

Often we think that we know this being. "I think, therefore I am." But the awareness of thought is not in itself sufficient to establish our sense of being. Our whole being arises out of the full congruence of our persons. We cannot *be* through cognition. It is not enough to exist only in the abstract. We must know that we exist through our participation in our living. And we find such participatory knowledge only in our ordinary experience of living.

The rational process alone cannot confer being; being involves all parts of us and our environment. If we see ourselves as separate from our world, as we do in an observer-object mentality, we make objects out of ourselves. *Participatory thinking, feeling, and behaving go into our ordinary being*. Real experience happens only when all three parts are integrated and congruent. Being is always *whole* in this sense.

Meaningful experience occurs in a relationship with an *other*, whoever or whatever that other happens to be. The act of experiencing involves self *and* other. If I love you in my head but not with my arms, obviously I have diminished my capacity for full human being. There is no real being when there is no real other, any more than we can have real experience with only one part of ourselves.

Of the windows to experiencing, there are four which most assure our *being*. They are: 1. Responsibility for Self 2. Self-discipline 3. Congruence 4. Presence. We can briefly summarize each one:

• RESPONSIBILITY FOR SELF *Self-responsibility* literally means to respond to oneself. Self-responsibility means that we are aware of our inner world, and we claim it as our own, of our own choosing. The opposite of being responsible for self is *dependency*, which means to respond primarily to what is outside ourselves.

• SELF-DISCIPLINE   *Self-discipline* means to learn out of love for oneself, to be loving disciples of ourselves. The opposite of self-discipline is *rebellion*, to war against ourselves or others, or *compliance*, to live by outside rules. When we are self-disciplined, we guide ourselves to wholeness.

• CONGRUENCE   *Congruence* means that we come together as a person. We are harmonious in the sense that our thinking, feeling, and behavior are integrated and consistent. When we are *incongruent*, we are not a harmonious whole. One or more components of our being are fixed or stuck and prevent us from being whole.

• PRESENCE   *Presence* means to be in the here-and-now and literally to be with the other person. The opposite of presence is *absence*, which means to be away in time or space, to be disinterested and distant.

Someone who is fully *being* is harmonious and present. She is herself while she is with others; she lives openly and in full view of life, as herself. She deals with essentials, and learns out of love and respect for herself. She responds to her own person as the primary basis for her living and being in this world. Contrast such a person with the one who is at war with himself, hides his real self from others, lives caught up in external systems, and does not love himself enough to learn from himself. He has little selfbeing and thus has no new or real experience. Without *being*, wholeness is impossible.

Beyond Being

In the midst of the word he was trying to say
In the midst of his laughter and glee,
He had softly and suddenly vanished away—
For the Snark was a Boojum, you see.

—LEWIS CARROLL,
"The Hunting of the Snark, An Agony in
Eight Fits"

Being, however, is not enough. There are people who may *be* in the fullest sense of the word but whose being is in a world that is self-created. They do not live in the world as it really exists, or with others as they really are. We call these people psychotic or character disordered. Such being does not move one to wholeness, irrespective of its power. Although psychosis sometimes has within it a thrust to growth and change, it is not a movement to fuller selfbeing.

Daydreaming is also a form of being that is isolated from the world. It is being within ourselves. But, unlike in psychosis, in daydreaming we eventually return to the real world. And perhaps some of that being—the playfulness, the risking, and the creativity we find in our daydreams—will manifest itself in our subsequent being in the world. If, however, we do not translate that daydreaming into our experience in the real world, the experience is little different from the disconnected fantasies of the psychotic person.

Nor, in some ways, are we in the "real" world when we sleep and dream, although dreaming *is* a real part of our natural selves. Our dreams are a creative factory of experience that can be used consciously or unconsciously in our waking hours to expand our selfbeing and our experience in the world. Dreams also provide us with the most direct method of working through our day-to-day disturbances. We repeat our unfinished daily experiences in our dreams in order to clear our psychological decks for a fresh tomorrow. They help to free our waking hours of the psychic baggage of yesterday, making us more available for full experience today. We can finish our yesterdays in our dreams instead of living them again in our todays and tomorrows. Again, however, if we do not bring our dreaming experience into our waking world, we remain disconnected.

There are many kinds of what we might call states of *pseudobeing* that hinder and limit our capacity for real *being* in the world. These states are all manifestations of a lack of internal integrity—congruence, presence, self-responsibility, and self-discipline. All those ways of being in the world that prevent internal integrity will diminish selfbeing, since they block experiencing of the new and real. All such ways of living shutter many windows. We cannot actually divide them into neat categories, but a simple listing may assist in showing how common they are. For example:

LACK OF SELF-RESPONSIBILITY
  A. *Issues of dependency*
      Obligatory living—the person who cannot say no to others
      Paying too little attention to oneself—the person who lives a role
      Being overresponsible for others—the person always taking care of others
      Living in response to others—the person who is an external placater
  B. *Issues of irresponsibility*
      Untrustworthiness—the person who cannot keep her word or intention
      Lying—the person deliberately destroying integrity
      Being a martyr—the person who enjoys indicting others
      Fickleness or inconsistency—the person forever changing his mind
      Unreliability or eraticism—the person who cannot be depended on
  C. *Issues of blaming*
      Alibis—the person who always says, "It wasn't me."
      Excuse making—the person who always has a reason for everything
      Halfhearted living—the person who does not give full effort

LACK OF SELF-DISCIPLINE
  A. *Issues of obedience*
      False duty—the person who always does what he is supposed to
      Living without resolve—the person unable to maintain choices in life
      Paying too much attention to others—the person looking to others before living himself
  B. *Issues of selfishness*
      Vanity—the person who spends his life in front of a mirror
      Being messy—the person who uses disorder to avoid responsible living
      Capriciousness—the person who impulsively breaks commitments

C. *Issues of self-denial*
  Uncertainty—the person who always second-guesses herself
  Hesitancy—the person who cannot decide
  Vacillation—the person who is always changing decisions back and forth

LACK OF CONGRUENCE
  A. *Issues of Fixed Behavior Patterns*
    Perversions—the person addicted to behavior
    Compulsions—the person who lives in her behavior
    Rigidity—the person locked into certain behavior patterns
    Judgmentalness—the person who lives to teach others
  B. *Issues of Fixed Feeling Patterns*
    Sentimentality—the person who lives in her feelings
    Conformity—the person formed by others
    Rebellion—the person who is a covert conformer
    Appeasement—the person who believes being alive is dangerous
    Masochism and sadism—the person constantly making fun of his parents
  C. *Issues of Fixed Thinking Patterns*
    Obsessing—the person who feels safer thinking than feeling or behaving
    Prejudgmentalness—the person who always already knows
    Preconstruction of worlds—the person with his own special world and rules
  D. *Issues of Personal Dishonesty*
    Incoherence—the person who uses confusion to avoid being honest
    Dissonance—the person at odds with herself
    Living for others—the person who makes fun of others

LACK OF PRESENCE
  A. *Issues of Absence*
    Withdrawal—the person who leaves you whenever you are there
    Substance abuse—the person living in alcohol, illegal drugs, or prescription drugs

Cowardice—the person who lives frightened and pleading

Head living—the person always thinking instead of living

Recreational drug use—the person fooling himself

B. *Issues of Temporal Displacement*

Procrastination—the person living by wishing

Anxiety—the person trying too hard to be there

Depression—the person living in the past

Hypomania—the person living in the future

C. *Issues of Spatial Displacement*

Disconnection—the person who lives without relation to the context she is in

Premeditated living—the person who lives the same regardless of context

Being lost—the person who is never really where he is

What if—the person always wanting the other choice

Usually we can recognize our pseudobeing. It is almost always followed by a depressed feeling, a sense of isolation, and a general irritation with our world. It is not difficult to understand why states of depression, isolation, and irritated disappointment are so frequently described by those in the aftermath of unhealthy behavior or living—the alcoholic after a binge, the Don Juan after the latest affair, even the lover who has been less than honest with her partner. There is always a feeling of coming down from what we could be as persons, which, in fact, is exactly what we are doing.

In the World

The second necessary component of full experiencing is to be *in the world.* This involves our natural connection to the whole universe that surrounds and nourishes us. It involves our living in a world of reciprocity with the other. Our preconscious awareness of this natural connection constantly reassures us of our belonging in a world of interdependence, a world of *relational being.* Without such connection, we would live in a state of constant solitude.

The windows that are most related to our experience of being *in the world* are: 1. Personal Surrender 2. Attentiveness 3. Free choice 4. Reciprocity. They can be summarized briefly:

• PERSONAL SURRENDER   *Personal surrender* or *making do* is the capacity to live in the space we are in at any given moment, at the time we are there, and with whatever other is present in that space and that time. *Making do,* in the deepest sense, means *to make open.* It opens us to the learning and growth available in any moment. The opposite of making do is *begrudging:* resentfully putting up with our world.

• ATTENTIVENESS   *Attentiveness* means to extend ourselves actively to the other. Tenderness is the essence of attentiveness. In attending, we *listen* to the other, we lean toward them. The opposite of attentiveness is *neglect.* Its literal etymology of "not to gather fruit" points directly to the barrenness of our not attending to others.

• FREE CHOICE   *Free choice* means to perceive and then to choose; originally it meant to dearly try, to taste. When we are free, we taste life and then choose. We become our own friend. Only out of freely choosing can we be genuinely loving and at peace. The opposite of free choice is *obligation,* control, and the blandness of never really tasting life.

• RECIPROCITY   *Reciprocity* means that we are all in this world together and that *we are all connected.* It defines a willingness to give *and* take, to go back and forth, to work both ways. The opposite of reciprocity and connectivity is to be disconnected—only to take or only to give, both of which maintain our *separateness.*

A person who is *being in the world* opens his relationships to the growth process. He is a person who stretches out to the other, offering himself tenderly. He lives in his world peacefully, choosing to be who he is in his environment. Such a person is connected, lives in a world that moves back and forth, and is willing to give *and* take. The person who is not being in the world is one who is forever destroying relationship. She neglects the other, cannot listen, and has no interest in gathering the fruits of life. She does not wish to choose and is not at peace inside herself or with her world. She is separated from the other, and adverse to fostering any growth. She does not give and take but remains isolated.

The following are the ways in which we are not *in the world*—manifestations of a lack of personal surrender, attentiveness, free choice, or reciprocity. Again, these are but simplified examples of how such ways of living shutter particular individual windows.

LACK OF PERSONAL SURRENDER
    A. *Issues of Self-Righteousness*
        Having to be right—the person still trying to please the parent
        Argumentativeness—the person who must have the last word
        Belligerency—the person forever angry
        Contrariness—the person who disagrees as a way of touching others
        Antagonism—the person living by always taking oppositional positions
    B. *Issues of Neediness*
        Having to have one's way—the person still looking for limits
        Selfishness—the person confused about what being a person means
        Demanding living—the person who relates to others as a demand
    C. *Issues of Being Begrudging*
        Living with resentment—the person who would rather be right than loved
        Insubordination—the person who cannot be dependent
    D. *Issues of Being Closed*
        Living with an aversion to new experience—the person afraid of being crazy
        Narrow-mindedness—the person afraid of growth

LACK OF ATTENTIVENESS
    A. *Issues of Negligence*
        Distraction—the person who cannot attend to one thing
        Disregard for others—the person who cares nothing for himself

Thoughtlessness—the person who is afraid to look at life

Being a lackey—the person who still wants Mother

Being a sycophant—the person consumed by the other's voice

B. *Issues of Carelessness*

Recklessness—the person without limits

Laxness—the person waiting for someone to care

Forgetfulness—the person living in make-believe

Absentmindedness—the person who thinks too much and without care

C. *Issues of Aloneness*

Loneliness—the person who waits for the world to come to him

Solitariness—the person who withholds herself from the world

Misanthropy—the person who separates off from others and lives in hate

LACK OF FREE CHOICE

A. *Issues of Addiction*

Substance dependency—the person without choice

License—the person who lives out of control

Sexual addictions—the person who must be turned on from outside herself

Eating disorders—the person using food as love and relationship

Perversions—the person using sex as a substitute for relationship

Excitement—the person living for the rush

B. *Issues of Fear*

Phobias—the person who fears what she desires

Anxieties—the person who wants to be but is afraid

Denial—the person who cannot acknowledge how he feels

Refusal—the person who will not try

Rejection—the person who rejects the choices available to her

C. *Issues of Obligatory Living*

Rote obedience—the person who lives through outside rules and decisions

Enmeshment or entrapment—the person whose life is a fragment of another's

Authoritarianism—the person who lives by permission

Servitude—the person who lives for the benefit of another

Subjugation—the person who lives as a shadow of another

D. *Issues of Codependency*

Living through other's unhealthiness—the person who cannot be angry

LACK OF RECIPROCITY

A. *Issues of Blaming*

Prejudice—the person who lives as a bigot, either blatantly or subtly

Chauvinism—the person without his or her other side

Sexism—the person afraid of him- or herself

Religious fanaticism—the person without spirituality

B. *Issues of the Inability to Give*

Greed—the person unable to give

Stinginess—the person who guards his emptiness

Separateness—the person who sees himself as not one of his fellow humans

Emptiness—the person who lives as if she has nothing to give

C. *Issues of the Inability to Take*

Isolation—the person who cuts herself off from others

Solitude—the person who lives only within himself

Martyrdom—the person who accuses by suffering

D. *Issues of Disconnection*

Disagreeableness—the person who touches in a poor way

Living without communality—the person drifting to death

Living without mutuality—the person who lives as an untouchable

Living without being *in the world* will never lead to wholeness. If my being exists only in a special world of its own, it can never learn and grow from the rest of what exists. We usually know when we are living in our own idiosyncratic worlds because we feel an aloneness, an emptiness, and a lack of freedom. We are angry that no one seems willing to give us what we need, and, likewise, that no one seems willing to take what we have to give. We develop an increasing fear that we might truly end up all alone.

In Good Faith

I (Pat) do not have a window looking out on the garden at our clinic. My office is on the opposite corner of the building and overlooks a shopping center parking lot. The pollution of noise, sight, and smell coming from there show me how distant we are from learning the quiet lessons Dad has watched in the garden. As a culture, we are increasingly cut off from both our human and universal natures. It often seems to me that we pay little attention to our being, have little sense of our connectedness, and are far removed from any real faith. But the individuals I see in therapy bring me back to my hope. They bring into my office dreams, joys, and rebirths that help remind me that we *can* save ourselves. And that is the true meaning of keeping the faith.

In good faith is the third necessary element of experiencing. It is the most difficult of the three components to describe because it is less behavioral and involves value judgments. Perhaps the difficulty has mainly to do with the fact that it is the unconscious component of our path to wholeness. The unconscious involves *universal being*, not just *individual* and *relational* being. The windows through which we primarily live *in good faith* are a part of *all of nature*, not just human beings. The unconscious, in this sense, includes all the "isness," not just the human component.

The notion of *good faith* has two major qualities: acceptance and innocence. Although it is inconceivable to some, the opposite of living in good faith is the denial of death. Denying death manifests itself in the loss of hope and spirituality. Continued existence, which is the core issue involved in universal being, requires faith and hope. Faith and hope energize us, providing the momentum that carries each of us from moment to moment in our living and experiencing. Out of faith and hope, *self* is constantly regenerated. Natural life is characterized by faith. To attempt to transcend natural life (to rise above it by denying death) is to lose faith. And without faith there is no way to understand life itself.

Faith is not conscious; it is intrinsic. Its reality seldom reaches even the preconscious mind. Experience, since it is so natural and pragmatic, requires a risking faith. That concept may be difficult to understand, much less accept, since faith seems to us today rather ephemeral. Nothing, however, could be further from the truth. Faith is natural, pragmatic, and functional. It is the basic energy in the universe.

The root meaning of *experience* includes the concept of peril, of waiting with fear, trying out new aspects of growth. The word *hope* has much the same connotation. *Faith* means, literally, to trust. To have faith, to experience with hope, means, then, to trust that our perilous waiting will work out. In order to risk, one *must* hope and *must* be willing to wait with fear. That is not ephemeral; it is courageous and pragmatic. And it is much more passionate and promising than living in the nonexperiencing world of the faithless and hopeless.

Without our innocent acceptance of the essential unity of nature, a unity of which we are an intricate part, we can never participate in the beautiful and grand experiment of living. We can never experience our lives. We are forever alienated. Aristotle described hope as a waking dream. Hope is, indeed, the unconscious brought into our ordinary living. Faith is a form of trusting the connected and connecting pattern of life. At some deep level we know that it is in our relationship with all else in nature that we can meet all of our experiential needs. In spiritual terms, faith is a form of knowing that God, whatever God is to us, accepts us. Such faith motivates us to risk perilously and, thus, to live fully. Without risk there is no experience, and without faith and hope there is no risking.

Good faith differs from the pretense of *blind faith* and the captivity of *bad faith*. Blind faith is nonparticipatory—for example, believing that our relationship with our lover is going to get better without any involvement on our part—and nonparticipants can never truly experience. The blindly faithful do not care to choose. Not caring enough to be ourselves is very costly. It prevents us from ever being whole. Since it is not really possible not to choose, we simply live our lives by default. We then see our lives as the fault of others.

Blind faith pretends. These are people who sit in their shuttered rooms, hoping that their blind decisions will somehow fix things outside themselves. They leave living up to chance. For example, the lonely person who always remains at home, as if believing someone will come by and save him from his loneliness, avoids choosing. He refuses to recognize his own good-ness and thus denies his own God-ness.

The price of bad faith is even higher. Bad faith assumes that life is divisive and untrustworthy. In bad faith, one takes a position as being above it all, as a pseudo-God, in a world separate to oneself. In bad faith, one needs to control life; in good faith, one feels the need only to live it. Attempting to control life is the essential quality of all selficide.

In good faith, we realize that we live as a significant, integral part of all nature. We live as part of the God-stuff, and, therefore, participate in all of life. We know that what we need is already there, and that we can actualize ourselves in that connected wholeness. Our unconscious provides us with the momentum for our becoming. It pushes us into our wholeness, into the natural connections we have with the universe surrounding us. It overcomes the inertia of nonexperience. We move. Without good faith, we feel the pain of alienation from our nature. We do not know we are part of all that is, and, thus, we lose the ability to participate in the power and energy continued in that wonderful matrix that is *being in the world in good faith.*

The windows that are most important to being in the world *in good faith* are: 1. Acceptance 2. Naturalness 3. Play 4. Aesthetic Morality 5. Risking 6. Creativity. These particular windows seem to have a distinctive relevance to the unconscious. Again, they can be briefly summarized:

• *ACCEPTANCE Acceptance* means to receive or take into oneself. It involves receiving others into ourselves—*as they are.* The opposite of acceptance is *judgment,* the accusing of others, blaming them for being who they are.

• *NATURALNESS Naturalness* comes from *natura,* "to be born." It means living in the world without a preset agenda. The opposite of naturalness is *artificiality*—being technical, inert, or inactive. Being artificial includes being self-conscious, phony, or embarrassed, as well as the obvious opposites of being natural: unnaturalness and guilt.

- *PLAY* Play means being involved in living itself, rather than viewing life from the outside. Play is nonintentional being: the gratification gained from experience is an experience itself, without any intent of accomplishment or triumph over others. As Walter Pater said, "Not the fruit of experience, but experience itself, is the end." To play is to take joy in the process, and so to pay attention to ourselves. The opposite of play is *work*, to use activity for its results, but, more specifically, to not pay attention to ourselves.

- *AESTHETIC MORALITY* Aesthetic morality describes a morality that is inner-created, based on whether what we are doing feels right to us, feels beautiful, and makes us more whole, as opposed to feeling wrong, ugly, and not really part of us. The opposite of *aesthetic morality* is *moral anesthesia*, meaning quite literally a lack of such sensing and, subsequently, a lack of feeling and being alive.

- *RISKING* Risking is our willingness to go outside the ordinary norms of our living, to be different in a way that is consistent with an inner desire and new sense of ourselves. Its arises from the word *risqué*. To be risqué is to delight in ourselves even in the face of the admonitions of society to be more careful and more fully aware of what is expected of us. Such risking is a physical participation in life. The opposite of risking is to be *proper*, meaning in its root "to have a private possession." There is no risk involved in being proper. We take no chance of being different. Instead, we take care of our psychological property.

- *CREATIVITY* Creativity is the willingness to let old experience be finished so that we can have new growth and different experience. The opposite of growth is *stagnation*, which means to stand still or to stop flowing. The word graphically describes the lack of personal growth that comes out of an unwillingness to let old experience die in order to have space, energy, and time to let new growth occur.

Optimally, the person who is being in the world *in good faith* is able to accept in order to receive. She is capable of being born and reborn, and is aware of the importance of trusting the process of life. She is one who plays, who pays attention to herself and is willing in her play to speak loudly the truths of life. She lives her life in terms of her sense of the beauty or ugliness she feels in each moment. Her morality is in her living. She risks and is willing lovingly to follow her natural impulses. She trusts that her world has a place for her. She is willing to set aside her past experiences, to put an end to what needs to be ended, and to come to a new beginning. She allows herself to grow into the new space provided by the death of old experience.

The person who is not being in the world *in good faith* is judgmental, accusing, and an agent of some outside system. He is artificial, self-conscious, manipulating, and unnatural. He is constantly in the process of dying, since he has no hope for new life. He pays no attention to beauty or ugliness, either in himself or in his world. He is bored, sad, tired, and always serious. He is stifled in his own soul, his own body, and his own relationships. He takes no chances and can let nothing go. He relives his same old life over and over, constantly fearing death.

The following are ways in which we do not live *in good faith*—manifestations of a lack of acceptance, naturalness, play, aesthetic morality, risking, and creativity. These are, once again, only simple examples. Each one actually clouds many of our windows.

LACK OF ACCEPTANCE
    A. *Issues of Righteousness*
        Feeling superior—the person living as if he is better than others
        Being opinionated—the person living so full of her ideas there is no room for new ones
        Prejudice—the person living jealous of others
        Condescension—the person living down to others
    B. *Issues of Judging*
        Blaming—the person faulting the other for being who he or she is
        False toleration—the person resenting others for being as they are
        False acquiescence—the person who goes along with others as a way of being superior
    C. *Issues of Rejection*
        Closed-mindedness—the person unable to open himself to what is outside
        Using others—the person who makes objects of others
        Stubbornness—the person unable to let go of her rightness

Obstinacy—the person who is captured by internal neediness

D. *Issues of Insatiability*

Personal greediness—the person who cannot get enough

Personal neediness—the person who cannot be filled up

LACK OF NATURALNESS

A. *Issues of Oversocialization*

Pomposity—the person full of himself

Pretentiousness—the person always being someone else

Primness—the person afraid to get dirty

Studied sophistication—the person once removed, always commenting on life

B. *Issues of Insincerity*

Cynicism—the person who mistrusts life

Manipulativeness—the person who sees others as objects for his or her own use

Lying—the person who cannot accept what is true

Conceit—the person living in narcissism

Envy—the person who always wants the other's life

C. *Issues of Artificiality*

Overmanneredness—the person with predefined responses to others

Posing—the person pretending to be a person

Seductiveness—the person who lives as a tease

Machismo—the man who lives without gentleness

D. *Issues of Self-Consciousness*

Guilt—the person who lives as an appendage to others

Embarrassment—the person who never knows how to be

Social anxiety—the person afraid to be part of the group

LACK OF PLAY

A. *Issues of Seriousness*

Stuffiness—the person who cannot let go

Solemnness—the person who cannot laugh

Staidness—the person who cannot play

Living without humor—the person who cannot respond to life

B. *Issues of Boredom*

Depression—the person not fully there

Sedation—the person who lives without passion

Weariness—the person who lives without energy
Ennui—the person who lives without joy
C. *Issues of Goal-drivenness*
Workaholism—the person who lives through her work
Living in roles—the person who lives in his assignment or task
Living in stress—the person who lives in her problems
Social climbing—the person always going to be

LACK OF AESTHETIC MORALITY

A. *Issues of Gracelessness*
Evil—the person without feelings
Vileness—the person who wants to be bad
Cruelty—the person who lives pissed off at his parents
Distortion—the person who confuses beauty and ugliness
B. *Issues of Insensitivity*
Not caring—the person who does not care, even about not caring
Opportunism—the person who uses experience instead of living it
Rudeness—the person who hurts others before they can hurt him
Coarseness—the person who lives without sensitivity
Personal anesthesia—the person dead to beauty or truth
C. *Issues of Integrity*
Living without ethics—the person who never feels beauty or ugliness
Hypocrisy—the person who pretends to know beauty and ugliness
Personal dishonesty—the person who avoids beauty and ugliness

LACK OF RISKING

A. *Issues of the Search for Security*
Properness—the person who always stays within the rules
Carefulness—the person who lives overcautiously
Materialism—the person owned by possessions
Covering up—the person owned by image

Trying to look good—the person owned by outside response

B. *Issues of Fearfulness*

Shyness—the person always waiting to be noticed

Timidity—the person who is passive toward life

Protectiveness—the person who makes believe that he is fine

Overquietness—the person who will not say who she is

Appeasement—the person who lives by placating others

Passivity—the person who uses helplessness to bring Mother back

Living without courage—the person who just gets by heartlessly

C. *Issues of Recklessness*

False bravado—the person who takes pseudorisks

Foolhardiness—the person who takes foolish risks

Compulsive activity—the person who cannot be still

D. *Issues of Unphysical Living*

Lassitude—the person who will not move

Head living—the person who watches life instead of living it

Lack of activity—the person who waits for life to happen

Apathy—the person who goes through the motions

LACK OF CREATIVITY

A. *Issues of the Fear of Death*

Search for immortality—the person waiting for the great parent

Barrenness—the person living dead

Desolateness—the person who abandons living, feeling he has tried and failed

B. *Issues of Fear of the New*

Mass production—the person living the same feeling or thought over and over

Infertility—the person who will not give birth to the new

Shallowness—the person who lives life walking on tippy-toes

Imitation—the person who lives as others live as a way of life

Stagnation—the person stuck in the old
C. *Issues of the Lack of Imagination*
Homogeneity—the person who lives like her surroundings
Living without animation—the person who lives without spirit
Laziness—the person who will not try
Dullness—the person turned off or turned down

The Anxiety and Despair of Being

Most people can imagine *being* without trepidation—being congruent, responsible for self, self-disciplined, and present to others. It may seem like a great deal of work, but possible. They are the qualities that form our idea of what a down-to-earth person is, what we feel a mature person can be. Integrating thinking, feeling, and behaving into a centered person, present and responsible, is often seen as the main task of psychotherapy. As a *conscious* process, *being* seems knowable, even achievable, to us. Normally the anxiety it creates seems surmountable; what fear it creates, conquerable. We feel we *could* have identity if we were willing really to try.

However, as we move *in the world*, we usually begin to feel much greater anxiety. Our fear grows. The development of reciprocity, attentiveness, freely choosing, and personal surrender become much more problematic. We fear making our own choices and being responsible for them. We fear ongoing connections, as if the resultant relationship would make us more vulnerable to the other. This fear is *preconscious*, as if almost on the tip of our tongue. We step back into old patterns. It is a frightening paradox that in many ways people prefer the security and familiarity of unhealthy life. Whereas preconscious process frightens us, old unhealthiness is predictable and we know what to expect. But there is no healthy nonrelational living: in our shuttered room, we are not living freely out of our choices in a real world, a world full of others to whom we are intimately connected.

We see the wise person as one who knows this truth and who

lives in relation to her world. That person understands what R. D. Laing meant in *Self and Others* when he said:

> It is ironical that often what I take to be most public reality turns out to be what others take to be my most private phantasy. And that which I suppose is my most private "inner" world turns out to be what I have most in common with other human beings.

But most of us usually see such living as a demanding and lonely responsibility. We see the wise person as suffering in isolation, and we hesitate to walk in those footsteps.

As we move to living *in good faith*, we become even more frightened, now with an *unconscious* fear. We see the faithful person as mystical, and avoid him, afraid he will cause something to happen in us. It is as if we are afraid that in being near such a person we might be too near to God. The *unconscious* frightens us deeply. The mystical person appears to be in direct contact with the "All," that is, the "isness." And, indeed, to be intimate with the unity of life is frightening. It is the ultimate risk.

Confusing "fear and trembling" with anxiety and despair, we feel we will be consumed, displaced, and captured by that "All." This is both our sin and our sadness, as Kierkegaard so cogently described in *The Sickness Unto Death*. He identified the basic despairs of all humans: the despair of being (conscious fear), the despair of not being (preconscious fear), and the despair of becoming (unconscious fear).

The Levels of Consciousness

These levels of consciousness generally accompany each of our sets of experiential windows. The windows most related to facilitating *being*— responsibility for self, self-discipline, congruence, and presence—are characterized primarily by *consciousness*. They are recognized in the individual at a conscious level. It is probably also true, despite the fact that most of us live as if it were not, that these qualities are learned, or relearned, at a conscious level.

On the other hand, the windows associated with facilitating being *in the world*—personal surrender, attentiveness, free choice, and reciprocity—appear to operate primarily on a *preconscious* level. For the most part, they are learned and relearned on that same preconscious level. We are, therefore, even more resistant to the idea that we can change those parts of ourselves.

Lastly, those windows that contribute to and facilitate our being in the world *in good faith*—acceptance, naturalness, play, aesthetic morality, risking, and creativity—are operative in our persons mostly on a totally *unconscious* level. As such, they are the experiential substratum of life. They characterize the natural living in good faith we see present in children until the age of three or four. We all lose them to some degree as our socialization proceeds. But to become fully human, we have to regain that good faith as adults.

What are these levels of existence? By *consciousness* in the whole sense, we mean being aware of ourselves and our unending connections in the world we live in. However, consciousness in this sense of the word has many dimensions and levels. How are we aware? We are obviously aware in the awakened sense of *being conscious*. We see, hear, smell, taste, and feel—documenting in our waking state through our senses the world as we at any given moment live in it. We are, in a similar way, aware of our internal world, sensing the thoughts and feelings that come to the surface. This awareness we also refer to as *being conscious*.

There are, however, two other broad areas of awareness that are equally important, if not more important, than the conscious state of knowing—the preconscious and the unconscious. *Preconscious* awareness is somewhat different from cognitive awareness in that it has intuitive qualities and is more a vague sensing than an actual knowing. It represents something emerging from more deeply within the person, the place where signals sent out from the conscious and unconscious meet, offering vague intimations of meaning and memory. For example, a shudder may tell us more about the truth of a situation we face than any conscious opinion. These intimations are enormously important in our living. In many ways, they are more important than our conscious cognitive states. Certainly, in our intimate and close relationships, we pay more attention to these intimations than we do to the data that we are aware of in a conscious manner.

In addition to the conscious and the preconscious, there is the *unconscious*. The unconscious is that part of our being which modifies our life unendingly, but of which we have no real awareness. The unconscious may be said to be the center of both our physical and personal being. It is the physical center because it regulates our heartbeat, breathing, and digestion, and controls our physical being in the world. Participating in the intricate dance of nature, the unconscious regulates the chemistry within our bodies with a beautiful perfection and proficiency. It is also the personal center, because it contains the history of our evolution as living beings. There are within each of us awarenesses that were characteristic not only of our human antecedents, but of our evolutionary process as a whole. These are not individual but collective memories; they are what Jung called *archetypes*.

Archetypes account for the fact that, despite their separation by space, time, and language, primitive societies develop with remarkable consistency many of the same basic social and cultural systems. They may have varied customs and religions but, despite those conspicuous differences, the archetypical patterns of community (as well as those of individuals) will be remarkably similar. The archetypes represent universal patterns of life, patterns of real experience in the collective participatory unconscious.

The unconscious also contains all of the memories of our own *individual* lives. It carries our important early memories, long repressed from consciousness and irretrievable except metaphorically. Yet those memories are enormously significant in our living. Our important early experiences are constantly resident in our persons. They directly affect our emergence as selves, as well as all of the ways in which we open or shutter the windows of experience.

The windows of experience related to living *in good faith* are probably learned, or relearned, on a totally unconscious level. Acceptance, naturalness, play, aesthetic morality, risking, and creativity are all descriptive of the young child before he or she is trained. Even with variations in degree, inclination, and intensity arising from our innate constitutions, they are natural aspects of life, seen in the rest of nature and distorted in the process of socialization. Sadly, humans have not yet learned how to create community *naturally*.

We see people in therapy struggle with these different aspects of living. Some seem best able to learn about *being* through the experience they have with the therapist on a personal level, as a conscious learning experience—an aspect of close relationship. Those who learn about living *in the world* can also grow and learn through the experience they have with the therapist, although what happens may occur more on the preconscious level. Such interactions—often nonverbal or involving humor—are aspects of intimate relationship.

Experiences related to living *in good faith* may occur in the therapeutic relationship, but not in the ways described above. There are no *intended* experiences in the relationship that seem directly to help develop these unconscious windows. There is no counseling of one's consciousness or therapy for one's preconscious that seems to directly affect the unconscious at all. Something does, however, appear to happen: an unfolding, of their own devising, occurs in clients. This unfolding is fostered by participation in a relationship containing the *union* of those close and intimate aspects. This blossoming may then come, for example, out of dreaming, or from the multitude of new experiences they are having because of increases in their being and expansion in their connectedness to the world in which they live. They begin to recall the child within. Without being consciously aware, they return to those ways of being in good faith that are so beautifully characteristic of young children.

Only a minute portion of psychotherapy occurs in therapists' offices. The vast majority of psychotherapy occurs among people in their relationships, both close and intimate. Such psychotherapy can happen with strangers, while we are reading a book and interacting with characters in it, or when we are looking at a painting or sitting in a movie and suddenly find ourselves tearful about something that we cannot quite identify. Psychotherapy occurs with the environment, animals, and plants. These epiphanies are never labeled psychotherapy, but that is what they are. The many hours, months, and years of the process of life are far more effective in helping us learn what we need to know of the *windows to experience* than are the few hours spent in a chair in a therapist's office. Therapy can be but a guide, but *life* is the biggest window of all.

If you happen on that window, stop and look. Go outside, outside from where you have been to where you might be. You will be leaving the dimness of what has been, moving to the lightness of full being. Life and the world need you. The shuttered windows are making the sunlight dim, and leaving life feeling lonesome and useless. Come out in the sunlight. Sleep and dream in less darkness. Wake tomorrow and live in the lightness of being in the world in good faith.

Epilogue

For we are the local embodiment of a cosmos grown to self-awareness.

—Carl Sagan

Both of us are deeply concerned with ecology—personally as well as professionally. It does not seem possible to us to be therapeutic, in any sense of that word, without being concerned about ecology. Our concerns involve not just what we do or fail to do about our forests, air, soil, water, and animals, but also about our religion, our education, our art, our economics, our politics, and how we say hello and good-bye to each other. In short, the total *psycho-ecology* of our universe seems to be the individual responsibility and concern of each of us.

The core determinant of how we as individuals will carry that responsibility—whether we will unshutter our windows or not—seems to be our basic concept of the point of life. Our answer to that particular *spiritual* question will be crucial in determining whether we begin to see clearly through our windows and move to greater wholeness in our lives. Do we see the point of life as *joy* or *success*? Are the two opposites? Must we choose between them?

We would suggest that the two are not opposites and that we do not have to choose one over the other. We do need, however,

396

to become much clearer about the relationship between the two. If we live out of joy—that is, *being*—we will naturally succeed. For example, if we have a talent, we will enjoy using it to its fullest—we will manifest what we *are* in what we *do*. If, instead, we live for the sake of success—that is, *doing*—there is no guarantee we will be joyful at all. It does not really matter what our idea of success is—that is, what our *doing* agenda is. While it may seem clear that security agendas that make us depressed or anxious are unjoyful, it is also clear that the agendas of money, power, and status can make us equally unhealthy, unhappy, and without joy. *Being* must always precede *doing*.

Our inner *self* knows that truth. To find wholeness we must relearn to listen to him or her. In listening, we will begin to know our real voice and can begin to follow it. We can also begin to hear and know our many false voices and cease to follow them. The question therapists usually hear is "How can I know which is which? How can I know who the real me is?" In truth, it is much easier than we think to tell them apart. The false voice is rigid, inflexible, controlling, and static. It contains no joy, only agendas. The real voice is open, flexible, free, dancing, and joyful—even if it is dealing with sadness, fear, or other "hurting" but real feelings. It *moves*. We have only to listen and experience it.

The emergent person always moves. Movement in the *whole* sense—physical and emotional, behavioral and intellectual, spiritual and practical—is the chief hallmark of selfbeing. Since self is always relational, that is, exists only in relationship, selfbeing *always* involves movement and change. The emergent person is energetic. He or she participates in life's energy as a full person, an ordinary being with equal standing in a universe of beings. For that is our *purpose*, to enable *being* to emerge—naturally and joyfully.

Sometimes we wish the movement would cease. We are afraid or hurt and mistakenly believe that if we stand still we will be more secure, regain our energy, take a break from the demands of life. But in an emerging universe, stasis requires tremendous energy, as all self-diminishing people can attest. The drain of anxiety, depression, righteousness, incongruence, or any of the other ways we have of stopping movement is quite real. We feel the tiredness, the weakness, and the malaise, and have the sensation that life is passing us by. Not changing is, of course, as much a *process* in the purely phenomenological sense as changing. Just as there is no way to *not relate*, there is no way to *not change*. But *experientially*, the process does stop, and as a result no learning, growth, or movement takes place. No person emerges. We miss the point of life.

Stopping the experiential process of life is selficidal. It destroys more than us alone because each of us is part of the creation of the universe. We are not just *creations* but also *creators*, and thus our failure to experience diminishes both ourselves and our world. Sadly, too few of us live out this understanding in the world. Full selfbeing requires our participation in life both as creations and creators. There is no *fully living* alternative. In the continuing process of life, new areas of the unconscious are made manifest to us, more of what *is* becomes known. That process is the nature of emergence.

Our tragedy is that we would rather control life than live it. Thinking we can make ourselves secure, we step outside the experiential process in order to *do* something. We give up selfbeing for this doing something and then wonder why we feel so unalive and unwhole. Naturalist Rachel Carson reminded us in *Silent Spring* that, "the 'control of nature' is a phrase conceived in arrogance, born of the Neanderthal Age of biology and philosophy, when it was supposed that nature exists for the convenience of man." Neither nature in this sense nor human nature is under our control. To insist otherwise is self-destructive and futile. It poisons the psychoecology.

Einstein showed that energy and matter are in essence different faces of the same process. In the same way, information—information in its grandest sense as an organizing principle—is another face of energy and matter. All of life is a dance of the ever-changing universal essence—energy/matter/information. The dance of life is not controllable because we are part of the dance. As dancers, we can participate, but we cannot step off the dance floor and choreograph living from the sidelines. We create what we examine just as we examine what we create. We are controller and controlled at the same time. We have only ourselves, and as Montaigne said, "the greatest thing in the world is to know how to belong to oneself."

Wholeness is a journey toward belonging fully to ourselves. The whole human is one who is wise enough to see both the complex and the obvious in life, and faithful enough to know that life cannot be controlled, only lived. The journey is neither short nor easy, and there is no final destination. But it is a journey we *can* make, and, it would seem, a journey we *must* make if we are to save ourselves as joyful individuals *and* as a species. In truth, the two experiences are the same.

Further Reading

The following list contains books from many fields: science, art, philosophy, psychology, literary criticism, theology, and general literature. These books are not meant to be used instructionally as "how to" manuals, but are instead starting points for individual journeys. Many of the authors have published other books, and the bibliographies in each book will provide further resources.

Allport, Gordon W., *Becoming.* New Haven, Connecticut: Yale University Press, 1955.

Bach, Richard, *Illusions.* New York: Delacorte, 1977.

Bateson, Gregory, *Mind and Nature: A Necessary Unity.* New York: E. P. Dutton, 1979.

————, *Steps to an Ecology of Mind.* New York: Ballantine, 1972.

————, and Mary Catherine Bateson, *Angels Fear.* New York: Macmillan, 1987.

Becker, Ernst, *The Denial of Death.* New York: The Free Press, 1973.

Berger, John, *Ways of Seeing.* London: Penguin, 1977.

Berman, Art, *From the New Criticism to Deconstruction*. Chicago: University of Illinois Press, 1988.

Berman, Morris, *Coming to Our Senses*. New York: Simon & Schuster, 1989.

————, *The Reenchantment of the World*. New York: Bantam, 1984.

Bettelheim, Bruno, *A Good Enough Parent*. New York: Vintage, 1988.

Bion, Wilfred R., *Seven Servants*. New York: Jason Aronson, 1977.

Bloom, Harold, *Ruin the Sacred Truths*. Cambridge, Massachusetts: Harvard University Press, 1991.

Boeke, Kees, *Cosmic View: The Universe in 40 Jumps*. New York: John Day, 1957.

Bohm, David, *Wholeness and the Implicate Order*. London: Ark Paperbacks, 1983.

———— and F. David Peat, *Science, Order, and Creativity*. New York: Bantam, 1987.

Briggs, John, and F. David Peat, *Turbulent Mirror*. New York: Harper & Row, 1989.

Brown, Norman O., *Life Against Death*. Middleton, Connecticut: Wesleyan University Press, 1970.

Buber, Martin, *I and Thou*. New York: Charles Scribner's Sons, 1970.

————. *The Knowledge of Man*. New York: Harper & Row, 1965.

Calvin, William H., *The Cerebral Symphony*. New York: Bantam, 1990.

————, *The River That Flows Uphill*. San Francisco: Sierra Club Books, 1986.

Campbell, Joseph, *The Power of Myth*. Garden City, New York: Doubleday, 1988.

————, *The Hero with a Thousand Faces*. Princeton, New Jersey: Princeton University Press, 1949.

Capra, Fritjof, *The Tao of Physics*. New York: Bantam, 1977.

Caputi, Natalino, *Guide to the Unconscious*. Birmingham, Alabama: Religious Education Press, 1984.

Carroll, Lewis, *Through the Looking Glass and What Alice Found There*. London, 1896.

Carse, James P., *Finite and Infinite Games*. New York: The Free Press, 1986.

Carter, Forrest, *The Education of Little Tree*. New York: Delacorte, 1976.

Casti, John, *Paradigms Lost*. New York: Avon, 1989.

Chodorow, Nancy, *The Reproduction of Mothering*. Berkeley, California: University of California Press, 1978.

Comfort, Alex, *I and That*. New York: Crown, 1979.

———, *The Nature of Human Nature*. New York: Harper & Row, 1966.

———, *Reality and Empathy*. Albany, New York: State University of New York Press, 1984.

cummings, e. e., *The Enormous Room*. New York: Liveright, 1922.

Dahl, Gordon, *Work, Play, and Worship*. Minneapolis, Minnesota: Augsburg Publishing House, 1972.

Doi, Takeo, *The Anatomy of Dependence*. New York: Kodansha International, 1973.

———, *The Anatomy of Self*. New York: Kodansha International, 1985.

Dubos, René, *A God Within*. New York: Charles Scribner's Sons, 1972.

Dyson, Freeman, *Infinite in All Directions*. New York: Harper & Row, 1988.

Eagleton, Terry, *Literary Theory*. Minneapolis, Minnesota: University of Minnesota Press, 1983.

Eco, Umberto, *Travels in Hyperreality*. New York: Harcourt Brace Jovanovich, 1986.

Eliade, Mircea, *The Forge and the Crucible*. New York: Harper Torch Books, 1971.

———, *The Myth of Eternal Return*. Princeton, New Jersey: Princeton University Press, 1991.

Elkind, David, *The Hurried Child*. London: Addison-Wesley, 1981.

Felder, Richard, and Avrum Weiss, *Experiential Psychotherapy: A Symphony of Selves*. New York: University Press of America, 1991.

Fossum, Merle A., and Marilyn J. Mason, *Facing Shame*. New York: W. W. Norton, 1986.

Foucault, Michel, *The Archaeology of Knowledge*. New York: Pantheon, 1972.

———, *Madness and Civilization*. New York: Vintage, 1988.

———, *The Order of Things*. New York: Random House, 1970.

Frank, J. D., *Persuasion and Healing*. Baltimore: Johns Hopkins University Press, 1961.

Frankl, Viktor, *Man's Search for Meaning*. New York: Pocket, 1963.

———, *Psychotherapy and Existentialism*. New York: Washington Square Press, 1967.

Fromm, Erich, *The Art of Loving*. New York: Harper, 1956.

———, *Escape from Freedom*. New York: Rinehart, 1941.

———, *Man for Himself*. New York: Rinehart, 1947.

———, *The Sane Society*. Greenwich, Connecticut: Fawcett, 1970.

Gardner, Howard, *The Mind's New Science*. New York: Basic Books, 1985.

Gardner, John W., *Self-Renewal*. New York: Harper Colophon, 1965.

Geshe, Rabten, and Dhargyem Geshe, *Advice from a Spiritual Friend*. London: Wisdom Publications, 1977.

Gilligan, Carol, *In a Different Voice*. Cambridge, Massachusetts: Harvard University Press, 1982.

Gleick, James, *Chaos: Making a New Science*. New York: Viking, 1987.

Gould, Stephen Jay, *Ever Since Darwin*. New York: W. W. Norton, 1977.

———, *Hen's Teeth and Horse's Toes*. New York: W. W. Norton, 1983.

———, *The Panda's Thumb*. New York: W. W. Norton, 1980.

Groddeck, George, *The Book of the It*. New York: Vintage, 1961.

Gustafson, J. P., *The Complex Secret of Brief Psychotherapy*. New York: W. W. Norton, 1986.

Haley, Jay, *Strategies of Psychotherapy*. New York: Grune & Stratton, 1963.

Hampden-Turner, Charles, *Maps of the Mind*. New York: Collier, 1982.

Hardison, Jr., O. B., *Disappearing Through the Skylight*. New York: Penguin, 1989.

Havens, Leston, *Making Contact: Uses of Language in Psychotherapy*. Cambridge, Massachusetts: Harvard University Press, 1986.

Hesse, Hermann, *Siddhartha*. New York: New Directions, 1951.

Hoffer, Eric, *The Ordeal of Change*. New York: Harper & Row, 1952.

Hofstadter, Douglas R., *Gödel, Escher, Bach*. New York: Basic Books, 1979.

———, *Metamagical Themas*. New York: Basic Books, 1985.

———, and D. Dennet, *The Mind's I*. New York: Basic Books, 1981.

Horney, Karen, *Neurosis and Human Growth*. New York: W. W. Norton, 1950.

———, *Self-Analysis*. New York: W. W. Norton, 1942.

Huizinga, Johan, *Homo Ludens: A Study of the Play Elements in Culture*. Boston: Beacon Press, 1955.

Hunt, Morton, *The Universe Within*. New York: Touchstone, 1982.

James, William, *The Varieties of Religious Experience*. New York: Longmans, Green, 1935.

Jay, Martin, *The Dialectical Imagination*. Boston: Little, Brown, 1973.

Jaynes, Julian, *The Origins of Consciousness in the Breakdown of the Bicameral Mind*. Boston: Houghton Mifflin, 1976.

Jourard, Sidney, *Disclosing Man to Himself*. New York: Van Nostrand, 1968.

——, *The Transparent Self*. New York: Van Nostrand Reinhold, 1971.

Judson, Horace Freeland, *The Search for Solutions*. New York: Holt, Rinehart, & Winston, 1980.

Jung, Carl, *Modern Man in Search of a Soul*. London: Routledge, 1933.

——, *Man and His Symbols*. London: Aldus, 1979.

——, *The Undiscovered Self*. New York, Mentor, 1958.

Keen, Sam, *Fire in the Belly*. New York: Bantam, 1991.

Kierkegaard, Søren, *Fear and Trembling/The Sickness Unto Death*. Garden City, New York: Doubleday/Anchor, 1954.

Koestler, Arthur, *The Act of Creation*. New York: Dell, 1973.

Kohut, Heinz, *The Analysis of Self*. New York: International Universities Press, 1971.

——, *The Restoration of the Self*. New York: International Universities Press, 1977.

Kongtrul, Jamgon, *The Great Path of Awakening*. Boston: Shambhala, 1987.

Kopp, Sheldon, *An End to Innocence*. New York: Bantam, 1981.

——, *If You Meet the Buddha on the Road, Kill Him!* New York: Bantam, 1976.

Kuhn, Thomas, *The Structure of Scientific Revolutions*. Chicago: University of Chicago Press, 1970.

Kundera, Milan, *The Unbearable Lightness of Being*. New York: Harper & Row, 1984.

Laing, R. D., *The Divided Self*. London: Penguin, 1965.

——, *The Politics of Experience*. London: Penguin, 1967.

——, *Self and Others*. Baltimore: Penguin, 1969.

Langer, Susanne K., *Philosophy in a New Key*. Cambridge, Massachusetts: Harvard University Press, 1979.

Leakey, Richard E., and Roger Lewin, *People of the Lake*. New York: Avon, 1978.

Leonard, Linda Schierse, *The Wounded Woman*. Boston: Shambhala, 1985.

Lerner, H. G., *The Dance of Anger*. New York: Harper & Row, 1986.

——, *The Dance of Intimacy*. New York: Harper & Row, 1989.

Leshan, L. Y., and H. Margenau, *Einstein's Space and Van Gogh's Sky*. New York: Macmillan, 1982.

Lévi-Strauss, Claude, *The Savage Mind*. Chicago: University of Chicago Press, 1966.

———, *Structural Anthropology*. Garden City, New York: Doubleday, 1967.

Lewis, Thomas, *The Lives of a Cell*. New York: Viking, 1974.

Lindbergh, Anne Morrow, *Gift from the Sea*. New York: Vintage, 1965.

Lorie, Peter, *Wonder Child*. New York: Fireside, 1989.

Malone, Michael, *Handling Sin*. Boston: Little, Brown, 1986.

Malone, Thomas P., and Patrick T. Malone, *The Art of Intimacy*. New York: Prentice Hall Press, 1987.

Margulies, Alfred, *The Empathic Imagination*. New York: W. W. Norton, 1989.

Maslow, Abraham, *Motivation and Personality*. New York: Harper & Row, 1954.

———, *Toward a Psychology of Being*. New York: Van Nostrand, 1968.

May, Rollo, *The Courage to Create*. New York: W. W. Norton, 1975.

———, *Love and Will*. New York: Dell, 1969.

———, *Man's Search for Himself*. New York: W. W. Norton, 1965.

———, *The Meaning of Anxiety*. New York: W. W. Norton, 1977.

———, *Psychology and the Human Dilemma*. Princeton, New Jersey: Van Nostrand, 1967.

———, Ernest Angel, and Henri Ellenberger, *Existence*. New York: Basic Books, 1958.

Mead, G. H., *Mind, Self, and Society*. Chicago: University of Chicago Press, 1934.

Merton, Thomas, *The Way of Chuang Tzu*. New York: New Directions, 1965.

Miller, Alice, *The Drama of the Gifted Child*. New York: Basic Books, 1981.

Miller, David L., *Gods and Games*. New York: Harper Colophon, 1970.

Miller, Jean Baker, *Toward a New Psychology of Women*. Boston: Beacon Press, 1976.

Mitchell, Richard, *The Gift of Fire*. New York: Fireside, 1987.

Moltmann, Jürgen, *Theology of Play*. New York: Harper & Row, 1972.

Morrison, Philip, and Phyllis Morrison, *Powers of Ten*. San Francisco: W. H. Freeman, 1982.

Nachmanovitch, Stephen, *Free Play*. Los Angeles: Jeremy P. Tarcher, 1990.

Needleman, Carla, *The Work of Craft*. New York: Alfred A. Knopf, 1979.

Needleman, Jacob, *A Sense of the Cosmos*. Garden City, New York: Doubleday, 1975.

Nozick, Robert, *The Examined Life*. New York: Touchstone, 1989.

Ogilvy, James, *Many Dimensional Man: Decentralizing Self, Society, and the Sacred*. Oxford, England: Oxford University Press, 1977.

Ouspensky, P. D., *In Search of the Miraculous*. New York: Harcourt Brace, 1949.

Pagels, Elaine, *Adam, Eve, and the Serpent*. New York: Vintage, 1989.

———, *The Gnostic Gospels*. New York: Vintage, 1989.

Pagels, Heinz R., *The Dreams of Reason*. New York: Bantam, 1989.

Percy, Walker, *Lost in the Cosmos*. New York: Farrar, Straus & Giroux, 1983.

———. *The Message in the Bottle*. New York: Noonday Press, 1990.

Piaget, Jean, *The Construction of Reality in the Child*. New York: Basic Books, 1954.

———, *The Origins of Intelligence in Children*. New York: International Universities Press, 1966.

Pirsig, Robert M., *Zen in the Art of Motorcycle Maintenance*. New York: Bantam, 1975.

Polanyi, Michael, *Personal Knowledge*. Chicago: University of Chicago Press, 1962.

———, *Science, Faith and Society*. Chicago: Phoenix Books, University of Chicago Press, 1964.

Postle, Denis, *Catastrophe Theory*. London: Fontana, 1980.

Prigogine, Ilya, and Isabelle Stengers, *Order Out of Chaos*. New York: Bantam, 1984.

Proust, Marcel, *Remembrance of Things Past*. New York: Random House, 1981.

Reagan, Charles E., and David Stewart, (eds.), *The Philosophy of Paul Ricoeur*. Boston: Beacon Press, 1978.

Reich, Wilhelm, *Character Analysis*. New York: Farrar, Straus, 1949.

Rogers, Carl, *Client-Centered Therapy*. Boston: Houghton Mifflin, 1965.

———, *On Becoming a Person*. Boston: Houghton Mifflin, 1961.

Rorty, Richard. *Consequences of Pragmatism*. Minneapolis, Minnesota: University of Minnesota Press, 1982.

———, *Contingency, irony, and solidarity*. Cambridge, Massachusetts: Cambridge University Press, 1989.

———, *Philosophy and the Mirror of Nature*. Princeton, New Jersey: Princeton University Press, 1979.

Rucker, Rudy, *Infinity and the Mind*. Boston: Birkhauser, 1982.

Sanford, John A., *The Invisible Partners*. New York: Paulist Press, 1980.

Satir, Virginia, *Conjoint Family Therapy*. Palo Alto, California: Science and Behavior Books, 1967.

Singer, June, *Boundaries of the Soul: The Practice of Jung's Psychology*. Garden City, New York: Doubleday/Anchor, 1973.

Storm, Hyemeyohsts, *Seven Arrows*. New York: Ballantine, 1972.

Sullivan, H. S., *Conceptions of Modern Psychiatry*. New York: W. W. Norton, 1953.

————, *The Interpersonal Theory of Psychiatry*. New York: W. W. Norton, 1953.

Suzuki, Shunryu, *Zen Mind, Beginner's Mind*. Tokyo: Weatherhill, 1970.

Teilhard de Chardin, Pierre, *The Phenomenon of Man*. New York: Harper & Row, 1959.

Tillich, Paul, *The Courage to Be*. New Haven, Connecticut: Yale University Press, 1952.

————, *The Eternal Now*. New York: Charles Scribner's Sons, 1963.

Trungpa, Chogyam, *Glimpses of Abhidharma*. Boulder, Colorado: Shambhala, Prajna Press, 1978.

————, *The Myth of Freedom*. Berkeley, California: Shambhala, 1976.

Wallace, B. Alan, *Choosing Reality*. Boston: Shambhala, 1989.

Watts, Alan, *The Book: On the Taboo Against Knowing Who You Are*. New York: Pantheon, 1966.

————, *Nature, Man, and Woman*. New York: Mentor, 1960.

————, *Psychotherapy East and West*. New York: Pantheon, 1961.

————, *The Wisdom of Insecurity*. New York: Vintage, 1951.

Watzlawick, Paul, *The Invented Reality*. New York: W. W. Norton, 1984.

————, John Weakland, and Richard Fisch, *Change*. New York: W. W. Norton, 1974.

Whitaker, Carl, *Midnight Musings of a Family Therapist*. New York: W. W. Norton, 1989.

————, and William Bumberry, *Dancing with the Family*. New York: Brunner/Mazel, 1988.

————, and Thomas Malone, *The Roots of Psychotherapy*. New York: Brunner/Mazel, 1953.

Williams, Paul, *Das Energi*. New York: Warner, 1973.

Winnicott, D. W., *The Maturational Processes and the Facilitating Environment*. New York: International Universities Press, 1982.

————, *Playing and Reality*. London: Tavistock, 1971.

Winson, Jonathan, *Brain and Psyche*. Garden City, New York: Double-day/Anchor, 1985.

Woolf, Virginia, *A Room of One's Own*. New York: Harcourt, Brace, 1929.

Yalom, I. D., *Existential Psychotherapy*. New York: Basic Books, 1980.

Yutang, Lin, (ed.), *The Wisdom of Laotse*. New York: Modern Library, 1976.

Index

Depression (*cont.*)
lack of bonding and, 337
as nonexperience, 181
unwillingness to take risks and,
142
Descent of the Goddess, The
(Perera), 175
Desiderata (Ehrmann), 73
Destructiveness, self-. *See* Self-
destructiveness
Detachment, systemic, 157–160
Dickens, Charles, 257
Differences, 320–322
Dinesen, Isak, 364
*Disappearing Through the Sky-
light* (Hardison), 340
Discipline. *See also* Self-
discipline
defined, 115
meaning of, 120
Discovery of the Asylum, The
(Rothman), 118–119
Discrimination, lack of, 58–59
Displacement of affect
spatial, 188–189, 377
temporal, 179–187, 377
stress and, 191
Displacement of context, 192–193
Divine Milieu (Teilhard de Char-
din), 302
Doi, Takeo, 60
Doing, play as, 267–268
Drama of the Gifted Child, The
(Miller), 71, 214, 314
Dreams, 364–366, 374
remembering, 357, 366
Drucker, Peter, 173
Drugs
abuse of, 274
effect of, on presence, 194–195
Dryden, John, 194
Duty, 121–123, 234–236
chosen, defined, 235
to oneself, 122
origin of word, 121
sense of, 271
true (*see* Commitment)
Dysfunctional families, 155, 296

Eating disorders, 123–125
Eckhart, Meister, 367
Eco, Umberto, 276
Ecology, 396
Education, versus training, 20
Educational system, 214
Effective Executive, The
(Drucker), 173–174
Ego
matriarchal, 175
patriarchal, 175
Ehrmann, Max, 73
Einstein, Albert, 36, 215, 271,
398
Eliade, Mircea, 149
Eliot, George, 225
Eliot, T. S., 44, 345
Elliot, Harriet Wiseman, 89
Emergent persons, 397
Emerson, Ralph Waldo, 19, 213
Empathetic Imagination, The
(Margulies), 166, 239
Empathy, 237–240
defined, 237
lack of, 238–239
reciprocity and, 316
Empowerment
free choice and, 213
of others, through making do,
222–224
personal surrender and, 234
self-discipline and, 126–128
true intimacy and, 231
"End point" living, 201–202
Energies of Men, The (James),
245
Energy, enhancing, through let-
ting go, 350
Enthusiasm of passion, 27–28
Environment, healthy, and play,
281
Epiphenomenological child, 110–
111
Ethics. *See* Morality, aesthetic
Euripides, 113
Evil and ugliness, 45–46, 300
Existential Psychiatry (Yalom),
349

relationships to others and,
90–91
self-responsibility and, 90–91
Self-experience, refinding responsibility through, 112
Self-fullness, versus selfishness,
224–226
Self-help books, goal of, 14
Selficide, 29–30, 212
absence of presence and, 42
boredom as, 120–121
concept of, 19
connections as insurance
against, 63
cultural, 160, 170
group, 196
hyperactivity as, 120–121
lack of new experiences and,
32
obedience as, 118–120
other terms for, 32–35
and overcoming personal inertia about change, 30–32
self-consciousness and, 167
Self-images, distorted, 104
Selfishness, 113, 375
versus self-determination, 302–
304
versus self-fullness, 224–226
versus self-love, 114–115
Self-love, 41
self-discipline and, 117, 133
versus selfishness, 114–115
Self-nourishment, 44
growth and, 248, 259
lack of, in relationships, 256
Self-perception
as basis for self-responsibility,
90
defined, 90
Self-relating, healthy, 232
Self-responsibility. See Responsibility for self
Self-sacrifice, for security, 21,
24
Self-talk, 81–82
negative, 232
Serendipity, 31

Seriousness
damage done by, 280–281
defined, 279
Sexual feelings
lack of, 33, 60
versus love, 201
Sexuality, 275–278
foreplay, 278
owning, 190
play and, 45, 275–278, 280
religious beliefs and, 293
society and, 277
Shakespeare, William, 20, 147
Shamanism (Eliade), 149
Sharing, 257
Shaw, Robert, 28–29
Sickness Unto Death, The
(Kierkegaard), 391
Social Contract (Rousseau), 325,
346
Social demands, and congruence,
168–170
Social systems. *See also* Society
behavior as reflection of, 23–24
compromised healthy functioning in, 24
lack of knowledge about, 169–
170
and lack of self-responsibility,
108–110
Socialization, 300–301
healthy, 169, 227–228
Society, 281
and art, 58
on individuality, 259
lack of growth in, 203
lack of responsibility and, 109
lack of support for wholeness
in, 14, 16
need for change in, 239–240
self-destructiveness of, 20
Sociopathic behavior
incongruence in, 165
Socrates, 299
Solomon in All His Glory
(Lynd), 270–271
Solzhenitsyn, Aleksandr, 58
Some Like It Hot (film), 226

About the Authors

THOMAS PATRICK MALONE received his Ph.D. from Duke University and his M.D. from Emory. Along with Carl A. Whitaker, he founded the experiential concept of psychotherapy and authored the ground-breaking book *The Roots of Psychotherapy*. Dr. Malone has been in private practice at the Atlanta Psychiatric Clinic since 1955.

PATRICK THOMAS MALONE received his M.D. from the University of North Carolina. He was Chief of Psychiatry at Orlando Naval Hospital for four years and in 1975 joined his father at the Atlanta Psychiatric Clinic. In addition to his private practice at the Clinic, he is the Medical Director of the Mental Health Division at Northside Hospital. He is coauthor with his father of *The Art of Intimacy*.